# POLITICS AND CHANGE
# IN DEVELOPING
# COUNTRIES

# POLITICS AND CHANGE IN DEVELOPING COUNTRIES

STUDIES IN
THE THEORY AND PRACTICE OF
DEVELOPMENT

EDITED BY
## COLIN LEYS

FOR THE
INSTITUTE OF DEVELOPMENT STUDIES AT
THE UNIVERSITY OF SUSSEX

CAMBRIDGE
AT THE UNIVERSITY PRESS
1969

Published by the Syndics of the Cambridge University Press
Bentley House, 200 Euston Road, London N.W.1
American Branch: 32 East 57th Street, New York, N.Y. 10022

Library of Congress Catalogue Card Number: 78–85725
Standard Book Number: 521 07602 1

Printed in Great Britain by
Alden & Mowbray Ltd at the Alden Press, Oxford

# CONTENTS

# CONTENTS

# NOTES ON CONTRIBUTORS

J. P. NETTL Reader, University of Leeds, 1965–7 and Professor of Sociology and Political Science, University of Pennsylvania from 1967: died October 1968.

Author of *The Eastern zone and Soviet policy in Germany* (1951); *Rosa Luxemburg* (1966); *Political mobilization* (1967); *The Soviet achievement* (1967); *International systems and the modernization of societies* (1968).

JOAN VINCENT Lecturer in Political Sociology, Makerere University College, 1966–7 and Assistant Professor of Anthropology, Barnard College, Columbia University from 1968.

Author of *Status and power in an African community* (1969); and articles on plural society in Zanzibar, cooperative development, local government and administration in Uganda.

ALEC NOVE Professor of Economics at Glasgow University from 1963.

Author of *The Soviet economy* (third edition 1968); *Was Stalin really necessary?* (1964); co-author of *The Soviet Middle East* (1967); *Economic history of the U.S.S.R.* (1968).

DAVID FELDMAN Member of the Economic Mission to Tanzania, 1965 and Fellow of the Institute of Development Studies at the University of Sussex from 1967.

W. H. MORRIS-JONES Director of the Institute of Commonwealth Studies, University of London from 1966.

Author of *Parliament in India* (1957); *Government and politics of India* (1964); contributions to *Politics and society in India* (C. H. Philips, ed., 1963); *A decade of the Commonwealth, 1955–64* (W. B. Hamilton, D. Robinson and C. D. Goodwin, eds., 1966); and *India and Ceylon: unity and diversity* (P. Mason, ed., 1967). Editor of *Journal of Commonwealth Political Studies*.

MARTIN STANILAND Fellow of the Institute of Development Studies at the University of Sussex, 1967–9.

Author of articles on local administration in the Ivory Coast, on the political writings of Frantz Faron, and on South African novelists. Has also written a study of the development of political parties in Dahomey.

BERNARD SCHAFFER Senior Lecturer in Politics, University of Sussex, 1965. Reader in Politics, University of Sussex from 1967 and Fellow in Development Administration, Institute of Development Studies at the University of Sussex from 1968.

Joint author of *Top officials in two states* (1963); *Decisions* (1964). Part author of *Specialists and generalists* (1968). Sometime associate editor *Public administration* (Sydney).

R. E. DOWSE Lecturer, University of Exeter from 1964, and Visiting Professor, State University of New York 1968–9.

Author of *Left in the centre: The I.L.P. 1893–1940* (1966); *Ghana and the U.S.S.R.: A study in political development* (1968). Joint editor of *Readings on British politics and government* (1968).

COLIN LEYS Professor of Politics, University of Sussex from 1965 and Fellow of the Institute of Development Studies at the University of Sussex since 1967.

Author of *European politics in Southern Rhodesia* (1959); *A new deal in Central Africa* (with R. C. Pratt and others, 1960); *Politicians and policies* (1967); contributor to *Development* (D. Seers, ed., forthcoming). Joint Editor of *Journal of Commonwealth Political Studies*.

# EDITOR'S PREFACE

These papers were originally presented to a conference held at the University of Sussex in June 1968, and they owe a great deal to the contributions which were made there. The authors would like to express their appreciation to all the participants and in particular to the chairmen and commentators who led the discussions: Prof. D. E. Apter, Dr E. A. Brett, Dr R. J. Chambers, Dr R. A. Chapman, Prof. J. S. Coleman, Prof. R. P. Dore, Prof. S. E. Finer, Prof. B. D. Graham, Prof. A. H. Hanson, Mr G. Ionescu, Dr A. R. Jolly, Mr J. M. Lee, Prof. W. J. M. Mackenzie, Dr D. Mitrany, Prof. P. H. Partridge, Dr R. R. Rathbone, Prof. K. J. Ratnam, Prof. C. G. Rosberg.

Warm thanks are also due to Miss Patricia Howard, our Conference Secretary; to Miss Andrea Hopkinson for valuable assistance with references; and to the secretarial staff of the Institute of Development Studies, without whose willing support the deadlines would never have been met.

*Stanmer*                                                    C.T.L.
*October 1968*

*On 25 October 1968, Peter Nettl was killed in a plane crash in the U.S.A. To those who had the good fortune to work with him the loss of this brilliant and warm-hearted colleague, at the height of his powers, was a heavy personal blow. We would like this book, to which he contributed much more than his own paper, to be in some measure a tribute to him.*

# INTRODUCTION

## COLIN LEYS

*I can read anything which I call a book. There are things in that shape which I cannot allow for such. In this catalogue of books which are no books—biblia a-biblia—I reckon Court Calendars, Directories, the works of Hume, Gibbon, Robertson, Beattie, Soame Jenyns, and, generally, all those volumes which 'no gentleman's library should be without'.*

Lamb's prejudice against 'things in books' clothing' must be shared to some extent by anyone who has suffered from the outpouring in recent years of collections of papers in the social sciences; and so the rationale of this book ought as far as possible to be explained. It is by British writers; and it has to do with the so-called 'revolution in political science' as it bears on the study of development.[1]

The existence of a long record of work by British writers on the politics of countries in Africa and Asia needs no advertisement; it is an important part of the standard literature on these areas. At the same time it is obvious that it has now been greatly surpassed in volume by the work of the very large numbers of American scholars, backed by impressive resources, who moved into these areas, partly as a result of the American decision to become deeply involved in Third World problems after the Second World War. This work has to a very large extent been based on quite different methodological presuppositions, those of 'behaviouralism'; and between these two bodies of political literature there existed, until quite recently, an abysmal gap of mutual incomprehension: a situation perfectly expressed by the remarkable fact that David Apter's classic monograph, *The Gold Coast in transition*, published in 1955, was not even discussed in the only other study of comparable quality on modern Ghanaian politics, Dennis Austin's *Politics in Ghana 1946–1960*, published in 1964.

The passage of time has done something to bridge this gap. The brilliant research successes of what Professor Mackenzie has called 'partial theories', and generous American financial support for British students to study in the U.S.A., have deepened understanding in Britain of the sources of 'behaviouralism', and made possible some discrimination between its different varieties and their different aspirations.[2] This has been reflected in teaching.

[1] I am very grateful to Prof. H. S. Bienen, Prof. B. D. Graham, Dr B. B. Schaffer and Mr T. F. Mars for invaluable comments on an earlier draft.

[2] W. J. M. Mackenzie, *Politics and social science*, Harmondsworth 1967, p. 77.

At first the new territory mapped out by behaviouralists was added to existing syllabuses based, so to speak, on maps drawn by cartographers using quite different projections (not to say flat-earthers)—thus 'political culture' or 'elites' would become marginal new topics in an old course on 'political institutions'; but later whole new courses began to be offered, with titles like 'political sociology', which began to convey some understanding of the point of view which makes sense of books on political culture like *The civic culture* or books on elites like *Politics, personality and nation building*. The last, unfinished phase is a re-shaping of the whole approach to political studies in Britain in which some of the gains made by behaviouralism, both in general and in particular, begin to be reflected in the work of British political scientists themselves.

This phase could obviously be interesting and productive. There are some particular intellectual resources on which British students can draw in coming to terms with this almost wholly foreign-made methodological revolution—the British tradition in political philosophy, for example, and in political history. A fusion of the theoretical and empirical preoccupations of behaviouralism with these traditional British modes of political study could be fruitful, especially in the study of developing areas, where the strengths and weaknesses of both approaches have been clearly revealed. But certain conditions need to be met. There must be no supercilious British parasitism, and above all, the inquisitive and speculative drive which is the secret of behaviouralism's vitality must not be smothered.

This brings us back to the behavioural movement, about which a great deal has been written.[1] Much of this has, unfortunately, been highly

---

[1] The best statement of the behavioural position known to me is Heinz Eulau's *The behavioural persuasion in politics*, Random House, New York 1963. The following summary gives the essentials of the general position.

'The orientation to the study of political science that I identify by the term political behaviour (1) rejects political institutions as the basic unit for research and identifies the behaviour of individuals in political situations as the basic unit of analysis; (2) identifies the "social sciences" as "behavioural sciences", and emphasizes the unity of political science with the social sciences, so defined; (3) advocates the utilisation and development of more precise techniques for observing, classifying, and measuring data and urges the use of statistical or quantitative formulations wherever possible; and (4) defines the construction of systematic, empirical theory as the goal of political science' [Evron M. Kirkpatrick, 'The impact of the behavioural approach on traditional political science', in Austin Ranney (ed.), *Essays on the behavioural study of politics*, Urbana 1962, p. 12.]

A useful list of writings on behaviouralism in politics is given in the same article, p. 3, n. 3. See also R. A. Dahl, 'The behavioural approach in political science: epitaph for a monument to a successful protest', *American Political Science Review* 55 (1961), 763–72; and James C. Charlesworth (ed.), *The limits of behaviouralism in political science*, American Academy of Political and Social Science, Philadelphia, October 1962; especially the article by David Easton, 'The current meaning of "behaviouralism" in political science', pp. 1–25. For a hostile view see the famous 'Epilogue' by Leo Strauss in H. Storing (ed.), *Essays on the scientific study of politics*, New York 1962, pp. 305–28; and the review by J. H. Schaar and S. H. Wolin and the reply by Storing and Strauss and others in *APSR* 157, 1 (March 1963), 125–60. For the impact of behaviouralism on the study of development politics see especially David E. Apter, *The politics of modernisation*, Chicago 1965, and David E. Apter and Charles Andrain, 'Comparative government: developing new nations', *Journal of Politics* 30, 2 (May 1918), 372–416.

polemical, and the associated argument about the nature and purpose of political science has at length begun to bore even political scientists. This is unfortunate because an extended analysis by a sympathetic student of scientific history is badly needed; especially because so many attempts to 'adopt' behaviouralism without understanding the many (and possibly, in some cases, contradictory) strands of theory and methodology that produced it lead to a peculiarly awful kind of formalism. But not even a crude attempt will be made here to classify or analyse the different elements in behaviouralism. Taking a good deal for granted, we will instead offer a few opinions about some of the most general characteristics of behavioural political science as revealed in the study of development.

Of the many springs from which behaviouralism flowed, three stand out in this context; the belief that the concepts in terms of which what is studied empirically should be organized must be derived from explicit theories about political behaviour; the view that political behaviour is intimately related to social and economic behaviour; and the particular influence of Max Weber. In the study of development, these influences seem much more important than some others (e.g. the drive for quantification). This is due partly to the nature of the subject-matter. Political behaviour in decolonizing countries was less accessible and less easy to measure than in developed systems; or rather, before the question of measurement could be tackled at all there was a fundamental prior problem of characterizing what the significant elements in behaviour were. For this the behaviouralists turned to theory, and especially to the rich stock of analytic concepts provided by general sociology, and especially Max Weber. It may also have been important—it is a matter for research —that many of Weber's major ideas had been introduced to American students by Talcott Parsons in whose writings they were strongly associated with the behavioural aspiration towards a unified science of society, transcending both cultural and disciplinary boundaries; early behavioural work on the politics of new states was often a conscious expedition across cultural boundaries which, it was hoped, would prove the worth of the cross-cultural analytic equipment carried by the expeditionary by enabling him to bring back findings fit to be added to the corpus of *general* social scientific knowledge.[1]

Parsons also taught a particular form of functionalism; and whether from this source, or from Robert Merton, or from a more direct encounter with structural-functionalism in anthropological writings on the developing countries that was entailed by the determination to see political behaviour only as one dimension of social behaviour, an important group of behaviouralists embarking on the study of new states adopted a

[1] See especially Talcott Parsons, *The social system*, Glencoe 1951, and (with E. A. Shils) *Towards a general theory of action*, Cambridge, Mass. 1951.

structural-functionalist position.[1] The merits and demerits of functionalism do not matter for the present discussion; but it does seem to be true that functional explanations do not rest on quite such a straightforward relationship between hypothesis and evidence as is required, in theory at least, by some other models of scientific explanation.[2] A further aspect of Weber's work, which is possibly even more emphatically reflected in Parsons and very marked in the behavioural literature on new states, is the use of 'ideal types', which need not be associated with a functionalist approach, but very commonly is. At all events, these schools of thought within the behavioural movement have been extremely influential in the study of development politics and have been associated with an unusually pronounced tendency towards theoretical experimentation and typology-construction.[3]

These ideas led to two kinds of literature on developing countries: theoretically oriented political monographs (the studies of Binder, Apter, and Pye stand out among early examples of this type),[4] and attempts at very general theory (the most influential being, of course, Gabriel Almond's, but proliferating year by year in the pages of *World Politics* and other journals, and promising to culminate in the long-awaited final volume of the distinguished series on political development published by the Comparative Politics Committee of the American Social Science Research Council.)[5] Neither kind of work has had any significant British

[1] For an account of Parsons's functionalism, see William Mitchell, *Sociological analysis and politics, The theories of Talcott Parsons*, New Jersey 1967, pp. 67–68. See also R. K. Merton, *Social theory and social structure* (2nd edn), Glencoe 1957, chapter 2; the locus classicus for the doctrine of functional equivalence applied to the politics of developing countries is Gabriel Almond's Introduction to G. A. Almond and J. S. Coleman, *The politics of the developing areas*, Princeton 1960.

[2] An excellent bibliography of the literature on the problems of functionalism is provided by the footnotes to R. E. Dowse, 'A functionalist's logic', *World Politics* XVIII, 4 (July 1966), 607–22.

[3] 'Even an empirical study of politics and government in a single little-known country is no longer complete without its general theory, or suggestions for one, as prologue or epilogue.' Ruth Ann Willner, 'The underdeveloped study of political development', *World Politics* XVI, 3 (April 1964), 470. Dr Willner drew attention to the limiting effect of influential general concepts on the pattern of research, an effect due to factors other than the scientifically established value of the concepts, and therefore to be distinguished from the 'paradigms of normal science' which form the turning points in scientific revolutions as described in T. Kuhn, *The structure of scientific revolutions*, Chicago 1962 (see below, p. 7, n. 1).

[4] L. Binder, *Iran: political development in a changing society*, Berkeley 1962; D. E. Apter, *The Gold Coast in transition*, Princeton 1955; L. W. Pye, *Politics, personality and nation-building; Burma's search for identity*, New Haven 1962.

[5] In the early 1960s hardly an issue of *World Politics* did not contain a largely theoretical discussion of some aspect or other of development politics. Among the most frequently cited contributions on this subject are: D. A. Rustow, 'New horizons for comparative politics' (July 1957); Martin L. Kilson, 'Authoritarian and single-party tendencies in African politics' (January 1963); Robert E. Ward, 'Political modernisation and political culture in Japan' (July 1963); S. N. Eisenstadt, 'Modernisation and conditions of sustained economic growth' (July 1964); Robert A. Packenham, 'Approaches to the study of political development' (October 1964); Samuel P. Huntington, 'Political development and political decay' (April 1965); C. S. Whitaker, Jr., 'A dysrhythmic process of political change' (January 1967). It seems almost superfluous to list the titles of the S.S.R.C.'s Committee on Comparative Politics series, published by Princeton

counterpart until very recently, as a glance at the contents of the British political science periodicals will confirm. The first type resulted from a prolonged graduate training (unavailable in Britain) in the relevant fields of sociological theory and method, and a particular way of pursuing research, quite alien to British traditions, by looking for facts to illuminate a theory rather than the other way round (to put it crudely but—as will be seen—not unsympathetically). The second type, very high-level theorizing, required a faith in a particular scientific ideal, and a consequent willingness to suspend the demand for normal standards of clarity or consistency during the supposedly pioneering stages of theory-building, for which again nothing in the British intellectual inheritance provided the slightest support.

The most immediately important point about both kinds of literature, for present purposes, is perhaps that they already seem dated. It is doubtful if anyone of intelligence is now pursuing either field research or theory-building with the same unreserved commitment to the original behavioural ideals that infused, say, Apter's early work on Ghana or even his much later theoretical work on modernization.[1] In field studies, especially, there has been a reaction against the procrustean spirit of the mid-1950s; the work of people like Zolberg on the Ivory Coast or Kilson on Sierra Leone or Brass or Weiner on India shows a continuing preoccupation with theoretical problems—their interest is in no sense parochial, but constantly seeks to interpret findings in terms of general and comparative concepts—but they have been much more willing to allow 'the situation' to determine what is central in their studies, and are content with quite modest or even with negative contributions to the existing stock of theory.[2]

But before considering this as a welcome trend with fruitful possibilities for a *rapprochement* with British political scientists working in developing areas, we should consider what may be lost, both in the research ethos of early behavioural field work, and in the realm of theory.

[1] David E. Apter, *The politics of modernisation*, Chicago 1965.

[2] A. R. Zolberg, *One party government in the Ivory Coast*, Princeton 1964; M. Kilson, *Political change in a West African state: a study of the modernisation process in Sierra Leone*, Cambridge, Mass. 1966; M. Weiner, *Party building in a new nation: the Indian National Congress*, Chicago 1967; Paul R. Brass, *Factional problems in an Indian state; the Congress party in Uttar Pradesh*, Berkeley 1965.

University Press: Lucian W. Pye (ed.), *Communications and political development* (1963); Joseph LaPalombara (ed.), *Bureaucracy and political development* (1963); Robert E. Ward and Dankwart A. Rustow (eds.), *Political modernisation in Japan and Turkey* (1964); James S. Coleman (ed.), *Education and political development* (1965); Lucian W. Pye and Sidney Verba (eds.), *Political culture and political development* (1965); and Joseph LaPalombara and Myron Weiner (eds.), *Political parties and political development* (1966). The final volume (edited by Coleman, LaPalombara, Pye, Weiner and Leonard Binder) is announced as *Crises in political development*. This casual way of alluding to the development of development theory in American political science is bound to do unintentional injustice to the leading role of others; names such as Edward A. Shils (especially his *Political development in the new states*, The Hague 1960) and F. W. Riggs (e.g. his *Administration in developing countries*, Boston 1964) come immediately to mind.

To take theory first, it seems rather obvious that the value of the theoretical work done by behaviouralists on new states is substantially independent of the validity of the claims actually made for it. The ideal of a unified science of society or even the less ambitious goal of a science of comparative political analysis may not have been brought much closer to realization by this work, yet its contribution has been of first-class importance. This is partly due to the organizing power of some of the analytic concepts that have been used, such as Parsons's achievement/ascription, universalistic/particularistic 'pattern variables', Weber's authority types, and so forth; but above all, I suggest, to the fact that the behavioural commitment to theorizing restored speculative political thinking as an intellectually legitimate activity—something which, for most political scientists, it had ceased to be for at least half a century.[1]

This last remark cannot be properly documented here, but perhaps this much will be agreed; even where (as in Britain) the idea of a 'value-free' political science had few supporters, a fairly clear distinction existed in practice between students of government (or 'institutions') and political theorists. Political theory appeared to most students of government or institutions as a quite separate kind of activity, concerned primarily with 'great books' written in days when speculation and exhortation were not disentangled from observation and comparison. The virtual disappearance of this class of literature from current publishers' lists was noted as a striking fact, deplored by those who found it stimulating to read;[2] its reentry into political science from general sociology through behaviouralism was less noticed.

Yet this is, surely, a fundamentally important aspect of the behavioural movement. Talcott Parsons's complete apparatus may have been too complex and obscure for most people; what mattered, however, was the identification—by him and other behavioural theorists—of formulae for speculative thinking with the ideal of a science of society. By a 'formula' I mean an intellectual procedure, a programme of discussion, description, abstraction, and so forth, in relation to a given subject-matter, that is to some degree accepted as a valid or reasonable way of treating it; in this sense the various schools of behaviouralism may be seen as providing formulae for speculative thinking about politics similar to the famous formulae of classical political theory such as Natural Law or the Social

---

[1] Leonard Binder's Introduction to his *Iran* is most frequently, and with justice, cited as an example of almost impenetrable abstraction. For another type, see Apter's *Politics of modernisation*, p. 249. But both are saying some important things which, though they could be said in plain English, have not on the whole occurred to plain English speakers.

[2] See, e.g., A. Hacker, 'Capital and carbuncles: The "great books" reappraised', *APSR* 48, 3 (September 1954), 775–86; also 'Political theory and the study of politics: a report of a conference', Rapporteur H. Eckstein, *APSR* 50, 2 (June 1956), 475–87; and a symposium: D. G. Smith, 'Political science and political theory'; D. E. Apter, 'Theory and the study of politics'; and A. A. Rogow, 'Comment on Smith and Apter, or whatever happened to the great issues?', *APSR* 51, 3 (1957), 734–75.

Contract.[1] Behaviouralists not only felt free to theorize, they felt an obligation to do so, and had a good range of conceptual building materials to hand, and a variety of approved ways of going about it.

The results were sometimes vacuous, often confused and rarely very readable; but they were, quite simply, the means by which an exceptionally talented group of scholars were able to lift the study of politics out of the rut, in which it was preoccupied almost exclusively with institutions and very largely with their forms, at a level of concern and understanding determined almost wholly by the policy-concerns of political actors.[2] Professor Oakeshott's diagnosis was exact: '. . . a curriculum of study of unimaginable dreariness. . . which could have no conceivable interest to anyone except those whose heads were full of the enterprise of participating in political activity or to persons with the insatiable curiosity of a concierge';[3] and he correctly perceived that to add newly fashionable items to the curriculum, without a fundamental reorientation of intention and the acquisition of an appropriate method, was only to make the rut deeper and greasier. But whereas he did not see any such possibility, and recommended only a retreat back into history and philosophical criticism, the behavioural theorists were utterly convinced that a new synthesis of ideas and knowledge was not only possible but imminent; and in the process of trying to create it, they asked entirely new and interesting questions, and developed new and challenging canons of what would count as answers.

It may be objected that the behavioural movement in political science proper can be sufficiently explained without reference to its general theorists, and that its main stream consists of the succession of field

---

[1] Formulae are not, I think, the same as the 'paradigms of normal science' (see above, p. 4 n. 3); at any rate they have occurred when the discipline is in the state discussed by Kuhn in *The structure of scientific revolutions* at pp. 13–16, which appears to be pre-scientific (in his usage). His description of the effect on a discipline of acquiring a paradigm (pp. 18–21)—i.e. the movement away from books towards articles, written in esoteric language for the circle who take the paradigm for granted, and other associated tendencies—is interesting in this connection; the phenomenon has occurred in behavioural political science, but seems to have been rather deliberately manufactured. The hoped for convergence of the next generation of scholars around the paradigm does not seem likely to occur, at least not in the clear-cut way some protagonists have wished. One is inclined to think that we are still in the run-up stage towards the emergence of paradigms in most branches of the subject.

[2] For example, the preoccupation with the viability of British constitutional machinery for British colonies after independence which led to such enterprises as the Legislative Council series edited by Margery Perham; or the curious faith in the significance of electoral studies of the Nuffield variety, extended to newly independent countries (e.g. D. C. Mulford, *The Northern Rhodesia general election, 1962,* Nairobi 1964, or G. Bennett and C. G. Rosberg, *The Kenyatta election; Kenya 1960–1961,* London 1961). This tendency has almost certainly been reinforced and rationalized by the demand (not unreasonable when other things are equal) for 'good', 'simple' English; as Peter Nettl aptly remarked, it helps to ensure that 'our nose is grimly kept a bare inch above the squiggly furrow of facts'—facts conceptualized and selected by certain of the political actors, as a rule (J. P. Nettl, *Political mobilisation,* London 1967, p. 23).

[3] Michael Oakeshott, 'The study of "Politics" in a university', in *Rationalism in politics and other essays,* London 1962, p. 324.

studies, in developed and underdeveloped countries, in which theory plays on the facts in a particular way. This view seems unhistorical, however; although there has been some division of labour, even the best-known general theorists such as Gabriel Almond or Karl Deutsch have been closely involved in empirical studies and in the field of development this is especially true. The fact is that for more than 10 years a particular group of academics, and a very large body of imitators and students, have been dedicated to the proposition enunciated by David Easton in 1953, that empirical research and general theory-building are essential to each other.

The kind of empirical work which they and their research students attempted can only be understood as an expression of this point of view. General theory provided a sense of participation in a major programme of discovery, and the hope of contributing, by the hours of 'fanatical boredom' devoted to some aspect of the politics of some obscure state, to our understanding of politics in general; a sentiment which was essential for sustaining the peculiar demands of fieldwork carried out under the behavioural canon.

This approach, which I have already called procrustean, in which the researcher brought to the field a set of theoretically derived hypotheses to be investigated in relation to appropriately selected facts, involved a phenomenal effort of self-denial; facts not relevant to the hypothesis had to be ignored, or at least set aside, however much more interesting or accessible or in a vulgar sense 'important' they might seem to be. Often far from any professional companionship, the researcher had to pursue his chosen course supported entirely by his own—or his supervisor's—conviction that his true contribution to knowledge would be made, not by reporting and interpreting things that seemed on the spot to be 'central', but by faithfully accumulating just those specific data which would confirm or disconfirm the hypotheses which he had travelled so far (and so expensively) to test.

This is, of course, an idealized and somewhat exaggerated account of the behavioural research canon in its application to developing areas. The starting point, in most cases, was the obligation to produce a 'dissertation proposal' for a behaviourally oriented dissertation committee; once in the field, the more intelligent researchers would, after a period of unsuccessful struggle, fasten on to some more tractable set of problems and emerge with a publishable study bearing little relation to the original proposal, although the level of theoretical concern in it might be equally great. But not all researchers had the independence and ability to adjust in time or completely; the results could be pathetic and barren (few of the many 'negative returns' have, in fact, been published); and it was also not surprising that many researchers were tempted to look for facts which would confirm 'their' hypotheses, albeit perhaps with qualifications, rather than those which might disconfirm them.[1] Nonetheless we should again count the cost of the reaction against this approach.

The beauty of the best work which it produced is its single-mindedness. Seldom, perhaps, has it either established or destroyed some key theoretical proposition about politics with the finality and clarity which the behavioural ideal would imply. But there is a depth and tension in the best of such writing that is absent from other equally learned and often better-written books about politics; a sense of the persistent pursuit of something important and elusive, by means which may be faulty or even crude but which are still methodical and explicit and not wholly inappropriate, which makes the result stand out as at least a sustained attempt to penetrate to levels of order and regularity in political life, without denying the existence and importance, at another level, of its diversity and uniqueness. This is to some extent a personal matter; one either senses and responds to this dimension of works like, say, *Who governs?*, *Leaders, factions and parties* or *The political kingdom in Uganda* or one doesn't; although it is perhaps beginning to be an observable fact that such books are, in the end, the ones to which most of us return in preference to other sorts of books about more important and attractive cities than New Haven, more edifying and hopeful political systems than the Philippines, or more topical encounters between traditional and modern structures than those of pre-independence Uganda.[2] At all events few students who came to David Apter's *The Gold Coast in transition* from previous books on the Gold Coast, or indeed on other colonial areas generally, could fail to grasp that here was an entirely new, ambitious and extraordinarily exciting approach, which lifted the discussion out of the parochial plane, and that the study of African politics at least was about to be revolutionized, as indeed it was. Engels's retrospective comment on the effect on the Young Hegelians of Feuerbach's new philosophy—'One must himself have experienced the liberating effect of this book to get an idea of it. Enthusiasm was general; we all became at once Feuerbachians'—could fairly be applied to the effect of the early behavioural political monographs on graduate students in the late 1950s.

The causes of the partial retreat from both general theory and the 'hard-line' field research ethos are well known. The construction of comprehensive theoretical systems can degenerate into an uninspired and pointless scholasticism; like all social theory, behavioural theories rest on ideological presuppositions which may become less fashionable[3]; at the same time, the

---

[1] Pye's important and deservedly influential *Politics, personality and nation building* can be faulted on this ground, for example.

[2] R. A. Dahl, *Who governs? Democracy and power in an American city*, New Haven 1961; Carl H. Landé, *Leaders, factions and parties; the structure of Philippine politics*, New Haven 1965; D. E. Apter, *The political kingdom in Uganda*, Princeton 1967.

[3] This view rests, I would argue, on quite general arguments about the relation between social experience and the language of social analysis. I do not subscribe to the frequently expressed view that structural functionalism is an inherently conservative method of analysis, nor even that it has always been used as a matter of fact to support a conservative viewpoint.

ideal of completing, by sheer deductive effort, an 'over-arching' social-scientific conceptual web which would then require only to be 'filled in' with the findings of appropriately conceived research, strikes more and more people as based on a methodological and psychological error—a once fertile one, perhaps, but no longer capable of inspiring useful work.[1] Theoretically inspired research, for its part, *can* easily become trivial or indeed meaningless; and it is characteristic of a science to try to reduce its methods to rules and consequently to acquire a large fringe of people who can follow the rules, but without inspiration or insight, leading to mediocre results, the more dispiriting for being presented under the banner of 'science' or 'analysis' ('blessed word', as Oakeshott scathingly remarks) or—worse still—'scientific rigour', meaning, sometimes, the faithful counting of what can be counted.

But these are risks attending the behavioural approach; they are the price that has been paid for its achievements. For this price it has established the study of politics on an independent footing, provided it with a set of methods, and in a number of directions has set in motion a very impressive accumulation of reliable scientific knowledge at a quite high level of generality.[2] Above all, and especially in the study of developing countries, it has enabled political scientists to ask questions that were of general interest and importance; so much so that we have possibly learned more about politics from studies of underdeveloped countries than from studies of developed ones in recent years.

This creativity and innovation and capacity for comparison and accumulation are the things which have been so conspicuously lacking in the institutional and historical tradition of British political science, and which restricted its work in developing areas for so long to the cultivated writing of history too recent to be guided by criteria of relevance furnished by a reliable historical perspective, or to the reporting of institutional changes of real significance only to local actors; which, in short, made it parochial. American political scientists may be moving towards a less ambitious and more pragmatic conception of behaviouralism, but they will certainly not abandon its commitment to speculative theory, and theoretically inspired field work; these are now part of a deeply entrenched tradition, and are supported by the great strength of American sociology. But in Britain these are still very new ideas and they could conceivably be stifled, at least partly, unless the real gains of behaviouralism and the

---

[1] This view, which I personally share, is certainly debatable; and it refers specifically to 'overarching', not to 'partial' or 'middle-level' theorizing.

[2] A good example of this process in current work on developing areas is the study of factionalism; see R. W. Nicholas, 'Village factions and political parties in rural West Bengal', *Journal of Commonwealth Political Studies* 2 (November 1963), 17–32; the work of Brass and Landé, already cited; B. D. Graham, 'Change in factional conflict. The case of the Uttar Pradesh Congress Party, 1964–65' (mim. University of Sussex 1968) refers to most of the relevant literature.

The most obvious example in the study of developed polities is the work which led up to A. Campbell *et al.*, *The American voter*, New York 1960.

limited character of the changes occurring in it in the development context are understood.

Given this understanding, however, British political scientists may have a contribution to make to the next phase of political studies in developing areas. There are certain obvious possibilities. The continuing strength of history in the undergraduate training of most political scientists in Britain might help to keep a sensible balance between the theoretically absorbing and the historically significant in the focus of research, and to ensure that middle-level or general theories are not built out of purely short-run models. It is probably also important that economics still plays a large part in the early training of many students of politics, having been in many universities the 'parent department' of political science and being often still closely related to it in the curricula. There are also areas of special expertise, relevant to development, in which there are relatively strong British traditions: Soviet historical studies, with their obvious yet hitherto only superficially exploited relevance to understanding contemporary efforts to develop; economic studies; Marxist studies; and above all, social anthropology, with its own special ethos of field research and intense concern with theory.

The papers in this book were written partly to explore the value of some of these intellectual resources for the study of politics in developing countries. Some—Alec Nove's, Joan Vincent's, and David Feldman's— suggest in a very explicit way the possibilities of convergence between different disciplines in the development field. The others are by political scientists representing, certainly, a spectrum of methodological viewpoints, but nonetheless sharing a good deal of common ground—just how much, the reader must judge. The gap between, say, Peter Nettl's uncompromising commitment to speculative analysis, and the sceptical reconsideration of a particular bit of empirical explanation by Martin Staniland, may seem very wide. Yet both are centrally concerned with theory and with understanding politics in terms which disclose their significance at the widest level of generality appropriate to the subject-matter. The gap between them, significant as it is, is no wider than the equally significant gap that separates both their points of view from that of strictly historical, not to say anti-behavioural, writers. At the same time, some common elements in these two contributions also seem to distinguish them from at least one strand of American writing on the politics of development; a strong sensitivity to the ideological component of theories of development, for example, and a pronounced historical perspective.

As for the question, what do *we* mean by development, the idea itself is the major theme of Peter Nettl's paper. As Joan Vincent suggests, it is quite possible to do without the word, with its strong ideational and teleological overtones, and maybe we should. Nonetheless, it does refer conveniently to a very definite, if infinitely complex, fact of life; a compound of private and collective actions and their intended and unintended consequences, through which a society moves from one state of organization and one system of beliefs and ideas and stock of equipment to another, in the context (more or less dimly perceived) of others which have followed or are following a similar, though far from identical, route with similar, though also differing, hopes and fears; a thing as important to understand as it is moving to observe.

# STRATEGIES IN THE STUDY OF
# POLITICAL DEVELOPMENT

## J. P. NETTL

In the social sciences the self-conscious formulation of methodology generally lags a little behind actual developments in real life. Problems arise; attempts at solution follow. The basic theoretical reformulations in the study of any subject thus seem to reflect tendencies initiated in real life some time earlier; theory catches up with real life. This process of catching up has all the appearance of dramatic novelty, the sort of *Umwälzung der Wissenschaft* which Thomas Kuhn has analysed in *The structure of scientific revolutions*. Previous emphases are suddenly discarded and replaced by new ones, new arguments are formulated, new systems are created. In this way even quite gradual processes of societal change become the subject of apparently dramatic dissents and theoretical reconstruction. The reason why re-emphases and changes are more frequent and perhaps less dramatic in the social, as opposed to the natural sciences, is of course that in the first case the requirements of formal rigour are so much less; hence there is much less commitment to a paradigm, the options appear more open. Even so, the drama of conceptual change often hides the constraints of incrementalism of real life, and it is the task of the historian to even things out—to heighten the drama of gradualism by summation, to lessen the impact of revolution by emphasizing continuities and highlighting antecedents. The skill of the political scientist or sociologist consists partly in sensing forthcoming political and social changes and helping to bring them about. The secret is to recognize them early.

But in any science or para-science generalizations must of course be based on evidence. In social matters evidence—in so far as we are not dealing with history—takes time to accumulate. Hence 'early' generalizations tend to be indistinguishable from speculation. The most powerful system of predictive socio-politics in modern times, that of Karl Marx, began as a philosophy and finished in detailed multifaceted empirical specification. Inevitably we are faced with something of a vicious circle. Evidence needs time to accumulate, to be garnered and to be digested; this means delay, and delay means that the social scientist willy-nilly becomes an historian.

Occasionally the reformulations are powerful enough not only to capture the recent past, but in doing so to extrapolate into the future. Success, though very rare, may in such cases be self-fulfilling; the prediction becomes the blueprint, as with Marx or Keynes. I think that a good definition for this rare phenomenon is philosophy; the difference between philosophy and history would then primarily be one of time. While history provides explanations of past events, philosophy throws forward its system across the barrier of the testable past, through the merely sensory present into a problematic, at best probable, future; time ceases to be the primary independent variable.

It seems to me that we are now due for some 'philosophy' in the area of socio-political development. At the moment we are in an impasse. Recent theories of development, almost all from America, have certainly defined the problem areas—and very well too. But they have left the problem or problems largely unsolved, especially the problem of *what* constitutes development and how it is to be attained. In this the theories are closely tied to actual events in the so-called developing world; difficulties in the theory are matched by failures in the 'real' world, and moreover the shape of the difficulties is matched by the shape of the theories. We can say with confidence and with Gunnar Myrdal that the problem of development in the Third World, however defined, is further away from solution than it has ever been.[1] On the level of analysis one of two things may now happen; either there will emerge a theory of development with universal or at least large-scale application (though it may not be a very optimistic one), or development, like totalitarianism, will go out of conceptual fashion and be replaced by—what? Statics once more? Empirical discreteness, the willingness to live with unbridgeable diversity at least until new evidence accumulates to make possible a major reformulation of problems? Theories of non-development, which focus on an ordering and interrelating of the complex uniformities responsible for the inability of, say, black Africa, to 'develop' in any meaningful way at all?[2] Or indeed an end to the expansion of Third World studies, a return to the fascinations of industrial and post-industrial societies and (something of which there are definite signs already) a theory of development concerned with the leading instead of the lagging societies of the world?[3] The pull of the modern sector in determining the emphasis of socio-political theories of development is a perennial problem.

[1] The relationship between existing development theories and the bias of the Western view of underdeveloped countries is brought out clearly in Gunnar Myrdal's monumental *Asian drama: an enquiry into the poverty of nations*, New York 1968, esp. vol. I, pp. 5–127. The burden of the book, however, is the failure of 'development' and its causes.

[2] This is implicit in Hugh Tinker's notion of 'broken-backed states'; *Ballot box and bayonet*, London 1964. Cf. also the recent discussion and summary of problems by Aristide R. Zolberg, 'The structure of political conflict in the new states of tropical Africa', *American Political Science Review* LXII, 1 (March 1968), 70–87. In my view theories which explain failure to develop are not simply symmetrical opposites of theories of development; they do not have the same assumptions and do not deal with the same problems.

[3] Amitai Etzioni, *The active Society: a theory of societal and political processes*, New York 1968, is precisely such an approach, and a very fruitful one.

But let us assume for the moment that there will emerge an adequate theory of development. When we have looked a little more closely at the present impasse, we might try to investigate the sort of *needs* such a theory would have to fill. Unfortunately, it is not yet possible to sketch out what sort of theory it is likely to be.

## THE CONCEPT OF DEVELOPMENT

The concept, and hence the problem, of development is historically a very recent one, and it is worth remembering that it is not at all native to underdeveloped areas but is strictly a Western notion, one that looks out from the 'us' of modernity or industrialization or what have you, to the have-nots of that same what have you. The history of country A setting itself the goal of catching up with country or countries B is as old as the hills, and reached its most specific policy application in Japan in the second half of the nineteenth century and the Soviet Union in the twentieth. Historians who come up against the heavily (in their view often excessively) conceptualized proceedings of social scientists express an uneasy feeling of *déjà vu*; in what way do modern theories of development differ from the many individual plans for 'improvement' of backward colonies, from Indian agriculture to African constitutionalism? *The concern* is surely as old as knowledge of the non-European world, and a feeling of at least moral responsibility for it.[1] But all this is not quite the same thing as development today. In the past it meant particular courses of action for particular societies that might be chosen as options among many others. But now development has become, at any rate conceptually, a universal priority, a self-generating aspiration resulting from status inequalities in the international system.[2] We must not fail to distinguish between the universality of the pressures for development, and the problem of how societies respond to this pressure, which is what this paper is mainly about. It is the unity and universality of the pressures for development that have led people to see the world as divided into two categories of society, developed and less developed. This universalization, this coherence of categories, is new, as is the passionate involvement in the problem of many leaders in developing countries themselves. But it does not follow that because the actors involved perceive the situation in this fashion, our analysis of the responses to the pressures must also be carried out in terms of these same concepts. The concept of development, as it has itself developed, carries a number of implications which need to be examined. They can be summarized under four headings:

[1] The point was forcibly made by Professor Low in criticism of this paper.

[2] For this, and the substantial literature on measurements of intra-societal statuses and its application to the study of relations between nations, see part III, 'Modernisation and international systems', in J. P. Nettl and Roland Robertson, *International systems and the modernization of societies*, London 1968.

(a) A set of definitional priorities which constitute the meaning of development as a process and the notion of being developed or underdeveloped as a state.

(b) A set of values which make development desirable if not mandatory.

(c) The interconnection between the two categories of developed and underdeveloped societies.

(d) The recognition of an implicit rank order of development—at least in the mind of the analyst, but possibly also in that of the participants.

### (a) Definitional priorities

The original foundation of the concept of development was economic—the result of a distinction between growth (a much older, pre-war pre-occupation in the West which took the starting point for granted), and a focus on more fundamental, generic changes in socio-economic categories of which industrialization was the most important (the Soviet Union providing the menacing example of rapid, deliberately managed transformation to which less painful and more democratic responses had to be found). The early analyses recognized to a greater or lesser extent the importance of socio-political factors, but saw them as separate, though associated—*either* as prior conditions *or* as subsequent results. The literature of the fifties, which debated the order of these problems, now seems grossly out of date, especially since the Third World countries made their own decisions in the matter. They tended to regard national independence almost universally as a pre-condition of economic development, in some cases even as a sufficient condition. Following independence, the revolutionary countries generally opted for socio-political priorities, the 'democratic' ones for a more distinctly economic or economistic solution. (It is a matter of degree, of course; economic priorities imply the acceptance of a distinct economic rationality which cannot be wholly subsumed under socio-political priorities. I am assuming that since the capacity of developing countries for social manipulation and control is very small compared to industrial countries, rigorous economic planning in such countries can be regarded as an interesting exercise in socio-political mobilization, but not necessarily as conducive to economic development or growth.)[1]

In practice the regimes which saw themselves as revolutionary soon ran into mountainous economic difficulties and drowned their failures in increasingly non-economic ideologies and justifications which, as in Indonesia, Algeria, and Ghana, ceased to bear much relation to any of the existing academic models and hypotheses of development. The non-revolutionary, more 'pluralist' states struggled on and are still struggling today, but the success of their development in an economic sense is very much in doubt. Ironically, the countries with failed revolu-

[1] See J. P. Nettl, *Political mobilisation*, London 1967.

tionary regimes are being guided back to more orthodox economic priorities (Ghana and Indonesia), while the economistic democracies like India are increasingly held to be incapable of development without major social and political upheavals. This in itself reflects the hesitant and discordant divisions of development theories into socio-political and economistic priorities, and also the seesaw between historical analogy and abstract models of utilitarian or rational emphasis.

In the last decade the specification of development has increasingly shed its early teleological assumptions according to which a Western-type industrialization was both essential and inevitable. As both the democratic perspectives and the economic hopes were eroded, a search for alternative models began—both by the leaders in developing countries and by academic analysts—with Japan, the Soviet Union and even China (for a time) as possible models. At the same time, to counteract the imposition of European history abstracted into developmental stages (or, in the Soviet case, developmental upheavals) on to their very un-European societies, the countries of Asia, Africa and Latin America searched their history for glosses that might be grafted on to the imported model, hoping to provide politically possible and economically successful local versions of development theories.[1]

Thus as the teleology receded out of development theories, breaking up both the deterministic economic priorities of Rostow and the democratic priorities of, say, Lipset, an increasingly relativistic concept of development emerged, which took into account the individual diversities and cultural constraints of different societies.[2] Instead, people saw development as having to do with what was hopefully described as the attainment of specific and identifiable societal goals. Moreover, these were regarded as more and more self-consciously influenced by awareness of different societal assets and 'capabilities'—means—of which the developmental analyst increasingly took note. Thus the political development of Pakistan was seen to differ markedly from that of Tanzania: both in turn differ substantially from that of India or Indonesia or Latin-America.

But the loosening of the teleological hold of the Western model did not simply make it less relevant. Rather it led in turn to a re-conceptualization of the Western experience in more differentiated socio-political terms (the relaxing of the domination of economics making itself simultaneously felt in the study of Western history as well), and this produced new conceptual categories intended to be applicable across national boundaries. As we shall see, the time factor came to play an important role. Western

[1] African and Asian socialism, what might be described as African and Asian 'traditionalist integrationism' (no classes, community instead of materialistic society, etc.), Latin American 'developmental nationalism' (invented in Brazil), and so on. The literature has been noted in the West, but rarely analysed with any consistency.

[2] W. W. Rostow, *The stages of economic growth*, Cambridge 1960; S. M. Lipset, *Political man: the social bases of politics*, New York 1960, ch. II.

historical development came to be regarded as a series of inescapable crises and responses to crises whose sequence and timing constituted the process of development. To this extent the West now became not so much a precise blueprint for development as a model of steps towards the attainment of modernity which today's developing countries would have to emulate—if not by specific institutional or quantitative replication, at least through functional equivalence. This was the period of theoretical–empirical area analyses, of which Pye's study of Burma was the first and best known, in which a specific theory of developmental change towards modernity was set out and tested as far as possible.[1] In any case, the developed world (increasingly including the Soviet Union) still furnished the raw material for the meaning of modernity, though the means of reaching it were now seen as much more varied than before. At about the time that the notion of different paths to socialism began to make a serious breach in the universal applicability of whatever happened to be called Leninism in the Soviet Union at the time, the notion of different paths to development made itself felt in the West.

This process of 'desimplification' of the concept of development raised definitional problems which remain unresolved. With the gradual loosening of the immediate causal connection between economic growth and various categories of development (economic, social, political, even psychological), industrialization came to be regarded as a separate issue from development. Even within an economic perspective, problems of priorities between agriculture and industry, between balanced and unbalanced growth, between measures of collective and individual 'betterment' further eroded confidence about meanings. To these difficulties of conceptualization was added the intrusion of the more recent category of 'modernity'—a relativistic concept if ever there was one. Various relationships between all these categories have been proposed, but it is certainly significant that such conceptual problems should arise at this time; it is surely evidence of ideological uncertainty. A possible non-economic meaning for development, suggested below (p. 25) with the long-term implication that the economies of developing countries would remain stagnant, and focused primarily on the socio-political consequences of such stagnation, is regarded as either a reactionary recommendation or an unsound prediction by many scholars to whom the primary purpose of development is still economic. Thus the basic contrast between a normative and a logical/empirical ordering of categories remains, in this as in almost every area of social science.[2]

[1] Lucian W. Pye, *Politics, personality and nation building: Burma's search for identity*, London and New Haven 1962; also the country analyses of David Apter, Leonard Binder, Jean Grossholtz and others.

[2] For a discussion of the categories, and one solution for a meaningful ordering, see Nettl and Robertson, *International systems*, part I, 'Modernization, industrialization or development?' David Apter has suggested a different, hierarchical order: Industrialization as the lowest, most

## (b) Values

Concurrently with the change in definition of what constitutes development there has been a connected change in the identification of societal
goals in developing countries. Indeed the question of values and goals as
such only became a research problem once the teleological assumptions
of the Western model were found wanting. For instance it was possible
at one time to regard Burma as an example of the conflict between
'traditional' and 'modern' values—both on the macro-level of society
and the micro-level of the individual. Today we would be more likely to
regard Burma as a special case in which policies and results should be
appraised in terms of the values evidenced by its chosen international role
of withdrawal and 'privatization'.

With the attempt to focus on the values and goals of the society under
study an intervening variable was thus placed between the hitherto more or
less agreed meaning of modernity (or 'state of being developed')—that is,
approaching the levels of development of the West—and the study of
the process, as well as evaluation of the chances, of achieving this modernity.
While the measurement of progress was still tied to the state of the West,
the means of getting there varied, became 'functionalized'. This was the
period of Parsonian pattern-variables and their empirical specification
(and occasional adaptation to circumstances); analysts looked hard for
evidence of functional differentiation. Above all it was recognized that
the actual goals of a society might in fact not be wholly conducive to
economic growth or modernization in spite of the rhetoric; both democracy
and development (especially economic development) came to be regarded
as in conflict with what was actually happening, above all with what a
good part of the leadership in the Third World seemed to want most
immediately. It was the first period of disillusion—too many armies,
too much bureaucratic parasitism, too much unequal distribution and
not enough production, too much concentration on display projects and
neglect of infra-structure, too much articulation of conflicts between
communities, in short too much politics for the élites, not enough authentic
participation for the masses. For anything but the very long run, the
Western model began to be regarded as unattainable, especially given the
absolute character of the values and goals of many Third World leaders.
Indeed, some analysts now began to view the Western model as destructive;
destructive, in particular, of stability, which had slowly become the
unconscious but dominant preoccupation of Western analysts. And the
immutability of the Western world as a value in itself was also challenged
from within Western society; far from the state of ultimate perfection

empirical category, contained in a broader category of modernization which includes non-
economic components, while development becomes a purely logical category (as suggested in
this paper) in which particular processes of change, possibly related to a means–ends dichotomy,
are accommodated.

which it appeared to be so long as it was a model for developing countries, it looked instead to be heavy with problems of its own. A new emphasis on societal goals on the part of leaders in developed countries was matched by academic preoccupations with the problems and values of so-called 'post-modernity'. The scene in the West acquired a new dynamic; the absence of protest in allegedly fully integrated societies was replaced by a new wave of anti-system alienation—beginning, perhaps, with the Civil Rights movement and the Berkeley campus events of the early 1960s.

### (c) The connection between the developed and less developed world

Quite apart from the problems of imperialist penetration—real or imagined—both the theories of development and the actual situation in the world for the last twenty years have necessarily laid heavy stress on the interdependence of the two worlds. Indeed, theories of development may be regarded as a fugue on this theme. As long as the industrial West was regarded as a model to be emulated, it necessarily served also as a standard of performance, both for whole societies and for individual projects, technological innovation, administration and so on. The notion of comparative standards of performance at all levels is a basic concept in industrial society and as such is inherent in the whole idea of development. After the erosion of the linear/teleological idea of development, the absence of any adequate substitute for comparative attainment caused the developed world to be retained as a generalized image, even if no longer as a detailed model of process. This image varies, however, according to often conflicting views about the nature of development. Here are the main variants reflected in the literature.

1. The now declining view of the West as the inevitable and/or best example of the process of industrialization—the linear teleology.

2. The somewhat similar conceptual distinction between developed and underdeveloped (or modern and non-modern) without the linear teleology. The crystallization and specification of development and underdevelopment as two distinct analytical categories is common to much American literature. Here the actual process of development is sometimes regarded as a transitional mix of the two categories, occasionally elevated to the status of a distinct category in its own right, like the prismatic one of Fred Riggs.[1]

3. A whole spectrum of analyses clustering round the central concept of imperialism, which regards the Third World as the new locus of the traditional class struggles in industrial societies, and the revolution of the Third World against the First or Western World (sometimes also against the Second or Soviet World) as the new variant of the proletarian revolution.

[1] F. W. Riggs, *Administration in developing countries*, Boston 1964; 'The theory of developing politics', *World Politics* XVI, 1 (October 1963), 147–71.

This approach reflects the division between capitalist and anti-capitalist ideologies in the analysis of capitalist industrial societies.

4. The recent reconceptualization of Western socio-political history as a series of necessary crises or stages which must be passed through in order to attain modernity. This variant of functionalism—the crises are in fact functional exigencies which must be met, though how, when and in what order, are empirical problems whose solution governs success or failure— makes much use of time scales. Certain minimum intervals between the different crises are essential, and the order in which they appear is also important. Almond's work is significant in the development of this approach; Lipset and Rokkan's introduction to their recent volume on parties and voters provides the most sophisticated conceptualization of Western history in this manner.[1] What this amounts to is a rewriting of European, American and even Soviet history for developmental purposes. The modern world is no longer so much a goal or a process model but an historical abstraction of functional 'events' which, one way or another, must happen and be coped with by all countries aspiring to modernity.

5. Finally, the dismissal of the model and history of the existing developed world as only marginally relevant to today's Third World in terms of any general theory of development—though, of course, the two 'worlds' remain closely connected in regard to interaction, exchange, influence and even control in empirical terms; a position which I myself have adopted.

### (d) Rank order of development

The early teleological perspectives and the search for specific developmental indices gave rise to a number of academic exercises in rank ordering. Initially these were mainly economic, but several attempts were made to produce increasingly independent socio-political rankings with their own non-economic indices. Thus the primacy of economic factors as relevant to notions of development was questioned, and so was the related identification of wealth with democracy. As the construction of indices and rank-orders becomes more sophisticated, however, the difficulty of giving an adequate definition of social and political development not tied too closely to 'extraneous' economic and ideological factors becomes more and more apparent.[2] In so far as an interest in scaling or rank ordering remains, it is likely to focus increasingly on organizational criteria like capabilities of the political system to control or coerce, or on a wide sweep of economic, social, political, and cybernetic indices which provide hard

---

[1] S. M. Lipset and Stein Rokkan, 'Cleavage structures, party systems and voter alignments: an introduction', in Lipset and Rokkan (eds.), *Party systems and voter alignments: cross-national perspectives*, London and New York 1967, pp. 1–64. A recent statement of problems is Eric A. Nordlinger, 'Political development: time sequences and rates of change', *World Politics* XX, 3 (April 1968), 494–520.

[2] See the comments by Deane E. Neubauer, 'Some conditions of democracy', *APSR* LXI, 4 (December 1967), 1002–9.

data without any commitment to professed institutional or processual em-phases—summations or aggregates of individual characteristics.[1] How-ever, since any rank ordering implies a commitment to the validity of common factors throughout the scale, growing doubts about regarding development as a continuum based on Western indices are likely to reduce interest in producing such rank orderings. If development is indeed a highly differential process according to particular societies and their goals, then rank ordering comparisons become meaningless.[2]

We may indeed be approaching the end of a phase of developmental analysis. The unities are breaking up, both in terms of cross-disciplinary priorities and indices as well as cross-national relevance. One may well question whether the notion of developed and less developed worlds is as meaningful as it appeared even five years ago. Much of the consciousness of unity and similarity of situation in the Third World, which under-pinned the validity of the conceptual category of 'less developed countries', was expressed in practical terms by the attempts on the part of the Third World to speak with a single voice. These have largely failed; the failure in turn throws doubt on the value of the overarching concept of a Third World. In addition, there has been a shift back to problems of 'develop-ment' in the industrialized world, as regards both policy and analysis. This renewed self-absorption in many developed countries is matched by a declining interest in the economic and political events of the Third World (the minimal reporting of the 1968 UNCTAD conference in the Western press was significant evidence of this). Political uncertainties in the West and the Soviet bloc, the raising of problems long regarded as finally settled in consumer societies, a new awareness of poverty and the need for 'aid' at home, have all reduced the immediacy of Third World problems. The Third World, to put it bluntly, is being left to stew, or bubble, or seethe, according to individual taste in culinary metaphors. All this seems to suggest that development as a concept and as a problem may be going out of fashion.

### SOME REQUIREMENTS OF A NEW THEORY
### OF DEVELOPMENT

But to those who are well aware that the area of concern has not become less important or less interesting, the problem is rather the extent to which

[1] For the former, see the forthcoming work of Karl von Vorys, *The theory of political development*. The latter approach is to be found primarily in the work of Karl Deutsch, 'Social mobilization and political development', *APSR* LV, 3 (September 1961), 493–514.

[2] The Russians have had somewhat similar troubles with their scale of 'development' in a Marxist or neo-Marxist sense. See T. P. Thornton (ed.), *The third world in Soviet perspective*, Princeton 1964; more recently Herbert S. Dinnerstein, 'Soviet policy in Latin America', *APSR* LXI, 1 (March 1967), 80–90. Elizabeth K. Valkenier, 'Recent trends in Soviet research on the developing countries', *World Politics* XX, 3 (July 1968), 644–59.

the current development theories are in difficulty owing to the failure of one particular approach and its various, increasingly sophisticated echoes. In spite of growing scepticism, a growing relativism and above all greater sophistication in universalizing Western developmental history, the formulation of problems of development still takes place within a fundamentally similar framework to that of fifteen years ago. Certain epistemological hurdles remain which are unlikely to be surmounted by the accumulation and analysis of empirical data. I would suggest, instead, that a fundamental restructuring of our conceptual framework is required within which data can in future be analysed more effectively. Perhaps the best way to identify these hurdles is to enumerate some of the problem areas which have hitherto been neglected or inadequately dealt with.

### (a) The interrelated world

The first problem is to shift the meaning of the notion of a single world away from model images and historical abstractions provided by allegedly advanced for allegedly retarded nations, to an understanding of interrelatedness which focuses on what is really relevant—in terms of similarities as well as contrasts. The interrelatedness of societies and groups of societies is above all an empirical fact. It can be broken down into various layers. One layer consists of the manifold strategic–diplomatic factors and processes of interaction, ranging from the activities of the United Nations to the relationship of economic aid and exchange and finally to the genuine problems of neo-imperialism caused by the economic and cultural penetration of small countries by large and powerful countries. This huge and growing arena of interaction is primarily a matter of empirical investigation, but certain general conclusions and hypotheses are being drawn from it, such as the relationship between socio-structural proximity and conflict, or between strategic alliances and transaction flows of different societies.[1] Such hypotheses and generalizations would provide one of the building blocks of development theory, though nothing very relevant has emerged so far.

Another layer is the uneven but vital spread of technology and the demand for it. Here we have to face a problem that is simply not understood at present: the accessibility of information and of sophisticated technological objects to societies which consume them but cannot produce them. We tend to regard the problem of technology as a notional level of attainment which, once reached, is irreversible, whereas in fact the situation is one in which technological consumption is much more readily

---

[1] For the first, see for instance the work of Rudolph J. Rummel and R. Tanter on the dimensionality of nations, and Johan Galtung's studies of structural dimensions of conflict. For the second, Stephen J. Brams, 'Transaction flows in the international system', *APSR* LX, 4 (December 1966). In addition, many of the strategy and power formalizations of relations and conflicts between nations presumably have relevance to the Third World, even though most of the focus has been on the West.

available than the industrial–scientific base to produce it. This fact, coupled with very uneven levels of technological capacity, is crucial in any theory of development, for it cuts right across the very idea of uniform levels of development as between one group of societies and another, and incidentally knocks away one of the main props of the relevance of the Western experience.

One example may help to illuminate this problem area. Some of the technologically most backward societies operate reasonably efficient airlines with very sophisticated equipment. This has a number of implications. For one thing, it creates an enclave of 'high modernity', which may absorb such small pools of modern human resources as the society possesses without having hitherto been aware of it. There is evidence that certain families tend to run the airlines of developing countries.[1] Secondly, it structures the consumer perceptions of masses in ways which differ fundamentally from the incrementalism, particularly as between generations, which is normal in the West, where things have to be invented and tried before they can acquire mass usage. Thirdly, it skews both investment and import strategies in strange ways, reinforcing (inter alia) the neglect of agriculture. Similar problems arise with regard to weapons; in many countries the technological gap between available weapons and the prevailing levels of technological know-how is greater than at any time in history. The same is true of communication media like television.

Yet another layer of what might be described as the *monde fini*, the wholly interrelated world, is the amount of information about other countries circulating in a world-wide information system, and the consequent relative freedom of elites and leaders to select models unfettered by geographical continuity or cultural similarity. It can be argued that this leads to a world of multiple modernities, within which selection is a much more complex notion than it was in the days when there seemed to be a consensus about what constituted the most advanced society. This in turn, however, creates a gap between elite and mass of hitherto undreamt-of proportions.

The whole problem of leadership in developing countries can be regarded as an attempt to resolve the conflicts between the 'overlayer' of 'modern' objects made available from outside (both technological and social) and the indigenous 'underlayer' of social resources. Shall change be internally generated or exogenously imposed? Is the modernity inevitably located *within* societies? If the latter, does the existence of a small and fragile island of modernity clustering round the government, the army and certain sectors of industry lead directly to a basic instability

---

[1] See David Corbett, *Politics and the airlines*, London 1965, pp. 303–23, for evidence on India and Latin America. The general economic theory of imbalanced growth may be found most clearly expressed in the work of Albert Hirschmann, *The strategy of economic development*, New Haven 1958; *Journeys towards progress*, New York 1963.

in the relation between overlayer and underlayer, with the former 'floating free' of any societal base and therefore available for easy capture, at least temporarily, by anyone willing and able? Looked at in this way, the bothersome problem of so-called political instability in developing countries assumes a different shape, and ceases to appear as the embryonic or misshapen reflection (according to ideological taste) of the 'stable' processes of developed politics and government.

As against these layers of positive inter-relatedness in the contemporary world, there are equally important negative contrasts which also constitute a form of inter-relatedness. Most important perhaps is the increasing doubt regarding the universality of the Western experience of industrialization. In spite of all the internal differences between 'developed' countries, they still constitute a relative unity in historical experience and present situation compared with the rest of the world; while there is such a thing as post-industrial modernity, its absence does not provide an opposite category of similar uniformity and common characteristics. Moreover, post-industrial modernity may be seen as a unique but parochial phenomenon. Not only are there at least three distinct internal models of industrialization—West European, Russian, and Japanese—but one may well doubt whether some or even any form of industrialization is an inevitability. This would imply that the difference between industrial and non-industrial countries may be very long-lasting and may come to be regarded as less crucial a stimulant to socio-economic change or development than we presently think. As I suggested, the direct conceptual connection between industrialization and development has been largely broken already, partly because no simple or direct relationship is discernible between levels of economic growth and socio-political structures or processes, and partly because at a conceptual level sociologists and political scientists will not be tied in their work to *ex ante* or *ex post* economic priorities. Accordingly future theories of development might increasingly discard the economic components of the Western experience and learn to live with the assumption that socio-political 'development' in many countries in the world today might have to take place in a situation of industrial stagnation or even regression.

Once this hurdle is crossed, various possibilities suggest themselves. Increasingly specific theories of socio-political development would focus more and more on problems of control rather than structural change. As I shall argue in the next section, the traditional societal units might give way to new ones as new forms of social and political control face up to chronic instability in the presently existing national or governmental units of the Third World. An alternative approach is to face up to the question of a possible international system in which both industrial and non-industrial collectivities or units (mostly but not necessarily 'nation-states') would fulfil necessary systematic functions and become connected by some form of organic solidarity which would tie presently irreconcilable diversity into the *modus vivendi* of a world system. The industrial world might supply sophisticated technological objects and services, the non-industrial world 'primitive' products like textiles and raw materials and labour. The imbalance of relative incomes might be partially rectified by substantial equalization payments (as in the French community of African states). In this way our current, almost total, conceptual dependence on the causal ring between production and consumption within given national–societal units may be ultimately broken. The mutual concessions and bargains necessary to underpin such a system, it should be stressed, would have to arise not out of moral considerations, but from the pressure of functional necessity, including fear of destruction of the 'North' by the hungry and revolutionary 'South'. It is worth stressing that behind every theory of development lies a more or less explicit theory of international relations; what we may be approaching is a situation in which a theory of development follows from a theory of international relations.

### (b) *Stability and Instability*

Another problem is our obsession with the primacy of stability as a necessary condition of development  The implications of this built-in assumption in our thinking are very important. For one thing they incorporate what are really low levels of specificity into what we tend to regard as significant. Thus we regard regimes as significant; most of our major classifications of politics are still based on types of regime. In the history of the West and the Soviet Union changes of regime are taken—no doubt correctly—to imply and reflect major changes in the societal nature of the unit studied. A theory of Western development is therefore at least in part a theory of the nature of socio-political regimes; Marxism joins traditional forms of analysis in this respect. In many parts of the world today, however, regimes come and go with bewildering rapidity. Similarly we tend to regard electoral systems and the nature of party systems as significant, but these too are things that come and go rapidly in parts of the Third World.

The problem can be illustrated most effectively if we look closely at the literature about the military in developing countries; Dowse's paper in this volume shows the weakness of many of the theories, paradigms, and typologies about the military. Finer, in his published work, has perhaps pushed systematization as far as it can go without falling foul of empirical accuracy. Yet apart from a few really very obvious statements (like discipline, concentrated presence, and possession of arms), the analogies and comparisons are strung out in a chain of tangential dyadic similarities: the situation of $A$ resembled $B$ in regard to $x$ and $y$, $B$ resembled $C$ in regard to $y$ and $z$, while it is instructive to note that $C$ has in common with $D$, $E$, and perhaps $F$, though $F$ is a special case because of the predominance of *n*, etc., etc. But the difficulties of such a procedure are not due to any methodological or intellectual failure but to the weakness of the concept of 'the military' in developing countries. With all due allowance for differences in historical development and tradition among European armies, these latter are sufficiently similar to permit systemic comparative analysis; the armies in developing countries are not. By focusing on the military in the first place (in anything beyond a recital of facts and events) we may be committing ourselves to systemic assumptions which are unwarranted (e.g. that military coups are an abnormal and illegitimate means of changing regimes, signifying a breakdown of 'normal' processes—when in fact orderly elections are the deviant form or breakdown of normality in, say, Africa; or that the military are 'non-ideological' etc., etc.). By focusing on such structures, which in many developing countries are *not* in fact structures within the strict meaning of the term, we build a finding of instability into the asking rather than answering of the questions. This then is the basis for our tendency to consider the Third World as unstable.

Even approaches that surmount overt preoccupation with political structure and concentrate on the functions supposed to be necessarily performed by all systems are equally anchored in an ideology of stability. If we do not know what structure fulfils what function, we cannot conduct a sociological form of systems analysis at all. Instead, we tend to see a rubbish-bin of undifferentiated primitiveness, which—in so far as systems analysts are historically minded—is equated with our own dim and distant past.

Regimes, party systems and electoral participation may, therefore, prove to be unsuitable components for any theory of development in the Third World, simply because they imply a level of specificity meaningful only for ideologies of relatively great stability. Some recent theorists have become aware of this problem and have tried to use the notion of process at a higher level of generality. Integration, nation-building, commitment to the universalism of a societal level instead of the parochialism of the village, achievement instead of ascription, mobilization, institutionalization and other such processes have figured in recent approaches to theories of development. In focusing on these processes, traditional categories of analysis like parties, bureaucracies, governments, etc. have had to be emptied of the contents with which our own history and tradition has filled them; to retain them as structural identifiers at all has required stretching their meaning far beyond the range of meaning hitherto accepted (and as Staniland's paper in this volume indicates, sometimes too far to be helpful).

But in spite of these concessions to unpredictable change the ideology of stability remains very strong. The problem is to find a way of acommodating into the analysis structures that may dissolve before our very eyes at any time, without at the same time jeopardizing the status of all theory. For instance, we must accept that we may be studying nation-states which may cease to exist—for there is no continuing reason why some of the new states should survive for any length of time (though it must be noted that the high level of inter-relatedness in the world today does act partly to maintain national survival, since the climate of opinion in the international system does not favour the disappearance of national actors, except possibly by an amoebic, dividing process). New states as well as parties and movements tend to appear. Perhaps the first classification we should make is into states with high, even and low chances of survival (for which the ratio of population growth versus resource growth would be one crucial index). Finally we must regard periods of lengthy warfare, civil as well as international, as a normal feature of political and social development in many areas of the world. At present we regard war as a breakdown of order. Though it carries possible consequences for theories of development we have not made it a basic part of any such theory, but relegated it to a special discipline concerned with conflict.

An alternative to the use of process in building theories of development free from the inhibiting constraints of relying too much on stability is to focus squarely on problems. One such approach is indicated by Barrington Moore's recent study of comparative modernization which asks the conceptually simple but empirically very complex question: *cui bono?*[1] Here the drive for modernization and large-scale social change—defined as a distinct transformation of status-dominated agricultural self-sufficiency to production for the market—is related to an historical analysis of who the carriers of such changes were and what benefits they expected and actually did derive from them. Although Barrington Moore's analysis is primarily concerned with the past, it is perfectly possible to envisage a middle-range theory of possible changes in developing countries based on asking who really rules and who gets what benefits from ruling in, or from overthrowing, the existing system. This approach ties up very interestingly with the much more *ad hoc* irascibility of writers like Rene Dumont who excoriates the elites of Africa and India for maintaining a system which offers them direct benefits and hence a stake in the *status quo*, but which inhibits development in the sense of a large-scale improvement of living standards.[2]

### (c) Population

The very difficulty of using the habitual categories of socio-political analysis, and of adjusting existing knowledge to the peculiar juxtaposition of continuities and discontinuities in the world today, makes the search for new factors of significance all the more urgent. Thus we hear a great deal

[1] Barrington Moore Jr., *Social origins of dictatorship and democracy: lord and peasant in the making of the modern world*, Boston 1966.

[2] René Dumont, *False start in Africa*, London 1966; *Terres vivantes: voyages d'un agronome autour du monde*, Paris 1961.

about the population explosion and a certain amount about the possible demographic, agricultural, and economic strategies which must be adopted to prevent disaster. Yet we know next to nothing about the socio-political consequences of demographic explosions. If the Cassandras are right, the politics of developing countries will probably be governed to a considerable extent by the rapid increase in population; there is at least one recent study which puts forward an international policy for the United States in which population problems are the main component.[1] It is remarkable that with the great paucity of literature on this particular subject, one of the very few comparitive studies of political systems, written by anthropologists, comes to the conclusion that no relationship can be discovered between population density and political organization. As against this, an attempt, as far as I know the first, to argue with any evidence and vigour for the existence of such a relationship, has recently appeared in America; but this is not yet anything like a conceptual correlation, much less a theory.[2] The discovery of meaningful relationships between demographic and socio-political change may, however, eventually enable us to formulate a theory of development applicable to the present time and the near future which will subsume the relatively epiphenomenal problems of structure, process, regime—and perhaps even national identity. For instance, the Vietnamese situation, particularly the strategy of the North Vietnam government and the N.L.F., appears to be based on a strategically interpreted relation between demographic growth and acceptable casualties—a strategy that is quite new in the history of what might be called development theories, and which upsets all existing Western theories of cost-effectiveness and growth. If such an approach to the strategies of development politics becomes widespread, the previous perception of the possible or acceptable limits to instability will dissolve before quite new forms of conflict, flux and change as a normal feature in the politics of the Third World. Analysis and theory, then, must needs follow such new reality. At present there is no academic theory of development of which I am aware that accommodates the Vietnam war as anything but a huge setback—i.e. does not view it from the American–Saigon point of view.

[1] William and Paul Paddock, *Famine—1975!*, London 1968. This suggests a policy of *triage* for the U.S.; helping the marginal survivors and abandoning those who in any case will, or will not survive—on the assumption that there is not enough aid for all.

[2] The negative relationship between population density or change with political structure is argued by M. Fortes and E. E. Evans-Pritchard in their classic *African political systems*. For the recent counter-argument see Robert F. Stevenson, *Population and political systems in tropical Africa*, Columbia University Press, New York 1968.

To avoid misunderstanding, I should perhaps make it clear that the literature of anthropology has always been directly concerned with the effects of changing populations, in size as well as composition, on culture and political system. But whereas for anthropologists this is a constituent part of the depiction and explanation of cultures, for political scientists it is a possible variable of correlation and causality, as yet largely unexplored. Cf. Vincent's paper in this volume.

Connected with this are the often significant differences in age structure between elites and populations of developed and developing countries. Once again the ageing population of modern societies and the 'resultant' politics (assuming that there is a connection) are assumed to apply to developing countries only in so far as Western politics are considered relevant. Yet it could surely be argued that interventionist or planning-conscious parliamentary democracy is not so much the political super-structure of capitalism as that of an ageing population. At the moment no theory of which I am aware can accommodate the political problems result-ing from age differences between elites; though there is at least one lengthy statement of a particular generational problem in developing countries which is faithfully echoed by political scientists who do their homework.[1] It may well be, therefore, that the politics of the developing countries will become more systematically comprehensible in terms of the shape and size of the age cohorts in positions of power there. Since the problem of institutionalizing generational conflicts in modern consumer societies is now also beginning to raise its head, a general effort to incorporate such problems into theories of development appears all the more desirable.

### (d) Race

One of the crucial issues in the study of process—especially with regard to such processes as nation-building, mobilization, and integration—has been the form which collective self-definition will take. Some evidence is appearing which suggests that it may well be race, at least in the long run. While much of the communal conflict in India and Africa is best under-stood in terms of ethnic discontinuities and ethnic group-consciousness, one of the consequences of the interrelatedness of nations in the world may well be the 'grossing up' of ethnic consciousness into heightened consciousness of race. If the crucial division within and between nations in the second half of the twentieth century is indeed to be race, then clearly new strategies and tactics as well as more imponderable societal changes are likely to result. The very pride of many intellectuals in developing countries in the absence of classic European class problems may simply be based on the substitution of race for class divisions. There are numerous examples of attempts to adapt to a racial setting the classic European revolutionary tradition based on class.[2] And the Chinese contribution to 'international relations' has been precisely this formal identification of

---

[1] S. N. Eisenstadt, *From generation to generation*, is, of course, the major statement with functional correlates for industrial societies. For an echo of this see e.g. Lucian Pye; 'The non-Western political process is characterized by sharp differences in the political orientation of the generations through lack of continuity—in the circumstances under which people are recruited to politics', 'The non-Western political process', in H. Eckstein and D. Apter (eds.), *Comparative politics*, New York 1963, p. 660. For a case study see Jean-Michel Wagret, *Histoire et sociologie politique de la République du Congo (Brazzaville)*, Paris 1963.

[2] Probably the work of Frantz Fanon is the best known in this regard.

the relationship between developed and developing countries as the modern, international version of the Marxist class struggle, and its reinforcement by superimposing on it a race cleavage involving the same classes; this superimposition of different conflicts on top of one another being a means of exacerbating them which is well known in sociology. Interestingly both theories and policies of this kind are almost all confined to the revolutionary variant of development specified under heading 3 on p. 20 above, that is to say in a tradition wholly at odds with orthodox Western developmental theory. The study of race, even at an empirical level and taken on its own, is usually confined to patently racialist societies like South Africa.[1]

It seems likely, therefore, that theories of development must eventually attempt to accommodate racial conflict or at least racial differences. At present, however, we have really no tools for analysing the societal impact of race problems. Class and race hang together very badly, and the attempts to explore racial disjunctions and exploitations in class terms have led to great difficulties. There is an immediacy of primary identification and interpersonal conflict which is quite lacking in class formation and confrontation between classes; the very violence of personal conflict between black and white obviates the intervention of sociological collectivist notions as a means of creating identities and then hostility. Problems such as this indicate that, quite apart from the objective importance of race conflict in the modern, interrelated world and its influence on development in different societies, a focus on race will produce new methodological and conceptual categories. It is worth noting, however, that the long preoccupation with anti-semitism in European history made little or no contribution in this regard; it has simply been ignored in most current sociological or political theory.

## CONCLUSION

In stressing the unsolved problem areas and difficulties in the current state of development theories, above all in suggesting that we are reaching the end of a phase rather than a take-off point from the groundwork prepared during the last decade, I do not want to minimize the importance of the contributions that have been made. The idea that there should be such things as theories of development at all has helped a great deal to overcome the parochialism of individual studies of societies and has helped to relate our conceptual apparatus to the real world. Interest in theories of development was due simultaneously to policy requirements on the part of governments and international organizations, and to the interest taken

[1] See, for instance, Leo Kuper, *An African bourgeoisie: race, class, and politics in South Africa*, for a careful study of 'integrating race into the normal analytical tools used by sociologists of development'.

by academics in the countries newly inducted, somewhat naked and bereft, into the international system. Moreover, the study of development has brought political scientists, sociologists and economists somewhat closer by differentiating between their respective autonomies and contributions. The 'pure' economic theory of development which simply abstracts from all socio-political factors, such as Tinbergen's recent book, has now become something of a curiosity. The study of development has also contributed substantially to the infusion of a dynamic approach to the study of society generally; we have become fascinated by change. Finally there is no doubt that the salience of developmental problems has made social scientists more historically minded, and has helped to produce highly ingenious theories of how we ourselves became what we are.

But the very division of the world into strata of developed and developing countries has imposed constraints which have proved conceptually and empirically misleading. The disruption of linear teleology still left the industrialized world as the supplier of concepts which were imposed on the non-industrial world as tools of analysis, means of change and goals of development. Even today the whole analytical apparatus brought to bear on the study of development is redolent with Western concepts—just as Soviet analysis of development reeks of their own experience. The recognition of today's Third World as a unique category—however differentiated it may be within itself—requires a new set of concepts which will not only accommodate the peculiar forms of substantial interrelatedness between different sectors of the world today but at the same time will allow for the uniqueness and the remarkable parochialism of processes in the industrial countries. The virtual disintegration of the Third World as an operative bloc in world politics, the resultant disillusionment with the very notion of a bloc of developing countries, still do not obviate the need for a special category in which to place societies which are not industrialized and regard themselves as distinct and different from countries that are. On the contrary, I think that the strategic failure of the Bandung concept of bloc action actually facilitated analysis of the Third World as an analytic category, for it directed attention to more important continuities and discontinuities behind the façade of cohesiveness in international strategy. One of the crucial discontinuities is the actual experience of decolonization, ranging from polite hand-over to protracted and hence integrative struggle.[1] 'Underdeveloped' may thus be a useful analytic category of self-identification but has little to do with processes of 'catching up' which cannot be measured, let alone ranked.

I have indicated three possible approaches to theories of development in these circumstances—assuming that the concept will not be abandoned altogether, that we do not finish up with 'mere' systematic explanations of

---

[1] For an analysis of the long-range effects of this see Nettl and Robertson, *International systems*, section II.

non-development, and finally that we do not relapse into the study of individual and unique discreteness for each society or subunit.

First a focus on structure which conceivably will retain familiar names like party, bureaucracy and so on but will assign new meaning to them.[1] For instance the concept of 'party' will have to accommodate processes and phenomena vastly different from the cleavage–structure approach, the most recent and sophisticated approach to historical political sociology in the West. Similarly the Soviet conception of 'party' hardly applies; it can be argued that the failure of mobilization regimes like that of Nkrumah, Sukarno, and Ben Bella was due to an excessive if unconscious reliance on the Soviet model of party exclusiveness and hegemony without the unique religious quality and ideological compactness of Bolshevism, or the circumstances and traditions in which it grew and conquered. The type of parties emerging in Tanzania, Zambia, and elsewhere in Africa try to provide something quite new. It is too early to say what it is in conceptual terms or whether these parties contribute anything to political development over time; a mere confrontation of rhetoric with reality in itself tells us little about failure or success. At present party regimes appear to be on the wane, and are being replaced by makeshift forms of military and political leadership. But those which do survive may effectively provide answers to the unique integrative problems of 'instant nations'; load-bearing structures acting as a nation's inner shell, means of political socialization in 'inadequate' societal circumstances, channels of mobility in still relatively unurbanized and disjunctive societies, recruitment agencies for political elites and so on. I am still inclined to believe that some variant of 'party' will prove to be the peculiar contribution of the Third World to the solution of its perceived and perhaps even unperceived statistical and processual problems. Why? Because the gap between individual institutions and the societal whole, between imperialistic islands of modernity and their indigenous base, is so great in developing countries that totally disparate levels of development are possible, and may indeed have to be encouraged. Thus the typical political party in developing countries may be one that keeps itself insulated from 'its' constituent society, except in terms of recruitment inwards and control outwards, for a considerable period; one that fulfils no obvious societal function presently known to us, one that in fact substitutes for society in large measure. Elections, in turn, may come to serve the function of intra-party recruitment instead of inter-party legitimacy, thus opening up very necessary doors to a new view of minimal participation and legitimacy. The state may wither away in Africa before it withers in the Soviet Union. And if so, a theory or theories will, perhaps after some initial lag behind actual

---

[1] The search for self-conscious neologisms as a result of an implicit recognition of the difficulty in handling traditional concepts is already defended in the work of people like Riggs.

events, emerge to explain these phenomena systematically and specify the necessary conditions for success.

Secondly there is the possible concentration on processes, of which a few have been mentioned. Here we have to be sure that the processes selected for study are meaningful and significant. For instance, in my own focus on mobilization I found myself assuming a validity for the national units within which such mobilization took place which may well not prove justified in the event. In any case, phenomena which are recognized as significant in the West, and which contribute substantially to the shape and form of society, may prove to be merely ephemeral in developing countries. This would mean that we must study processes of change at levels of abstraction for which we simply do not have the data; hence the element of speculation is likely to loom large.[1]

Finally there is the problem-approach, which in a sense is more abstract still; the study of consumption versus production of technology, of the relationship between socio-politics and population, general disjunctions and race (to name only three), requires digging even further beyond the obvious furniture of the social and political scene. This is why I have suggested at the very beginning that we may be at least as much in need of a philosophy of development as of a proliferation of detailed empirical studies, however accurate, along conventional lines.

Underlying this check-list of unsolved problems there is the suggestion of a strategy or choice of strategies. Developing countries, weighed down by the impact of their environment, may have fewer choices than we have tended to think. We as students of development do have strategic choices to guide us towards adequate theory. I use the word strategy deliberately to imply a set of consequences to which one is committed by a prior decision. The by-products of the analysis of modern, industrial, Western *or* Soviet society are not enough. Either we must abstract still further to the highest common factor of process, or we must extrude the Western experience from our conceptual apparatus altogether while adding it to the analysis as an empirical fact and vital influence. The reason I have talked of strategies is because the decision on how we choose to regard problems is, in the last resort, ours; it is not an objective datum of the problems studied. At present our approaches still tend to be far too determinist.

[1] See for instance the discussion of institutionalization versus mobilization as factors for and against stability in Samuel P. Huntington, 'Political development and political decay', *World Politics* XVII, 3 (April 1965), 386–430.

# ANTHROPOLOGY AND POLITICAL DEVELOPMENT

## JOAN VINCENT

Anthropology, like political science, stands at a crossroads in a revisionist mood. One way of understanding this is to examine the ideas and data which it offers to political scientists and others concerned with development, and also the effect on anthropology as a discipline of an increasingly explicit concern with the problems of development.

Such an examination will not necessarily focus on what are, possibly, the finest anthropological studies of politics, such as the work of Barth among the Swat Pathan, Bailey on political change in Orissa, or any other of the close empirical studies made at the micro-level of society.[1] It may be that, in the long run, the distinctive contribution of anthropology to the study of political development will prove to have been through the influence of case studies such as these on the general character of political science or on particular fields of analysis within it, not necessarily confined to its applications in studies of development. However, by its nature, anthropology confronts the empirical situations which give rise to a concern with development, and in recent years this confrontation has been more and more explicitly recognized, both in the problems anthropologists choose to study and in the widening of their frame of reference. This essay is about this confrontation and its consequences. Reviewing the literature of the present decade, it discusses the anthropological approach to structural change at the macro-level, that of political development.[2]

The essay is both selective and interpretative. It considers contemporary anthropological writing on the most general level of society, a literature which has its roots in nineteenth-century evolutionary theory and which appears today in many different guises on both sides of the Atlantic.[3]

---

[1] F. G. Bailey, *Politics and social change*, Berkeley 1963; F. Barth, *Political leadership among Swat Pathans*, London 1959.

[2] Annotated bibliographies, each of over 250 items, relating to the anthropological study of development include V. Rubin, 'The anthropology of development', B. Siegel (ed.), *Biennial review of anthropology 1961*, Stanford, California 1962, pp. 120–72; B. J. Siegel, 'Some recent developments in studies of social and cultural change', *The Annals* (of the American Academy of Political and Social Science) 363 (1966), 137–53; R. Murphy, 'Cultural change', B. J. Siegel (ed.) *Biennial review of anthropology 1967*, Stanford, California 1967, pp. 1–45.

[3] As Mair has observed, 'The nineteenth century anthropologists, who thought they could trace a series of phases through which all societies had passed, were in one sense on the right lines, though we seldom mention them now except to laugh at them...But isn't there a sense in which it is true that, in historical times, human societies have trodden very largely the same path?' 'How small-scale societies change', *Penguin survey of the social sciences*, Baltimore 1965, p. 26.

[ 35 ]

The macro-sociological level is becoming increasingly important in social science generally and it is not at this level that anthropology has hitherto succeeded. However, the anthropological contribution to a number of topics of 'developmental' interest—national integration, cultural pluralism and elite structure—is considered below, within the general framework of stratification theory. The essay concludes with a discussion of three related themes that are less obviously central, but nonetheless cannot be ignored: a current questioning of the unit of analysis and an increasing emphasis on ideology (both indications of a growth in the cultural element in societal analysis); a re-examination of the colonial situation in the light of contemporary events; and an increase in European and Latin American ethnographies of peasant society which are heavily influenced by the politics of economic development.

'CHANGE', 'DEVELOPMENT', AND 'EVOLUTION'

The terms 'change', 'development', and 'evolution' are all within the repertoire of the anthropologist, 'development' being the least used. A review of the vocabulary suggests that *political change* usually refers to changes that can be observed and traced. These are often conceptualized as involving continually shifting alignments between individuals and groups. Not all political change involves development. The analysis of so-called 'development cycles' is, in fact, only a recognition of repetitive change or replication within the structure. A similar distinction underlies definitions of rebellion and revolution in anthropology. Involved are changes within the political or social structure and from this type of analysis dual-synchronic or 'process' models are derived.[1] In the past, anthropologists have been happiest with such studies, but it is difficult to perceive radical change (i.e. political development) from this close perspective.

The use of the term *political development* usually reflects a recognition of a major discontinuity in political structure. It appears prominently, for example, in *East African chiefs: a study in political development in some Uganda and Tanganyika tribes* and in M. G. Smith's essay on 'Kagoro political

[1] Distinctions between repetitive, structural, gradual and radical change, as well as distinctions between revolutionary and evolutionary theory, are elucidated by R. Firth, *Essays on social organization and values*, London 1964, pp. 7–29; F. G. Bailey, *Tribe, caste and nation*, Manchester 1960, pp. 251–5; P. Worsley, *The trumpet shall sound*, New York 1968, 2nd augmented edition, pp. 265–66; M. Gluckman, 'The utility of the equilibrium model in the study of social change', *American Anthropologist* 70 (1968), 219–37. See also M. Fortes, Introduction, J. Goody (ed.), *The development cycle in domestic groups*, Cambridge 1958.

The cultural view of the matter is presented by E. Wolf, *Anthropology*, New Jersey 1964; R. Murphy, 'Cultural change...'. A discussion of 'The strategy of social evolution in British social anthropology' is to be found in *Anthropologica* 4 (1962), 321–34, by R. Cohen. A seminal paper on the subject is A. Radcliffe-Brown, 'Social evolution', which appears in the volume edited by M. N. Srinivas, *Method in social anthropology*, Chicago and London 1958, pp. 178–89.

development' where the Kagoro polity is seen to operate 'in a new form and at a new level' at three phases of its history.[1] 'Development' signifies the marginal changes that may be recognized as marking system change, but it is doubtful whether such a distinction as that between changes within a system and system change does much to further the understanding of the mechanisms of change in which both anthropologists and students of political development are primarily interested. A sequence of system changes tends to be designated by the term *political evolution*.[2]

One might have expected some divergence between social and cultural anthropologists regarding the language of structural dynamics but, for the phase of literature under review, this is not very evident. The reason for this is the same as that which brings 'political development' (rather than 'change' or 'evolution') to the forefront of attention. Social anthropologists are concerned with the scientific study of the social structures of societies, that is, with the systems of persistent relationships between peoples and groups of people and the principles of organization which unite the component parts of the systems. They seek to abstract from the raw data of human behaviour and to construct 'a model of social reality' that may be compared with other such models independently of the actual content of the relationships which they would consider to be cultural and unique.[3] Cultural anthropologists, on the other hand, take the social structure of a people as but part of their field of study. Thus, in the culture of any given society there is not only a 'social system' to be found but also a 'value system', 'an economic system', and so on. Culture is, then, the totality of the interrelated systems.[4]

The coming together of cultural and social anthropology is due to a growing awareness that, first, static or equilibrium analysis is not the whole of the subject-matter of sociological inquiry and, secondly, that such an analysis must deal with more than the network of social relations. Moreover, there has been a trend since 1960 for anthropologists of both persuasions to deny explicitly the need for, and the validity of such a field as 'change' *or* 'development', since such an area of study is already preempted by the study of social structure. Thus Mair remarks that the kind of change observed and traced by social anthropologists is

---

[1] A. I. Richards, *East African chiefs*, New York and London 1960; M. G. Smith, 'Kagoro political development', *Human Organization* 19 (1960), 137–49. This usage is in line with the observation of J. LaPalombara that 'Little systematic attention has been accorded to the phenomenon of *political* development, i.e. the transformation of a political system from one type into another'. *Bureaucracy and political development*, Princeton 1963, p. 4.

[2] For cultural distinctions between 'development' and 'evolution' see W. Goldschmidt, *Man's way*, New York 1959.

[3] P. H. Gulliver, 'Anthropology', R. A. Lystad (ed.), *The African world*, New York 1965, pp. 58–62.

[4] See, for example, M. Sahlins's review of G. Murdock's *Social structure in Southeast Asia*, Chicago 1960 in the *Journal of the Polynesian Society* 72 (1963), 39–50 and M. Klass, 'Marriage rules in Bengal', *American Anthropologist* 68 (1966), 951–3.

from the point of view of social theory...interesting, not because it illustrates different social processes from those to be seen in what we may call a conservative society, but because it illustrates the same ones...The social pressures which operate in a rapidly changing society are the same as those that maintain social institutions in being.[1]

To the anthropologist who works within a structural framework, then (and this is the great majority of anthropologists, social and cultural, British and American) change and stability are corollary concepts. There can be no discussion of change without consideration of tendencies towards equilibrium. This leads to the study of the entire problem of structure. Just as change cannot be perceived without comparison with a stable structural matrix, so structure cannot be understood without an awareness of its changing nature. Even the most conservative society is not wholly still.[2]

If, then, the days of 'Stop the world, I want to make a sociological analysis' are past, the use of the terms 'development' and 'evolution' to describe structural change is an index of the distance of the investigator from his data. With the explicit recognition of the temporal dimension, the meticulous dissection of short-term change in small social units has expanded in scope towards what has been called 'middle range abstractions and universal development theory'.[3] Anthropological analyses of the involuted political development of Indonesia, a country of over ninety-seven million people, or of the growth of West African states in the nineteenth century, reflect the discipline's expansion into the realms of political science and history.[4]

### THE ANTHROPOLOGISTS' STARTING POINT

It has been suggested by one political scientist that 'One common developmental tendency does stand out: the aggregation of independently defined, specifically outlined traditional primordial groups into larger, more diffuse units whose implicit frame of reference is not the local scene, but the nation—in the sense of the whole society encompassed by the new civil state'.[5] Few anthropologists would argue with this conclusion, although they might want to alter its wording, since the processes by which such aggregation occurs have been the subject-matter of their discipline from its beginning. The question of the origin and the nature of the state is an anthropological question *par excellence* inasmuch as it is the ethnographer who controls first-hand data on nascent states. The development of the

---

[1] L. Mair, *New nations*, Chicago 1963, p. 15.

[2] R. Murphy, 'Cultural change...', pp. 1–2.

[3] C. W. Anderson, F. R. von der Mehden and C. Young, *Issues of political development*, New Jersey, Prentice Hall 1967, p. 3.

[4] C. Geertz, *Agricultural involution*, Berkeley and Los Angeles 1963; D. Forde and P. M. Kaberry (eds.), *West African kingdoms in the nineteenth century*, London 1967.

[5] C. W. Anderson *et al.*, *Issues of political development*, pp. 153–4.

state—old or new—holds a key position in political anthropology. Approaches differ: studies of *Primitive government* or *The evolution of political society* may be placed alongside analyses of *New nations* or *The Third World*; but the underlying processes, which involve the increasing complexity of interaction between groups and individuals within society, are common to both.[1]

The periodical literature of political science is full of edicts on the relation of 'tradition' and 'modernity', two constructs which the anthropologist today considers to be of very little use. In their place the anthropologist distinguishes between systems of social relationships which contradict one another and those which do not. Such contradictions indicate the increasing complexity of social interaction.[2] Today the course of political development is perceived somewhat differently from the notion believed to be current in anthropology by one political scientist, with its echoes of unitary sequence and inevitability. 'Most comment on political development', he writes, 'still suffers from an evolutionist view of history: from barbarism to civilization, from tyranny to democracy, from force to reason, etc.'[3] Such constructs as egality, ranking, and stratification are currently employed to make developmental distinctions if the focus is upon the political community or, if the focus is upon the development of governmental forms, on minimal, diffused, and expansive organization.[4] Thus Mair's study of primitive government reveals how some stateless systems contain the prototypical governmental forms out of which states might develop. Having surveyed these systems as they function in relative autonomy, she then demonstrates how they have been articulated with colonial regimes.

Alternatively, a culture–historical approach may lead to the study of development in terms of 'socio-political levels of integration'.[5] Regularities

[1] L. Mair, *Primitive government*, London and Baltimore 1962; M. H. Fried, *The evolution of political society*, New York 1967; L. Mair, *New nations*; P. Worsley, *The Third World*, London 1964.

[2] The problem has been posed by R. Bendix, 'Tradition and modernity reconsidered', *Comparative studies in society and history* 9 (1967), 292–346, and J. Gusfield, 'Tradition and modernity: misplaced polarities in the study of social change', *American Journal of Sociology* 72 (1967), 351–62. One contemporary anthropological approach in terms of 'contradictions' is to be found in F. G. Bailey, *Tribe, caste and nation*, p. 239 and G. K. Garbett, 'Prestige, status and power in a modern valley Korekore Chiefdom, Rhodesia', *Africa* 37 (1967), 307–26.

[3] H. Glickman, 'Dialogues on the theory of African development', *Africa Report* 12 (May 1967), 38–9.

[4] The former terminology is that of M. H. Fried, 'On the evolution of social stratification and the state', S. Diamond (ed.), *Culture in history*, New York 1960, pp. 713–31; 'Anthropology and the study of politics', S. Tax (ed.), *Horizons of anthropology*, Chicago 1964, pp. 181–90; *The evolution of political society*; 'The State', *International encyclopedia of the social sciences*, London and New York 1968, pp. 143–50. See also M. G. Smith, 'A structural approach to comparative politics', D. Easton (ed.), *Varieties of political theory*, New Jersey, Prentice-Hall 1966, pp. 113–28; 'Pre-industrial stratification systems', N. Smelser and S. Lipset (eds.), *Social structure and mobility in economic development*, Chicago 1966, pp. 141–76; L. Mair, *Primitive government*.

[5] J. Steward, *Theory of culture change*, Urbana, University of Illinois 1955, sets out the theoretical basis of this approach. The three volumes, edited by him, which appear under the title *Contemporary change in traditional societies*, Chicago and London 1967, contain essays applying his

and alternatives of change are observed which may then be related to the
way in which over-rule was imposed, either by groups of indigenous
peoples or by aliens. Recently an effort has been made to develop and test
a systematic approach to problems of modernization in these terms. Its
application in a Tanganyikan society, for example, deals extensively with
social control and administration as problems of political development.
Other case studies of Asian and Latin American peasantry similarly
test this particular theory of cultural change. In all these studies, however,
the emphasis is upon the external factors of change with their resultant
structural changes. There is less attention to the processes of change which
involve contraditions for individuals and groups so that, as with Geertz's
ecological study of Indonesia, the work remains historical rather than
sociological.

Within social anthropology there is a comparable trend towards viewing
structured sequences within their larger interactional–ecological contexts.
A typical example is Barth's study of the ecological context of social
interaction among the Pathan which provides an explanation of the processes at work in a multi-ethnic society.[1] A re-examination of the literature
on segmentary lineages (such as those described by Evans-Pritchard among
the Nuer) similarly suggests that the processes by which they develop may
be discerned by viewing them as organizations of predatory expansion and
placing them within a wider ecological–historical perspective.[2] Thus it is
concluded that competition and external threats are a necessary condition
in the political ecology of any people if segmentary lineage systems are to
develop. The first group moving into any area is unlikely to develop a
segmentary lineage system, whereas the second to enter that area is more
likely to do so. This emphasis on structured sequences is most clearly
set out in an early textbook on the *Principles of anthropology* by E. C. Chapple
and Carleton Coon[3] and it is interesting to contemplate comparable
sequential analyses of army mutinies, *coups d'état* and irredentism within
ecological contexts.

A distinction between political development as a political goal and
political development as an analytical concept leads some social scientists
to argue that, besides assessing the magnitude of changes, indicating the
forces responsible and giving a guide to prediction, another objective

[1] F. Barth, 'Ecologic relationships of ethnic groups in Swat, North Pakistan', *American Anthropologist* 58 (1956), 1079–89.

[2] M. Sahlins, 'The segmentary lineage: an organization of predatory expansion', *American
Anthropologist* 63 (1961), 322–45.

[3] E. Chapple and C. Coon, *Principles of anthropology*, New York 1942. The 'Chapple–Arensberg
interaction scheme' which underlies this approach was first set out by Eliot D. Chapple and
Conrad M. Arensberg, 'Measuring human relations', *Genetic Psychology Monographs*, no. 22
(1940). Its use in a recent study of political development is discussed on page 62 of this paper.

framework of analysis to Africa, Latin America and Asia. The Tanganyikan study referred to is
by E. H. Winter and T. Beidelman.

should be to present a theory or approach to development which could itself be an instrument of change. Aware that changing times have brought with them the danger of anthropologists being viewed as subversive elements in the new nations in which they undertake fieldwork (since they may disclose discrepancies in the legend of national development) or of their seeking to escape into historical research,[1] most anthropologists seek an 'academic' definition of political development similar to that of Reinhard Bendix.[2] 'Modernization (sometimes called *social and political development*) refers to all those *social* and *political* changes that accompanied industrialization in many countries of Western civilization...The term *development* may be used where reference is made to related changes in both these spheres.' This definition is made operational by (*a*) attempting to establish the nature of the relationship between the political and social spheres and (*b*) focusing upon the structural analysis of *stratification*, which is perceived to be the crux of political development. This involves empirical inquiry into the degree of integration and the openness of any polity. The starting point for this is the recognition that stratification is not characteristic of all societies, but only of those which have undergone particular kinds of political development. This recognition leads to a new set of applications of long-established concepts and approaches in anthropology. Consistently with this, I shall consider first the anthropological approach to political development in pre-state, non-stratified societies and the bearing this has upon problems of political development in contemporary nation-states; and second, some aspects of the relationship between stratification and political development in the rapidly changing nations of today. I shall limit my observations to the last phases of any development sequences.[3]

The focus is, first, on the *integration* of the polity in its social and political aspects. Since government is the regulation of public affairs and the critical element in government is its public character,[4] anthropological analysis of political development begins with the nature and composition of that

---

[1] M. Freedman, 'A Chinese phase in social anthropology', *British Journal of Sociology* 14 (1963), 1–19.

[2] R. Bendix, 'Tradition and modernity', p. 5. Compare S. Eisenstadt's definition of modernization ('Modernization and conditions of sustained growth', *World Politics* XVI (1964), 576–94), which has grown out of his long familiarity with pre-industrial societies, and which M. Kilson adopts in his study of political development in Sierra Leone: modernization means especially 'the spread or dispersal of power—that is, the widening of the sphere of access on the part of a given populace to the institutions of authority, decision making, command, administration, force and coercion in a social system'. *Political change in a West African state*, Cambridge, Harvard University 1966, p. 282.

[3] But compare the anthropological analyses of early empires: K. Polanyi, C. Arensberg and H. Pearson, *Trade and market in the early empires*, Glencoe, 1957; feudalism to which full reference may be found in J. Goody, 'Feudalism in Africa', *The Journal of African History* 4 (1963), 1–18; civil wars and medieval law, M. Gluckman, 'Civil wars and theories of power in Barotseland', *Yale Law Review* 72 (1963), 1515–46; etc.

[4] M. G. Smith, 'A structural approach...', pp. 115–16; *Government in Zazzau, 1800–1950*, London 1960, pp. 15–16.

public and goes on to distinguish the processes by which it is established and consolidated. Many taxonomies of such publics have been drawn up; but, although this taxonomic phase in the study of comparative political development was necessary,[1] the emphasis in this discussion will be instead on the theme of continuity in change, the belief that 'the processes through which the changes of today are brought about are the same processes that maintained the small-scale societies in their relatively unchanging condition in the past'.[2]

## PRE-INDUSTRIAL STATE DEVELOPMENT AND THE CONTEMPORARY STATE-NATION

One area in which anthropological research into developmental processes in pre-state polities is relevant to an understanding of the problems of political development in the modern state is highlighted by Pflanze's distinction between the nation-state of nineteenth-century Europe and the new 'state-nations'.[3] In the embryo state-nations which decoloniza-tion has spawned, anthropological analyses of such social phenomena as nativistic or millenarian movements, cargo cults, prophets, ramage organization and ranking, witch-finding movements, barrio solidarity and so on help us to understand the dynamics of irredentism, 'liberation movements', rebel uprisings or peasant revolts in groups which do not participate fully in the civic culture of the state.

An analysis of guerilla insurgency might, for instance, be built im-mediately on anthropological insights into pre-state political organization. Charismatically led millenarian movements have been described as characteristic forms of political development both among non-centralized peoples in response to colonial rule and among others, such as peasants who, when confronted with the need to take joint action, are obliged to throw up a centralized political structure *de novo*.[4] Interesting comparisons

[1] For African polities, for example, see M. Fortes and E. Evans-Pritchard, *African political systems*, London 1940; J. Middleton and D. Tait, *Tribes without rulers*, New York and London 1958; P. Lloyd, 'The political structure of African kingdoms' and A. Southall, 'A critique of the typology of states and political systems', both in M. Banton (ed.), *Political systems and the distribu-tion of power*, London 1965, pp. 63–112, 113–37. For Latin America, J. Steward and L. Faron, *Native peoples of South America*, New York 1959; C. Wagley and M. Harris, 'A typology of Latin American subcultures', *American Anthropologist* 57 (1955), 428–51; E. Wolf, 'Types of Latin American Peasantry', *American Anthropologist* 57 (1955), 452–71, etc. For Asia, G. Murdock, *Social structure in Southeast Asia*, R. Nicholas, 'Structures of politics in villages of southern Asia'; M. Singer and B. Cohn, *Structure and change in Indian society*, Chicago 1968, pp. 243–84.

For divergent views upon the value and use of such typologies see M. Perlman, 'Methodological trends in political anthropology', and R. Cohen 'Political anthropology', both in *Rural Africana* 2 (1967), 3–10 and 11–12.                                    [2] L. Mair, *New nations*, p. 15.

[3] O. Pflanze, 'Characteristics of nationalism in Europe: 1848–1871', *The Review of Politics* 28 (1966), 129–43.

[4] P. Worsley, *The trumpet shall sound*, pp. 227–9. There is a large literature on this topic. The second edition of Worsley's study contains two bibliographies, that of D. A. Heathcote carrying the reader up to 1967. The relevance of this topic to anthropological theory and methodo-logy is discussed by I. Jarvie, *The revolution in anthropology*, London and New York 1964.

with the Congolese Kwilu rebellion and the political organization of Mau Mau immediately spring to mind. Research suggests that such interstitial movements must all be considered as part of the stream of political development. In the history of medieval Europe and nineteenth-century nation-building, all this is recognized.[1] Perhaps a greater concern with the past political development of the now stable states of Europe will provide a bridge between political science and anthropology in their convergence upon the new nations.

Because of this recognized need to understand the relation of subgroups to political development, some 'fresh avenues of exploration' proposed for political science by Aristide Zolberg sound like well-trodden ground to the anthropologist.[2] 'The most salient characteristic of political life in Africa', he suggests, 'is that it constitutes an almost *institutionless arena* with conflict and disorder as its most prominent features.'[3] This clearly calls for the study of the 'public' in which this state of affairs is to be found. Whereas, in the past, political scientists tended to work downwards, so to speak, dealing with vertical structures, anthropologists have always been concerned to work outwards from any point within an arena, dealing with horizontal structures. Moreover, it is the interstitial, informal aspects of government and politics that the anthropologist considers to be critical to the developmental process, as will be suggested later when elites and peasants are considered as marginal actors in the political arena. Characteristic topics emerging from such a focus are, for example, factionalism and patronage, the latter an area where, as Weingrod shows, the interests of political science and anthropology clearly meet.[4]

[1] E. J. Hobsbawm, *Primitive rebels*, London 1959.

[2] A. R. Zolberg, *Creating political order*, Chicago 1966. The six avenues he charts (p. 151) are: the colonial situation; law; the study of ideology; grass roots politics; the relationship between tradition and modernity; comparative studies.

[3] A. R. Zolberg, 'The structure of political conflict in the new states of tropical Africa', *American Political Science Review* 62 (1968), 70.

[4] A. Weingrod, 'Patrons, patronage and political parties' (unpublished manuscript). Anthropological studies of patronage include those of J. Boissevain, 'Patronage in Sicily', *Man*, new series I (1966), 18–33; J. Campbell, *Honour, family and patronage*, Oxford 1964; G. Foster, 'The dyadic contract in Tzintzuntzan', *American Anthropologist* 65 (1963), 1280–94; M. Kenny, 'Patterns of patronage in Spain', *Anthropological Quarterly* 33 (1960), 14–23; A. Mayer, Quasi-groups in the study of complex societies', M. Banton (ed.), *The social anthropology of complex societies*, London 1966, 97–122; S. Silverman, 'Patronage and community–nation relationships in central Italy', *Ethnology* 4 (1965), 178–89; E. Wolf, 'Kinship, friendship and patron–client relations', M. Banton (ed.), *The social anthropology of complex societies*, pp. 1–20.

The anthropological literature on factionalism includes B. Benedict, 'Factionalism in Mauritian villages', *British Journal of Sociology* 8 (1957), 328–42; W. Fenton, *Factionalism at Taos Pueblo, New Mexico*, Washington, Bureau of American Ethnology Bulletin 164, 1957; R. Firth, 'Introduction to factions in Indian and overseas Indian Societies', *British Journal of Sociology* 8 (1957), 291–5; R. Nicholas, 'Village factions and political parties in rural West Bengal', *Journal of Commonwealth Political Studies* 2 (1963), 17–32; and 'Factions: a comparative analysis', M. Banton (ed.), *Political systems and the distribution of power*, pp. 21–61; B. Siegel and A. Beals, 'Pervasive factionalism', *American Anthropologist* 62 (1960), pp. 394–417.

Leadership in sub-groups is of critical importance for the study of national political development. Possibly because of a concern with the application of direct or indirect rule by a metropolitan power, students of political development in colonial territories have tended to concentrate upon whether the pre-existing polity was a centralized state with a recognized ruler or whether it was an acephalous polity in which client chiefs had to be created.[1] This is an administrative perspective. But the centralized/acephalous distinction has not proved a very useful analytic tool. Its ethnographic basis lies in Evans-Pritchard's study of the Nuer. Nuer social organization rested on a system of segmentary lineages and at least one writer has seen in this a 'contingent polity'.[2] Evans-Pritchard himself, however, makes it clear that he is presenting a model of Nuer inter-group relations, a theory of political behaviour. His later monographs illustrate the differences between this and the actuality of social and political *organization*. Segmentary lineage systems are 'good to think', as Lévi-Strauss would put it, but they are not to be found on the ground. The distinction between political *relations*—a political system—and political *organization* is relevant to problems of contemporary nation-building. 'One of the problems involved in the creation and federation of new states', suggests Lienhardt, 'is essentially that of converting a political system of relations between once sovereign peoples within its boundaries into a more comprehensive political organization.'[3] An analysis of just such processes of political development among the Sanusi of Cyrenaica traces the structural integration of congeries of tribal systems into one state organization through the centralizing strategies of a religious confraternity.[4] There have, however, been few such studies.[5]

The reason for this neglect of the integrative aspect of political development lies partly in the history of the discipline. For much of the 1930s and 1940s the mainstream of political anthropology was identified for all

[1] But see M. Crowder, 'Indirect rule—French and British style', *Africa* 34 (1964), 197–205. On chiefs see K. Busia, *The position of the chief in the modern political system of the Ashanti*, London 1951; L. Fallers, 'The predicament of the modern African chief', *American Anthropologist* 57 (1955), 290–305; L. Mair, 'Chieftainship in modern Africa', *Studies in Applied Anthropology*, London 1957, pp. 37–9; J. Beattie, 'Checks on the abuse of political power in some African states', *Sociologus* 9 (1959), 97–115; P. Lloyd, 'Traditional rulers', J. Coleman and C. Rosberg, *Political parties and national integration in tropical Africa*, Berkeley and Los Angeles 1966, pp. 382–412.

The relationship between indigenous structures and bureaucratic norms is discussed by L. Fallers, *Bantu bureaucracy*, Chicago 1965; R. Apthorpe, *From tribal rule to modern government*, Lusaka 1959; 'The introduction of bureaucracy into African politics', *Journal of African Administration* 12 (1960), 125–34; P. Rigby, 'Political change in Busoga', *The Uganda Journal* 30 (1966), 223–5.

[2] D. Easton, 'Political anthropology', B. Siegel (ed.), *Biennial review of anthropology*, Stanford, California 1959, pp. 216–62.

[3] G. Lienhardt, *Social anthropology*, London 1964, p. 78.

[4] E. Evans-Pritchard, *The Sanusi of Cyrenaica*, Oxford 1949.

[5] Cf. the numerous such studies by political scientists. For example, K. Deutsch, *The integration of political communities*, Philadelphia 1964; E. Haas, *Beyond the Nation State*, Stanford, California 1964; A. Etzioni, *Political unification*, New York 1965, etc.

practical purposes with research carried out in African territories. Social anthropology, more than any other discipline, has always been a prisoner of its subject-matter and the British social anthropologist in Africa—unlike his American colleague whose training was the study of North American Indian culture wherein he viewed 'social action...in all its historic instability, conditioned by relationships with other groups and by adaptation to the environment'[1]—could naively and erroneously believe that anthropology was 'the study, not just of backward and primitive peoples, but rather of *colonial* peoples'.[2] Working within the stable administrative framework established by the colonizing power fostered an emphasis on stability and unity in the analyses of indigenous political organizations, frozen at a particular moment in time, instead of looking at the changing polities of Africa in terms of a moving frontier, as has been the case in Asia.[3] Working within a stable administrative framework also encouraged anthropologists to aim at the unravelling of intricate, but static, patterns of social and political organization in order to provide baselines for innovation and administrative change. It is recognized that a re-assessment is needed of the thinking that resulted from those conditions.[4]

This emphasis on static studies and the presentation of models[5] that is implicit in the whole concept of an 'ethnographic present' makes studies of 'traditional' African societies less useful for the study of contemporary political development than they might otherwise be. Ethnographic accounts of some Ugandan polities are a case in point. Colonial administrators tried to make indigenous political boundaries congruent with local government units and this has been seen as justification for a continuing anthropological role in the study of contemporary political development. Thus Fallers suggests

A primary task for political anthropology in the future is the detailed study of the ways in which the old societies, which must now be conceptualized as local ethnic units within the new national societies, relate to these new political institutions. Broadly speaking, it would appear that the traditional polities which in the colonial period were made to function...as primarily *administrative units*, in the period of independence, are coming to function primarily as *political units*.[6]

---

[1] R. Murphy, 'Cultural change...', p. 9.

[2] P. Worsley, *The trumpet shall sound*, p. 260.

[3] For example, in the work of F. Bailey, *Caste and the economic frontier*, Manchester 1957; E. Leach, 'The frontiers of Burma', *Comparative Studies in Society and History* 3 (1960), 49–68; and O. Lattimore, *Studies in frontier history*, Paris 1962.

[4] R. Firth, *Essays on social organization...*, pp. 11–12. See, however, M. Gluckman, 'The utility of the equilibrium model...', p. 234.

[5] For the use of the term 'model', see P. Cohen, 'Models', *British Journal of Sociology* 17 (1966), 70–8.

[6] L. Fallers, 'Political sociology and the anthropological study of African polities', *Archiv. europ. sociol.* 4 (1963), 329.

Yet, when we actually take up the ethnographies with this aim in mind, we find that it cannot be done. Fallers, for instance, saw the basis of the distinction between Nilotic and Bantu as lying in their indigenous political structures, the former having segmentary lineage systems, the latter centralized states. Because this neat dichotomy proved inadequate in Alurland, with its ethnic complexity, Southall was led to recognize an intermediate category of 'segmentary states'.[1] This is a wholly static approach for, as we have since seen, such political forms are characteristic of a *phase* in state development in which communications and bureaucratic efficiency are rudimentary, a phase clearly brought out in Evans-Pritchard's description of the emergence of the Azande state.[2]

The process is one of integration. Yet, as a result of the adoption of a static and synchronic approach, the works of Dunbar and Beattie tell us nothing of the marginal Banyala or Bachopi *within* the Banyoro state organization; nor do the ethnographies of Southwold and Fallers account for the integration of the Bagerere and Balamogi peoples within the states of Buganda and Busoga.[3] Since they are presenting the political systems as ideal types rather than focusing on the structural integration of marginal peoples or sub-groups within a larger whole, their work is useful for making taxonomies but not for understanding processes.

The recognition of the need to distinguish *structure* from *organization* is one of the theoretical advances of recent years. We owe the clearest statement of it to Raymond Firth. He writes:

In speaking of social organization we are not dealing with any isolable, concrete social identity. Our analysis refers to a field of social action which is identified in terms of pattern-sequence...In the concept of social structure, the qualities recognized are primarily those of persistence, continuity, form and pervasiveness through the social field...The concept of social organization has a complementary emphasis. It recognizes adaptation of behaviour in respect of given ends, control of means in varying circumstances, which are set by changes in the external environment or by the necessity to resolve conflict between structural principles. If structure implies order, organization implies a working towards order—though not necessarily the same order.[4]

Zolberg's perceptive observation, that political scientists have been focusing on political *structures* without seeing them as *organizations* operating in an environment not coterminous with the territorially defined nation-state, is to the point here.[5] Whereas political scientists have been taking

[1] A. Southall, *Alur society*, Cambridge 1956.
[2] E. Evans-Pritchard, 'The Zande state', *Journal of the Royal Anthropological Institute* 93 (1963), 134–54.
[3] A. Dunbar, *A history of Bunyoro-Kitara*, Oxford 1965; J. Beattie, *Bunyoro: an African kingdom*, New York 1960; M. Southwold, *Bureaucracy and chiefship in Buganda*, Kampala 1961; L. Fallers, *Bantu bureaucracy*.
[4] R. Firth, *Essays on social organization...*, p. 61.
[5] A. Zolberg, 'The structure of political conflict...', p. 133.

the nation-state as a given entity, trying to understand political behaviour within it, to understand this behaviour fully it is necessary to look at its goal-oriented character, realizing that these goals may be set by constraints which cut across, or are in a different dimension from, state boundaries. The study of the political development of Somaliland by an anthropologist, I. M. Lewis, illustrates this point very simply. The unit of analysis is not the Somali Republic (i.e. a culturally homogeneous unit which has been subjected to diverse regimes) but all Somalis.[1]

An analysis of the political *organization* of the Nuer, for example, as opposed to an analysis of its political *structure*, would focus upon leadership and support groups, on the source of political authority, on political choice and political manipulation.[2] A better understanding of non-hierarchically structured leadership and authority patterns leads to analyses of problems of political development not in terms of extending rule over peoples without chiefs, but of the distinct, structurally determined interests of the actors involved in the political situation at any point in time. Leadership in such societies is highly relevant to the study of political development in newly established independent states, since it provides the largest element in the leadership of the 'periphery', and this may well be a form of leadership different from that operating at the 'centre'. If one of the goals of political development is the re-structuring of the state-nation, its study is bound to hinge on local leadership.

Past emphasis in social anthropology upon political structure is now giving way to analyses of organizational strategies and integration. These reflect the cumulative advances of the last thirty years. Evans-Pritchard himself provides a dynamic account of the political development of the Zande state which was largely incorporated into the Anglo-Egyptian Sudan in the 1920s.[3] Prior to this, the indigenous polity had a population of over three million at various times in its history; covered between 60,000 and 100,000 square miles; and contained within its boundaries over twenty culturally distinct ethnic groups only some of which were totally assimilated. The variables singled out for analysis of Azande political development have a familiar ring. They include problems of succession; emphasis on personal allegiance to a charismatic leader; the questioning of relationships of authority and subordination; the exemption of certain categories (such as civil servants) from political office; variations in the degree of autonomy between provinces; the relation between the communications system and the government's effectiveness where there is great reliance on the personal control of the leader; the differential rate of

[1] I. Lewis, *The modern history of Somaliland: from nation to state*, London 1965.
[2] Such an approach was advocated by I. Schapera, *Government and politics in tribal societies*, London 1956, pp. 218–19. Case studies have been made by F. Barth, *Political leadership...*; and he has discussed further implications in *The role of the entrepreneur in social change in northern Norway*, Bergen 1963. See also F. Bailey, *Stratagems and spoils*, Oxford, 1969.
[3] E. Evans-Pritchard, 'The Zande state'.

expansion in different parts of the polity and the problems this raises for stability; relations between the central authority and the judiciary; general mobilization; intelligence; the spoils system and the balance of power; assassinations; reciprocity as a political mechanism; and so on.

Contributors to a symposium on West African kingdoms in the nine-teenth century also take the macro-sociological perspective required for a study of political development. To permit comparison, the most signi-ficant variables are set out as follows:

the earlier historical development of each kingdom...as a background to the main emphasis on the character of its organization in the nineteenth century and of changes during that period. The territorial structure of the state and its economic base in the control and exploitation of resources, and their distribution through tribute and trade, provide a foundation for the analysis of politically significant social groups and categories, of the prerogatives of politically dominant elements, and of the modes of incorporation of subject peoples. The principles of succession and of appointment at the various levels in the hierarchy of offices, and the modes of competition for power and the balance of power among offices and between different parts of the system, are also central themes. These involve consideration of the ideology and ritual of kingship, the admini-strative machinery of the state, and the organization and control of military forces. External relations of a kingdom have also, in some cases, played a dominant part in determining internal organization, and have called for special emphasis as a factor in its internal development and change.[1]

Clearly, organization as well as structure, competition, ideology and extra-systemic features are coming to be recognized as part of the anthro-pological perspective on political development. How then are they conceptually related?

The analysis of pre-state and pre-industrial state development has contributed not only to an understanding of continuity between phases, that is, to an understanding of processes, but has also brought about the methodological revolution already touched upon, which brings social anthropologists nearer to their culturological colleagues.[2] This is made explicit in Peters's study of the structural aspects of the feud among the Bedouin of Cyrenaica when he observes that the lineage model is the frame-

[1] D. Forde and P. Kaberry, West African kingdoms..., pp. xiii–xiv.

[2] E. Leach, Rethinking anthropology, London 1961, marks the beginning of this phase in social anthropology and essays on generative models by F. Barth, Models of social organization, London 1966, and 'On the study of social change', American Anthropologist 69 (1967), 661–9, may be taken as the furthest movement away from the earlier thinking. R. Firth suggests that 'The argument for a more dynamic theory tends to be based on two main premises: that "static" theory has assumed conditions of rest or return to rest in spheres where there was ongoing social movement; and that sophisticated analysis would reveal more, or more significant, forces in operation than have been shown. In a modern critique of social anthropology, if labels be ignored, both these premises are probably justified. Certainly in reviewing my own work I recognize the force of the argument at some points.' Essays on social organization..., p. 11. See, however, M. Gluckman, 'The utility of the equilibrium model...'.

work of the Bedouin themselves; it is not a sociological model.[1] He suggests that it should be abandoned since (a) it does not cover all areas of social relationships and (b) it does not make prediction possible. His ethnography adds fuel to the argument that a total social structure should not be viewed as composed of functionally interconnected parts, 'a delicately balanced mechanism rather like the various parts of a wristwatch', as Leach puts it, since this excludes any possible comprehension of changes save those present as part of the dynamics of a system; its only answer to change is to offer an account of a new, different system.

Peters suggests that if, instead, 'attention is focussed on the analysis of a field of components arranged in a specific fashion to meet the interests of men at a particular time, it then becomes possible to see how a shift in their positions, the addition of new components, or the elimination of others produces this or that effect'.[2] Thus, to the lineage model of social relations are added ecological, economic, demographic, and political contingencies in order to make it a sociological model. (What is at issue is not structural theory *per se*, but merely the Durkheimian model of social structure from which such key variables as ecology, conflict, dissonance, and extrasystemic relations are excluded.[3] A distinction between *social* and *societal* is long overdue in anthropology. As Etzioni has observed, although the term 'societal' is archaic, it usefully distinguishes macro- from micro-data, both of which are social.)[4]

## STRATIFICATION AND POLITICAL DEVELOPMENT

The historian C. E. Black has observed that

societies may be said to meet the problem of change by concentrating their efforts alternatively...on defending the existing conceptions and adapting them to an altered conception. It is not by chance that political struggles have come to be expressed in terms of an incumbent government and opposition, the ins and the outs, conservatives and liberals, parties of order and parties of move-ment. This fundamental choice between inflexibility and adaptation...reflects the accumulation of an infinite number of smaller choices that it is virtually impossible to trace in full detail and few of which in isolation would present clear-cut issues.[5]

[1] E. Peters, 'Some structural aspects of the feud among the camel-herding Bedouin of Cyrenaica', *Africa* 37 (1967), 281.

[2] Ibid., p. 281.

[3] I. M. Lewis, reviewing Gluckman's *Politics, law and ritual in tribal society*, Oxford 1965, which seeks to highlight the differences and similarities between tribal and modern societies, makes a similar point: 'Some of Gluckman's difficulties are inherent in the Radcliffe-Brown style of analysis which refers the functions of institutions to a holistic view of society and of social solida-rity, instead of merely relating them to a limited nexus of customary behaviour at a particular point in time', *Africa* 37 (1967), 98–9. The current trend in anthropology is to replace the concept of '*holism*' with that of '*context*'.

[4] A. Etzioni, *The active society*, New York 1968, pp. 47–8.

[5] C. E. Black, *The dynamics of modernization*, New York 1966.

The establishment and maintenance of a stratified social order are the distinguishing features of a modern state.[1] Political development (i.e. structural change) comes about with change in the established order, the main function of that order being to maintain the established system of stratification in the society. If we view the centre of the polity as the established body of persons which maintains, by coercion or consensus, its ideologically justified control over access to the valued resources of the society by defining and regulating the individuals and groups that are to compete legitimately in the political arena, we become aware of the crucial importance of the relationship of the stratification system to the state.

Stratification is a specific mode of social differentiation. Although all social structures may be viewed as status systems, only some of these are stratified. Societies which institutionalize equal access to positions of advantage are unstratified; they are decentralized societies in which political and status structures are coincident. Stratified societies vary in many ways (hence the complexity of development problems). In his cogent summary of pre-industrial stratification systems, M. G. Smith writes:

> In all cases, the principles that differentiate and regulate the unequal distribution of opportunities are identical with those that distinguish and regulate publics as corporate units of internal order and of external articulation. That is to say, the principles of stratification are basic to the political order...The widest span of the status system coincides with the limits of the widest effective political unit, as Nadel points out; and its basis and significance lie in the political sphere. For this reason, stratification cannot be adequately studied in terms of underlying value-orientations; it represents an order interdependent with the political order, based on certain concrete structural principles. In consequence of these principles, people might develop adjustive value orientations or protestant ones; but we must explain the values by reference to the structural principles that generate them, rather than the reverse.[2]

Thus, while some polities—stratification systems—are more stable than others, depending on the degree of consensus in their normative structures, this consensus itself is related to the 'character, congruence and inclusiveness' of the structural principles on which the stratification is based. Principles imposed upon a public by a small established minority, as in the case of Ruanda, for example, fostered a revolutionary situation. 'The wider the consensus and the more inclusive the legitimating ideology, the more absolute may be the tolerable differences between ranked strata and the wider the span of the stratification.'[3]

Having traditionally worked in more or less closed societies, the anthropologist is strategically placed to analyse society in terms of its openness

---

[1] The presentation in this section follows closely the argument of M. H. Fried and M. G. Smith whose writings have already been cited.

[2] M. G. Smith, 'Pre-industrial stratification...', p. 174.

[3] *Ibid.*, p. 175.

for the groups that comprise it. The earlier assumption that society is always integrated is now questioned and, once the integration of a society is regarded as questionable, the door is open for empirical inquiry as to how varying degrees of integration are produced and maintained.[1] Social quiescence and cohesion differ sharply from each other; so do regulation and integration, but if we begin by assuming that integration prevails it is virtually impossible to distinguish these conditions.[2]

The failure of political science to recognize degrees of integration and instability in society[3] is due largely to the particular sociological components that the discipline has drawn upon. The cultural and evolutionary view of the state, however, emphasizes flux and development; and the principles of stratification, in conjunction with the mode of integration which is the organizational reflection of this structure, provide the basis on which to distinguish types of polity, and thus furnish the starting points for analyses of political development. As we have seen, stratification— 'the principles that regulate the distribution of social advantage'[4]— parallels development processes aimed at building an integrated and open society. The following discussion will concentrate on two major issues of political development: first, the integration of diverse cultural groups within a polity (i.e. problems of cultural pluralism) and, secondly, the structuring of the elite and its counterparts, the masses and the establishment, within a developing society. The first issue focuses on factors which make for equilibrium; the second on factors which make for change. The anthropological perspective on each issue may be peculiar to the discipline: first, a questioning of whether cultural pluralism is, indeed, a useful focus of analysis, and a search for what might replace it; secondly, a view of the elite 'from below', as the cutting edge of societal change. In both cases we are led, through a concern with stratification, to *marginality* as the crux of development in the political sphere.

## CULTURAL PLURALISM AS AN ISSUE OF POLITICAL DEVELOPMENT

Cultural pluralism has been viewed as a major issue of political development in today's new nations and the plural society model as that most appropriate for an inquiry into the mode of integration in states made up of many ethnic groups.[5] A recent reviewer warned his political science colleagues that 'Concepts like pluralism and the plural society require *explicit* theoretical consideration, and they should not be so lightly applied

---

[1] This position is most clearly stated by F. Barth in his essay 'Processes of integration in culture', *Models of social organization*, pp. 12–21. Seminal articles for this approach to structural integration are to be found in the field of linguistics, notably in the work of André Martinet.

[2] M. G. Smith, 'Pre-industrial stratification...', pp. 145–6.

[3] A. Zolberg, 'The structure of political conflict...'.

[4] M. G. Smith, 'Pre-industrial stratification...', p. 142.

[5] C. Anderson *et al.*, *Issues of political development*.

to the complex issues of political development as they often are'.[1] A 'plural society debate' has been raging in anthropology for some time and here we can only review what is coming out of it, rather than all that went into its making.[2]

Adopting the anthropological approach to stratification outlined above, cultural pluralism becomes politically relevant only when differential access to positions of differing advantage is institutionalized in ethnic terms. The mere existence of social or cultural categories in the population is not enough to account for political cleavages; there must be politicization of ethnicity before we can talk of 'the politics of ethnicity'. Ethnicity *per se* is a cultural not a political variable. We must inquire, therefore, into the *process* of politicizing ethnicity and the ideology that validates it.

An early essay on the plural society suggested the dangers inherent in a facile use of the idea.[3] It is 'as a matter of convenience' (it suggested) that we speak of three societies in Malaya—Malay, Chinese and Indian—as a mere preliminary to a more realistic view of Malayan society as a whole, 'discarding the useful fiction that it is a plurality of societies'. None of the ethnic divisions has been politically autonomous; none has, in fact, constituted a unit; none has been a valid group. The Malay and Chinese may be described as 'meaningful cultural categories, all the members of which regard themselves as belonging to a kind of ethnic community. But it does not follow that each community is an organized entity.' The process by which Malays 'through the agency of a dominating political party have built up a hierarchy of power within their own ranks' allows us to speak 'fairly realistically of a unified Malay group within the setting of national politics [but] the Malayan Chinese have not attained the same degree of unification'.[4]

A distinction such as that made above between *valid groups* (i.e., in Nadel's definition, 'a collection of individuals who stand in regular and relatively permanent relationships') and *cultural categories* underlies most objections to the use of the plural society model.[5] Without the distinction,

---

[1] M. Stanley, Review of *The conflicted relationship*, *Journal of Developing Areas* 2 (1967).

[2] Reference is made in the following paragraphs to L. Braithwaite, 'Social stratification and cultural pluralism', *Annals of the New York Academy of Sciences* 83 (1960), 816–31; L. A. Despres, *Cultural pluralism and nationalist politics in British Guiana*, Chicago 1967; 'Anthropological theory, cultural pluralism and the study of complex societies', *Current Anthropology* 9 (1968), 3–26; M. Freedman, 'The growth of a plural society in Malaya', *Pacific Affairs* 33 (1960), 158–68; L. Kuper, 'Plural societies: perspectives and problems' (unpublished manuscript); 'Political change in white settler societies', paper delivered to Interdisciplinary Colloquium, UCLA, 1966; 'Conflict and the plural society', Paper delivered at the International Sociological Association meeting, 1967; L. Kuper and M. G. Smith, *African pluralism* (in press, 1968); J. C. Mitchell, *Tribalism and the plural society*, London 1960; H. S. Morris, 'Some aspects of the concept plural society', *Man*, New series, 2 (1967), 169–84; J. Rex, 'The plural society in sociological theory', *British Journal of Sociology* 10 (1959), 114–24; M. G. Smith, *The plural society in the British West Indies*, California 1965.

[3] M. Freedman, 'The growth of a plural society...'.

[4] *Ibid.*

[5] S. Nadel, *The foundations of social anthropology*, Glencoe, 1951, p. 146.

one is tempted to argue from cultural and racial appearances to social realities.[1] In its purest form, the plural society model ignores other cleavages between individuals and groups, including class cleavages. It tends to preclude any temporal perspective, denying the element of change and process. It obscures the fact that 'as the processes of change induced by national institutions and interactions with other subcultural groups eliminate or modify the alien ethnicity, distinctiveness follows lines of region, class, occupation and other factors. The definition of plural societies might subsume these modified groups'[2] and so prevent the analysis of development. Political analysis must be concerned with the process by which categories are turned into groups; that is, with the politicization of ethnicity.[3]

In short, there are better ways of approaching cultural pluralism. One has been outlined in terms of the variable relationships which produce groups of any kind and of the relationships of the groups to one another. 'In this context problems of racial and cultural diversity are of secondary importance, even if race and culture form some of the values about which the bargains in the relationship are struck.'[4] This approach, along with Barth's concept of 'transactions',[5] permits the observation and analysis of continually shifting alignments between individuals and groups, in some of which ethnicity may be a significant factor. Bailey's study of politics and change in Orissa illustrates such an approach and provides 'middle range theories' of political development.[6]

Nash, equally opposed to a dualistic or plural society model, presents instead a macrosociological *multiple society* model. His starting point was an empirical inquiry into economic and social development in Southeast Asia and Latin America. A multiple society, which he contrasts with a modern society, is one characterized by uneven development, whether it be of regions or of social groups. Cultural or ethnic groups may or may not form significant sectors in this respect. He contrasts the development problems of the two areas in terms of the need to maintain an integrated

[1] H. S. Morris, 'Some aspects...'.

[2] J. Steward, 'Comment', *Current Anthropology* 9 (1968), 21–2. This is a critique of the article by L. A. Despres in the same issue.

[3] Compare R. L. Sklar, 'Political science and national integration', *Journal of Modern African Studies* 5 (1967), 1–11. It may be observed in passing, however, that since the social scientist is himself an actor in the arena of inquiry, an emphasis on ethnicity may, in fact, bring about a degree of politicization of ethnic differences. As L. Dumont has observed ('Village studies', *Contributions to Indian Sociology* I (1957), 23–41), 'These studies will be a part of the people's own history; African societies will have been made conscious in the way that centuries of civilization have made India conscious and that consciousness will alter the facts themselves. To give a more precise example, the cultural unity of the Nilotic people demonstrated by Seligman, Evans-Pritchard and other workers cannot help but be transformed into some sense of social unity. To have been made aware that one is a Nilote and that there are others *like* one is to have at once a different attitude to them, to others and to one's self.'

[4] H. S. Morris, 'Some aspects...', p. 182.

[5] F. Barth, *The role of the entrepreneur...*

[6] F. Bailey, *Politics and social change.*

E

value and stratification system in Southeast Asia, and the need to re-order these in the face of 'modern' demands in Latin America.[1] Although Nash does not pursue the inquiry, it is interesting to reflect on the degree to which participation in the modern sector is itself based on a perpetuation of a closed system in the traditional sector.

Although the approaches of these various anthropologists—Smith, Morris, Nash and Steward—differ in some important respects, all fall broadly into a school which is reflected in the following extract from Leo A. Despres's study of cultural pluralism and nationalist politics in Guyana. His analysis clearly concerns the relationship between structure and organization, focusing on the organizational strategies of political groups. He writes:

In the organizational dimension individuals are more than units related to one another by virtue of the social structure in terms of which they interact and through which they express cultural values. They may be this, but they are also conscious agents capable of calculated action with respect to themselves as well as the social universe in which they operate. To state the matter differently, cultural sections are not in themselves politically functional. They may become politically functional only when individuals and groups make them so. Therefore, in order to understand the role of cultural sections in nationalist politics, we must look at the organizational activities of specific individuals and groups ...The creation of social alignment for political purposes...requires organizational strategy and organizational effort.[2]

Thus, we would conclude, as Morris does, that 'what sociological analysis requires of studies of plural, as of other social situations, is not that the models constructed should be all-purpose tools, but that the analyses should be based upon a satisfactory theory of group relations'.[3]

Is the plural society model, then, of no further repute in anthropology with its growing emphasis on process and development, just at the time

[1] M. Nash, 'Social prerequisites to economic growth in Latin America and Southeast Asia', *Economic Development and Cultural Change* 12 (1964), 225–42; *Primitive and peasant economic systems*, San Francisco 1966. For a critique of the diffusionist assumptions underlying this approach, see A. Gunder Frank, 'Sociology of development and the underdevelopment of sociology', *Catalyst* (1967), 20–73. Cf. J. Petras, 'U.S.–Latin American studies: a critical assessment', *Science and Society* 32 (1968), 148–68.

[2] L. Despres, *Cultural pluralism...*, pp. 27–9. M. G. Smith, who provides a foreword to Despres's study, describes it as 'a notable union of social and cultural anthropology' (p. xxiii). Despres calls it a study in political anthropology. 'It presents an analysis of a nationalist political movement with special reference to the sociocultural system in which it developed. That an anthropologist might be interested in the problems of nationalist politics may come as a surprise to those who are not familiar with the discipline. Anthropologists have a self-made reputation for being interested only in preliterate societies and cultures. However, for a very long time they have also been interested in the dynamics of sociocultural change. More recently, they have given increasing attention to the transformation of sociocultural systems from one type to another. The emergence of colonial societies as nation-states falls into this class of phenomena. Among other things, nationalism is a dynamic force by which diverse peoples are creating for themselves new types of social systems. Thus, the forces of nationalism offer the anthropologist an unusual opportunity to investigate the processes of sociocultural change' (p. xxiii).

[3] H. S. Morris, 'Some aspects...', p. 173.

when it is coming to the forefront in political science? Leo Kuper shows how it may have high relevance for the analysis of a specific type of polity; yet he, too, is critical of the model as it is currently used. Kuper distinguishes two antithetical concepts of the plural society: the Equilibrium Model of Kornhauser, Aron and Shils and the Conflict Model of Furnivall and Smith. Both focus upon the mode of integration: the former relying on consensus and cross-cutting ties, the latter on force and subjugation. In the Equilibrium Model, social forces counteract cultural pluralism; in the Conflict Model, 'cultural pluralism is the major determinant of societal structure, and all other factors are secondary to it'.[1]

It is to the Conflict Model of the plural society that Young adheres when he concludes that 'prolonged immersion into the multiple problems of cultural pluralism would seem to lead to gnawing doubts about the viability of the territorial state system'[2] in new nations, and it is this model that has been advocated for the study of political development in ethnically heterogeneous states.

Out of dissatisfaction with both models, Kuper significantly limits plural society analysis to polities in which the defence of the established order (i.e. the stratification system) rests in the hands of a dominant minority which relies on coercion as the mode of integration. He argues that cultural pluralism may provide an ideology of domination or of conflict in a struggle for power between different groups, the significance which the different groups attach to cultural differences varying with changes in the structure of their relationships with one another and, more particularly, with changes in relative power.[3]

The next step might be to recognize (as Peters does of the segmentary lineage system) that this is an ideational model and still not a sociological construct. Kuper does not pursue this line but, in subsequent papers, pleads for a restrictive usage of 'plural society'. He warns against over-emphasizing cultural pluralism even in societies in which ethnicity is politicized and differential access is institutionalized, as in South Africa.

Where the struggle has finally taken the form of racial or ethnic civil war, we tend to overlook harmonious interethnic relations which might have been the basis for other developments, in our preoccupation with the predominant and overriding forces. Yet these interethnic relations may be appreciable even in societies where there is extreme racial discord.[4]

Evolutionary as well as revolutionary development is possible in conditions of cultural pluralism; disillusionment with the 'erosion of democracy' in new nations does not call only for the analysis of conflict.[5]

[1] L. Kuper, 'Plural societies...', p. 8.
[2] C. Anderson et al., Issues of political development, p. 75.
[3] L. Kuper, 'Plural societies...', pp. 12–13.　　　　　　　　　　　　　[4] Ibid., p. 28.
[5] We may question to what extent the plural society model is culture-bound. The idea of society as a market-place in which groups compete for power is a free-enterprise model; com-

What, then, accounts for the differing anthropological and political science perspectives on cultural pluralism as an issue of political development? John Middleton, reviewing Lofchie's *Zanzibar: background to revolution* suggests why, in spite of Kuper's warning that 'few plural societies show the polar structure ascribed them in the ideologies of violence',[1] political scientists have tended to accept the ideologies as the basis of their model: 'This account is based largely on research among party leaders; research among the Shirazi peasants might have given him a somewhat different view of inter-party relations.'[2] The fundamental difference in perspective results from the anthropologist's view from the peasant village and the political scientist's view from the national capital. The way in which informants' sociological positions can distort the observer's analysis has been described by Lloyd, writing of African states.[3] Differences between upper and lower stratum perspectives have also been illustrated by the answers of Apter and Southwold to the same question: what is the future of traditional authority systems within modernizing states? Both worked among the Baganda, yet: 'Adopting the elite view, Apter phrases his response in either-or terms: either national integration or anarchy. Southwold, who looks out from the village, is able to show how a traditional authority system becomes incorporated within new national institutions.'[4] The village view emphasized diversity: the 'establishment' perspective of the politicians and the political scientist embraced a more limited range of alternatives.

[1] J. Middleton, Review of M. Lofchie, *Zanzibar: background to revolution*, Berkeley and Los Angeles 1966, *Africa* 38 (1968), 88–9.

[2] *Ibid.*, p. 89.

[3] P. Lloyd, 'The political structure...', p. 109. He refers to anthropologists who have relied too much on informants from the ruling classes. A comparison may be made of two anthropological analyses of politics in Ruanda: J. J. Maquet, *The premise of inequality in Ruanda*, London 1961, and H. Codere, 'Power in Ruanda', *Anthropologica* 4 (1962). Codere analyses the monopoly of power by a minority without the consent of the governed. This, in her analysis, is independent of the social order or is capable of shaping a kind of social order that becomes known to the people; revolution is a possibility. Emphasis is upon the maximization of power. The establishment can 'maintain superior communications and solidarity among the powerless; distinctiveness through the socialization of the children and this can increase, demonstrate and perpetuate their solidarity; they can use their power with maximum frequency and maximum intensity; they can multiply positions of power so that the powerless are subject to multiple relations with the powerful; they can pretend that chances of gaining power or influencing its exercise exist for the powerless when, in fact, such changes are virtually non-existent; they can develop and propagate ideologies, myths, cults and symbols that glorify and support established power' (p. 52).

[4] A. Weingrod, 'Political sociology, social anthropology and the study of new nations', *British Journal of Sociology* 18 (1967), 121–34; cf. D. Forde, 'Anthropology and the development of African studies', *Africa* 37 (1967), 389–406.

---

parisons with markets, ethnic groups, diversity and authority in China or the Middle East suggest that the model has far from universal application. Its use should be made explicit since other values in society are subordinated in the application of the ideal model. Cultural diversity alone should not lead to preference over a Marxist model of exploitation or any other model.

Exactly the same parallel exists in their respective approaches to cultural pluralism and to political development. Anthropologists are concerned with differences and paradoxes, wary of generalizations. Political scientists focus upon national integration *per se*; anthropologists on all that precedes and flows in the wake of integration—upon the field, the whole context in which political development occurs, upon the interplay of political with other factors which, in reaction to action, themselves become political. The interplay that is studied is of the political factors with all others, and of them upon each other. Horizontal as well as hierarchical concerns are the subject-matter of political anthropology. Attention centres upon the social *becoming* political or politicized rather than upon the analytically distinguished 'political'.

## POLITICAL DEVELOPMENT AND THE ELITE

The amount of space devoted above to cultural pluralism as one of the issues of political development reflects the vast anthropological literature on the subject. The space required for discussion of the anthropological perspective on development and the elite is smaller. Yet it is a parallel concern, as will be seen.

The relationship between the principles of stratification and the elite emerges clearly from Southall's exploratory discussion.[1] The elite, by his definition is a boundary-straddling category of social actors between the centre and the periphery. Stratification is then a matter of formal, institutional structures; the elite is a dynamic organizational concept, requiring parallel but independent study. This distinction between the 'elite' and the 'establishment' is an important one for anthropologists. The concept of an elite came into prominence in development studies when the stratification system which corresponded to the ideology of colonial rule, and which the colonial authorities had attempted to create and maintain, ceased to be effective. The rapid rate of development in the new nations brought into prominence people who only a short time previously had been of very low status, as well as yet another set of people who already challenged their newly established authority. Political development receives its impetus from those segments or groups that are strategically placed to move upwards within the system, and the elite concept operates in precisely this sphere where, as Lloyd has pointed out, because of social change or rapid social mobility, appropriate norms for social relationships have not been clearly defined.[2]

Elites may, then, be described as 'the growing edge of social activity... that which at any time is not yet institutionalized (although it inevitably

---

[1] A. W. Southall, 'The concept of elites and their formation in Uganda', P. C. Lloyd, *The new elites of tropical Africa*, London 1966, pp. 342–66.
[2] P. C. Lloyd, *The new elites...*, pp. 1–85.

will be if successful)'.[1] The anthropologist, as we have seen, is especially interested in such interstitial groups, those with influence but not yet power or legitimate authority, those in the process of politicization, perhaps, as well as 'those dynamic aspects of power and influence which are liable to elude formal analysis', such as patronage and corruption.[2]

The new nations of Africa, observes Southall, are 'for the most part open societies composed of a number of relatively closed traditional enclaves at various stages of integration'.[3] Anthropological interest is moving away from indigenous societies, in which leadership roles are relatively stable and formal within clear-cut corporate structures, towards societies in which new principles of stratification have yet to be determined. In the indigenous society, in which the relatively steady state could be analysed in terms of equilibrium, most change came from the outside; in today's developing societies, the polity itself is in flux, 'an almost institutionless arena', as Zolberg puts it.[4] The elite concept is a bridge by which the anthropologist—guided as always by the empirical data at his disposal—passes from the study of yesterday's relatively closed societies (which are today's micro-segments in a larger unit) to analysis at the macro-level.

Peter Lloyd's schema for the comparison of political development based on the nature of elites and the notion of men socially in movement has been thought by Mackenzie, who discusses it at some length, to have 'certain advantages, tactical, conceptual, and ideological for the study of political change in new nations.'[5] Emphasis is inevitably on the *continuities* of the development process:

The rapid rise of new ruling groups today can be compared with the much slower processes of past centuries which also made radical changes in the political system...Our task is to develop criteria and models which illuminate these changes, seeing them not as peculiarities of the mid-twentieth century, but as examples of processes that have long been known.[6]

Finally, in the light of my thesis that there is a growing convergence of social and cultural anthropology through their interest in change and development, it is interesting to observe that Lloyd compares his African elite model with a cultural analysis by Irving Goldman of 'Status rivalry and cultural evolution in Polynesia'.[7] As with Smith and Fried on stratification, and as with Mair and Sahlins on political leadership, the language

---

[1] A. W. Southall, 'The concept of elites...', p. 344.
[2] *Ibid.*, pp. 344–6.
[3] *Ibid.*, p. 348.
[4] A. Zolberg, 'The structure of political conflict...', p. 70.
[5] W. J. M. Mackenzie, *Politics and social science*, Baltimore 1967, pp. 353–7.
[6] P. C. Lloyd, 'The political structure...', p. 108.
[7] I. Goldman, 'Status rivalry and cultural evolution in Polynesia', *American Anthropologist* 57 (1955), 680–97.

and the proclaimed objective of the exercise differs, but there is extensive common ground between the two.

CONCLUSION

This discussion of anthropological perspectives on political development has dealt with the establishment, maintenance, and growth of the state form of political organization, emphasizing stratification and the control of key resources within the society. Continuities both of process and, in part, of content, suggesting the relevance of pre-state forms of organization to the political development of modernizing nations, have been stressed. An inquiry into degrees of integration and the mode of stratification, along with the study of mobility, marginality, and elite formation within the polity, makes possible cross-cultural and cross-temporal analysis of political development.

Let us pick up some of the threads we have lost in working so rapidly over such an extensive tapestry.

(i) *A questioning of the cultural unit of analysis*

There comes a time in every discipline when the participant needs to step back and ask himself whether what he is doing is meaningful. The units of ethnographic research are under such appraisal in anthropology today.[1] The concept of the tribe, for example, has come under scrutiny for several reasons. An apt illustration is provided by analyses of political events in the Congo; one wonders at the widespread use of 'tribe' as a relevant variable there, in the light of the anthropologist's use of linguistic groupings 'for lack of any clear criterion of tribal groupings'.[2] Douglas attributes political differentiation between groups to varying responses to colonial overrule. Nash's multiple society model, which is constructed essentially on this premise, might well be applied. Regional and class differences outweigh the 'politics of ethnicity'. Surely the 'tribe' may best be viewed as a colonial administrative unit given legitimacy, and, indeed, in some cases, reality, by colonial recognition?

(The multiple society model distinguishes between economic modernity and political development in terms of the openness and integration of the society. The United States of America is a multiple and not a modern

---

[1] See, for example, A. Capell, 'The Walbiri through their own eyes', *Oceania* 23 (1952), 110–32; E. Colson, *The Makah Indians*, Manchester 1953; M. H. Fried, 'On the concept of tribe and tribal society', *Transactions of the New York Academy of Sciences* 28 (1966), 527–40; P. L. Garvin, 'Comment on the concept of ethnic groups as related to whole societies', W. Austin, *Report of the Ninth Annual Meeting on Linguistics and Language Studies*, Georgetown 1958; F. M. LeBar, *Ethnic groups of mainland Southeast Asia*, New Haven 1964; N. Moerman, 'Ethnic identification in a complex civilization: who are the Lue?', *American Anthropologist* 67 (1965), 1215–30; etc.

[2] D. Biebuyck and M. Douglas, *Congo tribes and parties*, London 1961, p. 17. A similar case of different disciplinary treatments of the same data within one volume may be found in J. Middleton and J. Campbell, *Zanzibar: its society and its politics*, London and New York 1965.

society in these terms. We are reminded of M. G. Smith's observations on the relationship between the system of stratification and the 'long hot summers' now accepted as part of the American scene.[1])

Just as in contemporary political analysis ethnic categories have been given a concreteness they do not possess, so has the 'tribe' been given a false political reality in the past. The importance of shifting congeries is now recognized and the concept of cultural clusters provides a means of identifying cultural components hidden by the use of terms such as 'tribe' and 'ethnicity', especially if a criterion of 'mutually recognized commonality' be adopted.[2] Inquiry into ideology would lead to the analysis of cultural categories as well as social groups. The 'clan' as a unit of inter-action, for example, has been neglected as compared with the 'lineage', largely because of past emphasis on corporate groups. Attention is now shifting from descent to alliance and in the process new questions are raised as to the most useful units of ethnographic analysis.

### (ii) *An increasing emphasis on ideology*

Closely related to the study of development in new nations is an increasing emphasis on ideology. As Geertz has suggested, there are two sides to the coin.[3] First, the role of empirical research in the contemporary polity, distinguishing the ambitions of the leaders from the social instrumentalities by means of which their ends are sought. Mair's brief discussion of African socialism and Worsley's of elite ideology in the Third World provide a beginning.[4] Secondly, the precise determination of the ideological contribution of politics past to politics present. Much of this, presumably, is included within the rubric 'political culture'.[5]

### (iii) *Revisionist attitudes to the anthropological analyses of the colonial situation*

The two anthropological approaches to the colonial situation adopted in the past reflect the two levels of inquiry found throughout the discipline: first, the more particularistic approach to be found in the works of Balandier

---

[1] M. G. Smith, 'Pre-industrial stratification...', p. 176.

[2] The application of the culture-cluster concept to Africa has been discussed by P. H. Gulliver, 'The Karamojong cluster', *Africa* 22 (1951), 1–22; A. P. Merriam, 'The concept of culture clusters applied to the Belgian Congo', *Southwestern Journal of Anthropology* 15 (1959), 373–95; N. Dyson-Hudson, *Karimojong politics*, Oxford 1966.

[3] C. Geertz, 'Politics past, politics present', *Archiv. europ. sociol.* 8 (1967), 1–14.

[4] L. Mair, *New Africa*, London 1967; P. Worsley, *The Third World*.

[5] G. J. Bender, 'Political socialization and political change', *Western Political Quarterly* 20 (1967), discusses the anthropological contribution. He summarizes findings in education and reflects on the study of basic personality types. He provides an anthropological critique of the approaches of Hagen, Pye, and LeVine. He compares, for example, the work of Smith and LeVine in Nigeria and that of Pye and Margaret Mead in Burma. He stresses the dangers of ethnocentric and Eurocentric value judgements and suggests the falsity of a rural–urban dichotomy in considering cultural change. Anthropological studies of education are also cited in J. S. Coleman, *Education and Political Development*, Princeton 1965, where there is an excellent discussion of the issues involved in the concept of political socialization (pp. 18–25).

and Gluckman; secondly, the universalistic approach of Steward, Geertz and Worsley.[1]

A re-evaluation of the *context* of much past ethnographic inquiry is under way. Firth notes that

studies have often neglected the specific historical setting of the social forms they have described and so overlooked their contingent nature, their possibilities of change, their phase character in a developing situation. Sometimes with deliberate intent, they have concentrated on the traditional forms of institutions in the society, ignoring the concepts and actions of some groups or members of the society which, at the very period of study, were making for a radical re-evaluation of those traditional forms and a modification of them.[2]

Morton Fried attributes this to a lack of a macro-sociological approach: specifically, to the failure to deal with problems of sovereignty. He continues

This is a particular matter of concern when a society has been described as if it were politically autonomous when, in fact, it has been under the firm control of a superior political establishment... These studies have also been almost useless in furnishing guides to the developments that have taken place since the establishment of new states, especially in Africa.[3]

The anthropologist has been viewed as an authority on certain 'specialities' such as traditional rulers, pre-industrial societies or indirect rule. A move to remedy this is only just beginning.[4] However, while some anthropologists will remain content to work within this framework, others will inevitably challenge Balandier's dictum that 'Colonialism in establishing itself imposed on subject peoples a very special type of situation',[5] preferring to view colonialism as but one situation of dominance in a wider, historical perspective. The second, augmented edition of *The trumpet shall sound* reflects one anthropologist's broadening of his thinking in this respect, but the greatest failure at the macro-level, as Kathleen Gough Aberle points out, relates both to western imperialism as a social system and to the Communist world today.[6]

The opportunities that have been missed in anthropological studies of people under colonial rule are suggested by a recent study of a

[1] G. Balandier, 'La situation coloniale: approche théorique', *Cahiers internationaux de sociologie* 11 (1951), 44–79; M. Gluckman, *Analysis of a social situation in modern Zululand*, Manchester 1958; J. Steward, *Theory of culture change*; C. Geertz, *Old societies and new states*, New York 1963; P. Worsley, *The third world*.

[2] R. Firth, *Essays on organization ...*, pp. 11–22.

[3] M. Fried, 'The state', p. 146.

[4] See, for example, I. Wallerstein, *Social change: the colonial situation*, New York 1966; S. Diamond and F. Burke, *The transformation of East Africa*, New York 1966; V. Turner, *Profiles of Change*, Cambridge 1969.

[5] C. Balandier, 'The colonial situation: a theoretical approach', which appears in I. Wallerstein, *Social change*, p. 34.

[6] K. G. Aberle, *Anthropology and imperialism*, Ann Arbor, The Radical Education Project 1967.

social situation in a Pacific dependency.[1] Using the model perfected in industrial organization research by W. F. Whyte,[2] Appell sets out the structure of district administration in the colony and accounts for anti-administration activity and political instability there. The clearest state-ment of this approach, which appears to be creeping into British social anthropology through the Manchester school, is to be found in the Chapple and Arensberg monograph previously referred to.[3] Emphasis is upon the *measurement* of human relations: thus the study of interaction—actual contacts among people—involves specifications of frequency, duration, and origination. Actions, sentiments, and symbols are similarly treated in order to determine movement from one pattern of interaction to another. Such a procedure has been found useful for pointing out areas of stress and strain in social situations and for indicating possible ways of relieving such stresses. As early as 1943, W. F. Whyte advocated its application to the study of political organizations.[4] Close observation of a political organization as an interactive system would lead to the establish-ment of the *actual* relative positions of its members within its hierarchy and the analysis of their interactions at its various levels. Classic ethno-graphies which have resulted from the application of the 'Chapple–Arensberg interaction scheme' are *Street corner society* and Oliver's *A Solomon Island society*, a study of status and leadership.[5]

### (iv) *Studies of European and Latin American peasantry*

Each continent in turn appears to have fed into the mainstream of anthropological thought. Contributions to political theory have come predominantly from the African and Asian ethnographers whose work has been reviewed thus far. One future trend lies in studies of European and Latin American peasant societies where the anthropologist finds himself embroiled in a 'rural revolution'.[6] The closer familiarity of these anthropologists with the radical literature on economic development[7] and their manifest concern both with the urban situation and the village com-munities in terms of rapid socio-economic change, suggest that a major contribution of the 1970s will involve a shift from micro-level studies of

[1] G. N. Appell, 'The structure of district administration, anti-administration activity and political instability', *Human Organization* 25 (1966), 312–20.

[2] See, for example, W. F. Whyte, 'Patterns of interaction in union–management relations', *Human Organization* 8 (1949), 13–19.

[3] E. Chapple and C. Arensberg, 'Measuring human relations'.

[4] W. F. Whyte, 'Instruction and research: a challenge to political scientists', *American Political Science Review* 47 (1943).

[5] W. F. Whyte, *Street corner society*, Chicago and London 1965. This edition has an appendix entitled 'On the evolution of *Street corner society*' which discusses the methodology of the study. D. Oliver, *A Solomon Island society*, Boston 1967, is also a new edition of the classic work written in the 1930s.

[6] For a discussion of this, see J. Halpern, *The changing village community*, New Jersey, Prentice-Hall 1967, pp. 1–35.

[7] Such as the writings of Andrew Gunder Frank, James Petras and Fernando Cardoso.

patronage, factionalism and corruption towards macro-level treatment of populist movements, the urban proletariat in relation to the established elite and violent political change.[1]

To conclude, political science is moving rapidly into the sphere of social structure which formerly it viewed, as Zolberg so graphically puts it, as a blurry-edged film out of focus to political scientists as they trained their telescopic lenses on the political sub-system.[2] In this process it is bound to look for assistance from anthropology. In the past, however, anthropology has not been wholly sympathetic to its sister disciplines. Asked what is the contribution of anthropology to the social sciences, Geertz remarks that

The easy answer to this, still preferred in certain circles, is data, preferably anomalous data which will demolish some sociologist's high-wrought theory. But to accept that answer is to reduce anthropology to a kind of spiteful ethnography capable, like some literary censor, of disapproving of intellectual constructions but not of creating, or perhaps even understanding, any.[3]

This essay, with—to repeat—its neglect of much of the best that is anthropology (its tight empirical studies and its cautious contingent hypotheses), has attempted to come to grips with the macro-sociology of political development and so to answer such a charge.

[1] Besides the well-known work of Oscar Lewis, recent publications on peasant society include J. Ahumada, 'Hypothesis for the diagnosis of a situation of social change; the case of Venezuela', *International Social Science Journal* 16 (1964), 192–202; W. Carter, *Aymara Communities and the Bolivian agrarian reform*, Gainesville 1965; M. Diaz, *Tonala: conservatism, responsibility and authority in a Mexican town*, Berkeley 1966; E. Hammel, 'Some characteristics of rural village and urban slum populations on the coast of Peru', *Southwestern Journal of Anthropology* 20 (1964), 346–58; A. Leeds, 'Brazilian careers and social structure', *American Anthropologist* 66 (1964), 1321–47; J. Pitt-Rivers, *Mediterranean countrymen*, Paris 1963; N. Whitten, *Class, kinship and power in an Ecuadorian town*, Stanford 1965; etc.

[2] A. Zolberg, 'The structure of political conflict...', pp. 85–6.

[3] C. Geertz, 'Politics past...', p. 4.

# SOVIET POLITICAL ORGANIZATION
# AND DEVELOPMENT

## ALEC NOVE

No serious discussion of the politics of development can fail to give attention to the experience of the U.S.S.R. Here, if anywhere, is a case in which industrialization and politics were closely linked, in which a party imposed the necessary savings and mobilized the people for the tasks of reconstructing the economy on a new basis.

### A LITTLE HISTORY

One could argue that development was a major cause of the Russian Revolution. Rapid social and economic transformation was in progress in the last 25 years of the Tsarist empire. Modern industry was growing rapidly (as shown in Table 1). Agriculture, finally freed in 1906–11 from

Table 1.  *Industrial output (1900 = 100)*

| | |
|---|---|
| 1890 | 50·7 |
| 1900 | 100·0 |
| 1908 | 119·5 |
| 1913 | 163·6 |

Source: Raymond W. Goldsmith, *Economic development and cultural change*, April 1961.

Table 2.  *Crop output*

| | |
|---|---|
| 1861 | 51 |
| 1900 | 100 |
| 1911–13 av. | 141 |

Source: as Table 1. Figures relate to fifty provinces of European Russia.

the shackles imposed by the old communal system of tenure, was booming too (see Table 2). Banking, rural cooperatives, education, science, were all advancing, though admittedly from low levels. All this created acute social strains, strikes occurred frequently in cities, rural revolts accompanied the troubles of 1905. In 1914 a new wave of urban unrest was reaching a peak when the outbreak of war brought it to a halt which proved

[ 65 ]

temporary. It is sometimes said that if the growth rates of 1890–1913 were
extrapolated, Russia would now be a developed country, with a great deal
less sweat, tears, and suffering. This may seem statistically meaningful,
but in other respects the statement has little meaning. If Tsarism had
adapted itself to the social–political evolution of Russia, if Nicholas II
had been Peter the Great, if French and other foreign loans would have
been forthcoming for another 50 years, if the First World War had not
broken out, if a moderate and politically responsible reforming party
would have worked within the Tsarist system, if Rasputin had not
existed, then...But there must surely be some limit to the what-might-
have-been of history. Though it is not being argued that any event
subsequent to 1917 was predetermined, inevitable or 'necessary', the
collapse of Tsardom can hardly be treated as an historical accident.
This is not the only case of the kind. It could with considerable force be
asserted that the preservation of the Austro-Hungarian empire would
have been economically desirable. For a variety of social, political, and
military reasons, the Austro-Hungarian and Russian empires collapsed.

Development logic and Russian imperial policies were in frequent
contradiction. Examples abound. Gerschenkron has pointed to the restrictive policies towards the peasants after emancipation.[1] Seton-Watson
noted how the reactionary educational policies, continued until the end
of the nineteenth century, helped to maintain the deep gulf between the
gentry and the dark masses, which greatly contributed to revolutionary
ferment, contrasting this policy with the very different one pursued by the
Japanese under the Meiji restoration.[2] The memoirs of Count Witte
abound in examples of the opposition he encountered in Court and bureaucratic circles to his modernizing and industrializing policies in the 'nineties.
Yet the Wittes could not rely on effective support outside the official
classes. Many Russian writers, for instance the historian–politician
Milyukov, have discussed the weakness of the Russian middle class, and
also the negative attitude of much of the intelligentsia. It is a fact of
historical importance that many of the educated enemies of Tsarism were
also opposed to the mercantile spirit, to business, to money-making. In
other words, there was a notable lack of secure foundation for a modern
industrial state. This helps to explain why the very speed of the changes
which were in progress in Tsarism's last years exacerbated the contradictions and helped, along with the strains of war, to precipitate not merely
political revolution but also social collapse.

When, after the chaos of revolution and civil war, the Bolsheviks found
themselves surely in the political saddle, they had to find new answers to
old questions. Already under Tsardom the problem was how to industrialize
without many of the preconditions of industrialization, or else to cease to

---

[1] See his contribution to the *Cambridge Economic History*, vol. 6, part II.
[2] *The Russian Empire, 1801–1917*, Oxford 1967.

be a great power. For the Bolsheviks, the task was further complicated by the possession of power by a party ruling in the name of a small proletariat in a peasant country, lacking what orthodox Marxists supposed to be the preconditions of socialism. To the danger of war which worried Tsarist statesmen was added the deeply felt danger of anti-communist crusades from the West. The political–economic discussions of the 'twenties centred on such problems as these, and were further complicated by the nature of the peasant land settlement and the survival (indeed reinforcement) of the obsolete peasant commune as both an economic and political factor in village life.

It is worth drawing the attention of the historians of economic thought to the fact that development economics could be said to have been born in Russia in the 'twenties. There for the first time issues of investment strategy were perceived and debated, anticipating in remarkable degree the doctrines developed in the West in the 'fifties. The issues arose in this way because the state held the bulk of investment resources in its hands, and required to find criteria for their best use in the context of a development plan. Political ideologists such as Preobrazhensky urged that the expansion of the socialist as against the private sector be one of the principal aims of the investment plan. But in any event, in a society without landlords or capitalists (the 'privateers' were small men), it is clear that the role of political organs in the process of investment was bound to be predominant.

## WAR COMMUNISM AND NEP

Before going on to see how the party organized the industrialization drive, a few words are necessary on the early period of Soviet power, usually known as 'war communism'. Its causes and the confusion which it caused cannot be discussed in the present paper.[1] Partly under the stress of stern necessity, partly through ideological illusions, the Soviet regime sought to eliminate all private trade and manufacture, and virtually to confiscate produce from the peasants. In the process of so doing, the line between government and economic management was largely obliterated. The state and its enterprises were seen as a single whole. By 1920 payments between enterprises ceased, they simply moved such resources as there were on the orders of the state organs, with no money passing.

By 1921 this system was collapsing, and under the so-called new economic policy (NEP) the actual business of producing and selling goods was conducted by autonomous state trusts, which were given operational and financial autonomy and told to make a profit. True, the supreme council of the national economy, a government body, was supposed to be

[1] E. H. Carr and M. Dobb have devoted many valuable pages to analysing these years. Chapter 3 of my *Economic history of the USSR*, London 1969, is devoted to this period.

in charge, but, at least until the decline of NEP in and after 1926, commercial operations by state trusts were largely free of control. The private sector, in agriculture, trade, small-scale manufacture, and miscellaneous services, was quite unplanned.

Under this compromise system, a ruined economy recovered rapidly. Many of the party leaders looked with disfavour at the compromise with what they considered to be class enemies, and sought the opportunity to resume the offensive at the earliest date. To this extent recovery was achieved despite rather than because of the efforts of the Bolsheviks. Their main contribution, it could be argued, was that of abandoning the excesses of war communism and unshackling the energies of trust managers, private entrepreneurs, and peasants. There is some truth in this, but one other factor should not be underestimated: the maintenance of public order. Even the greatest admirers of the honest democrats who tried to rule Russia after the overthrow of Tsardom would probably agree that they lacked authority. It is not that they were notably less able than their western counterparts. On the contrary, a case could be made for the proposition that Martov, Dan, and Tsereteli (to name the leading Mensheviks) stood above MacDonald, Snowden, or Bonar Law in both eloquence and intelligence. Perhaps the decisive factor was lack of effective mass appeal, of any sense of legitimacy as successors to the awe-inspiring and remote Tsars. Nor does it help that their view of the revolution compelled them to act in coalition with the bourgeois parties, which themselves reflected the weakness of the middle classes. As for the biggest party of all, the Socialist-Revolutionaries, their political futility could be said to stem from the contradictions of the peasants' own views and of the party's reactions to them. The Revolution caught the peasants in a stage of transition: the more enterprising were beginning to reap the benefit of the Stolypin reforms of 1906–11, but the conscious majority seems to have resented these new-fangled notions, and as late as July 1917 a representative peasant gathering was still advocating communal control over land, periodical redistributions in accordance with 'mouths' and/or 'hands', the prohibition of purchase and sale of land, a ban on employment of hired labour.[1] Yet the stage was almost set for the emergence of a party advocating the interests of the growing class of commercially minded peasant proprietors. This class suffered severely in the Revolution.

Nor can any study of the activities of the Whites—of Kolchak and Denikin—fail to bring out their acute political weaknesses.

THE PLACE OF THE PARTY IN RUSSIAN DEVELOPMENT

The Bolsheviks were far from being the only, or the first, persons to advocate industrial development in Russia. Plans of various kinds were

[1] This was the policy adopted by the peasant congress which met in August 1917.

mooted by others, before, during, and after the Revolution. A particularly advanced plan for industrialization was produced by a talented engineer–technologist, Grinevetsky, in 1918, and his proposals influenced Bolshevik ideas of the time, though Grinevetsky himself was an anti-Bolshevik. An interesting recent article, which rightly praised Grinevetsky's ideas and showed no sympathy at all for communism, none the less noted that the communists contributed 'that strong, stable government, ruthlessly dedicated to the cause of industrialization, which Grinevetsky had been longing for'.[1] It is not that there were no other policies or alternative roads put forward which could, if followed, have led to success. Possibly *any* solidly established and powerful Russian government would have presided over a period of rapid economic growth. The point is that it was *this* government and party that succeeded in establishing order, and that they were ideologically particularly strongly committed to industrialization. It follows that a major service of the Bolsheviks to Russian development was that they saved the political unity of most of the former empire and imposed order. This requires to be set against the fact that they frequently pursued unsound or foolish economic policies.

What *was* a foolish and what a wise economic policy? The answer to such a question is by no means clear-cut in a developing country even today, after oceans of printers' ink have been devoted to discussing the complex issues involved. It must be recalled, in fairness, that the Bolsheviks were the first to tackle these issues, and could benefit neither from the post-1945 work on economic development nor from the economics taught at the time in the West, the latter being concerned in the main with static resource allocation, not growth.

The debate between 'genetic' and 'teleological' planners, which raged in the late 'twenties, was one which also concerned the role of the state in development strategy. Should plans be derived from a market analysis, or should they aim at transforming the social–economic (and market) situation? In either case the state, as the principal source of investment resources, would play a major part in the development process. However, 'teleological' planning carries with it much more far-reaching implications for the role of political authority; since it would have to be the agency of changes of structure, it would have in effect to fight *against* and subjugate market forces.

It is also clear that the state's role is affected by the *pace* of development, by the magnitude of the investments (and therefore savings) and by the *direction* of the investments. The reasons for the choices made by Stalin are beyond the scope of the paper. Suffice it to say that the choices included:

(*a*) The adoption of an extremely ambitious five-year plan, involving dramatic structural changes in the economy, very definitely 'teleological' in character.

[1] L. Smolinsky, 'Grinevetskii and Soviet industrialization', *Survey* 67 (April 1968), 113.

F

(*b*) Therefore a very rapid increase in total investments.

(*c*) The assigning of top priority to heavy industry. When difficulties arose with plan fulfilment, the investments designed for other sectors were further cut.

(*d*) This was all linked with the elimination of peasant control over land and produce, through a collectivization campaign which of its nature was coercive. It can be argued that without collectivization the necessary capital accumulation and agricultural procurements would not have been obtained on the requisite scale. (The consequences of the policy were, however, so drastic that a strong case can be made against it, but this is not the place to pursue the matter.)

(*e*) The mobilization of resources for the great leap forward involved also the liquidation of private industry and private trade.

(*f*) The resultant strains, sacrifices, shortages, led to the creation of an elaborate system of material allocation and central direction of resources, in order to implement the planned priorities of the state.

This was a 'revolution from above', and was so described by Stalin himself. It is inconceivable that it could be carried out or imposed without tough and ruthless political organization. For this the ordinary coercive organs, army and police, were essential but quite insufficient. One had to have a large body of devoted and disciplined political men, the party, imbued with an industrializing enthusiasm, to mobilize, inspect, exhort. The Communist party fulfilled this role.

The party was the dominant nucleus of every political and social organization. The party dominated the system of appointments through the so-called *nomenklatura* system, by which only those approved by appropriate party committees would have posts of any importance, whether in industry, civil service, journalism, or tractor stations. Its 'agit-prop' department exercised direct control over all means of mass communication. It used them to dramatize the five-year plans, industrialization, productivity, modernization, the onward march to socialism (the latter so defined as to require great new industrial construction). Incentives could be so arranged, and the moral standing of trades and professions so publicized, that the ablest usually went willingly into the areas of activity deemed important by the state and party: engineering, science, heavy industry. Trade, consumers' goods and services, agriculture, were neglected, and made do with poor-quality human and material resources.

The absence of private enterprise enabled the concentration of resources to proceed without any distracting claims on resources from the uncontrolled private sector, as has often been the case elsewhere. Even small-scale industry and workshops were either absorbed into the state's own industry, or forced into producers' cooperatives which were also under control; earning a living by private trade was simply equated with 'speculation' and made illegal. This could be described as the elimination, as far as this is possible in the real world, of economic pluralism. The state could decide the use of any material resource, and in providing or depriving any productive unit of materials or equipment it could enforce its own industrializing priorities and neglect other considerations.

This paralleled the striving for political–social monolithism. All publicity other than party publicity was banned. The elimination of competing parties, the total monopoly of the ruling Communist party, minimized the danger of organized protest against high rates of forced saving, against compulsory collectivization. The economic transformation undertaken in the years following 1928 naturally affected the various nationalities composing the U.S.S.R. very differently, and there would certainly have been awkward clashes with nationalist tendencies had these been allowed to manifest themselves. Indeed, so conscious were the leaders of this danger that they repeatedly purged the party itself of real or alleged 'nationalist deviationists'. The trade unions were wholly *gleichgeschaltet* at this period, with some of their leaders, such as Tomsky, branded as right-wing enemies of the general line of the party. The unions then used their influence to mobilize the workers to fulfil the plans of the party and state. All who disagreed could be coerced, by appropriate police measures.

The party at the very top controlled basic policy and the government. Within every ministry (people's commissariat), local government organ, economic enterprise or whatever, party groups had (and have) the duty to check, report, inspect. Locally, all the organs of government, including the judiciary and the local press, were and are under command.

To carry out these immense revolutionary-and-industrialization functions, the party had to be radically reorganized. The date of this reorganization can be disputed, and it certainly far antedated the first five-year plan. Some would argue that Lenin's original conception of a disciplined party of professional revolutionaries was peculiarly suitable for organizing 'social engineering' on a vast scale. Others would (rightly, in my view) stress the fact that Lenin's party was one within which argument still flourished, or at least was tolerated, as witness the fact that Lenin himself was on occasion outvoted, as in the trade union controversies of 1919–20. Probably the best way to express a complex evolution is to say that the party possessed some 'totalitarian' features from the first and that the civil war and the desperately difficult task of creating order out of chaos greatly strengthened the party's evolution towards becoming a ruling machine, designed for imposing order and its own social–political conceptions on a people largely indifferent to them. In a sense it gradually ceased to be a 'party', not only because of the suppression of all alternatives, but also because discussion and argument within its own ranks was gradually eliminated. This is no doubt explicable in terms of the logic of a one-party state, which requires periodic purges of those who are deemed to represent the views of the banned parties within the sole remaining legal political organization. In the U.S.S.R. this tendency was exacerbated by the consciousness that the party's social base was narrow, and that the 'petty-bourgeois' peasant masses would seek to find expression for their interests and aspirations in the party. But another important factor was that the desired transformation of society could only be forced through, against active and passive resistance, by a disciplined body who could act together and eschew the 'luxury' of discussions. So, if the party altered society, the party also altered its own nature. And since a disciplined party sailing stormy seas needed a strong captain at the helm, the emergence of Stalin was facilitated by his ruthlessness, his organizational abilities and by the widespread feeling among party activists that a supreme 'boss' was indispensable for survival.

Some might say: but if the party was well on the way to becoming a coercive and bureaucratized machine well before the launching of the first five-year plan and collectivization, then these latter events cannot be ascribed by hindsight as causes of the transformation of the party. This objection has only limited validity. It is true that a party ruling a largely peasant Russia in the name of the proletariat was impelled by the logic of its situation to organize itself as a machine for rule and for coercion. However, it was a party not only devoted to maintaining itself in power, but also to achieving social–economic transformation (without which, let it be added, its own philosophy showed that it could not maintain itself in power for long). This ideological–political commitment to drastic change was known and felt long before 1929. The poet Esenin, emotionally attached to peasant Russia, in his poem entitled 'Lenin's heirs', written in 1924, exclaimed:

> You, whose fate it is to force the raging torrents of
> Russia between banks of concrete.

Indeed, there were vigorous arguments in the 'twenties about how and how fast to proceed. But few doubted that big changes under party leadership and control were needed and that the party had to be able to cope with these problems, while continuing to suppress other organized manifestations of opinion or of social forces. These tendencies not only rendered possible the 'great leap' which began at the end of the 'twenties, but were themselves substantially strengthened by the actual experience of carrying through the 'revolution from above', as Stalin himself described it. For this reason, as well as Stalin's predilection for personal despotism, the party wore an increasingly monolithic look after 1929.

It is hard to avoid the conclusion that the crash-programme industrialization and forcible collectivization which characterized the period 1929–36 would have been inconceivable without the party machine. The latter was imbued not only with discipline but also with a modernizing fervour.

This aspect of ideology was certainly a highly relevant factor. The drive was maintained despite a dramatic fall in living standards, which reached their lowest peace-time point in 1933. Symbolic of the period was the forcible grain collection—partly for export—in the winter of 1932–3, which led directly to the famine in the Ukraine and North Caucasus. An unknown number of millions died, but exports were maintained so as to pay for imports of capital goods for the great plan. Resistance to collectivization led to a drastic fall in livestock numbers and in food supplies generally, but there was no relaxation in tempo. Official newspapers kept up a barrage of reports of great successes, and the very existence of the famine was not mentioned. Indeed to this day, so far as published documents, books, and newspapers are concerned, the famine has never been.

Stalin understood the immense strain which the high industrialization tempos imposed on the people, and in his well-known speech of 1931 insisted that tempos be increased, referring to external military danger as his principal justification and uttering his prophecy that only ten years remained in which to catch up the developed West. It would be wrong not to mention the national-security motivation as one factor which drove the party towards industrialization and which also affected both the planned rate of growth and the extent of the priority of heavy industry. By the middle 'thirties, Stalin also appreciated that nationalist feeling had to be harnessed in pursuit of his goals, hence the rewriting of history books and the stress on continuity and past glory. But the harshness of collectivization, the poor living standards and the total suppression of discussion within the party all contributed to an acute feeling of internal insecurity on the part of Stalin and his henchmen, and all this led to a tightening of police control and the spread of terror as a political and disciplinary weapon; this, like so much else in the Soviet polity, was already developing in the 'twenties, but it is surely evident that terror became much more open after 1929 and reached its apogee in the terrible years 1936–8. It will be argued for years by historians how far the system and the terror was due to circumstances, and how far Stalin established it to achieve his own personal dominance and the physical extinction of his actual and potential foes. I tried to discuss this question elsewhere;[1] it may be sufficient here simply to assert that harshness and repression were the necessary concomitant of the party's policies of these years *and* that Stalin did in fact achieve despotic power by terroristic means. (In passing, it is worth recalling that this dual function of terror has greatly embarrassed Soviet official historians; after a period of denunciation of Stalin's crimes following Khrushchev's 'secret speech' of 1956, the party line now is one of silence. How does one disentangle Stalin's excesses and crudities from the general policies and achievements of the party? It may well seem safest not to try.)

[1] *Was Stalin really necessary?* (first essay in the collection of that name), Allen & Unwin 1965.

## POLITICAL AND ECONOMIC COSTS

All systems involve a cost. A war economy of the western type, with controls and price-fixing, leads to a wide range of bureaucratic deformations and resource misallocation, even in relation to the aim of pursuing the war effort with optimal efficiency. None the less, for a number of cogent reasons, it was nowhere found possible to run the war in accordance with the principles and criteria of a free market economy. Stalin's economic model had much in common with a war economy, a point made by the Polish economist Oskar Lange. However, to the inevitable 'systematic' cost of centralized resource allocation must be added certain additional costs arising out of the peculiarities of the political system.

Thus, firstly, Stalin asserted the priority of political judgement over economic calculation. Even as late as 1952, in his last work,[1] he warned economists off the whole field of planning, which was reserved for officials and political men. In a sense, the choice of 'teleological' plans *was* a choice involving priority of politics over economics, in that current economic or market trends were to be disregarded or combated. However, in practice the denial of calculation led to the imprisonment of many talented economic and planning specialists and the choice of wasteful means of achieving given ends. Indeed, for a while there was an attitude of 'liquidationism' towards money as a measure.

Secondly, the general atmosphere of political terror had profound effects on planning itself. The decision to 'leap forward' was accompanied by such slogans as 'there is no fortress the Bolsheviks cannot take', which could be translated as 'the sky's the limit'. It carried with it the corollary that anyone who said that some plan was impossible or unbalanced was a right wing deviationist, a defeatist, maybe an agent of the class enemy. Such language was an everyday feature of articles and speeches in the 'thirties. This paralysed the critical faculties, or made silence much the safest policy. The result was the adoption of unnecessarily overambitious plans, as well as of technically unsound projects of many kinds. Heavy losses, and sacrifices, would have been avoided if warnings had been sounded, heard, and heeded.

Thirdly, these political pressures did particularly great harm in agriculture. Collectivization had, in the circumstances, to be coercive if it was to happen at all, since clearly the peasants would not voluntarily give up their land in order to deliver still more produce to the state at low prices. The huge investment programme in heavy industry made it impossible to offer material inducements for the change. But the political circumstances led to wild excesses. Some excellent Soviet historical work published in recent years provides much evidence on this score.[2] Peasants

---

[1] *Economic problems of socialism in the USSR.*

[2] The historians concerned are Danilov, Ivnitsky, Bogdenko, Vyltsan, and Moshkov. See also M. Lewin. *Russian peasants and Soviet power*, Allen & Unwin 1968.

had even chickens and rabbits confiscated, lest the local officials 'would be accused of right-wing deviation'. In fact there was mass dismissal of party officials who were thought to be soft on peasants, and those who replaced them ruthlessly collected and removed foodstuffs, thereby largely creating the famine of 1933. The terrible struggle of 1929–33, described by Stalin himself (in conversation with Churchill) as analogous to the struggle with the Germans in the last war, cast a blight for a generation on the regime's relations with the peasants and on agricultural efficiency.

The more purely political consequences of the Stalin model are well known: they led to the establishment of a personal despotism and to the physical elimination of all those suspected of dissent, actual or potential. The purge itself became a campaign which, like so many economic campaigns (of which more in a moment), developed its own momentum and went well beyond the purposes for which it was intended. The mass terror and great bloodletting of 1936–8 are subjects which do not fall within the scope of the present paper. However, they do have some relevance to Stalin's economic development strategy, and this in two very different ways. Firstly, the severities of the sacrifices and the social conflicts engendered by the strategy greatly added to the feeling of strain within the party, stimulated opposition and so led to the decision to eliminate all dissent by drastic surgery. Secondly, the purges themselves had economic side-effects. Growth practically halted in 1937–9. Many Soviet books and articles published since 1956 ascribe this (in part) to the disruptive effects of mass arrests on economic and technical decision-making. So many managers, planners, statisticians, designers, engineers, were arrested that there was a grave shortage of qualified personnel, and an equally grave shortage of persons willing to take responsibility.

### THE PARTY, THE STATE, AND THE 'STALIN' ECONOMIC MODEL

After the drama of the 'thirties came the war, and this inevitably led to even stricter centralization and rationing. After the war, and even more after Stalin's death in 1953, conditions became easier, but the political–economic system has remained unchanged in essence almost to this day. True, there were many reorganizations, some of them (like Khrushchev's ill-fated regionalization) of considerable scope, but in general it was a matter of 'changing the labels on the doors of the same officials', to cite the Soviet critic, A. Birman. So far we have been discussing the function of the party and state in times of tumult, of 'revolution from above'. But industrial growth proceeded also under this same system in quieter times, and it is worth casting an eye on how it worked.

The economy's place in the political set-up was different in important aspects both from the war-communism model and from NEP. It differed from the former because state enterprises possessed financial autonomy and legal personality, they paid for their expenditures out of revenues from sales of goods and services (the state providing a subsidy in the event of a deficit). Thus there was some degree of formal separation between the state and its enterprises, as there is between the British state and its coal industry, whereas the parallel with 1918–20 would be the British post office before its 1969 reorganization. The system differed from the state trusts of the NEP period by being more highly centralized, with resource allocation and production decisions belonging in principle to the state planning organs, expressing the will of the party. The role of the market forces was quite specifically denied.

On the face of it, the dominance of politics over economics was complete. Indeed, this was clear in matters great and small. There were nation-wide campaigns, especially in agriculture, where they were enforced upon farm management very largely through the party's local officials. Such campaigns concerned 'the transformation of nature', or rabbits, or an alleged rubber-bearing plant called *kok-sagyz* and grass rotations (all under Stalin's rule); and maize, 'overtake America in meat production', ploughing up virgin lands and eliminating grass rotations (Khrushchev period). They always went too far and caused economic losses. Campaigns were less common in industry, and the role of the state as distinct from the party machine was greater. None the less, decisions about the role of solid and non-solid fuels, of synthetics, about regional development, or the location of a particular factory, were frequently taken at high party levels, and interference or representations by lower party levels were extremely common.

There were, inevitably, some tensions and overlaps with the state (as distinct from party) hierarchy.

The state planning and ministerial organizations existed to carry out the wishes of the supreme political authority. Logically it should have followed that they would work out the most effective way of executing the orders received, and then act accordingly. In practice, the existence of party organs which duplicate state organs at various levels leads to some confusion. It might be asked why such duplication was and is allowed to persist. It is not a question merely of 'power', since logically the men in charge in the party bureaucracy would take over and thereby eliminate duplication. There seem to me to be two reasons for the survival of 'dyarchy'.

Firstly, the men responsible for running any sector of the Soviet (or any other) system quickly become identified with the interests of that sector, whether or not they have a party card in their pocket. This tends to be true of military chiefs, ministers of heavy machinery, republican premiers, and so on. Soviet experience clearly proves that 'the internalization of externalities' (i.e. taking into account the general rather than the sectional interest) presents great difficulties. The problem is not, as socialist thinkers once believed, bound up with private property. It arises out of necessary divisions of function and of responsibility. While it is true that the party's own sector or regional officials could also be affected by this 'disease', by intention—and to some extent in reality—the tighter all-union party discipline imposes a clearer view of all-union interest.

Secondly, the system as a whole lacks an *inner* dynamism, such as is provided much of the time by the profit motive under capitalism. People need prodding. Plans for great investments and increases in output are part of the prodding process. But there is much 'routine and inertia'.[1] The party is the prodder. Its job is to keep things stirring. Hence its tendency to insist on taut plans. Hence also party-led campaigns. The latter are intended to activate the party machine, to prevent it from getting routine-bound, to mobilize the mobilizers.

This question of campaign versus routine is germane to another more specifically economic issue, which helps to explain 'political' intervention into what might be regarded as the domain of the execution by the planning agencies of party intentions.

The planners, within the Stalin model, are deprived of the means of calculating costs of alternatives, owing to the fact that prices do not express economic relations, being in the main passive accounting-and-auditing magnitudes. So instead they use 'material balances' in an effort to achieve consistency between input and output. But these, like input–output tables, are derived from the experience of the past. Furthermore, the various ministries which compose the economic administration are in a real sense competitors for investment resources. The central planners often find it simplest to maintain existing patterns and proportions. It requires pressure from the very top to change them, to adjudicate between competing claims, to identify areas in which a campaign is needed to put right some sector which had suffered from neglect. Often such a sector is identified by reference to development in the western world. So it was with natural gas, synthetics, consumer durables.

Thus it would not be proper to assert, with Djilas, that the party within the 'Stalin' economic model loses its *raison d'être* and becomes merely parasitic, even though it will be argued in subsequent pages that circumstances do now call for reform of a kind which will greatly diminish the need for party interference with the functioning of the economy.

The 'Stalin' model bases actual administration on ministries, with Gosplan acting as coordinator (it is a state committee in name and status). Since the word 'minister' suggests a politician, a brief examination of the real status of the minister may help to clear our minds as to the

---

[1] On this see Gregory Grossman, 'Soviet growth: routine, inertia and pressure', *American Economic Review* 50 (May 1960), 62–72.

distinction to be drawn between politics and economics in this whole field. The heads of Soviet nationalized industries are ministers. But it is evident that their analogy in the British system is not a minister but the head of a nationalized industry. Since the results of Soviet elections are predictable, they very properly see no sense in having the equivalents both of the chairman of the National Coal Board *and* of a minister of fuel. But in this case one should see most of the Soviet council of ministers as a gathering of senior managers. Indeed, the top political leadership act for much of the time as super-managers of U.S.S.R. Ltd., the biggest firm in the world. When they, and the ministers, act in their managerial capacities, are they politicians? When the head of a western corporation identifies a future need for sulphuric acid and orders appropriate action to be taken, he is acting as an economic man. When the Soviet minister of chemical industry (or the head of Gosplan) identifies this same need and orders possibly identical action to be taken, is he imposing a political solution on the economy? Can a line be drawn, and if so, how or where?

To some extent, of course, the line is blurred in all countries. Certainly *all* statesmen are busy much of the time dealing with economic questions. None the less, in the 'Stalin' model there is a qualitative difference: the entire economy is not only regulated but both owned and *operated* by state organs, and the overwhelmingly significant criterion for managerial activity below the topmost level is 'the plan', that is, the systematized instructions of the centre. This is why so much detail has to be decided at what appears to us to be the political level. Yet such decisions are generally not only of a managerial–economic character, but are consequences of consequences, derived from past decisions through technological necessities. Indeed, they are often the consequence of representations from management. A Hungarian economist has asserted[1] that in a 'command' economy of the Soviet type the commands are usually written by the recipient, who then tries—often successfully—to persuade his ministerial superiors to sign them.

The essential point is that a large proportion of the economic decisions of Soviet political organs, either in initiating proposals or in countersigning them, are managerial or technical, in the sense that no identifiably political issues arise, or the issues are no more (or less) 'political' than similar decisions within large Western corporations. The organizational arrangements and pattern of incentives affect the *level* of decision and sometimes the decision itself too. Thus more tends to be referred upwards, there are far fewer small decision-making units, plan fulfilment in quantitative terms has hitherto played a much bigger role than profits in determining managerial bonuses (and this at industrial-ministry as well as at enterprise level). One could perhaps put the case as follows: if a decision is based primarily on *economic* calculation (whether it is mistaken or dis-

---

[1] In conversation with the author.

torted is another matter), then, regardless of who takes it, the decision could best be seen as economic. Thus if a highly promising mineral deposit is to be worked, investment is required in mining, transport, housing, etc. Of course, investment resources have a multitude of possible uses, and someone somewhere has to decide to devote them to this mineral complex. If the underlying calculation is economic or economic–technical in character, then the decision is best seen as a response to circumstances, consequential, induced, market-replacing, managerial in character. Of course political choices are made affecting investment and military policy in which the fact that politicians decide by reference to political objectives is beyond dispute. We can all think of examples in which the distinction which is here being attempted is exceedingly difficult to sustain. Yet it is surely worth trying to think clearly on this issue.

It may be objected that such an analysis leaves out of account the arbitrary decision-making concerning resource allocation which so distinguishes the 'Stalin' model. Elsewhere, the consequences of consequences do reflect, in at least some significant degree, consumer preference. In the U.S.S.R., it may be asserted, the system imposes 'planners' preferences' upon the consumer.

There is indeed an important difference here. But too much emphasis on 'planners' preferences' can be misleading, as I tried to point out elsewhere.[1] The top political leadership has a view as to rates of growth, the share of national income used for investment, the size and nature of the military budget. The last of these is the preserve of every government, which also decides the expenditures on education, health, and other social services. It has to decide, too, on terms of trade between village and town, but the briefest of looks at the farmers' lobby and price support in Britain, France, and the United States should convince us that this, too, is hardly peculiar to the Soviet system. For the rest, the logic of the situation requires:

(*a*) that the investments and the output of intermediate goods are such as to achieve the objectives of the authorities at least cost;[2] and

(*b*) that, save where 'political' judgements affect the issue (e.g. vodka bad, vitamins good), the production and distribution of consumers' goods should accord with consumer demand.

### POLITICS OF REFORM

Yet up to the present it is evident that neither (*a*) nor (*b*) is achieved. It is superficial to assert that this is because the planners prefer it so. Soviet economists, and officials too, tend to agree that such things are due to

[1] 'Planners' preferences, priorities and reforms', *Economic Journal* 76 (June 1966).

[2] Subject to possible modifications due to regional policy (Scotland, Uzbekistan, Mezzogiorno, Appalachians; examples transcend politics and ideology).

faults in the system, faults to be remedied. Investment decisions which are economically unjustified are usually seen to be wrong; they may be due to faults in the price system, or to intrigue among ministers seeking their share of the state investment cake, or the 'conservatism' of input–output tables. They are usually *not* due to a conscious desire of the top politicians to put arbitrary whim ahead of what they know to be the economically correct course of action. Similarly, we can note the system has been un-responsive to consumer demand, that the wrong product mix has often been provided, that shops are too few and the service sector starved of resources. But it is quite another thing to assert that the planners or leaders *wish* that there be too few hairdressers, that cloth be of poor quality, or that shoes or television sets actually wanted by the customer be unobtainable. *Pravda* recently reported that frankfurter-type sausages, in heavy demand, are very scarce, while there is plenty of salami. The reasons: plan in tons, price of frankfurters unprofitable, shortage of sausage casings. *Not* 'planners' preference'. Brezhnev and Kosygin would doubtless prefer that the citizens get the type of sausage they like.

The inefficiencies mentioned above are part of the cost of a centralized system of resource allocation. Inevitably so, because the sheer scale of the planning process makes it possible to concentrate only on key priority sectors, leaving (as A. Birman recently wrote) the entire consumption sector as a species of residual. The similarity to a Western war economy must again be mentioned.

Under Stalin, these arguments could not get a hearing, not only because that capricious tyrant imposed terror on his subjects, but also because he was engaged in *transforming the economy and society*. He had few years of 'normal' rule. Great leap forward, war preparation, war, recovery from war, took up the years 1929–50. He died in 1953. His system, geared above all to the imposition of political solutions, was dominated by the idea of struggle, emergency, campaign, battles on 'the economic front', to achieve industrial and military might quickly and almost regardless of cost. Of course many planners' decisions also under Stalin were 'managerial', but a great many fell on the 'political' side of the imaginary and ill-defined line. Among the many causes of reform is the fact that there is now no revolution, the regime is an 'establishment' (which rejected the erratic and unpredictable Khrushchev because he was erratic and unpredictable). There is a longing for order, efficiency, and other familiar bureaucratic virtues. It becomes more and more difficult to justify arbitrary inter-ference by party secretaries with resource allocation.

Party-state control, plans based on shortages, rationing, administrative allocation, are not a sound basis for micro-economic routine. This is increasingly understood. The decisions of the centre, of the government, ought to a great extent to reflect the demands of the citizens. As I was told in 1967 at the Institute of Mathematical Economics of the Academy of

Sciences, it is evident that the government has economic functions and duties, that to meet the citizens' needs for houses, amenities, coats, cars, hotels and so on it is necessary to make major investments, and these (in the absence of capitalism and of a capital market) will be the task of a central authority. This amounts to asserting the managerial and 'responsive' role of political authority in a reformed socialist economy, a role conditional (in the view of many reformers) upon the consumers' freedom to choose, 'to vote with the rouble', and enterprise managers' freedom to decide their product mix and their inputs in the light of customers' requirements.

The economic logic of reform and the economic reasons for its slow progress in the U.S.S.R. are another subject. Here I will confine myself to examining the political consequences of reform, and incidentally also the extent to which politics and the party are obstacles to change.

With the end of the revolutionary-development stage, there is need for reassessing the role of the party in the economy. If growth and economic decision-making could to a greater extent be routinized, many more decisions could be left to the managers at various levels. It then becomes a purely empirical exercise to determine at what levels. Decisions on cabbages and hair-curlers could be wholly devolved on to junior managers, guided solely by the market. Decisions on electricity generation in Siberia, the price of grain, employment in Central Asia, can only be taken at high levels, but at these levels could become to a greater extent supermanagerial, in the sense that the politicians would seek the economically most rational solution, without necessarily being more influenced by strictly political considerations than other statesmen in other countries (which is by no means insignificantly!).

But the party and state officials are unaccustomed to such an approach. For over a generation they have dealt with difficulties and shortages by administrative allocation based on priorities. In the absence of any automatically functioning economic mechanism, with prices ineffective as information carriers, the political machine has intervened in matters great and small. Sometimes their actions have been arbitrary or (in the communist jargon) 'voluntaristic'. Sometimes they have correctly responded to necessity. But even in the latter case they consciously responded by issuing an order. In much the same way, a general issues an order that greatcoats be worn; the reason, objectively, is that winter has come, but he still has the power to issue the order and possibly enjoys that power. Whatever the real content of planners' preferences, it could well be that planners and party officials prefer to be able to prefer. *This* preference can then be rationalized in terms of appeals to an outlook traditional among many Marxists: that the essence of socialism is the substitution of deliberate allocation of resources 'by society' for the 'anarchy of the market'. No doubt such sentiments and interests, as well as serious practical problems of transition, explain the slowness with which reform measures are being implemented in the Soviet Union.

In other words, there was some developmental logic in the Stalin 'revolution from above', and it could at least be argued that, during Stalin's lifetime at least, crises and emergencies, wars and reconstruction, justified the retention of centralized, politically dominated management. Its cost was always appreciable, but its advantages appeared to the leadership and the planners to be greater than the cost. Now loud voices are asserting the need for change.

But why should the Soviet system evolve, some may ask, when the principal objective of the party machine is to maintain its grip on power? If power is maximized under conditions of strain, shortage, and administrative resource allocation, why should not the party and the planning bureaucracy continue in the old way?

To this question there seem to me to be three answers. The first is that, though they are trying to retain important elements of the old system, the leadership want not only power but also results. Secondly, to put it a different way, power depends also on economic successes, therefore on greater efficiency. This clearly applies to power in the international field, but also to the power-position of individuals in Russia itself. Khrushchev was thrown out in the main for bungling economic policy.

Thirdly, for a system to survive in the face of strong criticism there must be some real sense of the necessity of continuing it, which is felt both by the men in charge and by at least some large segment of their subordinates. Men have a great capacity for self-deception and rationalization, but it must surely be admitted that changing circumstances do affect behaviour, and that the convenience of authority is not, by itself, a sufficient reason for expecting the indefinite continuance of obsolete methods of planning and control.

Yet the developmental dynamism provided by party pressures and campaigns may not be so easy to replace. Profit-maximizing socialist enterprises which many reformers are advocating could all too easily develop monopolist deformations. Neither a salaried manager nor his workers can be expected to have a long-term view. The whole question of risk-taking and its corollaries, the possibility of big gains in the event of success and bankruptcy in the event of failure, is still unsettled. Therefore, the active developmental role of state and party under social ownership may prove greater than some reformers expect.

## SOME MORALS FOR DEVELOPING COUNTRIES

It will be seen that the applicability of the Soviet 'model' to a developed Soviet Union may be regarded as questionable, to say the least. However, it is not the U.S.S.R. of Brezhnev and Kosygin which attracts the attention of developmental statesmen and theorists, but rather the 'Stalin model', or perhaps the whole Soviet period ending with Stalin's death.

High among key factors is the Communist party, which established order, provided the means of enforcing change on society and mobilized people for the job of reconstruction. It must be stressed that it transformed itself, even in a sense destroyed itself, in the process. The party which existed in 1917 was hardly suited to the task. It had, it is true, ideological commitment not only to economic development but also to a disciplined party ('democratic centralism', with the accent strongly on the centralism). However, its membership was small and very mixed: it included both tough men-of-the-people and cosmopolitan intellectuals, the latter much given to brilliant controversy and philosophic hairsplitting. Lenin, so to speak, bestrode both species like a colossus: an intellectual but a man of action with contempt for intellectuals, a Marxist but at the same time a successor of Russian revolutionary-populism. The personnel of the party expanded rapidly during and after the Revolution, and it naturally attracted ambitious 'doers', and reduced the importance and influence of mere agitator-talkers, though it is true that some of the intellectual wing of the party proved as tough as any sergeant-type in the 'class battles' of the revolution from above.

As with some developing countries today, a feature of the Russian scene at the time of the Revolution was the absence of a strong bourgeoisie, a fragmented and ill-organized petty bourgeoisie and an insufficiency of native private enterprise, a lack indeed of modern classes. As already indicated, this situation was changing in the first decade of this century, but the weakness of spontaneous social forces, especially spontaneous commercial forces, explains the traditionally very large role of the state in Russian economic development.

The Tsarist bureaucracy was in a sense above or outside class, regarding service to the monarch and the state as its principal preoccupation. Many of its members were concerned at the low level of economic development. But the bureaucracy as a whole lacked a modernizing motivation and was dominated by routine. It never established relations of confidence with the rising commercial class. The Soviet party official was imbued with the spirit of revolutionary change, which agreed with his beliefs and with party doctrine and agreed also with his direct self-interest. There was close association between plan fulfilment and promotion. Officials also found that their own careers and prospects benefited from the enlargement of the capital assets within their sphere, and this stimulated vigorous competition between officials, departments and localities for investment funds. Many of the party officials in these early days received a rough and ready training which gave the greatest emphasis to industrialization as an overriding goal. Experience also taught them that heavy industry was vitally important in the eyes of their superiors and that all non-priority sectors could and should be sacrificed. Of course, some Tsarist officials also pressed for change, and some Soviet officials have been routine-minded and conservative bureaucrats. None the less over the whole historical period it is clear that there was a marked difference both in motivation and in the dynamic qualities which so often impede the progress of less developed countries.

There emerged a Soviet or 'Stalin' model. Party and police dictatorship, the stern repression of dissent, the collectivization of agriculture, the imposition of a high rate of savings, the priority of heavy industry, the elimination of private enterprise and central control over resources, these were its essential features. The profit motive was downgraded, prices played a passive accounting role. The result was a transformation of the economy and society, achieved at an economic and social–political cost which no one can measure. It is understandable that some developing countries find interest and attraction in the achievements of the Stalin system, even while hoping that they would be able to detach its *economic* strategy from the harsh and cruel political coercion with which it was accompanied. Recent events underline the fact that the state and party in the U.S.S.R. gradually acquired the attitudes and status of an 'establishment', have become a conservative force alarmed by new ideas and resistant to necessary reforms. But this stage is in large degree one which relates to a period in which a great industry had already been built, and so is of less direct interest to developing countries. Some have argued that Russia at the time of the Revolution was already semi-developed, and that, therefore, its experience cannot be applied to the much more backward countries which are now starting to grow. In so far as the historical experience of every country is unique, the warning is well taken, and applies generally: what is there in common in the practical problems of Brazil and Zambia? Yet surely Russia's experience is one from which many useful lessons, positive and negative, can be drawn.

# THE ECONOMICS OF IDEOLOGY: SOME PROBLEMS OF ACHIEVING RURAL SOCIALISM IN TANZANIA

## DAVID FELDMAN

The analysis of political change in Africa has tended to concentrate on describing the development of a political elite, and the process of communication of their aspirations in the form of political decisions, through political and administrative structures. The mass of individual decision-makers within the society over which the elite strive for control tend to be examined only in so far as they react in a particular way to the various stimuli which originate from above them in the power structure. Although such an approach may have produced certain useful insights into the process of communication between the government and the governed, it has disregarded sources of change, generated independently of the government's decisions, within the rest of society. The emphasis on looking at political change 'from above' may, in fact, have created an exaggerated estimation of the power of leaders to mould the structure of African societies to the images they have determined. Thus theories of political change based on 'national consensus', or ideological relationships within leadership groups, only account for details of a part of the 'superstructure' and may ignore other determinants of the pattern of social organization.

This paper is an attempt to relate the decisions made at the 'grassroots' level of African society, i.e. those of the individual peasant going through a process of commercial and technological change, to the aspirations of the leadership about the patterns of society that are intended to emerge from this process. It is thus an attempt to look at political and social change from 'below'. The investigation was originally prompted by the need to evaluate agricultural policies against farmers' decisions in regard to the development of their own farming systems. It became clear that one is faced, in such a situation, with no single goal of government policy against which farmers' decisions can be evaluated, but by a complex of objectives that includes aspirations about the structure of society, as well as the more orthodox economic ends of achieving certain levels of output and income growth rates. The choice problem of partly conflicting objectives is fundamental to economics, yet its practical implications have only recently begun to concern economic planners.[1] Attempts to assign weights

---

[1] For a brief discussion on some of the economic issues see S. A. Marglin, *Public investment criteria*, London 1967, pp. 19–40.

to conflicting objectives in order to resolve decisions are open to objection:
policy-makers are unable to define these weights except implicitly by an
actual choice presented to them. Except for the goal of increasing income,
ideology has supplied goals for planners only negatively, by excluding
certain policies as unacceptable. Many policies, however, involve a conflict
between different ideological goals; attempts to determine the pay-offs
between these have not been taken very seriously, even in those developing
countries whose governments have articulated their goals in terms of
socialism. It is true, of course, that most such governments pay only lip
service to the development objectives implied by their ideologies, and
rarely go beyond exclaiming the right slogans. There is, however, a small
group of developing countries whose leaderships are more seriously
concerned with the quality of society that emerges from the changes of
economic development; Tanzania is one of these. Its leadership has
shown itself prepared to modify policies, even at the cost of reducing
its economic growth, in order to achieve long-term ideological aims.[1]
In such a situation, where these aims have been spelled out explicitly, the
adviser and the social researcher have a responsibility to examine the
implications of strategies designed to meet them. In particular it is necessary to indicate the costs of achieving a given objective in terms of the
extent to which others may have to be sacrificed.[2]

An assessment of the achievement of rural development objectives
in Tanzania shows the need to examine the implications of farmers'
decisions in the face of new economic opportunities. These need to be
evaluated not only in terms of achieving the aggregate output and income
targets set in the five-year plan, but also in terms of the quality of society,
which is also changed as a result of these new opportunities. This is the
interest which prompts this investigation.

The policy dilemma in Tanzania is a very real one. Up to the present,
the main weight of government effort to generate rural development has
been directed at encouraging the responses of individual producers by a
variety of incentives in order to achieve overall targets. The one major
attempt to by-pass this dependence on farmers' responses was a somewhat
disastrous village settlement programme.[3] Except for this, the policies

---

[1] These issues are discussed in a paper by Julius Nyerere, *Principles of development*, Dar es
Salaam 1966. In an appendix to this paper President Nyerere lists ten decisions, when policy
choices made by the Tanzanian government might have involved some material sacrifice in
order not to compromise other objectives.

[2] It is therefore possible to evaluate the achievement of aims which have no commonly accepted
measurement of progress by assessing the sacrifice involved in terms of more easily measured
objectives such as income or output growth. Any final choice between alternatives with no
common scale of value weightings, however, must be a normative one. The role of the social
scientist is not to make such a choice but to indicate the costs of alternative actions.

[3] The village settlement programme set up for the first five-year plan was an attempt to
transform the rural society and economy of Tanzania, by transferring people to live and work
on settlements designed by a government agency. Both the production systems and the social

adopted have been very successful. However, material progress is now seen to have been achieved at some sacrifice of the ideological goals of socialism that the political leaders of Tanzania set for the country. As Tanzanian rural society develops commercially it is becoming more fragmented and individualistic. Land markets are developing, and wage employment is growing. All of this conflicts with the ideals of the socialist society as defined by the leadership in Tanzania. The problem that needs to be faced is how to reconcile efficiency in economic growth with equality, coopera-tion, and the other aims of Tanzanian socialism; how to direct private energy in a way consistent with social good. Unchecked, the most efficient producer by commercial criteria may soon become a big landowner and employer. Class differentiation would characterize the countryside and socialist objectives would be frustrated.

There is not space to pursue all these issues in this paper. It will con-centrate on examining the implications of changes in social structure at family and village level which follow from rural economic change. These will be examined particularly in terms of farmers' decision-making about production and distribution at the farm level. This examination will be preceded by a discussion of the goals of rural socialism in Tanzania and an analysis of some of the assumptions in the Tanzanian ideology about the dynamics of social adjustment in the face of changing resource avail-abilities and economic opportunities. The main criteria suggested by this ideology will be used to evaluate the adjustments to new commercial-ized opportunities in a case study of tobacco farming. This will suggest a number of hypotheses which, it is hoped, may contribute to an agenda for future research.

### GOALS OF RURAL SOCIALISM IN TANZANIA[1]

The philosophy and directives of rural socialism in Tanzania are most clearly formulated in the speeches and papers of Julius Nyerere, and have been summarized in his paper entitled *Socialism and rural development.*[2] Nyerere's rural socialism is based on very firm assumptions about tradi-tional Tanzanian societies whose structures are supposed to allow con-tinuous evolution towards a modern socialist state. The basic social unit

[1] This paper is concerned with a very narrow view of socialism. It aims to provide a com-mentary on the structure of a commercializing rural society: in particular the work-organizations emerging with rural development. It therefore consciously ignores many other important aspects of socialistic development, such as the role of neocolonialism, state centralization and control of economic activity, overall development strategies such as intersectoral balances, and the growth of elite political groups.

[2] J. K. Nyerere, *Socialism and rural development*, Dar es Salaam 1967.

institutions were to be designed and managed by government officials. Most of the schemes that were established have failed to become economically viable and substantial amounts of govern-ment resources have been wasted.

in a traditional Tanzanian society is believed by Nyerere to be the extended kin group; what he calls the *ujamaa* family. We might characterize his brand of socialism as *ujamaa* socialism. There were, writes Nyerere, three basic assumptions underlying the traditional *ujamaa* system:

1. mutual respect by each member of the kinship group. This involved a recognition of mutual involvement in all activities, which was governed by rights and obligations fixed for all individuals;
2. the material goods of the group, such as land and other resources, were held in common and this prevented the development of economic differentiation;
3. there was an obligation on all members to work, that is, to contribute to the collective welfare of the group.

These three assumptions are argued by Nyerere to be the foundation of human security, practical equality, and peace in society. They are further assumed to be a sound basis for the development of a modern socialist society.

This idealistic representation of traditional Tanzanian society was tempered by the recognition of two major shortcomings: first, there was the subservient position of particular individuals within the family, such as women or younger members of the family, and second, there was extreme poverty. The latter is explained by Nyerere as being caused through ignorance and the small scale of operations. He implies that both of these shortcomings can be ameliorated without departure from the beneficial collective aspects of the *ujamaa* society.

The objectives of *ujamaa* socialism are thus equal rights and opportunities, peaceful existence without suffering, injustice or exploitation, and socially oriented individual motivation. By the alliance of *ujamaa* principles with the knowledge needed to defeat poverty, the standard of material welfare will be steadily raised. The principles of the *ujamaa* kinship group will be adapted and transferred to the larger social units of the village community and the state.

Nyerere recognizes that the changes at present taking place in Tanzanian society are not bringing it closer to the *ujamaa* ideal. In particular he recognizes that the spread of the cash economy has tended to encourage individualistic and acquisitive attitudes, and an increasing dependence on wage labour rather than on cooperative or communal work. He would wish to reverse this trend. Thus he wrote: 'Acquisitiveness for the purpose of gaining power and prestige is unsocialist. In an acquisitive society wealth tends to corrupt those who possess it.'[1] Capitalistic attitudes and methods are reflected plainly when he states that 'Tanganyika would reject the creation of a rural class system even if it could be proved that it

[1] J. K. Nyerere, 'Ujamaa—the basis of African socialism'—reprinted in *Freedom and unity*, London 1967, p. 163.

would give the largest overall production increase'.[1] However, he recognizes the role of individual progressive farmers in introducing new techniques and methods. In a speech made in October 1967 he argued that changes should not unduly restrict progressive farmers. The need was for empiricism and gradualism. The demand for changes must come from the farmers themselves, rather than just being imposed upon them.

Nyerere described the means to achieving his *ujamaa* ideals in his paper on rural socialism.[2] They involved the creation of new economic and social communities where an individual could live and work according to the principles of *ujamaa*. As the demand for such communities had to come from the people they would inevitably take a long time to spread. In the meantime policies should aim at modifying the worst effects of individualism in rural development, and at encouraging the acceptance of *ujamaa* ideals. There would thus be an emphasis on hard work, on democratic local government, and on the encouragement of cooperation in production and marketing. The development of land and labour markets would be inhibited in the pursuit of social and economic equality. There would at all times be an emphasis on situations where there was a significant divergence between private and social costs, or where the high initial costs prevented the establishment of local community enterprises. What is significant is the recognition of the relationship between economic policies and social goals and of the need to tailor economic policies to such goals. The national society implied by Nyerere's vision would be one where *ujamaa* farms and communities were characteristic of the rural economy and set the social pattern for the country as a whole.

This short summary does not do full justice to all aspects of the ideology of *ujamaa* socialism. It is presented only to emphasize certain important features which concern policy choices. First, there is the conceptualization of traditional Tanzanian society as an *ujamaa* society whose essential elements are desirable and appropriate as a base for economic development. Secondly, there is the rejection of a policy of modernization based on the encouragement of individual achievement, as leading to the growth of a rural class system with exploitation inevitably arising from land and labour markets. Finally there is the emphasis on gradualism, popular acceptance, and the minimizing of central direction.

## ECONOMIC STRESS AND THE TRANSFERABILITY OF TRADITIONAL SOCIAL STRUCTURES

Some of the conceptual issues raised by *ujamaa* socialism will be examined in this section and later an attempt will be made to illustrate the relationship

---

[1] J. K. Nyerere, '1963 McDougal lecture to the F.A.O.', reprinted in *Freedom and unity*.
[2] J. K. Nyerere, *Socialism and rural development*.

of traditional communal structures to economic change. Several questions can be raised at this stage. To what extent is the *ujamaa* conceptualiz-ation of traditional society in Tanzania valid? How far do the *ujamaa* features of traditional rural society, if they do exist, permit economic and technological development? To what extent will such elements survive in the face of economic and social change? To what extent can the creation of innovatory *ujamaa* organizations be expected to occur by popular demand?

This paper will not attempt an extensive anthropological review of the differing traditional rural societies in Tanzania. There are substantial ethnographic variations among different tribal groups. For many of these groups communal production and distribution activities based on kinship and neighbourhood were important for closely defined areas of the rural economy. One would not be justified, however, in suggesting that such communal action was the pervading characteristic of all economic action and all societies. We are really concerned with a matter of degree. Com-pared with the commercialized farming systems now emerging in the more developed parts of Tanzanian rural economy, traditional social structures were probably characterized to a greater extent by communal activity. Our query is not about the essential truth of the *ujamaa* description of traditional Tanzanian society, but about its operational utility as a guide to action. Thus we would argue that the first of the questions listed above becomes somewhat irrelevant. It does, however, lead to the more funda-mental problem of assessing how far traditional *ujamaa* features can be extended to the more commercialized and technologically advanced society implied for Tanzania by economic development. Following Kopytoff it is postulated that one cannot assume that such an extension is feasible.[1] The extension of the boundaries of cooperation from the kin group to wider groupings involves overcoming existing social and economic patterns. The tangible individual benefits and the effective group sanctions that sustained the traditional cooperation of the *ujamaa* family are unlikely to occur in larger-scale economic and social units.

The underlying hypothesis adopted here is that the characteristics, communal or individualistic, of traditional rural communities reflect an adjustment to a specific economic environment, typified by given resource availabilities, given technologies, and given economic op-portunities. Changes in these environmental factors such as population pressure or new market outlets will alter the course of economic develop-ment and consequently change the social characteristics of rural society. We will try to illustrate how in the face of new economic pressures the communal features of a traditional society will tend to break down. There is an accentuation of the sovereignty and the individuality of the

[1] I. Kopytoff, 'Socialism and traditional African societies', in *African socialism*, ed. W. H. Friedland and C. G. Rosberg, Stanford 1964, pp. 57–8.

more elemental social/production units at the expense of kinship, village, and district social links.

This hypothesis can find some support in the prevailing anthropological view, which tends to locate economic decisions about production and distribution in a network of social relations.[1] However, some anthropological writers make assumptions about causality which are the reverse of what is assumed here. Thus Dalton suggests that production and distribution decisions are merely the expressions of underlying kinship obligations, tribal affiliations, and religious and moral duties.[2] He goes on to explain that this dominance of social (i.e. non-economic) determinants is a feature of primitive societies where there is an absence of Western technology or market constraints. This implies some discontinuity when either of these factors is introduced; after that, presumably, economic determination becomes a real force. It is difficult to accept such a view. One observes a continuous process as rural communities adjust to their growing involvement in the commercial markets and new technology. There is no sudden switching from social to economic determinism but a continuous interdependence as social relations adjust to new economic conditions, and as the pattern of exploiting new opportunities is moulded by social institutions. One can, however, agree with Dalton when he concludes that the introduction of new techniques, of purchased inputs, and of crops for the market rather than for the family subsistence, involves changes in social values; and this creates a social disturbance.[3]

Our problem then is to identify the nature of this social disturbance and its bearing on the chances of preserving (or creating) the cooperative features of the traditional society or creating new socialist features for developing Tanzania. The question is when and how social relations change in the face of changes in the economic environment. We need to examine this at the level of the community and the production unit.

The concept of economic stress may be more useful than that of social disturbance in describing the adjustment process.[4] Economic development implies an opening up of a new range of economic opportunities. Exploitation of these opportunities can imply a breach of traditional social observances and this may be reckoned to have a cost. In so far as such costs mean that new opportunities are actually forgone, the opportunity cost values of social observances may be measured by the material benefits forgone. Conversely the measurement of the material benefits forgone to

[1] G. Dalton, 'Traditional production in primitive African economies', *Quarterly Journal of Economics* 76 (1962), 360–78.

[2] Ibid.

[3] Ibid.

[4] The ideas underlying this concept are based on discussions with J. L. Joy. He develops them in his essay, 'One economist's view of the relationship between economics and anthropology', which appeared in M. Banton (ed.), *Themes in economic anthropology*, London 1967, pp. 29–45.

maintain a particular set of values or pattern of relations is also a measure of the economic stress on the traditional social structure. As such stress builds up, conflicts will emerge as different individuals and groups find their interests threatened in different ways by the maintenance or the adjustment of the traditional social observances. When adjustment does occur, as the stress becomes too great, one would expect a less homogeneous and perhaps a differently stratified society to result.[1] This process is illustrated by reference to an ethnographic study by Gulliver of the Nyakyusa of Southern Tanzania.[2]

### SOCIAL CHANGE AND SOCIAL CONFLICT
### AMONG THE NYAKYUSA

Gulliver's study of the Nyakyusa is used to illustrate the problem of conflict and adjustment to the new opportunities of economic development within a tribal society. It is not meant to be a general commentary on the possibility for success or failure of the establishment of rural socialism in Tanzania, but merely an illustration of one aspect of the assumptions of *ujamaa* socialism, i.e. that traditional structures can be maintained in the face of changing economic opportunities. The Nyakyusa live in a fertile, well-watered area between the northern shores of Lake Malawi and the surrounding highlands. Their traditional social structure, whose main features continued undisturbed until recent times, consisted of village communities loosely grouped together into chieftaincies. Their subsistence needs made little demand on existing fertile land resources. The society progressed by age groups splitting off from the parent village to establish new coeval settlements. The land was held communally, and was distributed by the village headman to families who farmed the basic production units, and who would hold usufructuary rights over the land. Many features of this society would correspond to Nyerere's *ujamaa* ideal. Many activities were carried out communally, particularly around the patrilineal kin group, and social security was assured through the kinship and village structures.

Since the 1940s the Nyakyusa have been experiencing a growing pressure from land shortage, especially in the area close to the shores of the

---

[1] This description might imply that the analysis is concerned with an exogenous economic change, a mechanistic process in which adjustment to some new equilibrium inevitably follows, with some lag caused by the inertia of social institutions. Such a view is not justified. All economic changes do not necessarily involve social adjustment. Even if such adjustment is involved it might create further conflicts involving further adjustments. The process could therefore be de-stabilizing, as well as stabilizing. Ideally a dynamic, rather than a comparative, static approach is needed. There is a danger in emphasizing the partial equilibrium parts of a disequilibrium whole: that the model is confused with reality, rather than being confined to its real function—a heuristic device.

[2] P. H. Gulliver, 'Land tenure and social change among the Nyakyusa', *East African Studies* no. 11. E.A.I.S.R., Kampala 1958.

lake. This has been the result of a complex of changes, which typify the process of economic development. First, there has been growing population pressure. Second, there is an increasing demand for cash goods, which has led to the rapid expansion of cash-crop cultivation. This has led to increasing competition with subsistence cultivation for the available resources. Finally, there has been the introduction of new cultivation techniques, particularly the plough, which allow individuals to work much larger acreages than previously. Whereas output had previously been limited by the family's labour force, that limit was now extended. Increasing competition for available land has meant that abundance has changed to scarcity. By 1957, Gulliver recorded average population densities of between 400 and 600 per square mile.[1] There was no unused land available, and village sites had become restricted and unhealthy. It can be shown that many of the traditional features of Nyakyusa society were based on the existence of abundant land resources. The Nyakyusa have not readily adjusted all the features of their society to the changes in their environment. The result has been a growing conflict at all levels of Nyakyusa society, and in some cases enforced change of social institutions.

It is hoped to show how such conflicts have eroded certain features of the traditional rural society, particularly those collective features that Tanzania's leaders are so eager to preserve. Gulliver suggests that these conflicts are centred on the growing land scarcity.[2] In spite of growing pressure on the land, the concept of individual land ownership, and hence of purchase and sale, has not yet gained acceptance among the Nyakyusa. No land market has developed. This attachment to the traditional social value of land can be seen as a major feature of conflict arising over access to land.[3] The most critical of these conflicts is in respect of inheritance. Previously inheritance was not the normal means of settling land. Young men obtained land by forming coeval settlements on unused land. Other forms of property on a man's death passed first to his brothers, and then to their sons before the man's own sons. The growing scarcity of land meant that coeval settlement formation was impossible, so land inheritance

[1] Ibid.

[2] P. H. Gulliver, 'Land shortage, social change and social conflict in East Africa', *Journal of Conflict Resolution* 5, 1 (1961), 16–26.

[3] Gulliver describes this as a 'mystical attachment to the soil'. Such a description may beg a number of questions, but there are parallel conditions in East Africa where land is associated with mystical and other religious observances, particularly ancestor worship. Thus the Kikuyu of Kenya are said to believe that the souls of their grandmothers reside in the soil of their land. A Nyakyusa informant, Bismark Mwansasu, has stated that land is not considered by the Nyakyusa as a commodity for sale, and that it has social and religious functions in connection with their ancestors. Raymond Firth, in an unpublished paper, 'The influence of social structure upon peasant economies', presented at the 1965 Agricultural Development Corporation conference at Honolulu explains in more general terms that the development of a land market can be restricted by the overriding rights of the kin group in the collective interest of past and future members of the corporate group.

became common. This brought agnatic kinsmen into a new kind of relationship, in which old norms were irrelevant. The competition for scarce land conflicted with patrilineal solidarity. Sons who as young men had helped their fathers develop and cultivate land were unwilling to see that land pre-empted by their father's brother, on whom they became dependent for access when their father died. Equally the father's brothers became unwilling to take over the land for fear that their own land would revert to their nephews rather than their own sons when they died. This conflict was fairly simply resolved by the Nyakyusa district council changing the inheritance laws to allow sons to inherit direct from fathers. This was done, however, only at the expense of weakening the cohesion of the patrilineage and the practical cooperation that existed between its members. It suggests that the cooperative ideals of the traditional *ujamaa* kinship group may be related to such factors as the level of availability of the major economic resources. Thus, by encouraging land inheritance from father to son, the growing land shortage had discouraged the more extensive cooperation between the members of the patrilineage, and encouraged the solidarity of the more nucleated family groups.

The effect of the new inheritance law was to transfer conflict to brothers who now competed for the father's land. Attempts at equitable distribution soon led to unviable holdings; so the young went without. This led to accusations of greed and injustice. Temporary relief was again found by increased migration of young men to the mines and industries of Southern Africa and to the urban areas of East Africa. This relief was only temporary, partly as the young men were not prepared to live away permanently, and partly because of the growing political difficulties of migration southwards. Thus, without a more permanent adjustment to the changing economic circumstances, the traditional solidarity between brothers deteriorated as the brothers were in constant competition, and fair land shares only led to economic deprivation.

The effect of land shortage on village solidarity was also marked. In the village, land was owned corporately; individual rights to use specific parcels of land were obtained by continuous residence. These rights were forfeited if a man moved elsewhere, his land reverting to the village for re-allocation by the village headman. In the situation of land shortage, there was tremendous competition for such vacant land. Three groups were concerned: landless young men; older men with growing families and increasing material aspirations; and newcomers who, despite the land shortage, were still encouraged by the headman to settle in order to increase the size of the village and therefore the headman's prestige. There was increasing conflict between the villagers as a result of this competition for any available land. At the same time, the actual living space of the village was reduced, which increased the degree of physical interaction. Gulliver reported that unsuccessful land claimants made accusations of witchcraft and bribery.[1] Witchcraft allegations have increased in spite of a parallel spread of Christianity. The traditional means of meeting such a situation was for the suspected person to move away. This was now impossible, there being no empty land in other villages or between villages. So the accused have to meet the accusations, and accommodation is difficult.

Gulliver also reports that the growing competition for scarce land has led to a reaction against trends that had been leading towards a more open Nyakyusa society. Before land became scarce, economic development (particularly the increasing spread of coffee production) and the establishment of law and order had meant that individuals were increasingly breaking away from their close involvement in the village structure. There was no longer a need to rely on the village for protection, and it became increasingly common for individuals to establish their homestead on their perennial coffee orchard rather than within the village boundary. Very often these orchards were established in empty areas between the lands previously demarcated to particular villages. This trend, however, has been reversed as the growing scarcity of land has led to increasing inter-village conflict, particularly as boundary lines are vague and disputes are frequent.

Thus at all levels the solidarity of the smaller social units has been emphasized. The inheritance system has changed, kinship and inter-village cooperation has been eroded. New economic opportunities and changes in resource availability have led to increasing economic stress. This stress has caused conflicts of interest in which it pays some to uphold traditional rights and obligations and others to break away from them. However, it is still not sufficient to lead to the establishment of a commercial market in land. It could be suggested that the overriding right of the community to restrict the free market in land has been maintained because it is considered that the interests of the present and future members of the corporate group are more important than the interests of those individuals who would benefit from access to land through the market mechanism.[2] It will be interesting to observe what degree of economic stress will be tolerated before a more commercial attitude to land is recognized.[3]

Gulliver's observations show that among the Nyakyusa traditional forms of communal organization are vulnerable to the changes that have been brought about as a result of the new opportunities and growing

---

[1] P. H. Gulliver, 'Land shortage, social change and social conflict in East Africa'.

[2] See p. 93, n. 3.

[3] It is interesting to note that rural land markets have developed elsewhere in Tanzania only where land pressure is considerable. The most extreme example is probably Ukara Island in Lake Victoria. It is also found in the Chagga areas on Mt. Kilimanjaro. See H. D. Ludwig, 'Permanent farming on Ukara' and H. Ruthenberg, 'Coffee–banana farm on Mt. Kilimanjaro'; both are in H. Ruthenberg (ed.), *Smallholder farming and smallholder development in Tanzania*, Munich 1968.

scarcity of land resources. He also shows that the ability of these institutions to withstand the forces making for change varies. Thus new inheritance laws have been developed, but no land market has been established. Our conclusion is that it is not possible to assume that because cooperative structures exist in traditional society they can be extended to meet the new condition of economic development without modification and in their traditional form. This suggests that serious reservations need to be made about the assumption that the extension of traditional *ujamaa* relationships can be used to create a modern, but socialistic, society. If cooperation and other collective relationships are going to characterize the future rural society of Tanzania, it may well be necessary to give considerable thought to more innovatory types of organization.

## DECISION-MAKING, ENTREPRENEURSHIP, AND SOCIAL STRATIFICATION

The analysis so far has illustrated only a general relationship which affects the possibility of maintaining the traditional social structures in the face of changes accompanying economic development. It was suggested that when adjustment does take place a more stratified and less homogeneous society would probably result, because of the differences of interest between groups and individuals in relation to the traditional structures and the new opportunities. To comment further on the possibility of creating or maintaining socialistic *ujamaa* relationships in the new society that is emerging with economic change, it will be necessary to focus attention on the individual farm operator, in order to understand how he adjusts to the changes involved in rural development. In many ways it may be misleading to examine general changes in the behaviour of large groups in changing circumstances as observed by Gulliver. To apply concepts of economic stress to whole societies is dangerous. Variations between individuals may be great. Moreover, economic opportunities are not invariably in conflict with traditional social patterns. Indeed, it may be possible to exploit them by mobilizing and strengthening these patterns. For such reasons the analysis must be extended to look at the relationship between farm level entrepreneurial decisions and the emerging pattern of social relations.

Examining decision-making among a group of farmers produces insights not only into the economic development of their farming systems, but also into the pattern of social relations associated with that development. Choices made by farmers not only affect output, organization, techniques of production, and the pattern of distribution, but also the social links the farmer has, and the behavioural norms he observes. Such choices will then have implications for the whole social structure as well as for the individual production unit.

Farmers are assumed to act rationally within a concrete situation. The situation necessitates certain actions and precludes others. Rationality here implies actions appropriate to the actor's goals in the face of limiting constraints. The key actor in this process is the *entrepreneur*, in Barth's sense of entrepreneurship as a specific aspect of a role. The relationship between this concept and the subject-matter of this paper is explained in an illuminating passage by Barth:

> The occasional need for repudiating relationships points to possible connections between entrepreneurship and factionalism or social stratification. Both these forms of social division imply limitations or discontinuities of obligation and commitment. They are thus social barriers which may give strategic scope to certain kinds of enterprise, and may even be *generated* by the entrepreneur when the advantages he gains...outweigh the cost of repudiating the relevant relationships.[1]

The causal connection that we hope to demonstrate is between the changing economic needs of growing commercialized farming systems, the need to 'repudiate relationships', and the pattern of social stratification. In so far as the development of commercialization amongst the small-holders whom we are examining is typical of what will happen in the Tanzanian rural economy, then the social structure emerging from their decisions may illuminate some of the problems of attaining a socialistic society.

The short run decision-possibilities of the peasant entrepreneur are subject to a series of constraints. Some of these are determined by the physical production resources that are available, such as the amount and fertility of land, climatic conditions, his family's labour supply, and capital as both cash and physical productive assets. His ability to exploit these resources, however, will also be limited by less tangible factors such as his accumulated skills and social obligations. He also faces social and moral restrictions, which further limit his freedom of action.[2]

Not all these constraints are fixed beyond a very short time period. Thus the entrepreneur can accumulate more productive assets by producing a larger surplus over his immediate consumption needs. He can absorb new skills, and he can decide to ignore certain social claims or

[1] F. Barth, Introduction to *The role of the entrepreneur in social change in Northern Norway*, Bergen 1963, from whom the concept of entrepreneurship used here is taken.

[2] There can be some confusion between objectives and constraints in such an approach, which is made unnecessarily complex by Barth. One of Barth's criteria for entrepreneurial action is a 'single-minded concentration on the maximisation of one type of value'. It would be difficult to establish the empirical validity of such a characteristic without the use of rigorous psychological analysis. Thus the identification by a sociologist or economist of the attachment by an 'entrepreneur' to a particular social value, with his objectives, or his constraint structure, is an arbitrary one. The operational difficulties in economic analysis associated with multivalued parts of an objective function which are not linearly related, have meant that most non-money values that might be part of a farmer's objectives are treated as constraints. There would be no justification, however, to treat this methodological convenience as a reality.

moral restrictions. Costs as well as benefits are involved in all of these choices of action. Innovatory social links need not necessarily result in higher achievements of entrepreneurial profit; by maintaining traditional links, access to communal power and other resources may be mobilized for new activities.[1] The entrepreneur will be concerned to compare the payoff against the cost in any decision which conflicts with traditional norms.[2] The risk associated with such a choice is going to be a dominant consideration. Thus social security is obtained by maintaining traditional links, and a farmer who chooses to ignore traditional norms in order to pursue a new economic activity faces the risk that the new activity may not be successful, while his security in the community may be eroded.

The evaluations which individuals make of the costs and benefits of new activities, the choices of procedures to gain the new objectives and the risks associated with any choice, will not be uniform. Considerable differences may be expected in the organizational choices that are made in relation to new economic opportunities. The pattern of these differences will, however, have vital implications for the emerging social structure, as well as for the economic goals set at a national level.

### FARM ORGANIZATION AT IRINGA AND THE ACHIEVEMENT OF RURAL SOCIALISM[3]

We are now in a position to bring together the arguments of the preceding sections in relation to a particular case study, which concentrates on the choice of production organization for growing a new cash crop. It does not attempt to test the economic performance of the different organizations but aims to set these choices against the ideals of Tanzanian socialism. It concerns the economic decision-making process among a group of African tobacco farmers at Nduli in the Iringa district of Tanzania.[4] The study as originally conceived was partly aimed at evaluating these processes against the objectives of government policies; but the objectives then considered did not include those directly related to the achievement of rural socialism. The emergence of these as explicit and major governmental goals took place only in 1966, when the field-work was nearly completed. Thus, although a number of interesting and significant implications can be drawn from the field observations, they are not a

---

[1] Entrepreneurial profit does not need to be equated with commercial profit. It is merely a measure of the net benefits resulting from the entrepreneur's decision in terms of the particular value he is aiming for in his objectives.

[2] The economic analysis of Barth's constraint system within which entrepreneurial decisions are made has been developed by J. L. Joy in 'An economic homologue of Barth's presentation of economic spheres in Darfur', in M. Banton (ed.), *Themes in economic anthropology*, pp. 175–89.

[3] I am grateful to my wife, Rayah Feldman, whose parallel sociological research and insights into the organizational structure of agricultural systems have been invaluable for an understanding of the farming system described in this section.

[4] The study was made possible by a research grant from the Ministry of Overseas Development.

comprehensive commentary on the achievements of the *ujamaa* ideals of rural socialism in the area. In particular, there is no direct information on the degree of exploitation of labour, other than the size of the hired labour force, which is not adequate as a single measure of exploitation. A second major gap is that there was no attempt to test hypotheses relating social stratification to observed economic differentiation, and one hesitates to make too strong an assumption about this. Finally, the distribution of benefits from the production system is a third important aspect on which there is inadequate information. What can be done, however, is to examine how a heterogeneous group of Tanzanian farmers adjusted their production organizations to meet the changing needs of developing commercialized tobacco enterprises.

Attention will be concentrated on the patterns of cooperation and of family organization as these are adjusted to the demands of the new economic systems, and what these in turn imply for the *ujamaa* goals of rural socialism. To do this it is necessary to take a somewhat simplistic view of rural socialism, and to distinguish two sets of features which can be observed. First, there is the degree of cooperation in the ownership and control of production resources; and second, the degree of economic and social differentiation. The evaluation of organizational patterns against these criteria is not always simple. Thus it might be thought that the greater the equity in the distribution of assets, the greater the scale and scope of cooperation in decision-making, the smaller the dependence on hired labour, and the more equitable the distribution of benefits, then the closer will any particular system come to fulfilling the principles of rural socialism in Tanzania. In practice, evaluation may not be so simple, as there could well be choices that come closer to the socialist ideal in some respects whilst retreating from that ideal in others. Thus different organizational choices will have different implications in terms of each characteristic and these may not all be positively correlated. The evaluation problem may, therefore, be complex even if the goals of rural socialism are considered without reference to any other policy objectives; e.g. how are the collective benefits from the increased cooperation of a particular production organization to be valued against the increased dependence on hired labour that may also result from the same organization?

The observations were made among one hundred farmers, a thirty-six per cent sample of those growing tobacco in the Nduli area of Iringa. African smallholders have been growing flue-cured Virginian tobacco there since 1962. Prior to this, production was controlled by a licensing system, which effectively limited it to Greek settlers in the area. In 1962, twenty Africans, mainly ex-labourers on the Greek farms, established a cooperative production unit. A good deal of encouragement, advice and credit from government sources has since been received, and by the 1966/7 growing season there were nearly 600 Africans growing tobacco in the district. The situation has clearly been one of very rapid development, and this has tended to telescope the adjustments that are usually observed in the more gradual growth of rural commercialization. At the same time flue-cured tobacco is an extremely difficult crop to grow, process, and prepare for the market. Large quantities of purchased inputs are needed, as well as considerable technical, commercial, and organizational skills. These features have also accelerated the required changes away from more traditional production systems. The individual farmers concerned can therefore be considered as entrepreneurs in the classic economic sense as well as by Barth's criteria, which include: first, a willingness to concentrate on the maximization of one type of value or entrepreneurial profit;[1] second, actions on the basis of deductive prognosis of expected results, rather than expectations based on the accumulation of institutionalized experience; and third, a willingness to take risks by committing assets. A noticeable feature of this study of farmers' entrepreneurial behaviour is their willingness to experiment to a considerable extent in order to find production organizations that fit in with their social and economic needs.

The observed organizations show considerable variation. Production units may consist of cooperating family heads, extended family units of a more traditional form, or nuclear family farms, similar to a European peasant model. Heterogeneity is also reflected in the social background of the farmers.[2] Only about one-third have their traditional tribal homeland in the area. The rest have migrated to it from all over East Africa, searching for better economic opportunities. Except for a major difference between the local tribesmen and the migrants as a whole, there is little evidence to relate organizational differences to tribal origins.[3] The situa-

[1] See p. 98, n. 1.

[2] From a sub-sample of 49 farmers used for sociological research by Rayah Feldman the tribal distribution was:

| Tribe | Area of Origin | No. |
|---|---|---|
| Heye | Iringa | 16 |
| Kinga | Njombe | 10 |
| Bena | Njombe | 8 |
| Ngoni | Songea/Malawi | 6 |
| Mambwe | Northern Zambia | 2 |
| Nyakyusa | Rungwe | 2 |
| Sangu | Iringa | 1 |
| Zaramo | Dar es Salaam | 1 |
| Yao | Malawi | 1 |
| Luo | Kenya | 1 |
| Ganda | Uganda | 1 |

[3] Farmers from the local tribe, the Hehe, tended to be more cautious in adopting new organizational structures for growing tobacco. They also tended to be less commercially enterprising than migrants and they had a reputation, among agricultural extension staff, of being inefficient and half-hearted about growing tobacco. It could be hypothesized that they would be more conscious of traditional rights and obligations: and that their commitment to a new and exacting enterprise would be less necessary.

tion can therefore be characterized as fluid in so far as there is a considerable need to experiment among alternative organizations and, at the same time, there are only limited institutional constraints on the form that these experiments take. Because of the availability of empty land, tenure structures have not been a constraining factor. It is this fluidity that makes the area so fruitful to study. At the same time the significance of generalized conclusions may need to be modified in so far as this open characteristic is not typical of rural conditions elsewhere in Tanzania.

Three interrelated aspects of farm organization for tobacco growing are examined here. First, the structure of the decision-making unit; second, the involvement of family resources in tobacco production, which is directly related to the position of women and to the degree of reliance on hired labour; and finally, the integration of food production (which represents previous, but continuing, agricultural activities) into the new tobacco enterprises.

The three main types of farming organization at Nduli have already been listed. In terms of the criterion of cooperation alone, three main categories, cooperating non-family group farms, group farms of kin and affines, and nuclear family farms, might be assumed to be points on a continuum between the collective ideal and the individualism feared by exponents of *ujamaa* socialism. I shall argue, however, that such an interpretation could be misleading, partly because other criteria need to be applied, and also because the reasons for cooperation can be explained without reference to the ideological motivations of the country's leaders. It will be shown that in addition to their implications for achieving the goals of rural socialism, the variations in level of cooperation have other implications for the degree of utilization of family resources, and the creation of balanced farming systems. The distribution of the different forms of organization in the sample is shown in table 1. In this, cooperating groups are divided into those tobacco enterprises where a crop is cultivated, processed, and sold as a single unit, and those where the cultivation is done on separate plots, and where cooperation extends only to common land titles and the collective use of fixed assets, such as a curing barn, grading sheds, and baling presses.

The most interesting feature of the variations in farm organization has been a general fissiparous process among the different groups. There appears to be a tendency among the cooperating groups for them to get smaller as individual members either drop out of the system, or, if the group splits up, farm on a more individualistic basis. The change in the distribution of organizational forms between July 1966 and July 1967 is shown in table 2. The process is perhaps most clearly illustrated by the matrix in table 3. Each element outside the brackets of the matrix shows the number of farms that changed from one form of organization to some other form of organization between 1966 and 1967. The figures in the

H

brackets refer to the probabilities of a farm organization becoming any other organization during the same time period. Thus the numbers along the north-west/south-east diagonal show how many and what proportion of each farm type did change between 1966 and 1967. Numbers above the

Table 1.  *Distribution of main cooperation types among Nduli sample, July 1967*

| Type | No. | % of total |
|---|---|---|
| Cooperative groups—cultivation and processing | 5 | 14 |
| Cooperative groups—processing only | 6 | 15 |
| Total cooperative groups | (11) | (30) |
| Extended kin groups | 6 | 16 |
| Nuclear family groups | 20 | 54 |
| Total | 37 | 100 |

Table 2.  *Changes in farm organization, 1966–67*

| Type | No. 1966 | No. 1967 | % 1966 | % 1967 |
|---|---|---|---|---|
| Cooperative farms, 4 members | 6 | 0 | 16 | 0 |
| Cooperative farms, 3 members | 6 | 6 | 16 | 16 |
| Cooperative farms, 2 members | 5 | 5 | 14 | 14 |
| Cooperative farms, total | 17 | 11 | 45 | 30 |
| Extended kins farms | 10 | 6 | 27 | 16 |
| Nuclear family farms | 10 | 20 | 27 | 54 |
| Total | 37 | 37 | 100 | 100 |

Table 3.  *Organizational change matrix, July 1966–July 1967*

| | (1) | (2) | (3) | (4) | (5) |
|---|---|---|---|---|---|
| (1) Cooperative, 4 members | 0 (0·00) | 4 (0·67) | 1 (0·166) | 0 | 1 (0·166) |
| (2) Cooperative, 3 members | 0 | 2 (0·34) | 2 (0·34) | 1 (0·166) | 1 (0·166) |
| (3) Cooperative, 2 members | 0 | 0 | 2 (0·4) | 0 | 3 (0·6) |
| (4) Extended kin group | 0 | 0 | 0 | 5 (0·5) | 5 (0·5) |
| (5) Nuclear family group | 0 | 0 | 0 | 0 | 10 (1·0) |

diagonal show the extent of the fissiparous process, i.e. cooperating groups are becoming smaller or changing into more individualistic systems. Numbers below the diagonal represent the opposite tendency; and it is striking that there were none which moved in this direction.

The process appears to confirm Nyerere's fears about the relation between individualism and commercialization, and calls for some explanation. The original group of African tobacco farmers had consisted of twenty cooperating members. To some extent this size of cooperating group was determined by the legal need to form an association of at least twenty people in order to get access to institutional credit. Conflicts and other tensions within the original twenty-man group made it unworkable, and those who wished to continue to grow tobacco after the first unsuccessful year formed themselves into smaller groups of four. This was possible as it came to be realized that an association *between* production units was sufficient to acquire eligibility for credit. Thus a marketing cooperative was set up, to which all farms belonged, in order to channel government credit funds to the smaller production units.

Smaller cooperating groups have continued to be set up as others have started tobacco farming and this suggests that influences other than legal constraints are effective in determining this form of organization. The most noticeable of these is the existence of economies of scale. Few farmers have access to sufficient resources and expertise to grow more than one or two acres of tobacco in the first year. Because of the level of resources needed and the risks involved, expansion is cautious. By the third year of production 4 acres of tobacco may be grown; thereafter expansion can be more rapid. There are, however, considerable overhead costs involved in capital items such as curing barns, grading sheds, and baling presses. These are more efficient if designed for 4 acres capacity than for 1 acre. A number of farmers will, therefore, pool their experience and resources in order to utilize fully efficient processing facilities. Cooperators also appear to gain security from acting together rather than facing the new risks separately. It was indeed suggested by an agricultural officer that in the early years there were fears of witchcraft accusations because of the 'deviant' character of tobacco production.[1] Thus the deviants would band together to maintain solidarity.

There are other advantages to be gained from cooperation, particularly from the sharing of managerial responsibility. Thus there are periods of the year when a constant watch has to be kept on curing tobacco. There is also a need to direct the hired labour. By having a group of cooperating farmers, this burden can be spread. The risk that illness or journeys away from the farm will disrupt progress is minimized. Finally, there has been some political activity, which has tended to encourage cooperating production systems.

The fissiparous tendency, however, shows that there are other factors asserting themselves which discourage cooperation. First, the economies of scale that encouraged the original cooperation do not hold beyond certain limits. Once the group of four members is cultivating 16 acres of tobacco with four curing barns, each of 4 acres capacity, then there is no

---

[1] There is no other evidence for this.

technical reason why each of the four should not operate one barn and farm 4 acres separately. Secondly, within the small cooperating group, there is no hierarchy of decision-making, and no institutionalized bureaucracy to resolve conflicts. Suspicions of unequal effort lead to accusations of laziness. Imperfect literacy may also lead to conflict over accounts. Such grievances tend to encourage the breakup of the group. A further factor arises when there are significant differences in the objectives, in the degree of enterprise, and in the technical and managerial efficiency of the different cooperators. The more single-minded and efficient group member becomes increasingly restricted by his membership of the group, and unless he can completely control decision-making, he will wish to break away.

Further problems arise for cooperating groups if the farmers are to utilize existing family resources, particularly labour and equipment, that were previously used on the more traditional food farms. There is a clear reluctance among most wives to work alongside their husbands on the tobacco farm if other non-family members are also involved in the work. There is also a reluctance to abandon the traditional food farms, which are generally organized on a nuclear family basis, if separate family heads are organizing the tobacco farm. For this reason it has been very difficult to develop a balanced rotation of tobacco and food crops on the co-operative group tobacco farms. We shall have to return to this point later.

The process is thus away from cooperation among equal entrepreneurs, towards individualistic and perhaps more authoritarian enterprises. Although it should not be assumed that there is an inevitable conflict between cooperation and the efficiency needs of tobacco enterprises, and successful cooperation continues in some groups, the problem of establishing cooperative production enterprises as the dominant mode of organization at Nduli is clearly very great. All the tobacco farms are highly commercialized enterprises. Except in those cases where the tobacco enterprises are operated on an extended kinship basis, the organizations developed are innovatory, and in particular it is extremely difficult to find any direct influence of traditional *ujamaa* work patterns. This is particularly shown by the heavy reliance on hired labour for the peak seasonal demands of the tobacco crop, rather than the use of family labour, or the reciprocal work-parties which symbolize the *ujamaa* ideal.[1] There is some cooperation among farmers for heavy, expensive equipment, but this is limited, and most will try to buy their own as soon as possible. Any more permanent transfer of resources is done on a strictly commercial, contractual basis. This is quite common, and a well-organized farmer may contract out his labourers to others when he has completed his own work.

---

[1] It should not be inferred, however, that family labour is never used by cooperative groups. Many farmers in such groups may employ one or more for very short periods when the demand for labour is highest. They do not, however, constitute a significant part of the labour force.

This high degree of commercialization is in part the result of a credit scheme which gives farmers access to cash to pay wages. There are, however, certain structural reasons which ensure that the tobacco farm is run on lines which bear little relationship to previous more traditional agricultural pursuits. This is shown by the continued maintenance by most farmers of food-crop farms quite separate from the tobacco farms. A lack of integration between the different parts of agricultural production has meant that there has been no gradual adaptation of traditional work methods to the needs of modern production systems. There has rather been a sharp discontinuity which has allowed many of the features of rural capitalism to develop rapidly. Some of the implications of this are discussed below. At this point, however, it is necessary to try to explain the isolation of tobacco growing from the existing more traditional food production system.

The relation between food supply (mainly maize) and tobacco production affects the transference of *ujamaa* work patterns, as well as the technical efficiency of the farming systems. Maize is produced as a subsistence crop for family needs; as an alternative source of cash income when sold as grain or processed as beer; and as a wage good when labourers are hired.[1] It is also important for the social position of women, as they can maintain their economic independence through providing for their own children, and having their own independent source of income. Food supplies are generally assured either by purchase from the market or by producing food on a farm spatially separated from the tobacco enterprise, although it can also be produced within the crop rotation of the tobacco system. In its natural state, land suitable for growing Virginian tobacco is not suitable for maize production. Tobacco can be grown for 2 years on virgin land, after which a fallow period of 5 years is necessary. In the first fallow year there is generally adequate fertilizer residual left from the tobacco crop to produce a good crop of maize. As a result agricultural officers advise the farmers to grow maize in the third year of their tobacco rotation. The entrepreneur thus has to choose between this advice and alternative sources of food supply. To date very few farmers have exploited the suggested rotation system, and most continue to maintain separate food farms producing maize. Technically, the most efficient choice would appear to use the rotation as this allows the use of the same resources for both crops, particularly labour and farm implements such as ploughs. It also lessens the managerial problem by allowing the farmer to control both crops simultaneously.

A number of factors can be observed, however, which prevent this integration:

(*a*) The difficulties of tobacco production mean that only small acreages

---

[1] The modal monthly wage rate for hired labourers was 60 shillings if food rations were not provided, and 45 shillings if rations were provided.

have been grown so far. Thus there may not be adequate land available on the tobacco farm for the maize production required to meet the different needs that have been enumerated.

(b) The pioneering conditions experienced by farmers in opening up the tobacco land have led them to delay bringing in their wives and families until the farm has been fully established. The women, however, do the bulk of the food cultivation work.

(c) There are considerable risks associated with a new tobacco enterprise and the difficulties experienced have led to a reluctance by farmers to commit all their resources to these new enterprises. They have been eager to maintain previous income sources.[1]

These three factors might be expected to be effective only during the early stages of development. There are, however, a number of other factors which have a more permanent effect:

(d) Where there is a cooperating group of farmers working the tobacco enterprise, there may be a great deal of difficulty in organizing the cultivation of a crop which is not completely sold on the market. Subsistence needs may vary between the families of the different group members. Considerable difficulty would then be experienced in allocating the land made available from the tobacco rotation for food production, and this, in turn, suggests a great potential for disputes if food is produced on the group farm. For this reason, there is little chance that within cooperating groups individual farmers would give up their separate food farms in order to concentrate their resources on the tobacco farm.

(e) Tobacco-land is allocated under state-controlled freehold to farmers. Large quantities of credit are used. If a tobacco crop is not successful there is always a risk that the farm will be foreclosed by the credit agency, and the assets taken over in lieu of unpaid debts. Thus the farmer sees a need to maintain usufructuary rights in communal land systems outside the tobacco area in order to cover such an eventuality.

(f) Separate food farms are also maintained to provide inheritance for a number of heirs.

(g) The separation of the food farm is also closely bound up with the sexual division of labour, and the maintenance of women's traditional independence.[2]

---

[1] Such alternative income sources did not only consist of maize farms. Thus in the sample there were two farmers who continued to work as foremen on neighbouring Greek farms and one farmer who continued to operate a bar in the town 15 miles away.

[2] A distinction ought to be drawn between wives, who are not regarded, and do not regard themselves, as group members, and the adult sons and other younger male kin who may eventually be equal group members. The latter, while still subservient to the chairman in terms of decision-making authority, are nevertheless not totally deprived of rights. They have the security, and possible prospects of inheritance, which hired labourers do not.

The effect of maintaining separate food farms has meant the creation of completely commercialized work methods, e.g. the use of hired labour, on the tobacco enterprises. This has been more marked where tobacco is produced in a cooperative group organization than where it is produced within a family organization. This suggests an interesting direct relationship between the degree of cooperation and the degree of commercialization which would make overall evaluation in terms of *ujamaa* criteria difficult.

Cooperation is, however, not the only criterion of rural socialism. Among the tobacco farms worked by nuclear families or groups, there appears to be a markedly authoritarian approach to decision-making. The oldest male, with the title of chairman, generally has a direct managerial role in work organization, and this also extends to the distribution of profits. Both women and younger men hold subservient positions without even the contractual rights owed to hired labour. In terms of Barth's framework, this is a situation where the entrepreneur is exploiting traditional systems of rights and obligations in order to achieve his commercial entrepreneurial objectives. Such exploitation is comparable to the exploitation of a labour market which the advocates of Nyerere's rural socialism are afraid of. It suggests a further reason why a more innovatory social model than the traditional extended kin group is necessary if exploitation is to be avoided.

This authority structure has not encouraged families to integrate their resources for the new enterprise. Kinsmen are eager to maintain the rights they obtained from the traditional system, and this will affect the degree of integration of all the family's resources in the new tobacco enterprise.[1] This, in turn, affects economic efficiency. It increases the need to purchase inputs which might have been provided at no monetary cost from family resources; at the same time family resources are used to maintain non-tobacco enterprises although the economic returns from these may be less.[2] Thus the maintenance of certain previous social values and work relationships, and other factors such as risk, are seen to hamper the achievement of commercial profit and at the same time work against the maintenance or creation of *ujamaa* relationships.

---

[1] A similar problem has been analysed by J. Brain in regard to the position of women on the government-directed settlement schemes. He explains that part of the reason for the lack of productive efficiency of some schemes is that farming systems have been designed on false assumptions about the family labour supplies available, including that of wives, whereas there has been no attempt to give the wives an independent status in terms of rights on the schemes such as they had in their more traditional homesteads. They have thus been unwilling to contribute to the new systems. See J. L. Brain, 'The position of women on settlement schemes', and J. L. Brain, 'Observations on settler productivity and discipline at Kabuku with special emphasis on the role of women'. Both are unpublished papers (nos. 34 and 40) of the Syracuse University Village Settlement Project.

[2] Economic returns are here measured in terms of national objectives or in terms of commercial profit, not in terms of other values that might be used by the farmer or his kin.

The final aspect of tobacco farming at Iringa to be discussed is the relation of its development to economic differentiation and consequently to social stratification. This is of particular importance since the avoidance of a rural class structure is perhaps the ultimate criterion of achieving socialist ideals in Tanzania. The simple approach would be to equate economic differentiation with social stratification. One hesitates to do this, however. Implicit in the latter concept is the idea of social separation, and a conflict between the different strata. The growth of differentiation in economic achievement between different farmers, and the growth of a hired labour force, are certainly the basis of a potential class separation at Iringa. But this development is at an early stage, and neither competition for scarce resources, nor the establishment of a permanent labour force dependent solely on selling their services, has yet fully emerged. It seems likely that these other conditions are necessary for economic differentiation to develop into social stratification.

Economic differentiation between farmers is, however, marked. To some extent this is related to the different resources, particularly expertise and capital, which individuals had when starting to grow tobacco. The availability of substantial credit funds and land have, however, counteracted some initial individual advantages. Variations in managerial capacity, particularly in the ability to organize a large labour force, and the ability to handle credit in a commercially efficient manner, seem to account for many of the differences in farmers' performances. This, in turn, is largely explained by differences in their labour histories.

The extent of differentiation is shown by the marked variation in earnings from tobacco farming. Thus in 1965–6, returns varied from 200 to 15,000 shillings. Such results have a cumulative effect, as the less successful farmers who have substantial outstanding debts are unable to obtain current finance to harvest and process their crop. Thus at the harvesting period some farmers may be employing fifty labourers whilst others have insufficient resources to hire any, and their crop is mainly wasted. Differences are also shown in the rate of expansion of tobacco farms. Some have grown to 40 acres while others have hardly grown at all. Thus the most enterprising expand rapidly whilst the less experienced and less enterprising stagnate.

The speed of the emergence of differentiation in terms of commercial performance and scale of enterprise has therefore been very rapid. Differentiation in terms of social relationships does not seem to have progressed at quite the same speed. The basis of such an observation is admittedly impressionistic and suggests an interesting line of research. From observations of the activities of one of the most successful farmers and his relations with other less successful farmers, it appeared that he was treated as an equal and was seen as a source of advice. The hypothesis about the effect of competition for resources is related to this point, as his expansion has involved growing greater acreages of tobacco. As there has been adequate spare land available, this expansion has not been at the expense of the less successful in respect to land. In this sense economically disadvantaged groups may not yet attribute their position to the activities of the more advantaged groups. It could also be hypothesized that such a situation can last only until serious competition for scarce resources takes place. This process is in fact beginning in respect of the supply of credit funds. The latter are controlled by the marketing cooperative, whose executive in turn is dominated by the more successful farmers. Considerable maladministration of these funds has taken place, and dissatisfaction is growing among those farmers who have a less direct control of cooperative affairs. There are clear potentialities here for antagonism.

The second aspect of differentiation that needs discussion is the growth of the hired labour force. The technical labour requirements of tobacco growing and processing vary through the year. There is no possibility of substituting capital for labour at the peak periods of labour need during harvesting, curing, and sorting. The expansion of tobacco growing has thus involved considerable expansion of labour inputs at the harvesting season. This has been met mainly, as has been described, by increasing the amounts of hired labour. As well as the technical factors affecting labour inputs, the quantity of labour hired is affected by the choice of farm organization. A further determinant may be the farmer's leisure preference. Thus with finance available from credit funds, a farmer often appears to be willing to hire more labour even at the cost of reducing his overall returns. All these factors thus contribute to the growth of the labour force. In the 1966/7 season, the average size of the labour force per farm varied through the year from three to nine. At the peak labour period there were 300 hired labourers employed on the thirty-seven farms of the sample.

But no simple equation of the growth of this labour force with the extent of proletarianization, in the sense used to describe an industrial work force, would be correct. The labourers are generally migratory. They originate chiefly in the Njombe district, between 100 and 200 miles from Nduli. The local people do not like to work for others, nor are they popular with employers. The migrant workers generally maintain food farms and families in their home district, and will spend some part of the year with them. Many use the experience they gain from working on tobacco farms to set up their own tobacco enterprises. As there is still land available, this has not been difficult. For these reasons they are not dispossessed in the way Marx describes the labour force of a capitalist industrial society. These are good reasons for hesitating to equate the growing dependence on hired labour with social stratification. It could again be hypothesized, though, that this present situation is very temporary. Thus a more rigid rural class structure may be established when land is no longer available at Nduli for labourers to set up their own farms, when the migratory labourers find it in their own interest to live permanently off their wage earnings, and when the less successful farmers abandon their entrepreneurial activities to become labourers for other farmers.

This discussion of the implications of farm organizational decisions appears to justify Nyerere's fears about the possible course of social development in Tanzania. Most of these conclusions should, however, be treated with caution. They are suggested by observations of a very limited and specialized part of the rural economy, and the testing of the hypotheses suggested is not yet complete. The examination of the organizational structure has, however, indicated a number of contradictions between the *ujamaa* assumptions and the development of a prosperous, technologically advanced rural economy. It also suggests that within tradition-based systems conditions may not match up to the collective ideal. Examination shows a number of endogenous factors which encourage individualization in commercially developing agricultural systems, and a conflict between the achievement of different aspects of the *ujamaa* socialist goal. The implications are not, therefore, optimistic.

### CONCLUSIONS

This discussion has attempted to show how it may be possible to analyse the achievement of a particular form of socialist ideology in terms of the decisions of those who form the society, rather than the decisions of the politicians or the administrators whose aspirations are aimed at moulding that society. The minimum that may have been demonstrated is that the ethical values of a country's leaders are insufficient to ensure a particular form of social organization. Although this is not a very startling observation, it might need emphasizing in order to correct an over-estimation by earlier political commentators of the centralized power of the new African nations. Tanzania typifies the situation where the absolute limits of physical control are set by the weakness of the administrative structure.[1] The imposition of a particular model of social organization, such as collectivization in Soviet Russia, is therefore not a feasible policy. The role of political leadership is thus circumscribed, and the implementation of its policies directed at the rural economy and society is dependent on their acceptance by the mass base of society. This acceptance, in turn, is related to the extent that the structure aspired to by the leaders conflicts with the technological needs of the agricultural production systems and the aspirations of the decision-makers within these systems.

Two empirical conclusions and a further analytical one arise from our study:

[1] This is emphasized in H. Bienen, *Tanzania, party transformation and economic development*, Princeton 1967.

(a) Rural social organizations are in part a reflection of accumulated traditional rights and obligations, and in part an adjustment to environmental factors, such as resource availabilities, economic opportunities, and individual and social aspirations. There is no *a priori* reason to assume that particular institutions can be maintained if the balance between environment, opportunities, and aspirations is altered. The effect of developing commercialization in Tanzanian agricultural systems appeared to undermine their communal features, and to encourage individualism.

(b) The results of the field investigations suggest that the possibilities of maintaining *ujamaa* work organizations are limited by the farmers' own decisions, in situations where the technological and economic needs of the crop encourage innovatory commercialized organizations and discourage cooperative work. The implication of this is that if socialistic relations are desired then they need to be new ones, to fit in with the needs of the new economic processes. Appeal to traditional values will have little impact.

(c) The choice of production organization is moulded by production and distribution decisions, and in turn helps to determine the structure of rural society. It is thus the link between the needs of economic processes and social structure. The study of this choice is, therefore, essential to an understanding of the emergence of new social structures in developing situations.

These conclusions need rigorous testing by a coherent research programme. Such a programme should be a high priority for a country like Tanzania. The expansion of the rural economy in the last 20 years has shown the ability of its farmers to take advantage of changing opportunities. The quality of life that emerges with the processes of economic development needs to be questioned, however, and is a legitimate object of government policy. The present leaders of Tanzania appear concerned with this problem. There is thus an opportunity for economists, sociologists, and political scientists to work together in order to relate policy directives more realistically to social change, and thus make a valuable contribution to development.

# POLITICAL RECRUITMENT AND
# POLITICAL DEVELOPMENT[1]

## W. H. MORRIS-JONES

This paper begins with an examination of the concept of political recruitment. I wish in particular to clarify its relation to certain adjacent concepts and to argue its value as an instrument for the analysis of political process and as an indicator of systemic development. From this examination the paper moves towards specifying those aspects of recruitment which need to be investigated if we are to understand it as a process; certain subconcepts are developed for this purpose and I attempt to show what kinds of new light may be thrown on political life by research geared to these fresh approaches. Finally, some proof of the pudding is offered in the form of a brief outline, with preliminary findings, of my own inquiries into a particular recruitment process, the selection for the Indian general elections of 1967 of the Congress party's candidates.

The notion of political recruitment required no inventor; what has happened in recent years is simply that the term has gained greater currency and that several themes contained within the zone that stretches from participation through to leadership have been brought together within its span. We may, however, 'place' the idea in two ways. First, it represents a generalizing of separate recruitment processes with which political scientists have long been concerned. The study of political institutions already entailed a study of their recruitment procedures and their effects. Working perhaps on the model of the army, students of civil services, parliaments, and parties have inquired into the recruitment to these institutions, taking this aspect along with others such as structure, organization, procedures, training, and promotion. Recruitment clearly threw light on the style and performance of these institutions; policy concerns could therefore enter easily, and writers came to recommend changes in recruitment designed to alter the character and working of some particular body. Most frequently such changes have been proposed with a view to securing greater 'representativeness', to make a parliament, a party, or a bureaucracy more representative of society as a whole. Sometimes recruitment changes could be seen as ways of achieving what might (at the risk of introducing a contradiction in terms) be called specific

---

[1] The task of revising the paper for publication was made easier and more satisfying by virtue of the valuable comments offered both during and after the conference. Those of Professors Leys, Partridge, and Graham were particularly useful.

representativeness, as when a party might try to regulate recruitment to its ranks in such a way as to make it more representative of some specific class, caste, or tribal group—to enhance its proletarian or, let us suppose, its non-Brahmin quality. (It goes without saying that the latter concern would normally not be found in competitive political situations where a confined support could mean political suicide.) Sometimes, again, recruitment policies may be seen as instruments to achieve other goals such as increased professionalism in a bureaucracy. In any case, it is worth noting that such policy concerns match the fact that in the case of specific institutions recruitment is indeed a matter of deliberate manipulation and control to be determined from the top. As the notion becomes generalized into political recruitment at large, a characteristic not of a particular institution but of a system, the locus of such decisions is less clear.

The second manner in which political recruitment has to be 'placed' is as a derivative of elite theory. If elites are not unchanging, there must be some 'circulation' in the system; the critical points or junctures in the flow, upwards and downwards, can then be seen as recruitment (and dismissal) stations. If a system is regarded as headed by not one but several elites, one of which is a political elite (or, alternatively, if, as in Mills's *The power elite*,[1] there is one power elite which provides political as well as other kinds of leadership), then political recruitment becomes a way of referring to one relatively specialized selection process with its set of stations (or one aspect of a general social process of selection). If, further, one follows Bottomore in distinguishing between 'the political class' and 'the political elite' within the class, then one would expect to look for two main levels or stages of selection—into (and out of) the class and into (and out of) the elite.[2] Finally, the sociologist who identifies a political elite may go on to distinguish its several branches—bureaucratic, party, etc.—and study the distinctive recruitment patterns and procedures of each. (His different route probably saves him from ending up where the political scientist began.)

Whether we reach political recruitment by a generalizing route from institutional studies or by a specifying route from studies of social groups

---

[1] C. Wright Mills, *The power elite*, New York 1956.

[2] Bottomore, *Elites and society*, London 1964, pp. 8–9, himself focuses on the elite and makes surprisingly little use of the two stages which he clearly implies. He wants to arrive at a means of measuring recruitment flows ('what *proportion* of the elite is recruited from the lower strata?') and then comparing systems as regards their 'rates of circulation'. But clearly what happens at the 'class–elite' gateway is affected by what is in the 'class' reservoir.

The distinction between political class and political elite could have been made to serve more usefully in the puzzles about democracy which are raised towards the end of the book. If we are to assess Bottomore's statement that the belief that democracy is protected by competition between elites is 'one of the political myths of our age' we need to know more about the political class. While the elite consists of 'those who actually exercise political power' the class contains 'all groups exercising political power or influence and directly engaged in struggles for political leadership'. But it is not very clear whether class minus elite consists of the 'outs' as opposed to the 'ins' or of a whole layer below the top of the power pyramid.

and their mobility, what we have arrived at is a process which is at once strikingly universal and usefully definite. Every political system contains recruitment processes and each recruitment process is in principle well defined and susceptible of examination. Moreover, the importance of political recruitment does not vary greatly from one system to another.[1] Political recruitment is thus a strong candidate in the competition for good tools of comparative analysis.

Since some political structures run parallel to others while some are encapsulated within others, it follows that recruitment processes within a system are also related in these two different ways: some political roles are filled from among those who already fill other lesser political roles so that one selection follows 'on top' of another; others are separate flows along separate channels. The arrangements vary significantly in their combinations from one polity to another: in Britain, ministers emerge from among members of parliament who in turn emerge from party selection mechanisms, whereas civil servants come to their appointments by wholly different routes; in spoils and single-party systems, on the other hand, administrators may enter their posts through party channels. In all systems, however, it seems that certain parts of the political recruitment process are continuous or successive rather than parallel. In these cases the choice for selection at the higher level is limited by what has come through to the level immediately below. The situation is familiar, of course, in educational ladders but seems not to have been sufficiently noted in political life.

Recruitment, then, is not only a process common to all political systems; it is also a process which runs through several levels in each system. This is a further advantage in a tool for comparative analysis, for very often what we need is a way of understanding one part of a system by comparing it with other parts of the same system. Some of the functions designated as characteristic of political systems are often monopolized by particular levels or branches of the system and are therefore less serviceable as aids to intra-system comparisons.

The merits here seen as attaching to the process of recruitment are close to those seen by Nettl as attaching to the process of political mobilization. Indeed, 'one needs to focus on process—a process which operates universally in all societies at any time'; the object must be 'to bring developed and developing societies into one coherent discourse and to find a means of differentiating between them that is not culture bound' with a view to 'analysing the problem of political and social change'.[2] There is of course the difficulty that the term 'mobilization' has already achieved a certain

---

[1] This is more than can be said for some of the other 'functions' identified by Almond (e.g. in G. A. Almond and C. B. Powell, *Comparative politics: a developmental approach*, Boston 1966). Articulation and aggregation for instance may assume larger roles in some societies than in others.

[2] J. P. Nettl, *Political mobilization*, London 1967, pp. 19–25.

currency, through Apter notably, in a sense different from Nettl's—a sense, in fact, which makes it a characterizing feature of certain systems instead of one common to all.[1] But, leaving that aside, mobilization in any meaning of the term seems, when compared with recruitment, a somewhat awkward conceptual tool. Its co-ordinating power may be useful, but it fails to tell us precisely where we should cut into a political system in order to assess its character and style.

The relation between political recruitment and political socialization is a little more straightforward. We may here lean on Almond, but we have to do so with some care. Certain of his formulations[2] have been clear but misleading. 'The political recruitment function takes up where the general political socialization function leaves off'; 'the relationship between the political socialization function and the political recruitment function is comparable to that between Linton's "basic personality" and "status" or "role" personality'; 'political socialization is the process of induction into the political culture...[it] produces the basic attitudes in a society toward the political system'; 'the political recruitment function... inducts [members of a society] into the specialized roles of the political system'. These and other statements might convey the idea that socialization is at once prior or preparatory to recruitment and more general in character. The position is more complicated, as Almond's own qualifying statements indicate. Socialization of course does not 'leave off' when recruitment to political roles takes place; rather it takes fresh forms derived from these new roles. Moreover, socialization before recruitment could conceivably be so diverse and powerful that role socialization after recruitment would by contrast be more general. (For many if not most men becoming office-bearers in TANU, for example, it could presumably be said that the general political socialization function takes up where the specific political recruitment function leaves off.) Political recruitment, then, relates to socialization in two main ways. First, socialization, whether general or specific, may point in the direction of the recruitment (more or less specific) of the persons or groups concerned. In that sense socialization can shape the material for recruitment. Secondly, recruitment procedures and 'routes' can then in turn help to re-shape socialization; recruitment, a more or less institutionalized process, itself constitutes an agent of socialization which is a matter of attitudes.

---

[1] For Apter, the 'models...at opposite ends of a continuum of political systems' may be designated secular–libertarian and sacred–collectivity, while the 'empirically useful departures' from these pure models are respectively reconciliation and mobilization systems. The latter type 'implies a hierarchical system of authority', in it 'the goals of the state become sacrosanct', it is 'oriented toward the future', it usually contains 'a party of solidarity' (D. E. Apter, *The politics of modernization*, Chicago and London 1965, pp. 34–6, 357–61, and chapter 10, *passim*). It appears that Professor Finer and Mr Ghita Ionescu would favour a still more specific use of the term: mobilization systems would be systems of regimentation.

[2] G. A. Almond and J. S. Coleman (eds.), *The politics of the developing areas*, Princeton 1960, pp. 26–32.

These preliminary remarks may not take us very far. (It is rather surprising to find how little general discussion there has been on political recruitment as such. Neither in theoretical writings nor in studies of particular elite-selection is much said. Even Almond, who has probably done most to give the term currency, spares much less space to this function than to the others. The reasons for this are unclear.) Yet they may serve to suggest some of the questions which are worth asking and enable us to assess how far the literature takes us.

It is fair to say that what could be called studies in recruitment have mainly focused on either the outcome or the procedure. Examples of the former are in a sense legion, for every study of an elite group is looking at the characteristics of those who have emerged. The set of characteristics which attract most attention are those that indicate social background. Thus, when we inquire into who governs New Haven we inspect the social origins of those who have over a period emerged as holders of public office.[1] The same holds true when the scale changes and we look at, say, Britain as a whole or if we select a particular branch of the political elite and examine higher civil servants or legislators or party officials.[2] This preoccupation also marks the interest in political elites in developing countries.[3] The question, where have these leaders come from?, is surely interesting and most legitimate; the class, ethnic, educational or other background of office-holders has obviously some relevance to what is done by such men. But how much?[4] That depends of course on other factors: how powerful is role socialization and how independent is it of the social origins of the members? If such socialization processes count for anything there will in fact not always be a complete fit between origins and attitudes. British radicals who were upset by the way in which J. H. Thomas fell into the 'aristocratic embrace' of high political society were drawing attention to the real importance of a simple example of such role socialization. One might adapt and broaden the well-known French saying about deputies and say that there can be more in common between two holders of similar

---

[1] R. A. Dahl, *Who governs?*, New Haven and London 1961. This of course refers to book I only and the original contribution of the volume lies in the other parts.

[2] On these fields, I have in mind such studies as, respectively, W. L. Guttsman, *The British political elite*, London 1963; R. K. Kelsall, *Higher civil servants in Britain*, London 1955; D. R. Matthews, *U.S. Senators and their world*, Chapel Hill, N.C. 1960; S. J. Eldersveld, *Political parties: a behavioral analysis*, Chicago 1964; J. Blondel, *Voters, parties, and leaders: the social fabric of British politics*, London 1963.

[3] See, for instance, F. W. Frey, *The Turkish political elite*, Cambridge, Mass. 1965; M. Singer, *The emerging elite*, Cambridge, Mass. 1964; T. Kersteins, *The new elite in Asia and Africa*, London 1966.

[4] Since putting this question I have had the opportunity of reading some comments of Professor Sartori on the whole question of class interest as a supposed explanation of political conduct. His severe criticisms of much political sociology literature, especially on the 'jump' from origins to performances, is characteristically shrewd and lucid. See G. Sartori, 'From the sociology of politics to political sociology', in S. M. Lipset (ed.), *Social science and politics*, New York 1969.

I

offices from different social backgrounds than between two persons of similar social backgrounds who hold different offices.[1] If this applies to relations between origins and attitudes, there is still another gap between attitudes and actual behaviour in office; the latter may in turn be yet another and not wholly derivative thing—depending on factors such as accountability devices.

However, more to the point from the aspect of political recruitment is the fact that such disclosures of social origins form only a part of the story. If the British administrative class comes from Oxbridge, precinct leaders from the Italian community, and Ceylon legislators from among land-owners, this may not only do too little to explain why they behave as they do; it does not represent an effective focusing of attention on recruitment as a process. What would the latter require? An indication of what has been left out can be given by putting two questions in particular: first, from whom, effectively, were those who emerged chosen? Who else was entered for the race? Second, how are those who come into role *A* from group *X* differentiated from the other members of the same group *X* who by contrast moved into roles *B* and *C*? It is very strange that these questions have rarely been put in studies of political leadership selection.

Nor do studies which focus on procedure address themselves satis-factorily to these questions. For these studies concentrate on the mechanics of the operation and on the characteristics of the selectors. This would appear true, for example, of the work of Eldersveld, Key, David, Goldman and Bain, and Ranney.[2] Selectors' preferences and procedural constraints are important elements in the recruitment process but, even when taken in conjunction with studies of the selectees, still cannot be said to have covered the recruitment process as a process. Perhaps the missing areas can be indicated under three heads: *career routes*; *aspiration patterns*; *catchment areas*. These terms are closely connected and overlap considerably; they are probably best regarded as three approaches to one theme rather than as separate points. That theme is that the study of political recruitment is in need of some reorientation—away from the institutions towards the actors.

A start in this direction is made when interest is taken not simply in the selection procedures and the characteristics of those who get through, but in the *career routes* of all competitors, including those who get stopped at particular barriers or themselves decide not to proceed further, or choose

---

[1] 'There is more in common between two deputies of whom one is a revolutionary and the other is not, than between two revolutionaries of whom one is a deputy and the other is not.' (Robert de Jouvenel, *La République des camarades*, quoted by D. W. Brogan in his Preface to Bertrand de Jouvenel, *Power*, London 1948. I am grateful to Mr S. K. Panter-Brick for helping me to locate this.)

[2] Eldersveld, *Political parties*; V. O. Key, *Politics, parties and pressure groups* (4th edn) New York 1958; P. T. David, R. M. Goldman, and R. C. Bain, *The politics of national party conventions*, Washington 1960; and A. Ranney, *Pathways to parliament*, London 1966.

some other road. In a patchy, unsystematic way, there is a great deal to be learned from biographies. Systematic material is more scanty: Apter devotes a particularly stimulating chapter to 'Innovation, professionalism and careers', and although the use he envisages for the concept of career is related more to broad inter-system comparisons than to detailed uncovering of career selection and movement within particular political processes, his suggestions point to important lines of inquiry. Michael Lee has shown how historical investigation can reveal the movement of individuals from given social positions into a variety of political roles at different levels in the system. White has plotted the intricate steps in the ascent to one great political office. Eldersveld has a valuable chapter on career development and Frey included a cohort analysis in his study.[1] But there is much more that could be done. The study of career routes could cover not only direction but also rates of flow. Politics would be seen from this angle as a matter of who travels where, furthest, fastest.

It may well be that certain connotations of the word recruitment have impeded a balanced approach to its study. 'Recruitment' conveys the impression of initiative in the selecting agency: the army, the civil service, the party want men and they go out to get them; persons are inducted (passive voice) into roles. The reality is surely more of a two-way relationship: political roles are demanded as well as supplied. For every recruitment need on the part of a sector of the political system, there is a group of aspirants. In some situations—less frequently in established states—it is in fact *aspirant pressure* that characterizes the process of political recruitment. It is true that aspirant groups may be difficult to locate for examination, but it may be that no one has tried sufficiently. If we learned to think of the process, more bifocally, as aspiration–recruitment, we might find out more about the demand side of the relation. Robert Lane, with his sub-title 'Why and how people get involved in politics', represented an important move in this direction.[2] Less noticed but of considerable interest is Davies's *Private politics*.[3] More explicitly than Lane, Davies does constitute an attempt to tackle the process of '*entry*' (to use a term which has more neutral balance than 'recruitment') into political life from the actor's end. Following Adorno, Erikson, and others, the book is an exploration of socialization more than of entry, but the entry routes are in fact well disclosed and the relation between these and socialization clearly brought out. With this kind of inquiry we certainly get nearer to discovering how, out of a background shared with many others, some particular people, like Davies's 'second-drawer politicos', choose political routes.

In any area of social activity, selection and differentiation processes are

[1] Apter, *The politics of modernization*; J. M. Lee, *Social leaders and public persons*, London 1963; T. H. White, *The making of the President, 1960* and *The making of the President, 1964*, New York 1961 and 1965; Eldersveld, *Political parties*; Frey, *The Turkish political elite.*
[2] R. E. Lane, *Political life*, New York 1959.
[3] A. F. Davies, *Private politics*, Melbourne 1966.

continuous. In understanding and evaluating these processes it is necessary to ask who is selecting by what method for what purpose. But—and this is what is often missing in examinations of political selection—there is also the question of the nature of the 'field' from which the choice is to be made. (As noted earlier, the selected group at one level may constitute the field from which choice has to be made for a higher level.) A supposed bias in favour of Oxbridge training for admission into the administrative class of the British civil service may look different if it is shown that good candidates from Redbrick universities did not even enter the competition. The predominance of Italians among the precinct leaders may mostly indicate pressure of applications from that section. For certain purposes, admittedly, it may be useful to compare a chosen group with the population at large; but sometimes, and certainly if we want to focus on the entry process, it is in relation to its *catchment area* or 'field' that we have to make comparisons.[1] One of the few pieces of investigation which attempted to move in this direction was that undertaken by Valen.[2] The Norwegian process for the selection of parliamentary candidates is carried out at delegate conventions and the procedure entails not a simple choice but a ranking. Valen has tried to probe this *catchment area* in order to find out what qualities are regarded as necessary in an applicant, what factors actually sway the selectors, what features characterize those chosen and what features distinguish those given high as opposed to low rank. Although he collected data on the nominees and answers from local party leaders on the criteria, even Valen was not able to use the applicant group as such for his analysis.

At this point it may be appropriate to introduce a couple of refinements. First, we have so far spoken of recruitment and selection as interchangeable terms. In many if not most situations this seems harmless. However, it must be noted that a distinction in principle does exist and can sometimes be important: the use of criteria and the fact of deliberate exclusion are entailed in the process of selection but not necessarily in that of recruitment. Every selection includes a recruitment—except, of course, in the extreme case where all who are considered are rejected—but not every recruitment contains a selection; a party may be so literally 'catch-all' in character that it recruits without selection, that is, indiscriminately. Second, in directing attention towards the 'demand' for political roles, we have spoken of aspirants and of catchment areas. Clearly these terms need rather closer definition before they can become operational. The main ambiguity to be avoided can be indicated by making a distinction between aspirant

[1] After I had been thinking of this way of describing the applicant group, I found the term in Nettl's *Political mobilization*. The two uses are so different and unrelated that confusion seems unlikely to arise.

[2] H. Valen, 'The recruitment of parliamentary nominees in Norway', *Scandinavian Political Studies* I (1966).

and applicant. Or, using the other term, one must say that beyond every actual catchment area there is a potential catchment area. At the civil service examinations the unsuccessful candidates were clearly applicants and a part of the catchment area from which the winners were chosen, but beyond them were others who were eligible, could well have been attracted, and yet did not formally apply. Party selection committees may look at several possible parliamentary candidates before picking one, but there will have been other suitable aspirants who never got to the starting line. Clearly, in most processes of political selection, it is much easier to identify and examine the applicants than the aspirants. The composition of the latter is elusive because what constitutes eligibility for so many political roles is imprecise and the main variables are often supplied by personal disposition and temperament on the one hand and access to information and influence on the other.[1] Indeed, it may be that a further distinction is necessary for completeness and we should speak of eligibles, aspirants, and applicants.[2] In any full study of recruitment to political roles these distinctions would be by no means trivial. Nor are these areas impossible for investigation; only we have scarcely begun to explore them. That there is much to be learned about political life from this direction can scarcely be doubted. In what follows later we shall be dealing perforce with applicants strictly understood. But we shall have to bear in mind that this group is in some degree arbitrarily narrower than that of eligible aspirants, that it excludes for example those who did not apply because they thought that they stood no chance.

How does a reorientation on the lines indicated bear on the value of the concept in relation to political development? Almond is less helpful here than one might have expected. Although his recent book confesses that the earlier formulation of functional-systems theory was 'suitable mainly for the analysis of political systems in a given cross section of time' and 'did not permit' the exploration of developmental patterns, it does not add much to the recruitment function.[3] It is true that this function is now moved from its previous uneasy position as one of the input functions to a new status of independence, along with socialization, as the 'system maintenance and adaptation' level on which any system functions. The point is repeated from the earlier volume that recruitment criteria may be universalistic or particularistic, but otherwise only two further observations are offered: that recruitment procedures can be placed on a range from open to closed, and that systems also vary according to the degree to which

---

[1] Blondel's neat phrase 'selection by apathy' has a relevance here. See Blondel, *Voters, parties, and leaders*, p. 94 and chapter 4, *passim*.

[2] These are not necessarily groups wholly within groups. All applicants must be presumed to be aspirants, but not all applicants may be eligible (if the rules as to applications are inexplicit). More obviously, ineligible persons may aspire just as eligible persons may be without aspirations in the relevant direction.

[3] Almond and Powell, *Comparative politics*, p. 13.

the recruitment function is predominantly the concern of one particular kind of structure such as party.[1]

An important hint regarding the possible value of the political 'entry' process in the comparative analysis of development is contained in Rokkan and Valen.[2] There we find candidate recruitment selected as one index, along with turnout and party membership, of the 'mobilization of the periphery': how soon after their formal incorporation in the political system do new social groups make their appearance in the ranks of candidates for political office? (The question was good, but the investigation disappointing: it proved impossible to handle any variable other than sex on that particular index.) The notions of a time-lag in a developing system and the search for the 'catchment area' 'behind' the actual elected representative were valuable. But perhaps the most useful discussion of this whole matter is provided in Seligman's study of the case of Israel[3] from which some of the following is developed.

Political systems and social change cross and meet at the processes of political entry. These processes are reflectors of social change: they can mirror changes in values, aspirations, perceptions of opportunities, as well as changes in actual structures and roles. At the same time they exert their own influence in their distribution of status and prestige, their efficiency in selecting persons appropriate to the tasks to be carried out; by their flexibility they may contribute to system stability and development, by their rigidity they may create points of tension and breakdown.

One of the more obvious ways in which entry processes relate to political development is through the degree of importance attaching to political avenues as routes of social advancement. While it is probably untrue to say that in all developing countries political avenues acquire great importance, this is at least often the case, for clear historical and economic reasons. This results in the build-up of heavy pressures in the 'catchment areas'. These may be such that selection procedures break down; even if that does not happen, it ensures extensive frustration which becomes then a large fact of the political scene. In these situations it may be at least as important to see who is left behind at the barriers as to note who gets through.

Developing countries are often undergoing rapid social change and, since development 'distributes its gains unevenly',[4] the body of political aspirants can change composition fast—almost certainly faster than the elite itself can change. To acknowledge that the elite's composition will adjust only after some time-lag one does not have to assume that selectors are determined to reproduce themselves. But if we can inspect the catch-

[1] Almond and Powell, *Comparative Politics*, pp. 118–20.

[2] S. Rokkan and H. Valen, 'The mobilization of the periphery', in S. Rokkan (ed.), *Approaches to the study of political participation*, Bergen 1962.

[3] L. G. Seligman, *Leadership in a new nation: political development in Israel*, New York 1964.

[4] *Ibid.*, p. 8.

ment area group of aspirants, we may be in a position not merely to record movements of social groups into the arena but also to spot tomorrow's winners. As the backbenchers may be the catchment area to examine for the next cabinet but one, so the new entrants in the group seeking assembly tickets may, though unsuccessful on this round, be the best indicators of the next lot of representatives. Just how responsive the recruitment procedures are to pressures from fresh quarters, e.g. from rural groups challenging urban elites, will also indicate the adaptability of the system and give a guide to its capacity to endure.[1]

Regional disparities have importance in many states; in new states the differences are often very marked and politically significant. Sometimes it may be difficult to know whether to speak of regional parts of a political system or of separate political systems which are only loosely held together. Entry processes can make a useful focus of study in this connection. Inter-unit contrasts in the character of aspirant groups, their rate of change, their career routes and their fortunes at the points of selection can reveal much of relevance to problems of national integration.

Rather similarly, new states are often characterized by multiple political cultures and in particular by gaps between the values and attitudes at the base and those at the top of the political pyramid. In the handling of entry processes the contrasts in procedural norms between the higher and lower echelons of the same structure can illumine the scale and nature of these differences.

Inter-regional and inter-level comparisons in entry processes would normally be in the context of party organizations through which so large a part of the entry into non-bureaucratic political roles takes place. But the study of these processes could also be expected to throw light back on party itself as a political system. By their handling of recruitment or entry processes, parties can be compared in various ways: at what levels are the key selection decisions made? how narrowly guarded (a cooption mechanism) or widely distributed is influence over such decisions? how willing is a party to welcome and accommodate group interests or does it prefer to 'colonize' such groups with its own members? It is not suggested that such questions would throw up new categories for the classification of parties, but they could add a valuable dimension to existing categories such as sectarian/pluralist. Very important in single and dominant parties is the nature of intra-party competition and the character of factional groupings and their relations to each other. Party selection machinery, such as that for determining party candidates for elections, has the function *inter alia* of regulating these relations, and the working of the machinery should tell us a great deal about the party's internal power system. Party handling of selection problems will of course vary not only according to the character of the organization but also according to the

[1] *Ibid.*, p. 7.

system context in which it operates. Seligman in an unusual study of Oregon politics sought to relate, in the context of candidate selection, the internal cohesion or factionalism of party to the degree of competition it encountered in the political system.[1] His rather startling findings, contradicting earlier views put forward by Key, and suggesting that cohesion decreases and factions flourish as a system moves from dominance to competition, seem not to have been followed by other studies.

The foregoing remarks must not be seen as a prelude to an account of an empirical study which at once remedies all the shortcomings of our current literature. On the contrary, these too-random reflections were provoked by a desire to see how far some recently gathered and unusual material from India could be used in such a way as to complement previous studies. The answer unfortunately is that what is sketched below goes only a little way towards filling one kind of gap.

We begin with the assumption that in the Indian political system the body of persons who arrive at the position of member of parliament or member of a state legislative assembly (M.L.A.) constitute a significant element in the Indian political elite. This group of some 4,000 emerges from an electoral process which chooses them from a larger number (18,872 in 1967) of candidates contesting. This larger group is the catchment area from which the main streams of M.P.s and M.L.A.s are drawn. However, the Indian political system is not a familiar two- or multi-party system but a constellation system in which a number of parties move round a dominant party. The obvious fact that in single and even in dominant party situations candidate selection is the point of effective competition has been made several times.[2] Particular importance therefore attaches to that part of the candidate group which is composed of those who have the Congress party ticket. What is unusual is to be able to examine the total group out of which in turn this candidate group is selected. This is a catchment area which is usually neglected—perhaps because it is often inaccessible, perhaps because no one has been looking in that direction. Congress contested 4,164 seats in 1967, so that was the number of candidates to be selected. The average number of applicants per ticket was 4·7; so the number in the applicant group was about 19,000. This is the group whose characteristics, it is suggested, merit examination.

The general comparative analysis interest is matched by an interest arising out of the specific Indian context. To look at the working of a selection process internal to the Congress party is to look at part of what, before and after the 1967 elections, is still the hub of the Indian political

[1] L. G. Seligman, 'Political recruitment and party structure', *American Political Science Review* LV, 1 (1961).

[2] E.g. Key, *Politics, parties and pressure groups*; M. Duverger, *Political parties*, London 1954.

system. Moreover, its relative failure at the elections was in most areas and in large measure attributable to lack of internal cohesion and competition from breakaway organizations formed from its own ranks; these twin factors of dissidence and defection were in turn closely related to the outcome of the battles around the selection of candidates. The selection of candidates is relevant to the task of winning the election; it bears closely on the job of putting together a team that can engage successfully in the battles of wits in the assemblies; it determines the quality of the reservoir from which talent for manning governmental positions will have to be drawn; immediately, however, it is the supreme test of the skills of negotiation and reconciliation of the party managers. (From the viewpoint of the individual applicant it is of course a critical moment in the shaping of a political career.)

In some constituencies there was no tussle for the ticket; one person, usually the sitting member, would be in such a strong position that applications from others were seen to be futile or, if they were submitted, could be regarded as frivolous. But if we leave such constituencies to one side, most of the others witnessed manœuvres which were necessarily complex. Each applicant stands near the centre of a network which stretches both downwards to his sponsors or supporters and upwards towards those who are actual or potential patrons. And naturally the whole network trembles with sensitive response and purposeful activity during the period when the choice is to be made. To map completely the total activity of all persons concerned would be an enormous job. It was thus clear that a reasonably comprehensive and detailed account of why Sri *A* was preferred to Sri *B*, Dr *C*, and Smt. *D* could only be achieved for a few selected constituencies; even then one would need first-rate contacts as well as much patience and luck before one could feel confident that the inevitably conflicting versions had been sorted out and an objective account rendered. Fortunately, other approaches, sacrificing some of the intimacy of depth for the advantages of a broader picture, have their value, and it is one such approach that is taken in the study which is briefly described in what follows.[1]

The selection procedure, which is set in motion at a meeting of the party's central election committee (C.E.C.) some months before polling day, has to reconcile the intimate knowledge of the applicants which is possessed mainly by the local district committee (D.C.C.) with the influence demanded by the state committee (P.E.C.) leaders and with the inherited doctrine that the final choice resides with the central party leaders. Variations on these themes have been played in each of the four

[1] The full results of my study on the selection process in 1966–7 will appear shortly as a book. A briefer narrative account, 'Candidate selection: the ordeal of Congress, 1966–67', based mainly on press reports over a period of about 6 months, is included as a chapter in a volume of essays edited by Professor M. S. Rajan and presented to Dr Appadorai, to be published in Delhi in 1969.

general election periods (1951, 1957, 1962, 1967); the formal rules of the
1966–7 procedure were marked by an abandonment on the part of the
C.E.C. of any attempt to regulate the operation in detail. Applications,
instead of being filtered as in 1961 through to P.E.C., were to be sent
direct to P.E.C. and it was up to that body to determine how it was to
consult the D.C.C. executive and whether it would seek opinions from
other party committees. P.E.C.s did in fact ask D.C.C. executives for their
views on applicants for their constituencies, but otherwise practices varied
somewhat. In Maharashtra P.E.C. tours undertook the interviewing of
applicants alongside D.C.C.s. In states like Madras and West Bengal
consultation with lower local committees seems to have been kept very
informal. In states like Bihar and U.P., where the party was sharply
divided into rather institutionalized factions, there were parallel sets of
state–district links for each 'group'. Several states dispensed altogether
with P.E.C. observers sent out to D.C.C.s; it was often said that they
aggravated conflicts. The procedure laid down by the C.E.C. concluded
with the reassertion of overall central control: first, the C.E.C. would
appoint representatives who would attend the P.E.C. meetings at which
recommendations were being determined, and these central observers
would report to the Congress president; second, the final selection was to
rest with the C.E.C. which could make any changes in the P.E.C. list
and even select persons who had not applied for the ticket.

Apart from establishing procedural limits, the central leadership has
also pronounced upon the qualifications and standards it would wish to
have observed. Nehru's famous clarion call in 1951 for priority to be given
to 'integrity' was the first of such statements. In 1966 the list of criteria
was not unfamiliar: active membership (implying at least 2 years'
primary membership) of the party; agreement with basic policies;
record of relevant work in local bodies or welfare organizations; record of
disciplined behaviour and regular payment of party dues. Sitting members
were in addition to submit statements of assets and income and their
legislative record was to be examined. Not for the first time the aim of
ensuring a turnover of personnel through the retirement of about one-
third of the sitting members was declared, while 'adequate' representation
was to be ensured for women and minorities. However, already in the same
circular letter, the general secretary allowed that the criteria could not be
applied 'rigidly'. This may have been realistic, both in view of the antici-
pated need to try to accommodate rival group interests and in recognition
of the value as candidates of some who might hitherto not have been party
members, but it appears to have worried some rank and file members; a
non-official resolution moved at the September all-India Congress
committee (A.I.C.C.) tried to tighten the criteria, ensure ideological
solidarity and limit the pressures of factional groups. Even if only a small
fraction of all the scandalous tales told by unsuccessful applicants were

true, 'flexibility' of some kind often won the day! But to choose between applicants of ideological purity and organizational fidelity on the one hand and those of vote-getting power on the other is awkward, especially for a party of 'umbrella', 'catch-all' traditions. Not that this choice normally presented itself so clearly; more often than not the applicants—especially the prominent runners—were identified with rival groups; the decision would be shaped by the relative strength of the groups, though the arguments deployed might well be in terms of loyalty or capacity to win. It was a general impression among those engaged in the process whom I consulted that only in favourable circumstances would considerations related to a person's value as legislator be of weight.

Now the data gathered for investigation are of two kinds. First, there is biographical information on those who filed applications to be considered as the party's candidates. This information, derived from party records, is not neatly standardized across all states and for some states was unobtainable. Nevertheless, the majority of states are covered and the data usually include sex, age, education, party career, and public offices held. What is lost by unstandardized material is hopefully compensated for by the size of the group—some 10,000 individuals[1]—and the authenticity of the information which was of course presented before party officials who could not be easily deceived. Second, the data record the recommendations of the party at the three levels of D.C.C., P.E.C., and C.E.C. Between the two extremes of (a) the applicant who gets recommended right through and becomes the candidate, and (b) the applicant who is rejected by all three levels, there are a number of variations in these recommendation patterns.

The questions to be addressed to this material fall into two categories. One series of questions relates to the concepts developed above under the label of 'catchment area'. It is reasonable to think of sitting members as the pre-existing elite, the successful applicants who become new candidates as the freshly entered elite, and the unsuccessful applicants as composed in part of past and of possible future elites. These three groups will be compared in terms of the characteristics available and these comparisons will be done by state as well as on an all-India basis. It will thus be possible to see whether there are significant variations (in both the 'catchment area' and in the selected group) as between different parts of India— variations which may then be explained in terms of the different characteristics either of the different states or of the state party organizations or of the state party systems. In addition, the analysis will be pursued in terms of the constituencies themselves to see whether either applicants or selectees vary according to the party history of the seat or according to the

---

[1] This falls substantially short of the 19,000 mentioned earlier; some states have had to be omitted. Not all pradesh Congress offices were obliging or effective with regard to access, in a few cases shortage of time on my side prevented a proper approach.

census-based 'development' category of the district in which it is located.

The second series of questions uses the detailed recommendation data and will be used to throw light on the party itself. Thus we can 'place' states or *parts* of states according to their dominant recommendation patterns, indicating degrees of cohesion. Further, by including the election results themselves, we can observe if there is any relation between given recommendation patterns—e.g. complete accord at all levels—and actual success at the polls. It will also be possible (linking the recommendation data to the biographical data) to see whether there is a tendency for local units to have a stronger preference than higher echelons for a certain kind of candidate. Finally, information on post-selection behaviour of un-successful applicants is also being incorporated, thus permitting, for instance, a measure to be made of the exact extent to which disappointed applicants actually contested against the party.

It is not possible here to give more than a sample of the results which have emerged.[1] The sample chosen is confined to the first set of questions, those relating to the 'catchment area', and two states, Bihar and Maharashtra, are selected. Whether these two cases do in fact provide the most vivid contrasts was at the time of writing not yet clear, but it was at least likely that they would yield some differences of interest. Both states had Congress governments from the previous elections of 1962 up to 1967, but that was about the extent of their common ground. The Bihar government had survived with the utmost difficulty: its unpopularity had been increasing rapidly and during the pre-election period reached fever pitch with violent demonstrations, police firing, and smouldering resentment leading to demonstrations and a fresh cycle. The state government had not caused the famine, but its negligence (e.g. over well-construction) had helped to make it possible and its incompetence aggravated its consequences. But the violence came less from the rural areas than from the towns where students were ablaze in a fury. Their hatred (and that of the middle classes as a whole) of the chief minister and his close colleagues had something to do with the famine, more to do with price increases and corruption, not a little to do with their intense dislike and distrust of the extent to which government was relying upon the support of the 'backward' classes (i.e. lower castes) and thereby encouraging them to behave above their proper station—a twice-born or upper caste backlash, so to speak. In this situation opposition parties like Jan Sangh and the Samyukta Socialists seemed poised for a kill. In Maharashtra on the other hand, the Congress government, firmly resting on the support of the large and fairly homogeneous Maratha peasantry, scanned the political horizon and could

[1] I must here gratefully acknowledge the help received both from the Rockefeller Foundation which made my field trip possible and from the Social Science Research Council which financed the processing of the data. For the latter I am indebted to the patient and skilful work of Mrs Hadassa Gilbert who supervised the difficult coding operation and prepared the programme for the computer.

see no effective enemy in sight. It had performed responsively and responsibly, its skill and competence acknowledged outside the ranks of its supporters. Moreover, and of special relevance here, the internal affairs of Congress in the two states differed correspondingly: not even the most malicious gossip-monger could find a convincing deep split in party or government in Bombay, whereas in Patna factions had for long been engaged in open warfare which had reduced government to a clique and party headquarters to a scarred and sorry battlefield. The selection of Maharashtra's Congress candidates proceeded smoothly, in Bihar the tottering organization found the task an occasion for a further series of self-inflicted wounds.

Table 1

|  | No. of L.A. seats contested* | No. of applicants for Congress tickets | Average no. of applicants per ticket | No. of former Congress legislators among applicants† | No. of applicants securing ticket‡ |
|---|---|---|---|---|---|
| Bihar | 318 | 2,753 | 8·65 | 408 | 260 |
| Maharashtra | 269 | 1,439 | 5·35 | 263 | 243 |

* The number of seats in these legislative assemblies is 318 and 270. Congress contested all seats in Bihar; in Maharashtra elections were postponed in one constituency, Congress contesting the rest.

† Former legislators includes members sitting in the 1962–6 assemblies, but also (a) sitting M.P.s applying for L.A. tickets, and (b) former M.P.s and M.L.A.s, i.e. from pre-1962.

‡ The numbers in the final column fall short of those in the first. The records I used often failed to disclose the final selection stage but in such cases an attempt was made to trace the name of the chosen candidate in the list of applicants. In order not to miss the man who was in the end chosen for a seat different from that for which he applied, applicants within all the constituencies of the district were checked. It is therefore safe to say that all or almost all the 'missing candidates' must have been men who got the ticket without applying. (This makes an interesting fourth category to compare alongside applicants, former members and successful applicants and for the full study it may be possible to secure data on this group.) It is significant that in strife-torn Bihar the number is as high as 58, in more harmonious Maharashtra only 26; the better the ordering of party affairs, the greater the reliance upon regular procedures and thus the closer the approximation of the applicant group to the real catchment area.

While staying watchful for contrasts between the two states, we should, however, focus mainly on the extent to which in both cases we can observe differences between those who were already (or had earlier been) sitting members, those who became candidates, and those who sought to be candidates. Table 1 shows the six groups with which we are concerned in this sample. It should be noted that we deal here not with parliamentary constituencies but only those of the state legislative assemblies.

In both states the number of applicants per ticket is above the national average of 4·7 but in Bihar very markedly so. Other things being equal, applicant numbers would vary directly with the perceived chances of party success. These were certainly poorer in Bihar than in Maharashtra, but against this Bihar's internal party conflicts may have invited a rush of competitors, whereas the tighter discipline in Maharashtra may have worked in the opposite direction.

Tables 2–6 compare for both states our three categories of persons in

### Table 2. *Age*

| Age group | Bihar | | | Maharashtra | | |
|---|---|---|---|---|---|---|
| | *1* | *2* | *3* | *1* | *2* | *3* |
| Under 30 | 10 | 3 | 0 | 7 | 7 | 3 |
| 31–40 | 31 | 30 | 21 | 29 | 32 | 17 |
| 41–50 | 34 | 34 | 35 | 36 | 36 | 44 |
| 51–60 | 18 | 22 | 29 | 15 | 15 | 23 |
| 61–70 | 5 | 8 | 13 | 2 | 2 | 5 |
| Over 70 | 0 | 1 | 1 | 0 | 0 | 0 |
| Not known | 0 | 1 | 0 | 6 | 8 | 6 |
| | 98 | 99 | 99 | 95 | 100 | 98 |

### Table 3. *Education*

| Education level* | Bihar | | | Maharashtra | | |
|---|---|---|---|---|---|---|
| | *1* | *2* | *3* | *1* | *2* | *3* |
| Illiterate | 0 | 0 | 0 | 0 | 0 | 0 |
| Literate | 2 | 0 | 1 | 0 | 0 | 0 |
| Primary | 2 | 1 | 0 | 5 | 4 | 3 |
| Middle | 8 | 5 | 6 | 16 | 13 | 13 |
| High | 26 | 19 | 19 | 9 | 6 | 7 |
| Matric. | 23 | 23 | 23 | 18 | 18 | 18 |
| Inter. | 12 | 13 | 11 | 9 | 6 | 6 |
| Graduate | 8 | 12 | 12 | 8 | 11 | 10 |
| Postgraduate | 5 | 4 | 5 | 6 | 7 | 9 |
| Law | 10 | 16 | 20 | 15 | 25 | 22 |
| Not known | 4 | 5 | 3 | 8 | 9 | 8 |
| | 100 | 98 | 100 | 94 | 99 | 96 |

\* The levels are mainly as found in the records. 'Literate' may mean the same as 'primary' which is used to refer to 1st–4th standard (= class or form). 'Middle' refers to 5th–8th standard, 'High' to 9th–10th or 11th. 'Matric.' indicates the passing of the examination at the end of high school. 'Inter.' covers diplomas and degree examination failures as well as those who completed intermediate college. 'Postgraduate' means any higher degree including M.A. 'Law' refers to all who have law degrees; this includes some who would have arts degrees and these are counted under this head, not under 'graduate'.

respect of a series of characteristics. In each table column 1 refers to applicants, column 2 to successful applicants, and column 3 to former members within the applicant group. All figures are rounded percentages showing the distribution of characteristics within each of the six groups.

Table 2 shows that in Bihar the age distribution of the three groups varies steadily as one moves from 'yesterday's elite' (the former members) in column 3 to that of today (the successful applicants) in column 2, and on to the applicant group in column 1, most of whom will have to wait for tomorrow. In Maharashtra the pattern is the same in respect of the former members who are again older (though not as old as that group is in Bihar), but there is the interesting difference that here the successful men were slightly younger than the applicant group as a whole.

The contrasts between the three categories in terms of educational qualifications are less pronounced than might have been expected. However, while columns 2 and 3 run closely parallel in both states, it is clear that the applicant group contained a larger share of those with lower qualifications and a smaller share of the better qualified. This is more marked in Maharashtra than in Bihar, but then Maharashtra seems already to have more room for those with only a few years' schooling.

Table 4. *Local government positions*

| Position | Bihar | | | Maharashtra | | |
|---|---|---|---|---|---|---|
| | 1 | 2 | 3 | 1 | 2 | 3 |
| Office-holder, zila parishad | 0 | 1 | 0 | 3 | 5 | 3 |
| Member, zila parishad | 1 | 1 | 1 | 9 | 6 | 3 |
| Office-holder panchayat samiti | 0 | 0 | 0 | 6 | 8 | 1 |
| Member, panchayat samiti | 0 | 0 | 0 | 3 | 2 | 0 |
| Office-holder village panchayat | 15 | 9 | 6 | 1 | 1 | 1 |
| Member, village panchayat | 2 | 0 | 0 | 1 | 0 | 0 |
| Office-holder, district or taluka board | 2 | 5 | 6 | 3 | 4 | 5 |
| Member, district or taluka board | 4 | 5 | 9 | 3 | 3 | 3 |
| Office-holder, municipality | 3 | 2 | 2 | 4 | 5 | 5 |
| Member, municipality | 2 | 0 | 1 | 3 | 3 | 1 |
| No position given | 68 | 73 | 74 | 60 | 64 | 77 |
| | 97 | 96 | 99 | 96 | 101 | 99 |

With table 4, we move to information which was not directly sought of applicants. Applicants who included statements about positions they occupied (or had occupied) in local government did so because they deemed it relevant to their suitability as candidates. It is fairly safe to take it that those who made no such mention did in fact not hold any position. In view of the increased political significance of local elected bodies in most parts of India, it is not surprising to find that experience in such bodies is least among former legislators and greatest among the applicants. In Maharashtra such experience is rewarded in due measure; the proportion of 'local bodies' men among applicants is closely matched with that among the successful applicants. The relative prominence in Maharashtra of experience in the higher Samiti and Zila Parishad levels is simply due to the absence of those bodies in most districts of Bihar.

Table 5.   *Other public positions*

| Position* | Bihar | | | Maharashtra | | |
|---|---|---|---|---|---|---|
| | *1* | *2* | *3* | *1* | *2* | *3* |
| Public body A† | 5 | 9 | 7 | 3 | 7 | 6 |
| Public body B | 13 | 16 | 13 | 4 | 8 | 6 |
| Tribal, caste, community organization | 0 | 0 | 0 | 1 | 1 | 0 |
| Professional association | 0 | 0 | 0 | 0 | 0 | 0 |
| Office-holder, cooperative | 15 | 16 | 14 | 13 | 25 | 14 |
| Member, cooperative | 19 | 23 | 20 | 25 | 22 | 22 |
| University council | 1 | 5 | 5 | 1 | 2 | 2 |
| School board or management committee | 12 | 15 | 16 | 2 | 3 | 0 |
| Other educational administration | 34 | 34 | 35 | 16 | 25 | 21 |

* The positions listed here are of course not exclusive of one another; the figures simply show the percentage of each group who made mention of such positions held.

† 'Public body *A*' includes membership of committees, councils, etc., which either have an all-India scope or are state level bodies of some importance. 'Public body *B*' refers to membership of state level bodies of lesser importance or of bodies of smaller (e.g. district) scope. Most of these organizations would not be formally government bodies but would have close relations, sometimes of dependence, on government.

Here the differences between the three groups may not bear much weighty interpretation, though it does appear that the selected candidates score better in terms of public positions than the group from which they were chosen. In part it no doubt is the case that the party selectors attached importance to these positions as avenues of influence and support; partly, too, one could say that men of general political influence valued by the party would tend to be already found in such positions. Of greater interest is the clear picture which emerges of the outstanding importance of two areas of public life—education and cooperatives.

The information provided on length of party membership was surprisingly and significantly unsatisfactory: only in the case of some 15 per cent of the applicants was any clear mention made of record of service in the party. In view of this, the distribution pattern as between old-timers and recent entrants cannot be reliably seen; the most that one could say is that applicants with very long service are unlikely to have this omitted from their data sheets and that therefore the size of this group is probably accurate. In Bihar, 7 per cent of the applicants claimed pre-war membership, compared with 9 per cent of the successful applicants and 11 per cent of former member applicants. The corresponding figures for Maharashtra were 3 per cent, 2 per cent, and 3 per cent. The next oldest group, those with membership going back to pre-independence (i.e. 1939–47) accounted in Bihar for 3 per cent of the applicants, 4 per cent of the successful ones, and 2 per cent of the former members, and in Maharashtra for 2 per cent of the applicants, 1 per cent of the successful, and 1 per cent of former members.

Table 6.  *Party positions*

| Position* | Bihar | | | Maharashtra | | |
|---|---|---|---|---|---|---|
| | *1* | *2* | *3* | *1* | *2* | *3* |
| Member, mandal C.C. | 16 | 8 | 2 | 17 | 15 | 11 |
| Member, district C.C. | 10 | 10 | 9 | 4 | 7 | 5 |
| Officer,† district C.C. | 6 | 14 | 11 | 6 | 13 | 12 |
| Member, pradesh C.C. | 8 | 26 | 23 | 3 | 9 | 8 |
| Member, all-India C.C. | 1 | 6 | 5 | 1 | 6 | 5 |
| Officer, pradesh C.C. | 1 | 2 | 2 | 0 | 1 | 1 |
| No position given | 62 | 45 | 57 | 60 | 51 | 58 |

* Many persons are of course members of party committees at more than one level; such a detailed breakdown has been obtained, but this table in simplified form entails double counting of such persons who appear in more than one row.

† 'Officer' includes president, secretary, treasurer, and member of executive committee.

The positions in table 6 are arranged in order of importance from membership of the lowest committee (mandal) to office-holding in the state-level committee. It is of course evident, though more so in Bihar than Maharashtra, that holders of more important party positions are more prominent among former member applicants and successful applicants than among applicants as a whole; there is, that is, a measure of the extent to which progress in the organization assists, either by influence or in terms of 'qualifications', in securing advancement into legislative office. It is interesting to observe how prudence (combined with rules ensuring overlapping membership between the party's organizational and parliamentary 'wings') ensures that even the former members, those who have 'arrived', are still holders of party office. Yet it still remains striking that in all three of our groups and in both states, more than half the persons concerned could apparently show no very direct and active role in party affairs.

What has been set out in the above sample is no more than a small part of the results, omitting as it does the range of different states, much biographical data and the whole set of information on recommendation patterns. Still, it may serve two purposes. First, it suggests tentatively some of the findings that may emerge from the full study: for instance, that within the impressive all-India uniformity of the Congress party there are revealing marginal differences between states or regions, and that the Congress elite may be changing character but doing so only quite gradually. Second, the sample may show how some of the concepts used earlier in the paper can be made operational: it may suggest some of the ways in which we can get closer to seeing recruitment as a process, especially as a process central to the expanding political world which each developing country contains.

# SINGLE-PARTY REGIMES AND POLITICAL CHANGE: THE P.D.C.I. AND IVORY COAST POLITICS

## MARTIN STANILAND

A lot is written about African politics, but not much is said, and increasingly little new is being said. The main reason for the prevalent banality and circularity is a lack of alertness to the concepts we use, to their origins and their implications. The flat inconsequentiality of the literature is due to a double negligence in usage: first, the negligence involved in adopting uncritically the rhetoric of governing elites, giving this rhetoric a kind of analytic mandate: secondly, the negligence involved in using familiar concepts of analysis without looking at their assumptions and connotations.

The widespread use of the term 'single-party regime' in studies of African politics is one consequence of this negligence. The term, on examination, has no analytic value or depth. In itself it is significant only for those concerned with formal structure or with official rhetoric: it is often invoked as a crucial feature of political life while in fact it tells us nothing about actual political behaviour and provides no clues as to how we might start to find out. The same formalism has projected itself into comparative studies of African states, resulting in barren typologies of parties ('moderate'/'radical', etc.). What is lacking is a satisfactory framework for analysing politics as such, a framework that would provide the concepts of discrete levels and phases necessary for the analysis of long-term adaptive change.

In this paper I have experimented with concepts of this kind and the main concepts are discussed below. The problem which concerns me is that of the atrophying of various styles of political expression which developed in the late colonial period: these political styles—populist, representative, and consultative—emerged in connection with an overall territorial movement, the P.D.C.I., better described as a nativist than as a nationalist movement. Those who led this movement have taken over the bureaucratic structure against which these styles of politics were directed: not only is the structure itself perpetuated intact, but its principles are in process of extension to the party and representative structures which previously embodied values of popular expression.[1]

---

[1] In the present essay I have limited myself to describing this process and to exploring some of the concepts needed to deal with it: in a larger work, entitled *Politics without parties*, I shall set out the elements of a theoretical model that seems relevant to analysing this problem of post-colonial politics.

## ARENAS AND LEVELS

In order to conceptualize the type of political change that has occurred in the Ivory Coast, it is necessary to envisage politics as taking place at a series of levels and within a number of arenas. We ought to establish what the formal levels of authority are in the legal order and then find out who gets what, against whom, from whom, and for what. Levels are thus derived from formal structure: they are identified by particular offices and jurisdictions. The status of arenas is different: an arena is a locus of competition for some prize and the identity of an arena depends upon the observation of active competition and of the rules governing it. Level is a concept arising from the study of authority distribution: arena is a concept arising from the study of political competition.

It is important to stress the completely different status of the two terms. It is necessary to know what the formal offices are because very often they are the prizes of an arena, very often the units prescribed by formal structure are participants (as groups) in competition, and sometimes the jurisdiction of a formal unit (e.g. a constituency) is identical to the boundary of an arena. But the concept of arena is originally and ultimately an observer's metaphor: it has no logical connection with the institutions established by the formal legal order. It is relevant where we find competition: it is useful because of the questions it suggests. Mainly it requires us to establish what are the really valued resources (the prizes), what are the acknowledged effective ways of getting them, and who is eligible to compete for them. We then begin to detect different behavioural rules in the areas studied which may affect the performance of roles which are formally identical from one area to another. Formally, a *sous-préfet* is a *sous-préfet*, but some *sous-préfets* behave like frontier sheriffs, others like developmental Jesuits, and others again like bureaucratic moles.

## RESOURCES

The concept of a 'political resource' is used often. A resource is, by definition, a 'means of supplying a want'. A political resource is simply one that is perceived as relevant by politicians and it is relevant in so far as it can satisfy a want related to a prize or prizes in a particular arena. Political resources may be acquired through exchanges, in which they are seen as serving the mutual satisfaction of compatible wants. They may be inherited or non-contractual ('My country right or wrong'); but here it is arguable that the clientele is still receiving a return for its support, though one that is spiritual or emotional, and there may in fact be limits to the deployment of these, as of other kinds of resource.

What is perceived as a resource is conditioned partly by formal structure, partly by the actual environment of the structure: you need votes to be a deputy (if only the votes of the local party officials), but in some places the help of the chiefs is a way of getting them, while in others the big planters must be with you. Politicians rise by perceiving and appropriating resources: they flourish by detecting discontinuities between levels and arenas, making themselves agents of exchange between them and denying such transactions to others.

### GROUPS, FACTIONS, AND PARTIES

The procedure suggested above is used to reinterpret various phases of decolonization in one territory in terms of relations and exchanges between levels and arenas, and to indicate in what ways political entrepreneurs sought, through exchanges, to mobilize resources from other arenas so as to appropriate resources in their own.

Whereas various types of political group have appeared in Ivoirien politics, 'party' is on the whole a term of limited utility in this connection. Formally, the P.D.C.I. is a political party: in some areas at some times it actually performed as such in the sense generally accepted, but in others it did not. It is important always to bear in mind conventional usage and its implications when applying the term to a group like the P.D.C.I. and to specify the arenas in which it was performing, according to this usage, as a party.

The conventional use of 'party' is sometimes relevant, sometimes not. The term normally refers to the party group at a particular level or in a given arena. But the party group may be active in an arena without performing as a party. Equally, the presence of open competition between parties is in no way a precondition for use of the term 'arena': as long as there is scarcity of resources, there is competition and it will take place in arenas as defined above. An arena may, of course, itself become a group in a wider arena, as when representatives of a district try to get development resources for their area.

If not as 'party', how do we describe the groups competing? The term 'faction' raises problems, because, like the term 'party', its use depends on being able to identify at least two such units. In the Ivory Coast, social categories, that from an early period were observable in the party, began to crystallize into factions with the advent of 'single-partyism'. However, one of these embryonic factions, that of the old militants, almost completely eliminated the other in the years 1959–63. As a result, there seems to be little active or coherent factionalism within the formal P.D.C.I. organization.

But the lack of factionalism may be seen less as a sign of remarkable internal unity than as a sign of the atrophying of the party organization. This process has been masked by the imposition of compulsory membership upon all members of the population. The competition that might have taken place within the formal party organization has been diffused into a wider social category, which we might call 'the political class', and which comprises the P.D.C.I. officials, young civil servants, and district administrators. There is an incipient pluralism within this elite which is producing tensions between the respective bureaucratic hierarchies of party and administration.

These tensions not only take place in arenas that are formally identical to those in which the party fought the colonial administration: they are, to a large extent, the same tensions. The façade of 'single-partyism' breaks down under scrutiny. We find that, on the one hand, the party at the beginning was never really a 'mass party' in the sense of a vast, unified nationalist front and, on the other, that the reality of central–district relations has not been greatly changed by independence. Decolonization was a distraction from the really competitive issues in the country's politics: the young versus the old, the centre versus the periphery.

The pre-independence period (1957–60) contributed to the working out of these issues, by establishing and entrenching a new territorial elite. But it now seems a less significant event than the early 'mobilization' phase, which promoted this elite and first brought it into dealings between the arenas, and the inheritance phase since 1960, which has brought the elite round to face its own clientele and assimilated it to the system of relations established under colonial government.

The bureaucratization of the P.D.C.I., the growth of friction within the elite, and the reappearance of parochialism are aspects of political indigenization, the creation of a regime adjusted to its environment. If we ask, for example, what the P.D.C.I. does in the districts and villages, the answer is more like the answer one would have got in 1947 or 1950 than in the years just before independence. The party leaders say that, as under the colonial regime, it represents the interests of the population in relation to the administration. Just as in 1947, the observer sees that these 'representational' activities are a substitute for wider political participation, that they are a form of adjudication within and between elites. No doubt politics is universally like this; but in the pre-independence period the single-party system was presented as a novel kind of political institution.

## INTERPRETATIONS

If we look at writing on late colonial and post-colonial politics in Africa, we can distinguish two fundamentally different lines of interpretation.

The first interpretation holds that there were mass movements demanding independence in post-war Africa; that the granting of independence was largely due to the pressure of such movements; that the leaders of them were above all concerned with obtaining independence from an unwilling colonial power and with 'integrating' recalcitrant sectional interests into a wider community, 'the nation'. After independence, these leaders were interested as well in raising everybody's living standards: ideologically, they were said to be democratic and egalitarian. Further, •these leaders represented a somewhat evangelical interest, called 'the forces of modernization', which were engaged in a rather heroic struggle with an opposed interest, 'traditionalism'. The modernizers belonged to the national movement, were mostly young, and they usually lived in towns. The traditionalists lived in the countryside and were often chiefs.

The second interpretation (which I prefer) holds that colonial development brought into existence an indigenous group, an elite, the members of which were identified by their assimilation of values promoted by the colonial power. When the coercive capacity of the latter was reduced by war, this group was able to secure a measure of political participation at the territorial level (that of the colony). In attempting to enlarge this participation, it found itself in conflict with colonial interests and resorted to a tactical politicization of arenas below the national level. The form that this politicization actually took was a reciprocal commitment of resources by individuals in the respective arenas. Since the content of the exchanges in question varied considerably, only the vaguest formulation of *general* goals was possible or desirable (rigid definition would have made it harder to get so much support). The contribution of the local political entrepreneurs was to mobilize every relevant resource in the local arenas that was not committed to the colonial structure. Considerations of restructuring either at the local levels (district or village) were incidental to the maximization of support and they were, ultimately, subordinate to the terms of exchange between the principals involved. Decolonization consisted of a bargain between a seriously weakened colonial autocracy and the local 'inheritance elite'.

The second position is, in fact, a compound position: elements of it can be found in the writings of Martin Kilson and in writers of the Left, notably Frantz Fanon.[1] The concepts of 'entrepreneurship' and 'arenas' occur widely in the works of F. G. Bailey, and the first particularly has been developed in the work of Fredrik Barth.[2] The first interpretation is that typically adopted by members of what we might call 'the nation-building school'. One reason for the language of this school being so pervasive is that it is the common property of both political rhetoricians in Africa and an influential group of political scientists working in the continent. The most common terms employed by the school are 'modernization',

[1] Martin Kilson, *Political change in a West African state. A study of the modernization process in Sierra Leone*, Cambridge, Mass. 1966; *Idem.*, 'African political change and the modernization process', *Journal of Modern African Studies* 1, 4 (1963), 425–40; Frantz Fanon, *The wretched of the earth*, London 1966.

[2] F. G. Bailey, *Tribe, caste and nation*, Manchester 1960; *Idem.*, *Politics and social change: Orissa in 1959*, Oxford 1963; Fredrik Barth, *The role of the entrepreneur in social change in northern Norway*, Oslo 1963, pp. 70–82.

'nation-building', 'national integration', and 'political development'. Because they embody a confusion (or an inseparable junction) of the usage of participants and the conceptual elements of analysis, these terms can be exceptionally manipulative in the context of academic discussion. I have, therefore, eliminated them from this paper and I suggest that their intellectual credentials should in future be seen as extremely dubious.

## THE CASE OF THE IVORY COAST

There are already detailed studies of the recent political history of the Ivory Coast by Aristide Zolberg and Ruth Schachter Morgenthau.[1] I shall concentrate here on political development *below* the territorial level, especially in the period of grass-roots mobilization (1948–50) and since independence, so as to evaluate the account given of district politics in the existing studies.

The *Parti Démocratique de Côte d'Ivoire* (P.D.C.I.) is the oldest surviving 'single party' in West Africa.[2] When the party was officially created in 1946, social and economic conditions in the Ivory Coast were broadly typical of the territories of the French West African federation, of which the Ivory Coast was a part. The economic structure of the colony was dominated by agriculture—mainly subsistence agriculture. An atypical feature of the economic structure, however, was its relatively large cash-crop sector. Development of this sector began with the plantation of cocoa before the First World War and after 1929 coffee was introduced on a large scale. To assist the extension of cash-crop production, the French administration supported the establishment of European planters and used pressure on local chiefs to provide labourers for them. By 1947 European planters were producing about 9 per cent of the colony's exports of coffee and cocoa (these crops making up some 49 per cent of the total tonnage exported from the Ivory Coast).[3]

The *per capita* net national income of the Ivory Coast in 1951 was over three times the average for the other territories of the federation, and, on the whole, its position, judged by the same gross and strictly economic indices, is still very much the same. The country's economy has also

---

[1] Ruth Schachter Morgenthau, *Political parties in French-speaking West Africa*, Oxford 1964, especially part five, 'Planters and politics in the Ivory Coast'; Aristide R. Zolberg, *One-party government in the Ivory Coast*, Princeton 1964. An important study of the Ivory Coast, mainly economic, is Samir Amin, *Le Développement du capitalisme en Côte d'Ivoire*, Paris 1967.

[2] It was founded in April 1946. The *Parti Progressiste Nigérien* was founded some time in 1946; the *Union Soudanaise* of Mali in November 1946; the *P.D.G.* of Guinea in May 1947 (Morgenthau, *Political parties*, pp. 225, 275, 317, 318; Virginia Thompson, 'Niger', in Gwendolen Carter (ed.), *National unity and regionalism in eight African states*, Ithaca 1966, p. 159).

[3] Territoire de la Côte d'Ivoire, Ministère du Plan, Service de la Statistique, *Inventaire économique de la Côte d'Ivoire 1947 à 1956*, Abidjan 1958, pp. 35–6, 90; Samir Amin, *Développement du capitalisme*, p. 73; République de Côte d'Ivoire, Conseil Economique et Social, *Rapport sur l'évolution économique et sociale de la Côte d'Ivoire 1960–1964*, Abidjan December 1965, pp. 21 ff.

done relatively better than the economies of some surrounding territories in terms of matching production to population growth as shown in table 1.

But these statistics do not show certain characteristics of the Ivoirien economic and social environment which are important to understanding the territory's political history—characteristics that the Ivory Coast has (or had until recently) in common with some of its neighbours.

Table 1.  *Percentage changes in agricultural output, 1952/3–1963/4*

|  | Total agricultural output | Total food production | Per capita agricultural output | Per capita food production |
|---|---|---|---|---|
| Ivory Coast | 100* | 80 | 57 | 47 |
| Senegal | 58 | 58 | 22 | 22 |
| Soudan–Mali | 26 | 22 | 3 | 0 |
| Guinea | 36 | 31 | 1 | −3 |
| Upper Volta | 18 | 17 | −2 | −3 |
| Dahomey | 18 | 16 | −9 | −11 |
| Niger | 80 | 78 | 37 | 36 |
| Togo | 27 | 19 | −7 | −12 |

* All figures represent percentage increases except where indicated.
Source: E.C.A., *Economic Survey of Africa, Vol. 1. Western Sub-Region-Republic of South Africa*, Addis Ababa 1966, p. 35.

One such characteristic is *inequality of income distribution*. The economic resources of the country, impressive in global terms, were and are distributed very unevenly, both between regions and between segments of the population. So, *per capita* monetary income in the north was calculated to range from 1,100 to 1,400 frs. C.F.A. in 1950 and from 1,300 to 5,200 frs. C.F.A. in 1965: in the plantation areas of the centre, the corresponding figures were 8,800 frs. in 1950 and 12,400 frs. in 1955: in the oldest areas of coffee- and cocoa-growing (in the east), they were 16,500 and 17,500 frs. The average cash income in the east is about five times that in the north.[1]

Concentrating on the cocoa and coffee regions, the moderate growth of incomes is explained by an extension in the number of planters subsequent to the abolition of forced labour in 1946. The latter decision resolved a crisis concerning the allocation of a scarce resource, labour, to the benefit of both the established African planters (who had reached the limits of possible expansion using only the labour of their kinsmen) and peasants who had been prevented from becoming cash-crop producers by administrative pressures on them to work for European planters.[2]

[1] Amin, *Développement du capitalisme*, pp. 290–2 (1,000 fr. C.F.A. = approx. £1 10s.).
[2] Ibid. p. 277. See also Claude Meillassoux, *Anthropologie économique des Gouros de Côte d'Ivoire*, Paris 1964, pp. 315–17, 319–20, and Morgenthau, *Political parties*, p. 178.

Since 1946, what has happened in this sector is that the category of small planters has grown, subject to land and labour being available. This expansion has involved the opening up of new areas rather than competition over land or intensification of production in areas of established plantation. In the same period, the older planters have enlarged their holdings, using wage-earning labourers (who are usually from the north). So, within a broader expansion which involved the induction of an additional 30 per cent of southern population into plantation agriculture, there was a consolidation of those already committed to it in 1945. This double process is illustrated by the figures for migrant workers. The number of migrant workers rose from 35,000 in 1950 to 120,000 in 1965; however, of the latter group, two-thirds were employed by the richer planters, who constituted one-fifth of the total planter category. The aggregate income of the larger planters trebled within 15 years from 2,300 million frs. C.F.A. to 7,600 million frs. C.F.A., an average annual income of 380,000 frs. C.F.A. each.[1]

As Samir Amin writes, 'A real planter bourgeoisie exists there, similar to those found in Ghana or in south-western Nigeria. This bourgeoisie, unlike its counterparts in the two Anglophone countries, is very new, since it was still embryonic in the years around 1950'.[2] Its members represented only 5·8 per cent of the entire planter category in 1950 as against 20 per cent in 1965 (in 1950 29·1 per cent of the total plantation revenue accrued to this richer group, as against 36·6 per cent in 1965).[3]

This economic environment was not one that is normally associated with the appearance of 'mass parties', although Ruth Schachter Morgenthau remarks that 'there was the basis for a mass party in Ivory Coast'.[4] The urban and rural middle class was very small: there were considerable differences of income level between regions and within some of them. The great majority of the population was still engaged principally in subsistence agriculture, with little experience of the world beyond the village. The conditions of economic development and the level of education and communications were unpropitious for the organization of an articulate 'mass' movement.

## LEVELS OF AUTHORITY

To understand how politicians operated within this context it is necessary to start by identifying levels. The six that seem to me most important are:

---

[1] For definitions of large and small planters used here, see Amin, *Développement du capitalisme*, pp. 84–5, 89–92, 290–3. See also Meillassoux, *Anthropologie économique*, pp. 315–17.

[2] Amin, *Développement du capitalisme*, p. 92.

[3] Ibid., pp. 292–3.

[4] Morgenthau, *Political parties*, p. 182: Cf. Zolberg (*One-party government*, p. 185): 'The P.D.C.I. emerged as an organization for the masses rather than as a mass organization.'

1. the level of the French Union
2. the French West African federal level
3. the territorial/national level
4. the district level (*cercle, subdivision, sous-préfecture*)
5. the canton level
6. the village level.

The leaders of the P.D.C.I. eventually sought roles at all six levels. We can ask in relation to each: What roles were available? What kinds of resources (including qualifications to occupy them) did politicians need in order to appropriate these roles?

### Village, canton, and district levels

For the great majority of Africans, these were probably the only ones that had immediate relevance. At the village level, the formal structure provided for a village chief (*chef de village*), chosen within the community and preferably within a traditional chiefly line: the village chief was dependent on the colonial administration for recognition of his tenure. Above the village chief was a canton chief (*chef de canton*), who was responsible for implementing colonial policies and maintaining the authority of colonial government. The qualifications for this post (which, unlike that of village chief, was salaried) were expressed loyalty to the administration and some degree of general education.[1]

At the district level, the formal structure provided for a territorial administrator (a role analogous to that of district officer and called, in the Ivory Coast, *chef de subdivision*—at the provincial level, *commandant de cercle*). This official, known colloquially as *commandant*, had wide formal powers as a general administrator, supervising other civil servants and chiefs, as well as controlling development programmes, taxation, and the police. He also presided over the customary tribunal and the *conseil de notables*, whose members were nominated by him and which had a consultative role. The *commandant* had to be a graduate of the appropriate metropolitan training school and was appointed by and responsible to the governor: in practice, the position of *commandant* was universally held by Europeans until 1956.[2]

For all these roles, candidates had to be acceptable to the colonial administration: only aspirants to village chieftancy were subject to formal approval by their subjects, and an advantage lay with those who had an inherited title to the office. Candidates for the position of canton chief

---

[1] See Robert Delavignette, *Freedom and authority in French West Africa*, London 1950, chapter V, 'The native chiefs'; L. Gray Cowan, *Local government in West Africa*, New York 1958, pp. 44–6, 172–85; F. J. Amon d'Aby, *Le Problème des chefferies traditionnelles en Côte d'Ivoire*, Abidjan 1958, first section, *De la chefferie traditionnelle à la chefferie administrative*.

[2] *Encyclopédie mensuelle d'outre-mer* 70 (juin 1956), 250, *L'africanisation des cadres en Côte d'Ivoire*. Six African civil servants were selected at this time to serve as assistants to *commandants de cercle*.

did not have to possess a traditional title but did need to have acquired a certain level of literacy and some grasp of administrative techniques. Until 1956 there was no provision (except in the few larger towns) for elected councils or communes.

## The territorial level

At the territorial level there was provision for an assembly with between forty-five and fifty members: originally this body was called the *conseil général* (from 1952 it was known as *assemblée territoriale*). Since the territory was regarded as an overseas department of France, this assembly corresponded broadly to the general council found in metropolitan departments—with the governor corresponding to a prefect, responsible only to his minister (in this case, the Minister of Overseas France). The assembly, as a local government body, did not therefore have legislative power in its own right; however, it did have powers of deliberation over a number of matters, including development programmes, loans, public works, levels of taxation, education, and the organization of the local civil service. Further, the territorial budget required the approval of the assembly.

However, the power of the assembly was restricted, first, by the exclusion from its budgetary control of as much as 70 per cent of the total which came under the heading of obligatory expenditure; secondly, by the lack of any right to supervise the public services directly; thirdly, by the non-accountability of the executive before the assembly.[1]

Until 1957 elections to the territorial assembly took place in two electoral colleges. The first college comprised metropolitan citizens plus the Africans who had previously acquired French citizenship (in 1946 there were only 3,836 such persons in the Ivory Coast and Upper Volta together):[2] the second college consisted of those citizens without French civil status (the entire remaining adult population) who could claim to be *notables évolués*, members or ex-members of officially recognized assemblies and voluntary associations, members of cooperatives or trade unions with 2 years' standing, public servants, ex-servicemen, chiefs, licensed traders, and planters, owners of real estate, certain other licence-holders, or literate in French and Arabic. In 1951–2 the franchise was extended to heads of households. In the Ivory Coast the voters so defined elected between twenty-seven and thirty-two of the assembly members, while the first college voters (numbering only about 4 per cent of the total electorate) controlled eighteen seats. There was no official member in the assembly.[3]

To be a candidate for one of these seats, a man had to be over 21 and without legal disability: he also needed, obviously, to be literate in French

[1] See Gray Cowan, *Local government in West Africa*, pp. 101–10, especially pp. 107–10; Morgenthau, *Political parties*, pp. 56–7; P. F. Gonidec, 'Les Assemblées locales des territoires d'Outre-Mer', *Revue Juridique et Politique de l'Union Française* VI (1952), 327–38; VII (1953), 443–91.
[2] Morgenthau, *Political parties*, p. 396.
[3] Gray Cowan, *Local government in West Africa*, pp. 101–5: Zolberg, *One-party government*, p. 87.

and to some extent experienced in politics and administration if he was to participate effectively.

Apart from places in the territorial assembly, the only elective positions in the territorial arena were in the municipal councils of Abidjan, Bouaké, and Grand Bassam—and these positions were not created until 1953. The other important roles in the arena were those of the executive: the governor, the secretary-general of the colony, the various heads of services. All of these offices were independent of representative bodies. All of them were occupied by members of the metropolitan career bureaucracy: as Zolberg remarks, 'Not a single Ivory Coast African occupied a decision-making position in the executive of his territory until after the Loi-Cadre reform of 1956'.[1] There were Africans in auxiliary posts: but their number was minute—as late as 1960 there were only forty-five Ivoirien administrative secretaries in the civil service.[2]

### Federal and French Union levels

The federal level was provided with institutions nearly identical to those on the territorial arena. There was a grand council, to which each territorial assembly sent five of its members: the powers of this council, and its relationship with the executive (headed by a governor-general) were identical to those of the local assemblies. Its budgetary role was similar, except that the federal council had to decide on reallocation between territories of the proceeds from indirect taxes.[3] The grand council was essentially an intermediary body, as the governor-general was essentially an intermediary official.

The formal structure of the French Union allotted roles to Ivoiriens as deputies in the national assembly, as senators, and as *conseillers de l'Union française*.

Effectively, two places as deputies were reserved for Ivoiriens. Those recruited had all the advantages of metropolitan deputies, including rights of immunity, access to ministers, and eligibility to join metropolitan parties and to become members of the government. The powers of the senate and the *assemblée de l'Union française* were small beside those of the national assembly, which legislated for the entire French Union: the prestige and actual influence attaching to membership of the former bodies were proportionately less.[4]

---

[1] Zolberg, *One-party government*, p. 101.

[2] Thirty-two of them had been trained at the École Normale William Ponty in Dakar and Sebikotane: the total output of civil servants (doctors, clerks, and school-teachers) from Ponty between 1918 and 1945 has been estimated at about 2,000—naturally, most were natives of the territories with more developed primary systems, such as Dahomey, Togo, and Senegal (*Journal Officiel de la République de Côte d'Ivoire*, 10 December 1960, pp. 1427–37: Morgenthau, *Political parties*, p. 13).

[3] Most of which were reserved for the federal budget, the territorial budget being supported by direct taxes only.

[4] See Morgenthau, *Political parties*, pp. 75–9.

There was also a difference in recruitment to these roles which tended to reinforce the authority of the deputies. The latter were elected directly by the voters of the territory (acting in this instance as a single college): the senators and the *conseillers de l'Union française* were elected indirectly, by the territorial assembly.[1] Although the electorate represented only one-eighth of the adult population, this difference in manner of selection gave the deputies a plebiscitary character the other Ivoirien *parlementaires* lacked.

### The participant's view

It is fairly obvious what, other things being equal, would be the relative attractions and problems of each of these levels to an Ivoirien politician.

There was an extremely narrow pyramid. At the top, there were opportunities to influence the politics of France and the entire French empire, opportunities to participate in legislating for and communicating with a public of some 117 millions; opportunities available, however, to only two Ivoiriens. As long as one accepted the structure as a whole, appropriation of these places was obviously a goal of high priority: what was needed to secure it was an organization capable of ensuring support from the electorate. Equally imperative was a campaigning strategy which not only contained appeals to the common interest of the categories making up the electorate but also included themes calculated to attract a wider support, among the non-enfranchised. Since the latter were not accessible electorally, they could be seen only as a latent resource, a reserve capacity, but one which could be used indirectly (that is as a net of moral pressure about the enfranchised).

The opportunities available at the federal level were not so enticing—especially since the grand council was involved in a reallocation of resources which was already, in 1946, seen as disadvantageous to the Ivory Coast.[2] Yet, participation in federal politics was the means of acquiring a share in common services (such as those dealing with communications and public health). Again, a potential resource could be discerned in this arena, i.e., the possibility of tactical alliances with representatives of other territories.

The territorial level offered places in the assembly: these could be seen as desirable to the end of securing a platform from which to exercise leverage on the administration. Such a base was all the more desirable since at the district, canton, and village levels access to all positions was closed to candidates who did not have the express approval of the administration. Further, it was reasonable to suppose that membership of the territorial

[1] In both cases non-members of the territorial assembly could be candidates: each college in the assembly elected its own allocation of senators, but the *conseillers de l'Union française* were elected by the assembly sitting as a single college.

[2] See Zolberg, *One-party government*, pp. 89–92; Morgenthau, *Political parties*, p. 115; William J. Foltz, *From French West Africa to the Mali Federation*, New Haven 1965, especially pp. 29–30.

assembly would provide scope for appropriating resources that could be exploited to add to electoral support in the district arenas.

## PHASES

The perspective outlined here may not, of course, have been consciously entertained by any Ivoirien politician; it is a logical derivation from the formal structure, to which the politician had to pay some attention—unless he was intent on destroying it from the outset. Since, in fact, the leadership of the P.D.C.I. never adopted any position that remotely approached one of complete rejection, I think this perspective can provide a useful focus of interpretation.

So regarded, the history of the P.D.C.I. can be envisaged as a series of phases, characterized by distinct strategic options. Each option required a particular deployment of resources in particular arenas. What sort of analytic label we attach to the P.D.C.I. depends on which phase and which arena we are looking at. There were four principal phases:

1. the phase of electoral mobilization and monopolization (1945–47)
2. the phase of 'militancy' and grass-roots politicization (1948–50)
3. the phase of territorial dyarchy (1951–60)
4. the phase of party bureaucratization (1960–68).

### The phase of electoral mobilization

The creation of the P.D.C.I. was directly consequent on institutional changes within the French Union. They provided opportunities—in elections, first, to the post-war French constituent assemblies, and, secondly, to the representative bodies set up in Paris, Dakar, and Abidjan under the Fourth Republic constitution—for Félix Houphouët-Boigny and his associates to create the first nucleus of an unofficial political association in the territory.

Their electoral organization began as an alliance of various voluntary associations: the most important (and that in which Houphouët himself first became prominent) was the *Syndicat Agricole Africain* (S.A.A.), a planters' cooperative, and others included ethnic associations (notably one representing the west and an expatriate Senegalese group), the teachers' union, and intellectuals' societies.

These groups, like many of the voters, were located in the towns: the electoral committee used ethnic associations and S.A.A. officials (some of whom were canton or village chiefs) to extend its control into the sub-arenas of district politics.[1]

The platform on which Houphouët was elected to the constituent

[1] See Zolberg, *One-party government*, pp. 70–1; Morgenthau, *Political parties*, pp. 178–9.

assemblies and, subsequently, to the national assembly consisted of demands for better educational facilities, larger state investment in public works, easier procedures for Africans to register land, improved conditions for salaried workers, greater participation by Africans in decision-making at the territorial level, the creation of more urban communes, citizenship for the *évolués*, and the abolition of forced labour.[1] All would have been well calculated to appeal to the electorate as constituted.

By the end of 1946, the Houphouët organization had occupied nearly all the roles available at the French Union, federal and territorial levels. Houphouët and his friend Ouezzin Coulibaly were the two deputies; three senators and three *conseillers de l'Union française* were P.D.C.I. nominees, as were three of the five representatives designated for the grand council in Dakar. Twenty-five of the twenty-seven college seats in the territorial assembly were taken by P.D.C.I. candidates, who received 87 per cent of the total vote.

Moreover, the party leadership had acquired substantial credit outside the electorate (and outside the territory), as a result of Houphouët's having got the forced-labour regime abolished. By emphasizing this question, the party leaders had ensured the attachment to their organization of the existing planters (who felt that voluntary recruitment was more likely to work in their favour than the old system, under which European planters had received preference) and those who had been prevented from becoming cash-crop farmers by recruitment for European-owned plantations. The party thereby augmented its 'reserve capacity' at the territorial level. The credit enjoyed by the P.D.C.I. as a result of the abolition of forced labour was realized with the founding of the R.D.A., an interterritorial federation of parties, which, as Aristide Zolberg has said, was 'an extension of the P.D.C.I. to the superterritorial level'.[2]

The main feature of political recruitment in this phase was that the number of people qualified for office was fairly small. Qualification was largely a matter of education or, at least, of literacy. The situation was paradoxical in several respects. Although by economic indices (of national income, cash-crop agriculture, etc.) the Ivory Coast was the richest West African colony, it had before and after the war a relatively underdeveloped educational system. In 1947 only 3·7 per cent of children of school age (6–15) were actually in school. In 1951 the percentage had increased to 10·6, but this figure was lower than those for poorer territories, such as Togo (29 per cent), Dahomey (15·4 per cent), Oubangui-Chari (12·6 per cent), and the Middle Congo (46 per cent).[3] The average age of

---

[1] Zolberg, *One-party government*, p. 72.

[2] Ibid., p. 108; Foltz, *From French West Africa to the Mali federation*, pp. 54–6.

[3] Service des Statistiques d'Outre-Mer, *Outre-Mer 1958*, p. 188; Virginia Thompson and Richard Adloff, *French West Africa*, London 1958, p. 523.

territorial assembly members in the Federation was 45:[1] for the Ivory Coast, the probable percentage of people with primary education in the age-group 41–43 in 1946 was 3·0, and this indicates that the available elite in Ivory Coast was relatively small. No doubt people were left out who were qualified technically and would have liked to be elected: this was evidently one source of the earliest rival grouping to the P.D.C.I., the 'Progressistes', who were led by educated Agni from the south-east. But, compared to the situations in Dahomey and Senegal, where more people had been educated earlier, there was little intra-elite competition in the Ivory Coast: in this sense, Houphouët was a beneficiary of the restrictions on educational and economic opportunity for Africans in the Ivory Coast. He could both keep control of selection to places and maintain an impressively high level of recruitment[2] while yet not provoking the appearance of rival political entrepreneurs in the arenas concerned. This phase, then, involved both the politicization of the available elite at the territorial level and the consolidation of Houphouët's leadership.

Although by the end of 1946 the number of African voters in the Ivory Coast had increased from 15,101 to 128,525, it is important to stress that during this phase the P.D.C.I. was *not* active in district, canton, and village arenas. Its activities were devoted to occupying the positions made available by the constitution at the territorial and higher levels. The P.D.C.I., like the *Syndicat Agricole Africain*, 'grew from the top down'.[3] The only grass-roots support it sought was that of the voters: and it used their support only at the territorial level, not in the grass-roots arenas. Its connection with the voters was often made indirectly, via officers of voluntary associations and local chiefs. The P.D.C.I.'s support also derived from the top in the sense that Houphouët had the active support of the territorial administration at this time. With a small electorate and such patrons, grass-roots organization was felt to be unnecessary: on the whole, there is no evidence in district archives of party branches at this level before 1948.

It is important to stress these points because the very success of Houphouët in releasing the peasants from forced labour can obscure how little he actually proposed to give them in the way of formal political participation, as reference to his programme quoted above will reveal. He did *not* demand such reforms as the election of chiefs (he was himself a canton chief, like his friend, the late Léon M'Ba of Gabon), the creation of elected councils or *rural* communes, or changes in the structure of district administration. (How far, indeed, did Kwame Nkrumah, another

---

[1] Morgenthau, *Political parties*, pp. 401–11.

[2] Twenty-one members of the territorial assembly elected in 1947 were Ponty graduates (Morgenthau, *Political parties*, p. 402).

[3] Zolberg, *One-party government*, p. 67.

L

hero of liberation, ever make such demands?) Nor, at this stage, was Houphouët asking for universal suffrage: and, while his party got a high proportion of the votes of the total electorate, this is not indicative of 'mass support'.[1] On my calculation, the largest proportion of the population that voted for the party in this period was 3·4 per cent (in November 1946). Perhaps it would be better not to use the term 'mass party' unless it can be made clear whether it denotes some kind of verifiable reality and unless one can specify which (or whose) mass it is the party of.

### The 'militant' phase

It is in this phase that analysis becomes most seriously entangled with party mythology. It is certainly true that between 1948 and 1951 the leaders of the P.D.C.I. and the French administration in the Ivory Coast were mutually hostile; that public disturbances occurred in various places, as a result of which at least fifty-two people died, several hundred were injured, and large numbers were arrested. It is also true that the administration regarded this confrontation as one between itself and a Communist-inspired subversive movement; the official position of the P.D.C.I., for its part, was (and is) that it was 'a stage of combat, against an oppressive system' (colonialism). Philippe Yacé, the secretary-general of the party, recounted the official myth at the 1965 congress:

The goals and principles of the R.D.A. were to be exactly the same as those of the P.D.C.I., namely: the emancipation of our respective countries from the colonial yoke by the assertion of their political, economic, social, and cultural personalities, and their voluntary participation in a congress of nations and peoples...The means of achieving these goals were to be a widely based union, comprehending all ideological positions, all tribes, people of all social stations, and solidarity between the various countries engaged in the struggle.[2]

But the true significance of the period must be construed through questions about the location and substance of the conflict. Where did it really originate? In which arenas did it take place? What were the issues and were they the same in every arena? We must assess the mythology in relation to the answers to these questions.

First, it is clear enough that the opposition between the P.D.C.I. and the administration was at the French Union, federal and territorial levels (and in that order): it was *not* originally in district or village politics, although there were cleavages at these levels and these cleavages were subsequently aligned to the cleavage in the wider arenas. In a sense, the location of conflict was determined by the formal structure, as were the

[1] On the P.D.C.I. as a 'mass party', see Morgenthau, *Political parties*, chapter IX, *Towards one party states*.
[2] République de Côte d'Ivoire, Ministère de l'Information, *IVᵉ Congrès PDCI–RDA, 23–24–25 septembre 1965, Rapport moral du Secrétaire General du Parti*, pp. 25 and 46; see Zolberg, *One-party government*, p. 110.

hierarchy of opportunity and arenas of activity described previously. Once the P.D.C.I. had taken over the elective places allocated by the 1946 constitution, it became obvious how closely the constitutional hierarchy, once accepted, conditioned the forms of political organization adopted by participants. Despite a theoretical control by the territorial party over the *parlementaires*, so great were the advantages of the latter, especially of the deputies, over mere territorial politicians that in reality the locus of control was transferred to Paris.

Just as the party hung on the prestige of the deputy, so it inherited the deputy's enemies. Thus, Houphouët became involved in the party system in France, by allying with the Communist party: the R.D.A. accepted this affiliation: so did the territorial P.D.C.I. At first, this did not imply confronting the administration, since the P.C.F. was at the time (1945) a governmental party. But after the P.C.F. was expelled from government in 1947, the costs of the deputies' engagement became felt, and were felt more severely in the lower than the higher levels of the structure. The ultimate cause of conflict was the deputies' choice of party in 1945: as Aristide Zolberg says: 'The French government viewed the Ivory Coast, the bastion of the R.D.A., as another skirmish in its own Battle of Prague.'[1] Houphouët remarked that once the Communists left the government,

we were regarded as enemies of the regime. We were under attack, it was said, not because of our struggle for rights, which was seen as legitimate, within the framework of the Republic and the French Union, but simply because of our connection with the Communist group and our systematic opposition to the successive governments of the Republic...We never accepted the Communists' ideology. Not one of us ever preached class warfare in Africa or the redistribution of land, etc.

Every time we experienced set-backs in parliament, the majority of our African colleagues held us responsible, by reason of our opposition to the government and our co-operation with the P.C.F.[2]

In November 1948 Laurent Péchoux was appointed as governor, with orders to break the party.[3] Houphouët and the other R.D.A. leaders reacted by confirming their loyalty to the P.C.F. alliance and using the latter to develop the P.D.C.I.'s organizational structure. Formally, the hierarchy was to include P.D.C.I. committees in each village (or each *quartier* of the towns) and a *sous-section* at the district level, with a general secretary elected by the village representatives. The *sous-sections* would send delegates to annual congresses, which would determine policy and elect the *comité directeur* of the party; within the *comité directeur* a core group,

---

[1] Zolberg, *One-party government*, pp. 109–10.

[2] *Discours prononcé par M. le Député HOUPHOUET à ABIDJAN au cours d'une réunion tenue le 6 octobre 1951 au Stade GEO ANDRE* (manuscript).

[3] Morgenthau, *Political parties*, p. 188 and (for explicit orders of the same kind to his predecessor) p. 91.

the *bureau politique*, would be formed with a secretary-general presiding over it.

The decision to set up 'an all-encompassing mass organization' was made in response to criticisms by the P.C.F. that the P.D.C.I. was excessively urban-based.[1] The way the party worked diverged substantially from its official structure: in towns the ethnic associations continued as the cells of the party, while in the rural districts it seems that village committees were as often nominated (by *sous-section* officials and notables in the community) as elected. The composition of the *sous-section* bureaux was equally subject to improvisation: '...the *sous-section* became a sort of caucus of the original type, with a membership made up of representatives of the various ethnic groups that make up the town and its environs'.[2] In some places, general secretaries were appointed by decision of the *comité directeur*.

This failure of internal democracy at the district level necessarily undermined the provision for control at higher levels: whereas P.D.C.I. congresses were theoretically to be annual, in practice only four congresses have ever been held (in 1947, 1949, 1959, and 1965). Consequently, there has been almost complete immobility in the tenure of party offices (except for changes caused by personal circumstances and death).

However much P.D.C.I. leaders emphasize the grass-roots context of the militant period, historically the evidence would support an opposed hypothesis, one of deliberate involvement of people at the district level by leaders of a party at the territorial level in a conflict which originated at a still higher level. This period is described by people in the districts as 'le temps de politique' or 'pendant le mouvement politique': this suggests that their involvement was both abnormal and temporary. From this point of view, there was not a coherent, territorial, anti-colonial movement, but rather a series of emergency excursions into district politics by territorial entrepreneurs. The immediate (if not the only) purpose of this expedition was to mobilize enough resources in the grass-roots arenas to keep the P.D.C.I. team going in the territorial arena. The activities which the expedition provoked might well (ideally, would) involve the expression of local grievances, but they were not necessarily connected in the minds of those who instigated them with any more long-term strategy. Nor did they necessarily imply any wish to restructure fundamentally institutions at the grass-roots level, much less to facilitate entry into territorial arenas by what it pleases Ivoirien politicians to call 'la population'. For, as Martin Kilson remarks on the same phase in Sierra Leone,

nationalist myths to the contrary notwithstanding, there is no necessary harmony of interests between African elite groups and mass elements during colonial political change...No doubt there were periods when a relative harmony of

[1] Zolberg, *One-party government*, pp. 116–17.
[2] *Ibid.*

interests between these groups prevailed. But analysis of the different way in which colonial change affected elites and masses at different periods strongly suggests the unlikelihood of any automatic or universal harmony of interests between these groups.[1]

To show why I find this interpretation of the repression period more credible than the interpretations put about by the P.D.C.I. and the theorists of mass party nationalism, I should, of course, translate it and the others into questions to which evidence can be adduced.

The questions that seem appropriate are first those about *recruitment* (what kinds of people were active and prominent in party *soussections* and village committees?); secondly about *activities and demands* (in what ways was the party active? What demands did its members make? To whom were these demands addressed?); and thirdly about *conflict and opposition* (who was attacked by the party? What kinds of group were systematically opposed to the party?).

A basic issue here is how far party activities in one locality were repeated in other localities. I have therefore drawn on material from three districts in the Ivory Coast. The first district, Bongouanou, is in the old coffee- and cocoa-planting area of the south-east: it is peopled mainly by the Agni, a matrilineal group related to the Ashanti of Ghana and characterized by a highly structured chieftaincy system. The second district, Bouaflé, is on the border between the forest and the savannah: there are two major ethnic groups, the Gouro (who have a patrilineal, virtually acephalous social structure) and the Baoulé (an Akan group related to the Agni, though with a rather less rigid chieftaincy structure). The third district, Katiola, is in the orchard savannah: the population are nearly all Tagouana, a patrilineal group related to the Sénoufo, with chiefs at village and canton level and very limited cash-crop resources. In each district there are stranger groups: in Bouaflé and Bongouanou there are migrant labourers and northern traders (*dioulas*); in Katiola only a very small number of *dioulas*. The material is drawn from administrative archives and information provided by local party officials, chiefs, and others.[2]

The problem about discussing support and recruitment is that the first term is so hazy as an item of verification and the second provides only limited information about the social following of the party. How, after all, does one demonstrate support in a situation of narrow enfranchisement? Votes themselves are difficult enough to interpret: apart from

[1] Martin Kilson, *Political change in a West African state*, p. 191.

[2] On Bongouanou, see J.-L. Boutillier, *Bongouanou, Côte d'Ivoire: étude sociologique d'une subdivision*, Paris 1960; F. J. Amon d'Aby, *Croyances religieuses et coutumes juridiques des Agni de la Côte d'Ivoire*, Paris 1960. On Bouaflé, see Meillassoux, *Anthropologie économique des Gouros*; L. Tauxier, *Nègres gouro et gagou*, Paris 1924. On Katiola, see B. Holas, *Les Sénoufo (y compris les Minianka)*, Paris 1957; R. P. Clamens, 'Essai de grammaire sénoufo-tagouana', *Bulletin de l'I.F.A.N.*, XIV, 4 (1952), 1403–65 (this contains apparently the only published account of specifically Tagouana social structure).

voting, politics in colonial situations tends to take forms that are ambiguous and diffuse in meaning (such as riots, demonstrations, and sabotage) or (for analytic purposes) rather negative (such as tax-strikes).

However, the literature on 'national movements' provides four typical answers to the question: Who supported the party? The answers are not mutually exclusive; they are simply propositions, emphasizing particular sources of support, to be investigated, modified, eliminated, or combined. They are:

1. *The ethnic hypothesis:* that the party was mainly a vehicle for the expression of one ethnic group. In this case it has been argued that the P.D.C.I. was substantially controlled by the Baoulé, that the Agni and Bété groups tended to be dissident from the P.D.C.I. 'at least in part because of historic disagreements with neighbouring tribes'.[1]

Although the P.D.C.I. received strong electoral support in Baoulé areas, it did so also in the Gouro division of Bouaflé and in Katiola (Sénoufo). In Bongouanou (Agni), there was an active rival party (the *Progressistes*) which was closely related, in leadership, to an ethnic association. The leadership of the P.D.C.I. in Bongouanou, as elsewhere, was varied in its ethnic origins: most of the members of the *sous-section*'s bureau were local. Dioulas from Mali and the north were prominent, as they were in other districts.[2] It would be difficult to establish that specifically ethnic sentiments were responsible for the emergence of a rival party in Bongouanou or anywhere else.

2. *The 'modern young man' hypothesis:* that the party was mainly a vehicle of younger men discontented with traditional forms of social and political control and anxious to assert their own (educational and economic) resources within politics. This is a general hypothesis about 'national movements': it usually occurs in association with the hypothesis that such movements were systematically opposed to the colonial administration and its agents.

Many of the local R.D.A. leaders, particularly at the district level, were between 18 and 30 and in two of the three areas studied there were youth associations which were identified (by the administration) with the party.[3] But at village level, party representatives seem to have been of all

---

[1] Morgenthau, *Political parties*, p. 184.

[2] But Dioula families were sometimes split politically—as in the case of one Dioula family in Bouaflé, in which the eldest brother was in the bureau of the P.D.C.I. while the second, *A*, was in the opposing *Entente des indépendants de la Côte d'Ivoire* (Subdivision de Bouaflé, *Rapport politique, 1947*, 28 April 1948; personal communications).

[3] In 1947 at Bongouanou it was reported that: '...dans les villages les plus importants...des Sociétés de jeunesse se constituent'. By 1949 it was noted that: '...les Sociétés de jeunesse... étaient passées sous la bannière RDA'. At Bouaflé in 1950: 'Des groupements de jeunes ont commencé à s'organiser...Leur origine est manifestement RDA.'

ages: there was a sufficiently large number of older men in the district bureaux to make it absurd to speak of the P.D.C.I. as a 'young man's' party. Though there were many young men involved (as there would be in most active political organizations), their participation in P.D.C.I. activities varied greatly from one area to another.

The related hypothesis is equally invalid. Both 'traditional' and 'administrative' chiefs were among the party's leaders: at Bongouanou two tribal chiefs and two village chiefs were cited as P.D.C.I. militants.[1] At Bouaflé the situation was more clear-cut, with most of the chiefs opposed to the party; but the canton chief most admired by the administration was as opposed to the administratively backed *Progressistes* as to the P.D.C.I.[2] At Katiola the principal canton chief lost part of his salary for helping the R.D.A. and a second canton chief was an active supporter of the party.

In no case is either hypothesis completely irrelevant; but neither hypothesis provides a sufficient basis for an account of political development in any district, much less in all three.

3. *The 'administrative' hypothesis:* by this I mean the familiar notion of 'a small minority of troublemakers'. In this context it tends to postulate a confederation of deviants and foreigners.

This view was apparently taken in many Ivory Coast residences. The *chef de subdivision* at Bouaflé, for instance, described the P.D.C.I. as, 'the party of malcontents...any man who is dissatisfied with a legal decision, any sacked roadsweeper, any cuckolded husband who has been unable to recover his wife, etc.'[3] Classically, the troublemakers were identified as young and half-educated: 'a clientele of young self-styled *évolués*, of the ambitious, the embittered and all who have had trouble with the administration and the law'.[4] In fact, only a very small minority had any criminal record. In any case, as a sociological explanation of the P.D.C.I.'s opposition to the administration this hypothesis was rather circular: those who led parties opposed by the administration tended to acquire prison sentences anyway.

The administrators usually argued also that outsiders were largely

---

[1] One *chef de tribu* was dismissed by the administration in 1950: when the other died, the *chef de subdivision* recorded that, '...il avait...un pouvoir incontesté sur les six villages de sa tribu, pouvoir qu'il avait mis au service du RDA' (letters of *chef de subdivision*, Bongouanou, to Commandant de Cercle, Dimbokro, 2 August 1948, 15 July 1950 (62/C), and 11 November 1951).
[2] Subdivision de Bouaflé, *Rapport annuel, 1949.*
[3] Ibid.
[4] Subdivision de Bouaflé, *Rapport politique, 1947,* 28 April 1948.

---

At Katiola such activity seems to have been very reduced: a *Jeunesse R.D.A.* appeared only in 1956 (Subdivision de Bongouanou, *Rapport mensuel,* April 1947, p. 1, and draft on *Situation politique dans la subdivision,* 1949; Subdivision de Bouaflé, *Rapport annuel, 1950.*)

responsible (the *dioulas* and French communists especially).[1] Remove them and the actual indifference of the African to politics would quickly be revealed: 'He will go back to his round hut, to his interminable palavers about women and hunting round a pot of palm-wine, saying to himself: "All that be White-man's way", and politics will have no more hold over him than Catholicism, or Islam, health education or strictures on the moral value of labour.'[2] Although the *dioulas* were conspicuous, they did not monopolize the leadership anywhere: there was local support, generated by local issues.

4. *The 'middle class nationalist' hypothesis:* that the party was a vehicle of the class interests of a 'rising bourgeoisie'.

Among those who led the P.D.C.I. at district level there were planters, merchants, and teachers, to name only three categories that might be considered indicative of 'middle-class' support. But it is extremely difficult to establish the validity of any hypothesis involving the prevalence of a sectional interest, for various reasons. First, there is the lack of suitable data—data indicating the political attitudes of any large number of people in anything more than the grossest way. There is no evidence that in areas of relatively advanced cash-crop production the P.D.C.I. was simply the party of the rich planters.

It is impossible to devise one hypothesis that will account for P.D.C.I. 'support' in all of the areas studied. This becomes very clear if we look at the data concerning the activities and demands promoted by the party, and especially if we look at the conflicts in which it was involved. Two broad statements can be made in this connection. The first is that, whilst there was a basic similarity in actual organization from one area to another, the positions taken up by district party leaders on particular issues differed greatly. The second is that there seems to be a correlation between the degree of conflict in which the party was involved (as well as the intensity of party activity) and the level of economic development.

Both statements can be well illustrated by taking the question of chieftaincy. In one area (Katiola) there appears to have been relatively little trouble between the party and the chiefs: the chiefs, in consultation with other village elders, nominated party delegates from the villages. But then in Katiola there was apparently little trouble of any sort, little party activity or political conflict of the kind manifested elsewhere

---

[1] Bongouanou 'est une subdivision qui, si elle était livrée à elle même, resterait toujours calme; malheureusement la richesse et la crédulité de ses habitants y attirent fréquemment des trublions de tous ordres' (Subdivision de Bongouanou, *Rapport politique annuel, année 1950*, p. 9): while at Bouaflé,'...les militants locaux...ne peuvent avoir une clientèle que s'ils sont considérés comme les délégués ou les adjoints du chef suprême "HOUPHOUET"' (Subdivision de Bouaflé, *Rapport politique, 1947*, 28 April 1948); '...les mots d'ordre sont venus de l'extérieur de la subdivision "au nom d'Houphouet"' (*ibid.*).

[2] Subdivision de Bouaflé, *Rapport politique, 1947.*

in demonstrations, burning of property, violence, or incidents with the authorities. In Bouaflé the party was involved in attacks on the two main canton chiefs: village chiefs were driven out and party tribunals set up in their place. It seems that the actual institution of chieftaincy was under attack by the party, as well as the colonial authority which was seen as having imposed it, at least on the Gouro. There were no chiefs of any kind in the party bureau. There was conflict not only with the chiefs, but directly with a fairly repressive colonial administration,[1] with opposing parties, and with cash-crop intermediaries.

In Bongouanou the violence was just as intense and more extensive: villages split in half, large numbers of people were hurt and others left the area. On several occasions troops were called in. Yet, as regards chieftaincy, the alignment of conflict was quite different from that in Bouaflé. The main complaint of party officials was that the administration had interfered with succession; factions within villages were formed around rival candidates.

To show how far the positions of the 'territorial' party diverged to accommodate particular situations at the district level, one can juxtapose two statements concerning chieftaincy. At Bouaflé it was reported that the P.D.C.I. delegate, F. Kouamé, had visited one of the Gouro cantons: '...during his tour he said that all men were equal, that authority no longer existed, that the canton chief had gone too far and they would name other people to administer justice'.[2]

M. Kouamé remarked that an R.D.A. delegate might take the place of the canton chief, and that the P.D.C.I. general secretary would become *chef de subdivision*.[3] At Bongouanou the tone of a speech by Houphouët-Boigny was different:

The nomination of chiefs is your affair, not that of the administration which has no part in it...The chiefs should fall in with the party, they will become rich and happy, those who fail to do so will be doomed to misery...Don't be scared of being put in prison, you will get out all right and may become canton or village chiefs...I would like to pay the chiefs but the administration blocks the idea.[4]

---

[1] Accounts of African national movements seem to me to pay too little attention to the attitudes and resources of local administrators which in this case are regarded by observers and participants as having been important in determining variations in the militancy and following of the party. The political status of the P.D.C.I. appears in quite a different light when one reads administrative reports and sees how undermanned and poverty-stricken the local administration actually was. Its repressive *capacity* (to take only one resource) was quite a different thing from its attitudes and ambitions. Also, the myth of the mass party is often illuminated by comparing accounts of local observers with the *ad hoc, post hoc* rationalizations of administrators caught unawares.

[2] Assemblée Nationale (France), *Rapport fait au nom de la commission chargée d'enquêter sur les incidents survenus en Côte d'Ivoire* (Annexe No. 11348 of 21 November 1950), III, 886.

[3] *Ibid.*, p. 887.

[4] Reported in letter of *chef de subdivision*, Bongouanou, to *commandant de cercle*, Dimbokro, 3 February 1949.

There were similar differences between districts on such questions as tax-payment and the use of administrative facilities (such as schools and maternity hospitals). What is important is to stress the implications of this discussion for research strategy. The main implication is that in order to analyse politics, in situations such as those described here, it is essential, once we have identified the arenas involved, to treat each as analytically distinct in terms of political culture and behaviour. We must refrain from introducing concepts drawn from other arenas (e.g. nationalism, the anti-colonial struggle) or dichotomies drawn from 'grand theory' (such as that between traditionalism and modernity) until we have explored the connections between political, social, and economic structures in the arena studied and satisfied ourselves of their relevance and meaning within that context.

The differences in P.D.C.I. attitudes towards chieftaincy, for example, become much more intelligible when we investigate local family and pre-colonial political structures and the effects on them of cash-cropping. Hostility to chiefs in Bouaflé can be related to the pre-colonial acephalous political structure of the Gouro and to the scarcity of forest suitable for coffee-growing. The chiefs created by the French were in a position to expropriate and sell large areas of forest to the disadvantage of aspirant village planters. It happened that most of the forest available lay within Gouro areas of the district and one finds that party hostility was concentrated against those Gouro chiefs who had access to the largest concentrations of forest. There is almost no evidence of hostility to Baoulé chiefs, whose villages were located in the savannah area of the *subdivision*, although they were as much agents of the colonial power as, and certainly more 'traditional' than, their Gouro counterparts (and should therefore have been equally loathsome if we accept the anti-traditionalist or anti-colonial hypotheses).

The problem of chieftaincy in Bongouanou was related to the desire of junior heirs to thrones (stools) who had become successful planters to assert their economic autonomy in political terms. Thus an administrative report notes, in analysing the situation of five large villages where fission occurred, that 'the R.D.A. representative in four of these five cases is an influential notable, head of a compound, who covets the position of the village chief'.[1] 'Modern' and 'traditional' resources were involved here, but neither the party nor its opponents had a monopoly of either. Youth and education did not have any *immediate* relevance to explaining party support.

I have discussed the phase of grass-roots politicization at some length

---

[1] Letter of *chef de subdivision*, Bongouanou, to governor, 14 June 1951. A very pertinent study of parties in this type of traditional context is David E. Apter, 'The role of traditionalism in the political modernization of Ghana and Uganda', *World Politics* XIII, 1 (October 1960), pp. 45–68.

because it was in this phase that the most overt political conflict took place in district arenas. Such conflict provided the resources with which P.D.C.I. militants (and their rivals) acquired their entrepreneurial roles as well as their followers. An examination of this phase is also essential to understanding the basis of one of the two groups which are typically present in post-independence district politics.

### The phase of territorial dyarchy

The third phase began after Houphouët broke the connection between the P.D.C.I. and the French Communists in 1950.[1] Thereafter he stressed the normative theme, 'Co-operation with France for the economic betterment of all'. He consolidated his own resources within the French Union arena and gradually reacquired control at the territorial level—a control which had been severely impaired by the opposition of the French administration.

In order to appease the latter, however, he had to dampen militancy in the district arenas and to deny the ambitions of many local entrepreneurs, who expected that their loyalty to the old normative theme, 'Liberation from the colonial yoke', would be rewarded by election to the territorial assembly, etc.[2] Instead, after 1951 the rules for entry into the territorial arena emphasized economic and, particularly, educational qualifications. At the district level there was some delay before the local P.D.C.I. assimilated the abrupt redirection from above. At first the party leadership tried to represent it as a mere tactical ruse,[3] then the actual party structure began to change. In those districts where there had been genuine social and economic conflict *within an arena*, the moderates allied themselves to the administration and tried to remove the causes, where possible by the use of administrative resources. As a corollary the activity of the party *sous-sections* tended to atrophy and the more radically anti-colonial of the leaders tended to withdraw from public life.

The obvious problem here is to account for the ability of Houphouët to impose this realignment and at the same time to draw his rivals into the new union. A considerable part of the explanation is probably to be found in the willingness of the French administration to inject very large amounts of public investment into rural development, in a territory which had previously been considerably deprived. The administration became, as

---

[1] See Zolberg, *One-party government*, pp. 135-9: for an account of the third phase, see *ibid.*, chapter V, 'Union for development'.

[2] Zolberg, *One-party government*, p. 154; also Morgenthau, *Political parties*, p. 205.

[3] The *chef de subdivision* of Bouaflé, remarked: 'le "discours d'Abidjan" n'a été connu que par mes soins et la réaction ne s'est pas faite attendre: les adhérents RDA admettent le noirement mais y voient une manœuvre habile pour supprimer l'opposition' (Subdivision de Bouaflé, *Rapport politique, 1951*). Similarly at Bongouanou: 'Ce n'est que fin novembre 1951 que la nouvelle politique du parti a commencé à se faire jour dans la Subdivision; cette politique qui préconise la non-violence et le respect aux autorités désappointe vivement l'aile marchante du parti qui demeure toutefois fermement persuadée qu'il ne s'agit là que d'une ruse de guerre' Subdivision de Bongouanou, *Rapport politique annuel, année 1951*, p. 5).

Zolberg remarks, 'less a gendarme than an agency for education and for development'.[1] The actual resources were, however, mainly drawn from the local budget and this was possible because of high coffee prices between 1950 and 1954.[2]

Even when the scarce resources were not of a kind to be increased by the administration (such as forest), the development resources provided by the administration—such as schools—were sufficient to confine political disturbances to very limited areas. Simultaneously the attractions of public office became greater (because of the increase in resources at the *territorial* level) and, conversely, the deprivation involved in falling 'from grace to grass' became greater. Most politicians in this situation seem to have decided that their options were to comply with the new rules or to withdraw, as some did. There was no sign of a challenge to Houphouët.

Once the district politicians accepted the new rules, the problem of competition at the territorial level was a relatively minor one, since the number of people eligible under the rules was still fairly small and nearly everybody could be accommodated. The problem for Houphouët, then as now, was not how to deal with other parties of the elite at the territorial level: it was how to ensure that he could regulate movement from one level to another, as well as the allocation of resources between them. Of course, a thousand candidates might still put themselves forward for the National Assembly, as is said to have been the case in 1959.[3] But this deluge of candidates strengthened Houphouët's role as arbitrator, and allowed him to enforce his rules about educational and economic background more strictly.

There was, in fact, an overall shift in relations between levels of which changes in party recruitment were only one aspect. The more the territorial leadership of the P.D.C.I. gained control of increasingly large administrative resources, the more they could disregard individual political entrepreneurs in the districts upon whom they had relied earlier. As the leverage that could be applied individually by such entrepreneurs decreased, so did their collective capacity to get the kinds of structural reforms (administrative decentralization, the setting-up of local councils) which would have given them new platforms from which to assert themselves. As we shall see, the district caucuses were not anxious for such reforms, because of fear that they might be evicted from elective councils by the *jeunesse*.

Thus while most districts acquired substantial benefits in terms of schools, roads, credits, etc. between 1950 and 1960, they had exactly the same political institutions at the end of the decade as at the beginning

---

[1] Zolberg, *One-party government*, p. 171.

[2] The value of coffee exported (in millions fr. C.F.A.) was as follows: 1948, 2,501·8; 1949, 4,068·4; 1950, 6,675·1; 1951, 9,129·2; 1952, 10,619·9; 1953, 8,947·5; 1954, 16,491·3 (*Inventaire économique de la Côte d'Ivoire, 1947 à 1956*, p. 90).

[3] Zolberg, *One-party government*, p. 273.

(except that universal suffrage had been granted for territorial and departmental elections).[1] Although as a long-term goal *canton* chiefs were to be abolished, in many areas this seems in the short term only to have strengthened *village* chiefs as they became direct intermediaries with the administration. A provision for rural communes in the decrees applying the *loi-cadre* of 1957 was blocked at the territorial level by the argument that 'the people are not mature enough politically'. The district administration system was almost identical in 1960 (and in 1967) to that in force in 1950: the only change was a reduction in the typical size of the administrative unit. Since this unit was also the unit within which the party *sous-sections, conseils de notables*, etc., operated, the change, while facilitating some bureaucratic procedures, had the effect of trivializing even further the scope of the local politicians and reducing the leverage they could apply.[2]

Besides eliminating some of the grass-roots 'militants de la première heure', the insistence on giving equal rights to all educated men in recruiting to territorial positions led to the reconciliation of the party leadership with members of the elite who had joined rival parties during the second phase. This process of reconciliation was most noticeable at district level and particularly in those districts where some of the more prominent chiefs, planters, or civil servants had had post-primary education. How easily and quickly ex-opponents were accepted varied a great deal between districts: in Bongouanou the division at village level continued in some cases until at least 1957 and in a few until very recently.

In most districts there were two phases in the reconciliation. The first was a phase during which the old opponents made peace with the party. Sometimes there were 'mutual defence' alliances between individuals alienated from the party, as well as support-maximizing pacts that seem to have taken no account of theoretical dichotomies between, for example, 'traditionalists' and 'modernizers'. Thus at Bouaflé, *A*, who had been a fairly virulent enemy of the P.D.C.I., first set out to make peace with Houphouët. He was a graduate of the École William Ponty in Dakar and a senior civil servant and both things qualified him to participate in the 'union for development' phase. Within the district he made two significant allies: one was a Baoulé canton chief (also a Ponty graduate) who was regarded as a *Progressiste* by the local P.D.C.I., the other an aspirant canton

---

[1] After departments, on the French pattern, were set up in 1959, there were elected four *conseils généraux*. In practice they have never met: there are as yet no departmental budgets and the post of *conseiller général* is at present purely honorific. The details of the official structure are set out in the Loi 61–84 of 10 April 1961.

[2] The district administration system of the Ivory Coast is described in M. J. Campbell, T. G. Brierly, and L. F. Blitz, *The structure of local government in West Africa*, The Hague 1965; T. G. Brierly, 'The evolution of local administration in French-speaking West Africa', *Journal of Local Administration Overseas* V, 1 (January 1966), 56–68; and in my articles, entitled 'Local administration in Ivory Coast', in *West Africa*, no. 2649, 9 March 1968, p. 273, and no. 2650, 16 March 1968, p. 315.

chief and a relation of Houphouët. *A* was elected to represent his *cercle* in the territorial assembly with the help of votes secured by these notables, whose positions were subsequently eased and advanced (respectively) through *A*'s intervention with the administration.

In the second phase, the militants' control of the district arena was challenged by the appearance of more young people with post-primary education. Since the younger men on the whole became involved with the party after the older quarrels had been largely settled, one does not usually find an alliance formed between the ex-opponents of the party and the *jeunesse*, except in so far as both had an 'educated perspective' that the militants did not have and which they tended to scorn. The infiltration of the party by younger men was a slow process and what momentum it had achieved by 1959 was impeded by the counter-revolution of the old party militants between 1959 and 1963. But educated ex-enemies of the P.D.C.I., whether young or old, certainly took over party offices towards the end of this phase. Thus in 1958 *A* became general secretary of the Bouaflé *sous-section* and afterwards obtained a range of other posts within territorial and district arenas. In both Bongouanou and Katiola young civil servants became deputies (in 1957 and 1965), to the chagrin of the militants.

This phase also saw the consolidation of the territorial elite as against authorities at the federal and French Union levels. In 1950 the P.D.C.I. had made itself independent of the French Communist party, but its representatives continued to be affiliated to parties in the metropolitan assemblies. From 1957, however, the P.D.C.I. began to take over executive powers in the territory and renounced the federal arena at the same time as it withdrew from Paris politics. Only Houphouët remained in Paris, as a minister in the French government; after the *débâcle* of the Community he, too, withdrew.

From 1960 onwards, therefore, the P.D.C.I. ceased to be a participant in representative arenas outside of the territory: to the extent that relations continued with other countries in these arenas, they did so indirectly and, formally at least, in much the same way as with other foreign states. While P.D.C.I. leaders still called their organization a 'party', it was no longer an organization competing with others for power. Within the French Union and the federal arenas it had been a party in relation to the representatives of other territories and of France, and in terms of the structure within which it was conceived. Between 1945 and 1960, though decreasingly, it was also a 'party' in the territorial arena: it competed with such other parties as were available. Further, its leaders and apparently many of its sympathizers considered it to have 'party' functions in that it represented the interests of the Ivoirien people within an arena dominated by a colonial power.

After 1960, not only were two arenas eliminated in which the P.D.C.I.

had operated as something approximating to a political party in the conventional sense but also the P.D.C.I. became officially, if not constitutionally, the only organization admissible as such.[1] The significance of this phase is that the P.D.C.I. ceased to exist as a party in any arena and the accession of its leaders to control of territorial government enabled them to prevent other interests expressing themselves through the creation of new parties.

To what extent does a procedure emphasizing distinct levels and arenas cast fresh light on the emergence of such 'single-partyism'? This procedure can be justified by comparison with other examples of this phenomenon: for in nearly all cases the effective monopolization of a political arena by a party has followed a fairly radical change in relations between arenas— for instance, the expulsion of an occupying or colonial power (as in Africa and Eastern Europe) or a secessionist civil war (as in the United States). Pertinently, Key has observed that in the U.S.A.,

in reality the South has been Democratic only for external purposes, that is, presidential and congressional elections. The one-party system is purely an arrangement for national affairs...within the Democratic party in the southern states factional groups are the equivalent of political parties elsewhere. In fact, the Democratic party in most states of the South is merely a holding-company for a congeries of transient squabbling factions, most of which fail by far to meet the standards of permanence, cohesiveness, and responsibility that characterize the political party.[2]

By analogy, just as the P.D.C.I. was a party in relations between the territorial and the wider levels, it can be seen as an agent, even as an *apparat*[3] of the territorial arena in its dealings with the district, canton and village arenas. It does have an amalgam of characteristics, since local party leaders are also actors within these arenas; but increasingly since 1960 the party has become bureaucratized as an agency of the centre at the expense of the independence of local *sous-sections*, 'the most important instrument of government control, an *auxiliaire d'autorité*'.[4]

---

[1] The 1960 constitution states (Titre Premier, article 7): 'Les partis et groupements politiques concourent à l'expression du suffrage. Ils se forment et exercent leur activité librement sous la condition de respecter les principes de la souveraineté nationale et de la démocratie et les lois de la République.' Thus the one-party regime is not written into the constitution: 'freedom', however, is interpreted for the peasants at least as 'the recognition of necessity'.

[2] V. O. Key, *Southern politics in state and nation*, New York 1950, p. 16.

[3] See Ghita Ionescu, *The politics of the European communist states*, London 1967, p. 16: 'An apparat or apparatus can be defined as any centralistic organisation, which, in an oppositionless state holds, in proportion with its share of responsibility in the running of the state, a smaller or larger part of the coercive power of the state.' Ionescu says that there are usually eight such *apparats* and that they are 'all under the command of one, *main* apparat'. I am not sure whether such an *apparat* can be said to exist in Ivory Coast: perhaps the *Présidence* has this role. For comparative studies, see 'The dead-end of the monolithic parties', *Government and Opposition* 2, no. 2 (1967).

[4] Zolberg, *One-party government*, p. 318.

## Party bureaucratization

*The party oligarchy.* Between 1951 and 1960 the district organization of the party became rather dilapidated. Some *sous-sections* were without general secretaries; in others there was almost complete immobility where recruitment to party offices was concerned, those who had survived the repression coopting as necessary to bureaux that became, in effect, self-perpetuating caucuses. Apart from their work at election times, the activity of these caucuses was restricted to helping the administration and collecting party dues—and the latter became sporadic and ineffectual. When elections arrived, the *sous-sections* caucuses were involved in nominating candidates and getting in the vote: yet real control of selection was in Abidjan, and the inefficiency of the *sous-sections* in mobilizing the electors was exposed in 1957, when only 49 per cent of those registered actually voted for the P.D.C.I.[1]

As the P.D.C.I. leadership took control of the territorial executive, the weakness of the party machine became a matter of concern: the mood of 'apathie sympathique',[2] which had enabled the leadership to settle the terms of decolonization with a minimum of popular constraint, came to be regarded as an obstruction to consolidating and legitimizing the power acquired from the colonial government. A first step was to commit government resources to ensuring total support in the 1959 (and subsequent) elections. The resources in question were not just technical resources, such as government transport and communications, but also the ideological resources which the party now encompassed in government, such as appeals to civic duty and national unity. So in 1959 over 94 per cent of voters were recorded as having voted for the party: this result was significant at least in the contrast between its complete ambiguity to the observer, as evidence of mass support, and the complete assurance of the party leaders that it gave them all the mandate they needed to have.

As for the P.D.C.I. itself, a congress held in 1959 provided all the evidence the leaders needed of the dangers attendant on enlarging and revitalizing the popular basis of the organization. After complaints about the lack of internal democracy in the party and about grass-roots apathy, representatives of the youth organization, J.R.D.A.C.I., and the general secretaries of the district *sous-sections* were brought into the *bureau politique* and a revival of the *sous-sections* was announced. Subsequently, however, the secretary-general elected by the congress was edged out of his position by Houphouët and replaced also as Minister of the Interior (a post he had occupied since 1957) and the J.R.D.A.C.I. was brought firmly under the control of the party hierarchy.[3]

---

[1] Zolberg, *One-party government*, pp. 185–7, 190–4, 212–15.
[2] Zolberg, *ibid.*, p. 269.
[3] See *ibid.*, pp. 306–12, 314–18, and Morgenthau, *Political parties*, pp. 214–18.

Between 1959 and 1965, when the next party congress was held, the authority of the old party men was so thoroughly re-established (partly through the association of the youth leadership with a plot in 1963) that Philippe Yacé, the secretary-general, was able to impose the view that the 1959 congress was a shameful event in P.D.C.I. history. He could attack it as the source of opportunism, *ascencionnisme*, and subversion and could even reproach the rank and file for their lack of vigilance.[1]

Meanwhile, the party had been adapted in accordance with the spirit of M. Yacé's belief that popular participation should be conceived as 'active acquiescence in the policies of the government'.[2]

This adaptation has taken account particularly of the 'country interest' represented by the general secretaries, who demanded a larger share in the central organs of the party at both the recent congresses. There are now members of the *bureau politique* representing the *sous-sections* of each department (though this does not amount to the allocation of one-third demanded by one delegate).[3] More significant, however, was the decision to make the general secretaries into salaried officials: they now receive monthly payments ranging from 50,000 frs. C.F.A. to 100,000 frs. C.F.A. (that is, from about £75 to £150), according to seniority in the party.[4]

*Party finances.* The establishment of these salaries has caused a considerable pressure upon the organizational capacity of the party and, by exposing its inadequacies, led to increased reliance on the local administration. For the money required has to come from the sale of party cards: the general rate for these cards is 200 frs. C.F.A.[5] and in practice every adult is compelled to buy one. The proceeds are sent to party accounts in banks in Abidjan. For each card bought, 100 frs. are retained in the capital to cover 'costs of investment and equipment' and 70 frs. are reserved for paying the general secretaries and for 'the working of the *bureau politique*'. Of what remains (30 frs.), 20 frs. is returned to the *sous-sections* and 10 frs. goes to the village and *quartier* committees.[6]

In some areas this operation is a significant drain of financial resources. Supposing a *sous-préfecture*[7] with an adult population of 20,000, the total

---

[1] Ministère de l'information, *IVe Congrès PDCI–RDA* (hereafter cited as *IVe Congrès*), p. 22.

[2] Speech of President Yacé, opening national assembly, 27 April 1967.

[3] *IVe Congrès*, p. 291, speech of M. Niamkey Adiko (representing the general secretaries of the *département du Sud*). For other demands for greater consultation, and attention to the interests of *militants éprouvés*, see, *ibid.*, speeches by MM. Richard Pouho (p. 283), Vamé Doumouya (p. 260), and the unnamed representative of the northern general secretaries (p. 277).

[4] *IVe Congrès*, p. 35.

[5] *Ibid.*

[6] *Ibid.* This apportionment was established by a circular of 3 November 1964. The centralization of funds in Abidjan (instead of in district banks) was instituted 'to facilitate checks and to safeguard the good faith of the general secretaries' (Télégramme Officiel, no. 134 AN/Pt of 26 November 1965, Président, assemblée nationale to *sous-préfets*).

[7] The *sous-préfecture* is the basic unit of district administration, replacing the colonial *subdivision* and typically smaller than it.

M

collected by the sale of party cards would be 4,000,000 frs. (about £6,451), of which at least 2,000,000 frs. (£3,225) would remain in Abidjan. Then 1,400,000 frs. (£2,257) would be allotted to cover the general secretary's salary and the costs of the central *bureau politique*: 400,000 frs. (£644) would return to the *sous-section* and only 200,000 frs. (£323) would be left for the various village committees.[1]

The actual resources of the party are much greater than a calculation based on the general rate suggests, since a principle of 'from each according to his means' (if only that) operates, according to an official scale. Thus a member of the *Conseil économique et social* is required to pay 84,000 frs. (£126) annually into party funds; a deputy, 120,000 frs. (£180); and a minister or an ambassador, 180,000 frs. (£270).[2]

Similarly, all civil servants (and, in principle, all salaried employees in the private sector) have to make contributions proportionate to their income.[3] This levy on *fonctionnaires* is no doubt justified not only in terms of economic justice, but also because of their greater access to the facilities provided by the party in Abidjan with the retained half of funds collected. For, apart from 1,000-seat *maison des congrès*, this money has been used to build beside the lagoon a 'Club Houphouët-Boigny' where the militants can recharge their energies not only in various social facilities but also in a large swimming-pool, on volley-ball and tennis courts, and in aquatic sports.[4] Finally, the party has exacted an annual contribution from the entire adult population for the construction of three places of worship on a proposed *voie triomphale* in Abidjan: in 1966 the *per capita* rate seems to have varied, the lowest figure quoted being 400 frs., the highest, 1,000 frs.[5]

*Party and district administration.* The *sous-préfets* are not only required to buy a £7 10s. or £15 party card (depending on their rank), but they have

---

[1] Although the total available for paying the general secretary in this case would cover the services of even the most senior militant available (i.e., one costing £1,800), there is obviously a net transfer taking place in this respect between areas (since salaries are not related to the size of *sous-préfectures*, some of which have populations as low as 5,000).

[2] *IVᵉ Congrès*, p. 36; on the earlier operation of this system, Zolberg, *One-party government*, p. 193.

[3] The sliding scale is as follows (in frs. C.F.A.):

| monthly salary | party card |
|---|---|
| 15,000–25,000 | 1,000 |
| 26,000–50,000 | 2,000 |
| 51,000–100,000 | 5,000 |
| 101,000–150,000 | 10,000 |
| 151,000–200,000 | 15,000 |
| over 200,000 | 25,000 |

(Télégramme Officiel, no. 134 AN/Pt of 26 November 1965). Philippe Yacé remarked in 1965 that civil servants were contributing less to party funds than the deputies, etc.; this scale has since been introduced (*IVᵉ Congrès*, p. 36).

[4] *IVᵉ Congrès*, p. 37. In the suburb of Koumassi the P.D.C.I. has built 'Une maison...fort confortable...qui sert de logement à certaines personnalités politiques de passage dans notre pays' (*ibid.*).

[5] This was not, however, being collected in 1967.

increasingly the responsibility ('because of its complexity') for administering the sale of cards in their districts. Delegation of this kind seems to have begun in 1964 and to have taken place directly from the secretary-general, Philippe Yacé,[1] to the *sous-préfets*, without intervention by the Minister of the Interior. Theoretically there is a division of responsibilities, the general secretary disposing of all the 200-fr. cards and the *sous-préfet* collecting from all those subject to the sliding scale.[2] The practice differs from one area to another, largely depending on the administrative skill and local popularity of the general secretary. Invariably the subscriptions are late in arriving:[3] and in some areas the *sous-préfet* undertakes a tour in which he combines the roles of party-card salesman and developmentalist. On the occasions that I watched this taking place (in some thirty villages of one *sous-préfecture*) considerable time and temper were expended on the first role. The operation was in fact completely bureaucratized, each head of an extended family taking a clump of cards allotted to him according to the number of adults in his household. He was then required to pay or face *administrative* sanctions for 'indiscipline' or 'disloyalty to the nation'. Checks are also made on the occupants of vehicles in February and March by party representatives at road-blocks.[4]

Although it has led to inflamed relations between *sous-préfets* and general secretaries, the involvement of the administration in party affairs seems still to be growing. In the 1968 *budget spécial d'investissement et équipment*, there is an item in the section concerning the Ministry of the Interior entitled 'Maison de P.D.C.I. à Cocody...50 million frs. C.F.A.'[5]

There is also a concealed exchange of resources between party and administration in the party-card operation. Prior to 1959 the administration levied a head-tax on the population; in that year it was abolished, as a symbol of liberation from the colonial regime.[6] It is occasionally argued (by party and administrative officials) that the party card is a substitute for this tax and is justifiable psychologically in that it accustoms the population to making financial sacrifices (or rather, to continuing to make them). This substitution serves also to transfer control of the chiefs to the party, at least in the sense that previously village chiefs received a rebate on the head-tax: now, in some areas, whether or not they receive some of

---

[1] Who is also president of the national assembly.

[2] The original delegation was contained in Circular no. 1843/LT of 3 November 1964. The division of responsibilities is defined in Télégramme Officiel no. 134 AN/Pt of 26 November 1965.

[3] By 15 February 1967 (the official closing date) only 500,000 frs. C.F.A. of a required total of 6,000,000 frs. C.F.A. had been collected in the *sous-préfecture* where I observed the placing of party cards.

[4] I watched this happening at Gohitafla, near Bouaké, on 21 February 1967: in another district lorries were stopped and people without cards were sent to work on the roads for a day.

[5] *Journal Officiel de la République de Côte d'Ivoire*, 31 January 1968, Numéro Spécial, p. 156.

[6] See Morgenthau, *Political parties*, p. 213. This was possible because of the sizeable indirect taxation re-transferred to the territorial budget after the break-up of the French West African federation: and this taxation contributes far more to the budget than does direct taxation.

the 5 per cent returned to the villages depends on the extent of their cooperation in placing cards.

Three questions are prompted by this evidence of party bureaucratization. First, is it appropriate to speak of 'party' and 'administration' as separate entities? Second, if 'party' is distinct, what distinguishes it from the administration? Does it have a 'party' role any longer? Third, what effects has bureaucratization had on conflicts and factionalism within district party *sous-sections*?

### The distinction between party and administration

The P.D.C.I. and the administration are still separate in formal structure and in the eyes of prominent observers and participants: further, it is arguable that the regime wishes to keep them separate and so do the principal actors. At the district level, the fact that the party has had to depend on the *sous-préfets* to achieve efficient collection of party dues does not mean that the administrator is necessarily influential in other sectors of party activity (such as the nomination of election candidates) or that individual *sous-préfets* necessarily enjoy greater security as a result. Indeed, one of the chief results of this collaboration seems to have been a deterioration in relations between *sous-préfets* and general secretaries: typically, each official has a remarkably sharp perception of the distinction between his role and that of the other.

In fact, the present relationship at this level is a matter of generations more than of formal structures. Structurally, the administration has, as remarked above, the same role as under the colonial regime. Its immediate supplementary activities in relation to the party are due to a demand for rewards and recognition on the part of the older party militants and are therefore not due to any directed attempt by, for example, the Ministry of the Interior to 'take over' the party. Administrative intervention is due ultimately to the inability of local party organization to perform in its own image.

Informally, however, administrators have intervened in party affairs: for instance, successive *sous-préfets* in Katiola protested about the inadequacy of the *sous-section* bureau, and the replacement of the general secretary in 1962 and probably the replacement of the deputy in 1965 were due to alliances between the incumbent *sous-préfets* and younger elements in the party.[1] But a *sous-préfet* who so involves himself is seen by others as abusing his function and may provoke such a reaction from the offended interest that he loses his job.

This statement may seem paradoxical in view of what is said above

---

[1] One *sous-préfet* complained: '...les responsables politiques (le député...et le Conseiller Général et le pseudo Secrétaire Général de la Sous-Section...) étaient toujours absents et il n'existait de Sous-Section. Le Sous-Préfet s'était donc retrouvé seul en compagnie de son chauffeur pour entreprendre une vulgarisation de la culture de Tabac et du Coton' (letter to Préfet, Département du Centre, 1963).

about the ineffectuality of some party officials in collecting dues. On the whole, it is the case that those who are most effective in distributing cards are those who have shown themselves the stronger when conflict has occurred with an administrator. Certainly it is possible for a general secretary to provoke the removal of a *sous-préfet*, although I have been able to verify this possibility in only one case—that of the removal of a *sous-préfet* at Bouaflé in 1966, due to the intervention of *A*, the most forceful general secretary I have encountered. I have not found a case in which an incompetent general secretary has tried to remove a *sous-préfet*.[1]

There is, nevertheless, a basic structural point to be made: it is that the *sous-préfet*, like his predecessor the colonial *chef de subdivision*, is an impermanent official, without a local electoral base, and subject to revocation by decision of the Minister of the Interior. While he normally has greater immediate access to developmental and coercive resources from the territorial level than the general secretary, the latter usually has a range of allies within the district (including placemen in the administration), as well as in the cantons and villages, whom he can mobilize to circumscribe the political deployment of the resources that a *sous-préfet* has.

Both general secretaries and *sous-préfets* are conscious of the balance that exists between them. The former tend to favour the continuation of this balance: one general secretary remarked that a certain degree of tension was useful for maintaining the cohesion of the local party organization.[2] They evidently feel also that their present strength is favoured by the lack of elective bodies at the district and village levels: none of those interviewed wished to see communes or councils set up. Most *sous-préfets* felt the same way, but the reasons given were of a paternally developmentalist kind.

A much more difficult and basic question is how far people in the villages perceive a difference between the party and the district administration. All one can say is that the attitudes observed in the course of interviews with village chiefs and others tend to confirm the view expressed in studies of analogous situations elsewhere, that relations between the village and district officials are seen in a fairly undiscriminatingly extractive way.[3] The most relevant way of approaching the question might be to ask: who had been seen to give most, who to demand most? Objectively, the administration probably makes the most frequent and intrusive demands on the villages. But though it would be extremely difficult to get

[1] Though in two districts *sous-préfets* were allegedly removed in 1966 at the behest of deputies.

[2] The administration also favours such tension: *sous-préfets* who become too close to general secretaries may be moved on the suspicion that some kind of combination or corruption is developing.

[3] See Colin Leys, *Politicians and policies: An essay on politics in Acholi, Uganda, 1962–1965*, Nairobi 1967; and F. G. Bailey, *The peasant view of the bad life*, Presidential address delivered to the Nottingham Meeting of the British Association, 2 September 1966. For their comments on this and other sections of the paper, I am very grateful to David Feldman, Colin Leys, Theo Mars, Bernard Schaffer, and Geoff Wood.

evidence on the matter, it seems probable that questions about the difference between party and administration are peripheral in the village arena;
for they refer to activity in an arena with which the village is only inter-
mittently connected.

### Party processes in the P.D.C.I.

The same problems of access and verification arise when we try to assess
the overall characteristics and internal processes of the party.

To start with, it is not a voluntary association: membership is in
practice compulsory and the point has relevance if only because of the
annual ritual of financial exaction. Also, since everybody has to join,
membership of the party is indistinguishable from citizenship. The
P.D.C.I. lacks many of the features of participation that parties elsewhere
exhibit. Admittedly, the internal processes of the party are generally
invisible to outsiders; but there is some case material available. It suggests
that on strictly local issues (such as who holds party offices and which
villages get the development resources which are available) the district
party leadership is quite responsive to demands from the village level.
At and above district level, however, the party is highly centralized.

For example, if a village decides to change its delegates, this seems
to be accepted as its affair (though *sous-section* representatives may be
present at the election).[1] But to change a general secretary is impossible
without supervision of the election by delegates from Abidjan: a general
secretary under attack can thus hold on to his position as long as he has
influence with the territorial leadership. In 1966 a meeting of the Katiola
*sous-section* (that is, of the village and *quartier* representatives) voted by
23 votes to 11 to replace the bureau, including the general secretary.[2]
By July 1967 no delegation had been sent to Katiola by M. Yacé and the
incumbent general secretary was still recognized by the local administration and was still being paid his salary.

The same contrast applies to meetings and to the communication of
demands within the party. In all the districts visited, meetings are held
(if rarely) to which village delegates come and at which problems about
the running of the party and the needs of the district can be discussed.
Such meetings are often used by the general secretary or the deputy (very
often the same person) to transmit news or instructions brought by him
from Abidjan. But communication from district to territorial levels seems
to be meagre. None of the party representatives interviewed considered
that *sous-sections* had any role to play in offering advice or making demands
concerning general policy to the government or the *bureau politique*.
The reaction of general secretaries to questions on this subject was
remarkably similar to the reaction of the village chiefs to the question about

---

[1] Four villages in Katiola changed their delegates in March 1966.
[2] Katiola, *Procès-Verbal de la réunion des délégués des comités de village en date du 13 mars 1966*.

party and administration: the topic clearly lacked action reference and any question about it usually produced a very formal response.

At the territorial level, the secretary-general does occasionally mediate or arbitrate in disputes occurring within *sous-sections* and in conflicts between, for example, general secretaries and *sous-préfets*. In 1966 the general secretary at Bongouanou was summoned to Abidjan with members of his clan to explain his opposition to the deputy for the area: M. Yacé urged him to be less sectarian in his attitudes and to put the interests of the nation (as served by the deputy) before his own obscure feuding. The secretary-general seems, however, to control the P.D.C.I. very much in the manner of a squire administering his estate: he is protective of the general secretaries, but rarely leaves Abidjan and does not seem to have a full-time staff for party administration.[1] As for meetings, there are occasional sessions of a *conseil national* at which general secretaries and *sous-préfets* are present: the proceedings of the *conseil national* are private, but seem mainly to be concerned with the announcement and explanation of government policy-decisions.

The 'party' activities of the P.D.C.I. are thus narrow and occasional. The largest organizational effort regularly made by it, that of selling party cards, is also the most bureaucratized. There is only very indirect communication between levels in the party and little evidence of what political scientists have discerned in African parties as a 'mobilization function': it is the *sous-préfets* rather than the general secretaries who are the active evangelizers of modernization and it is they who are habitually the most earnest about 'the political education of the masses'.

### Conflicts and factions at the sous-section level

As is appropriate to a party which was historically intent on achieving only what Fitch and Oppenheimer have called 'a partial political revolution',[2] conflict and factionalism within the P.D.C.I. turn almost entirely on questions of office. Internal conflict of this kind is now all the more to be expected in a single-party regime which came to power when certain resources (notably education and private capital) were extremely scarce. One-party regimes are, in fact, a phenomenon especially related to situations where some such values are in very short supply, and 'single-partyism' is perhaps best seen as the ideology of those who have already monopolized much of what is going. However, once the party leadership moves into government, it is under pressure to increase these resources—to build more schools, to assist indigenous private enterprise, to help 'progressive farmers': when it does this it may, in fact, be undermining its own authority.

[1] Though he is alleged to have a personal militia drawn from ex-servicemen, of whose association he is president.

[2] Bob Fitch and Mary Oppenheimer, 'Ghana: end of an illusion', *Monthly Review* 18, 3 (July–August 1966), p. 23.

With the establishment of new secondary schools, it creates a potential challenge by the educated *jeunesse*, which will evaluate the party's intellectual claims to authority more critically: indigenous business men may acquire political ambitions as they become richer.

On the whole, of course, the Ivory Coast government has much more scope for manœuvre than the governments in some neighbouring countries with little or no resources to distribute. The point is that a study of the personal resources of the party leaders is useful for understanding the tensions in organizations like the P.D.C.I. The leadership has provided satisfaction for the older party men at the cost of ossifying the party itself: the authority of the party over the young has declined as the authoritarianism of the old has increased. While it is possible (and frequent) for younger educated men to be coopted as deputies or as members of *sous-section* bureaux, once recruited they have to accept the gerontocracy of the older militants, who continually assert the values of seniority, discipline, and past militancy, while denouncing the forms of ambition subsumed under the term 'Ascensionnisme'. Vice-president Auguste Denise gave the clearest of many expositions of this paternalist philosophy at the 1965 Congress (appropriately, since it was he who had been evicted by the *jeunesse* movement from the post of secretary-general in 1959). Deploring the tendency of the J.R.D.A.C.I. to make itself into 'a parallel party', he said:

Each of us, as an adolescent, had his revolutionary phase, whether nihilist or constructive. But there can be no question of electing, to all the posts of responsibility in the party, people who have not yet grasped that the work of construction is heavy and permanent...the place of the youth is to fight at the side of the grown men and of their elders, in one movement...those with experience will make their juniors understand that nothing is to be improvised, nothing worth having without patient and laborious work.[1]

M. Konan Bédié, speaking for the younger element in the P.D.C.I. denounced his ambitious contemporaries even more strongly:

We must expel resolutely all those who, moved by sordid and murky ambitions or by the deliria of 'Ascensionnisme', want to deny to the true artisans...the credit for and the desserts of their labour...There will be no more Catilinas in Ivory Coast. There will be no more Brutuses...Never will the youth of this country betray their elders. Never will the sons stray from the glorious and triumphal trail blazed by their fathers.[2]

The general secretaries for their part demanded: 'that only proven militants should participate in the direction of the party.—that only militants of at least five years standing should be elected to the assemblies'.[3]

---

[1] *IVᵉ Congrès*, p. 72.　　　　　　　　　　　　　　　　　[2] *Ibid.*, pp. 77–8.
[3] *IVᵉ Congrès, Rapport...des secrétaires généraux...du Département du Nord*, p. 270. See also *ibid.*, p. 269, report of M. Vamé Doumouya, representing the *Département du Centre*; p. 274, report

What this means is that from the point of view of younger men, office in the P.D.C.I. is effectively ascriptive within a generation: at the district level the surviving militants have imposed the criterion of age as the major qualification for office.

Nevertheless, there is an alternative 'faction', which typically recruits followers outside of the bureaux as well as among the younger cooptees inside the party hierarchy. This group might be called the developmental 'faction'. Its members are identifiable by their claim that the modern, 'rational' values they represent constitute the true interest of development and therefore entitle them (by virtue of their education or administrative training) to participate in politics, if necessary to the exclusion of the militants. Typically this group comprises a *sous-préfet*,[1] a younger deputy, one or two other *fonctionnaires*, in some instances a priest, and quite often a recently enstooled village chief.

Such a group can always be found in a district. The problem of political analysis is whether this group can be described as a 'faction', whether, in fact, even the term 'group' is justified. One element of this problem is that, although everybody is 'in the party' in the sense of being a compulsory member, by no means all of those whom I would identify as 'developmentalists' are 'in the party' in the sense of being officers or activists. If they constitute a 'faction', it is therefore not a faction within the formal P.D.C.I. organization, but one within the adult population of the Ivory Coast: they are perhaps a presence in the party rather than a faction.

A second, more intractable element of the problem tends to reinforce this distinction. To my knowledge, no 'developmental' group has ever achieved explicit, formal articulation in the *sous-sections* or in the congresses in the same way that the *anciens militants* have. The militants make claims on the party as such, recognize each other and are recognized publicly; whereas the members of the developmental group, though they can be recognized by an observer by their attitudes towards themselves and towards the militants, lack a public identity. They can be distinguished only by the difference of their individual attitudes from those of the militants and by their tendency to agree on a range of topics when they meet. Perhaps this category should be described as a psychological collation rather than as a faction, as a presence rather than as a group.

There is, of course, a simple reason why the developmentalists have not achieved formal identity within the party structure or elsewhere: it is that the *sous-sections* are controlled by the militants, militants dominate the central party organs, and most of the deputies in the National Assembly are militants. That there are young deputies and ministers of a

[1] Most *sous-préfets* are aged between 30 and 38.

of El Hadj Amoakon Dihye, representing the *Département de l'Est*; p. 282, report of M. Richard Pouho, representing the *Département de l'Ouest*; and p. 291, report of M. Niamkey Adiko, representing the *Département du Sud*.

developmentalist persuasion does not affect the general validity of this point. Furthermore, there are no elective bodies at a district level or lower which the developmentalists could exploit so as to acquire a communal identity: candidatures to the National Assembly and the *conseils généraux* are in the gift of the party organs, heavily influenced by the *sous-section* caucuses. The village, canton, and district levels thus lack institutional bases for the creation and consolidation of factions. There are clans among the militants and also some involving developmentalists. But these clans are essentially defined by attachment to the claims of a personality or an ethnic group in particular districts; they do not have the generalized, ideological character of the developmental category.

The ideological orientation of the developmentalists also may be partly explained by the situation within the party organization. Those whom I would define as members of this category tend to play down the official doctrine of the primacy of the P.D.C.I. as advanced by the militants. They are not, it should be stressed, necessarily any less authoritarian or paternalist in their attitudes to the population: further, they tend to share the militants' belief in the necessity of a single-party regime and to share the official view of development options (economic liberalism, cooperation with European private enterprise, etc.). They simply have a different view of instrumentality, emphasizing government rather than party, bureaucratic rationality rather than party 'mobilization'. There is no reason to believe that they would, once in control, alter substantially the present disposition of resources between arenas, aligned as it is to centralization in the territorial arena. Probably they would merely substitute the authoritarianism of an *apparat* based on the *Ecole Nationale d'Administration* for the paternalism of the P.D.C.I.'s 'inheritance elite'.

So 'development' in this connection denotes only the rhetoric of a potential counter-elite. In other parts of West Africa groups using this rhetoric have already moved into government. The rhetoric of the Ivory Coast developmentalists gives us no basis for predicting whether, once in power, they would be more or less devoted to the expansion of social opportunities in the country than the P.D.C.I. elite, or as little: or whether, intentions apart, they would be more or less capable of actually achieving it than the bureaucrats elsewhere, or as little: or how long it will take before ordinary Ivoiriens want to and can make politics more than a growth industry of elites and political scientists, more something they participate in and less something they have done for them.

The development of a political class, of which the party bureaucracy is only one component, is the major product of indigenization. So it seems now. But while the term 'political class' expresses a reality—the emergence of Ivoirien civil servants, administrators, and soldiers alongside the old party men—it is no doubt only adequate for this purpose, just as the earlier term 'single-partyism' was adequate to describe the phase in which the old party men superseded the colonial administration. It will become irrelevant if a more plural structure develops, if social and economic changes create a situation appropriate to a politics of vertical articulation and aggregation. Then the usage of class and party might become useful.

# THE DEADLOCK IN DEVELOPMENT
# ADMINISTRATION

## B. B. SCHAFFER

Over the last few years we have seen a big effort to establish something quite new called, distinctively, development administration: not, we shall see, the same thing as administrative development or as, merely, what administration actually happened to be like in less developed countries; but, rather, the establishment of a new way of conducting administration there or, at least, the setting up of conditions for the new form of administration by processes of research, advice or assistance.

There have been several factors at work. One was certainly the administration of economic development and planning[1] and, particularly, the problems of specific agencies like public corporations.[2] A second has been a far-ranging debate, sometimes about the comparison of public and private entrepreneurs,[3] sometimes about the neglect of administration by technical assistance agencies,[4] about what came to be called implementation[5] or about the dependence rather than the neglect or the defectiveness of administration as it was.[6] Thirdly, much more came to be known about the actual field problems, from the reports of expatriate assistance, of social anthropologists and of community and rural development.[7]

What was being sought was a new concept of what administrative behaviour should be, of why it ought to be changed, of how the alterations could be achieved but also of how all these questions could be tackled. Some of the stimuli were the actual experiences of planning, of agencies, of technical assistance and so forth. But another stimulus was the growth of the discipline of comparative public administration itself, particularly

---

[1] Royal Institute of Public Administration, 'Administrative organisation for economic development', *Proceedings of the Cambridge Conference*, London 1959.

[2] A. H. Hanson, *Public enterprise and economic development*, London 1959.

[3] J. J. Spengler, 'Public bureaucracy, resource structure and economic development' *Kyklos* 11 (1958), 459.

[4] H. Emmerich, *Administrative road blocks to co-ordinated development*, New York 1961; J. D. Montgomery, 'Field organisation, administrative relationships and foreign aid policies', *Public Policy 10*, (1960).

[5] K. William Kapp, 'Economic development, national planning and public administration', *Kyklos* 13 (1960), 172.

[6] F. W. Riggs, 'Public administration: a neglected factor in economic development', *Annals* 305 (1956), 70.

[7] E. J. Sady, 'Community development and local government', *Journal of African Administration* 11 (1959), 179; M. L. Thomas, 'The Philippines rural development programme', *Social Research* 22 (1955), 223; 'U.N. technical assistance operations', *Public administration aspects of community development programmes*, New York 1959.

from the mid-1950s onwards.[1] The point here was that a fresh approach to comparative public administration was excited by just this sort of data, with the explicit hope of less culturally or institutionally dependent comparisons and so with the hope of ultimately some accumulation of evidence and experience.

What was involved was very difficult: not only a better understanding of the differences between one administration and another, and so, perhaps, of how it could be changed, but also an understanding of the interplay between any administration and its environment and the way in which administration could be operated differently in the most difficult of circumstances.

That was what the whole effort or movement was about: relating some of the experiences of development to some of the hopes proffered by new approaches to understanding comparisons, changes and the relations between behaviour (political and administrative) and its setting. It is striking that the notion of a concept of development administration had, in fact, been established and received from 1960 or thereabouts. In Britain it seems to have met with some contumely, hostility, xenophobia or mere assimilation. In a footnote in his recent work W. J. M. Mackenzie doubted the need to consider development administration as a separate set of questions at all, despite the recent rapid increase of work apparently devoted to these matters. He assumed explicitly that development administration meant a concern with the improvement of public services and argued that there is no reason why such matters should vary from one case to another.[2] Somewhat different is the argument that it is wrong to distinguish public from development administration, not because it may be unnecessary, still less because it is meaningless, but precisely because it has a meaning and the meaning is dangerous. This certainly accepts the framework of reference. 'So significant for the well-being of the world is the present development era, and so important for the success of this

[1] R. Braibanti's movement to an understanding of the inherited traditions of administration is one notable example of scholarship and sympathy. See also the controversy between M. Berger and F. Heady, *Administrative Science Quarterly* (1957), 518 and (1959), 509, about the relevance of the Weber model. For the influence of comparative politics, see A. Diamant, 'The relevance of comparative politics to the study of comparative administration', *Administrative Science Quarterly* 5 (1960), 87. For wider sociological sources see S. N. Eisenstadt, *Problems of emerging bureaucracies in developing areas and new states* (UNESCO and University of Chicago), mim., Chicago 1960. An important early bibliography was F. Heady and S. Stokes, *Comparative public administration* (2nd edn), Ann Arbor. 1960. W. Sayre and H. Kaufman, *A research design for a pilot study in public administration*, 1953, mim., Bloomington 1966, was very influential; W. Siffin (ed.) *Towards the comparative study of public administration*, Bloomington 1957. That contained Riggs's landmark essay on 'Agraria and industria'. Riggs's own work in running the Comparative Administration Group and in acting as a one-man ideas factory has at times come near to constituting the whole movement. Many other people deserve credit. A good example would be Richard Gable, e.g., his *Plan for research and publication in public administration*, Washington 1961, which distinguished development, development planning, development assistance and development administration, and argued for research as a necessary condition of public administration in those fields.

[2] W. J. M. Mackenzie, *Politics and social science*, London 1967, p. 365, n. 2.

development are the processes which are involved in its administration that the present concentration of support for the concept of development administration as a special and peculiarly relevant type of public administration is understandable.'[1] The worry is not with the prescriptions or the need for them but with the pejorative implications for 'the traditional' [*sic*] or 'law and order and revenue collecting' functions of administration. That, it is implied, would be bad for administrators, overemphasize innovation and be unfair to the past, including the colonial record.

It has also seemed at times that the British attitude to the movement has been to treat it with suspicion as an invention with which to attack the colonial record or some particular notion like that mythical concept the 'generalist' administrator. Alternatively, people in the United Kingdom have acknowledged the words politely and assumed that they must mean something with which we are already familiar, like assistance for administrative training.

That clearly does not measure up to the anguished concern of Irving Swerdlow: 'There are, or should be, many important and clearly recognisable differences between public administration in a poor country, striving to attain self generated economic growth and public administration in high income countries. Officials must make enough different decisions, adopt enough different activities to warrant the distinctive designation.' It is not just an improvement of administrative conditions that is being sought, nor a particular section of administration, a planning unit or some so-called nation-building department. There is a sense of a need for different behaviour and different recourses in the face of different tasks.

As it happens, we are at a point of change in the development administration movement and the conditions which it faces. Changes are taking place in key sectors, such as the localization of the staff of those public service training institutes which have at least been centres for the discussion of development administration. Malaysia has decided that there is something here which it must adopt. Whether it is right or feasible, administrative systems like that of India seem prepared to consider major structural change in their machineries of government. Meantime, however, like other sections of development studies, the movement is concerned, almost guilty, about its extrinsic, technical assistance, Western or United States, orientation. There is worry about the outcome of national planning. There are worries about apparent commitments to anti-generalist or anti-inheritance slogans. There is an abundance of critical and despondent field reports, a paucity of fresh or attractive solutions. Hart and Meadows referred to development administration as 'the fascinating though capricious new field of entrepreneurial thought'.

[1] Compare J. LaPalombara, *Alternative strategies for developing administrative capabilities in emerging nations*, mim., Bloomington 1965, p. 38 with a forthcoming article by W. Wood in the *Indian Journal of Public Administration*.

My thesis is precisely that development administration has been capricious because of the movement's mistaken views of the relation of administration to development, including confusion about and sometimes hostility to administration itself.

In particular, there is confusion about strategies and means: for example, about whether technical assistance for administration is legitimate and possible, or dangerous and capricious. Yet nothing has happened to make Swerdlow's statement of concern less relevant.

It is a good moment to ask what the development administration movement has been and what it has tried to say about administration and about development; how and why there has been a deadlock; how we might resolve it.

## PUBLIC ADMINISTRATION AND
## DEVELOPMENT ADMINISTRATION

There has been a 'public administration movement' for just over 80 years. It started from Woodrow Wilson's definition of public administration as a practical science, from his particular agenda for research and teaching and from his recommendation that one should go on from reform to re-organization.[1]

The public administration movement was distinct from Cameralism or from Fürstenspiegel or from other schools of thought about official life, because of its interest in reform. Development administration has, above all, been involved with improvement.

Characteristically, research, a concern with action and change and an agenda went together.[2] Further, like the public administration movement, some parts of the development administration movement tended to exercise the certainty and optimism of the outsider. As Buck once felt he knew and could state briefly in a few 'standards' exactly how reorganiza-tion ought everywhere be conducted, so some parts of the technical assistance community felt they knew how, through the United Nations and other agencies, development administration ought to be conducted.[3]

Yet unlike the public administration movement, the development administration movement tended to ignore some of the theory and research that was most relevant to its interests. Riggs himself, for example, rarely mentions the work of Herbert Simon. The movement also got its motivation, its ideas, and its experience from non- or even anti-administration sources,

[1] B. B. Schaffer, 'Public administration and the political education', *Public Administration* 21 (Sydney 1962), 343; F. W. Riggs, 'The political context of administrative reform; re-learning an old lesson', *Public Administration Review* 25 (1965), 70.

[2] Gable, *Plan for research*, pp. 23 and 30–6.

[3] See particularly the two U.N. handbooks, *Standards and techniques of public administration, with special reference to technical assistance for under-developed countries*, New York 1951; and *Public admini-stration, current concepts and practice, with special reference to developing countries*, New York 1961. For A. E. Buck's 'standards' see his *Administrative consolidation in state governments*, 1919.

quite unlike the public administration movement which got its ideas from scientific management, or army reorganization and staff work.

However, there are two other common points. The public administration movement itself, in so far as it was connected with municipal reform, short ballot ideas, and even populism, did have many non-administrative and potentially anti-administrative sources, like the concern for mere retrenchment of many typical municipal reformers. Secondly, both the public administration and the development administration movements were closely involved in education. The American technical assistance device of employing universities on contract in the field has been particularly important. On the other hand, the development administration movement has operated in a public service training era. The public administration movement began before there was so much emphasis on training.

But the most important distinction of all has already been hinted at. Wilson and his followers argued for administrative reorganization from a sense of an achievement in administrative reform, from a highly relevant definition of the administrative function with a clear prescription or programme of institutional change attached to it, from a faith in the significance of those 'principles' for administrative change which Wilson was sure could be discovered, and in the end from a belief in the significance of administration within, at least, its proper scope. There was much unargued commitment, but there was certainly much that could be used, like a method of diagnosis, and much that could be experimented with (e.g. particular bits of administrative machinery), and hence much that could be spelled out, taught and applied.

It is exactly this clarity which is missing in development administration. A movement, as set up by a measure of agreed concern, has existed for, say, 10 years, and began to be most clearly expressed about 7 or 8 years ago.[1] But what is most striking beyond that concern is the lack of agreement about administration itself.

Some of what the movement itself sees as new is not so new. The perception that ecology explains administration was expressed a generation ago by John M. Gaus. Administrators specifically concerned with development were used as 'trouble-shooters' on projects in colonial Nigeria, and were recommended by the British select committee on estimates; a similar view of the task of administration was implied by the 1945 version of colonial development and welfare legislation with its provision for preparation of long-term 10-year planning.[2] Some such special posts have

---

[1] Irving Swerdlow (ed.), *Development administration, concepts and problems*, Syracuse 1953; A. Spitz and E. Weidner, *Development administration, an annotated bibliography*, Honolulu 1963; D. V. Hart and P. Meadows, *Directed social change, field reports and annotated bibliography*, Syracuse 1961; R. W. Gable, *Development administration and assistance, an annotated bibliography*, Washington 1961.

[2] J. M. Lee, *Colonial development and good government*, Oxford 1967.

N

persisted, as in Zambia. There has been a sort of coincidence of fresh experience, ideas and concerns comparable with the years after civil service reform in the United States at the end of the last century.

The problem can be better understood if we distinguish the coincident elements. In India, the possibility of discriminating between regulatory law and order, taxation and similar functions, on the one hand, and development administration, on the other, was inevitable with the introduction in 1952 of regulations which separated district administration from community development programmes below a certain administrative level.[1] However the community development movement's own agenda and concerns were something quite different, arising from another element: a growing sense of the need for substantive changes of programme. A faith in the effectiveness of governmental agencies, in the possible functions of public service personnel and structures in political mobilization, joined forces with the significance, for good and evil, of obstacles, scarcities and neglect. There was also a growing unwillingness to equate development administration with central decision-making.[2] Esman does indeed go on to reiterate what may be taken as a central part of the whole movement—its apparent point of agreement. 'This (that is development administration) supplants the traditional view of administration as a group of specialised auxiliary techniques.' But that is negative: one view is supplanted; what will the new one show?[3]

A further source has been the great debate about technical assistance for public administration. There have been two generations, so to speak, of thinking about the aims and values of technical assistance. The first saw confident western experts writing up reports (like Egger and Appleby in Pakistan and India), handbooks (like Emmerich) or training syllabuses. The second has been one of revaluation. That is scarcely surprising. What is more important is the complexity of the critique and then, finally, its uncertainty, ambiguity, and negativeness. It was one thing to show the irrelevance of some particular concept in western public administration.[4] It was another thing to argue that the priorities in assistance for administration were all wrong, as in an attempt to introduce performance budgeting in the Philippines,[5] or to argue generally that the whole heart

[1] U. Goswami, 'The structure of development administration', *Indian Journal of Public Administration* I (1955), 110.

[2] M. Esman, *Education for development administration*, Pittsburgh 1962.

[3] For the earlier view, see e.g. Max F. Millikan and W. W. Rostow, *A proposal: key to an effective foreign policy*, New York 1957.

[4] R. Braibanti and J. J. Spengler (eds.), *Tradition, values and socio-economic development*, Durham 1961 (J. D. Montgomery, at pp. 261 ff.), for a critical discussion of the policy–administration dichotomy and its effects on technical assistance in institutional policies in Taiwan, Vietnam, Burma, and Thailand.

[5] Malcom B. Parsons, 'Performance budgeting in the Philippines', *Public Administration Review* 17 (1957), 173. Parsons's article began an angry but interesting controversy with E. O. Stene and others.

of the trouble was the emphasis on organization and methods, fiscal management and personnel management.[1] Some writers seemed to imply that the answer was yet more emphasis on the technical assistance provided for administration. Those who argued in that way disagreed amongst themselves on the details of the solution (e.g. about the placing of administration experts in headquarters, missions, or project organizations);[2] and others, but not all, felt it necessary to go beyond a mere revision (of whatever sort) of the public administration content of technical assistance in favour of a wholly new entity, development administration;[3] but this was, once again, vague and unconvincing.[4] Yet others argued a still more different case; that the point was not to provide technical assistance for public administration in a different way (whatever in fact that might mean), or to provide assistance for another entity called development administration, but not to give the assistance at all. This clearly shows how far from the public administration movement the new movement had gone. The point was not how to improve things but that, as dependent variables in traditional societies, their administrative structures were inherently and inescapably different.[5] An increased flow of resources to them would not improve the structures or make their behaviour more Western but would simply weaken other political structures competing with them.[6]

This approach, however, was uncritical of the actual condition of Western administration and therefore over-critical of traditional administration: the comparison was with an abstraction, against which most cases might well appear to be given to corruption, delay, or aberrations from the ideal forms. The concern of its argument was not to tell administrators how they should behave or to tell others how they should help. It was to stress the need above all for strong political control. Now that may well have been an insight refreshed by the evidence of comparative

---

[1] E. Weidner, *Technical assistance for public administration overseas: the case for development administration*, New York 1963. A good example of what he was criticizing would be the essay by Westcott in Swerdlow, *Development administration*.

[2] Weidner and D. S. Brown.

[3] Weidner. An earlier version of his argument was his paper, 'Development administration: a new focus for research', in F. Heady (ed.), *Papers in comparative public administration*, Ann Arbor 1962.

[4] Victor Thompson, 'Objectives for development administration', *Administrative Science Quarterly* 9 (1964), 91. Thompson rejected the control-oriented model in favour of a crisis model. This did, at least, attempt to provide details of an alternative.

[5] See Riggs, 'Agraria and industria' in W. Siffin (ed.), *Towards the comparative study of public administration* (see above, p. 178, n. 1). For the working out of his ideas see esp. *The ecology of public administration*, New Delhi 1961; his collected essays in *Administration in developing countries*, Boston 1964; and in J. LaPalombara (ed.), *Bureaucracy and political development*, Princeton 1963, his essay 'Bureaucrats and political development, a paradoxical view'.

[6] Similar work has been done by Binder, Foltz, Pye, and Goodnow. For some important criticisms see LaPalombara, in LaPalombara (ed.), *op. cit.*, pp. 399 ff.; Braibanti, esp. in his *Asian bureaucratic systems emergent from the British imperial tradition*, Durham 1966; and F. Heady, *Bureaucracies in developing countries: internal roles and external assistance*, mim., Bloomington 1966.

politics and anthropology.[1] It may well have been relevant to problems of communication. But it was also, in fact, very Western, this assumption about a eufunctional primacy of politicians *per se*; and, at the same time, it was utterly different from that concern about designing an administrative style to supplant the 'traditional', to pick out the detail of the 'capricious new field' which was, we have argued, the central aim of the whole development administration movement.

Yet the problems of communication, and of the dysfunctions of technical assistance and field projects, much more than the so-called problems of implementation in planning[2] were what really aroused the concern of the development administration movement. The 'movement' had thus come to believe that improvement in administration (especially along familiar Western lines), which could be called administrative improvement or administrative development, was distinct from development administration. Secondly, technical assistance (and technical assistance for public administration in particular) was looked at critically and even suspiciously. Thirdly, less developed countries' transitional or prismatic systems indicated quite peculiar characteristics of the dependent administrative subsystems.

The content of the development administration movement can now be summed up. It has been a sense of the distinctiveness of administration for development programmes, policies, and plans in those conditions (traditional, transitional or newly independent, and less developed political systems) in which there are unusually extensive needs (which could coincide with urgently expressed demands of political elites, modernizing ideologies, and exercises in mobilization); precisely where there are peculiarly few resources and exceptionally severe obstacles to meeting the needs. The peculiarity of development administration lay exactly in that inconvenient combination: extensive needs, low capacities, severe obstacles.

Against this catalogue, the character of the 'deadlock' in development administration can be more clearly seen. Weidner's own discussion, for example, is really two distinct books; one a very experienced and pointed criticism of the actual record of technical assistance for public administration, the other a very different and generalized view of development

[1] E.g. E. H. Spicer (ed.), *Human problems in technological change*, New York 1952; H. M. Teaf and P. G. Franck (eds.), *Hands across frontiers*, Ithaca 1955.

[2] But see E. S. Mason, 'The role of the government in economic development', *American Economic Review* 50 (1960), 636, for an assumption of the advantages of public entrepreneurship; L. Mack, in *Economic development and cultural change* 7 (1959), 422, for a comment; E. Shils, in his 'The concentration and dispersion of charisma; their bearing on economic policy in under-developed countries', *World Politics* 11 (1958), 1, attempts an explanation. More work has been done by Waterston and his colleagues in the I.B.R.D. Economic Development Institute and in the Syracuse series edited by Gross. For Donald Stone's views, see his two lectures to the Indian Institute of Public Administration, New Delhi, 21 and 22 January 1963, 'Administration for development and development of development administrators'.

administration as something that is simply the answer to all the problems of technical assistance—a panacea. Another writer sees clearly enough that development administration is about the focus on achieving change in situations where change is difficult. 'Failure in the execution of development programmes persists'; and secondly that the concern with reforms in internal administration—with administrative development—is inadequate.[1] That is the heart and the core of the development administration movement, whatever the variety of its sources and concerns: the difficulty of change and the inadequacy, if not worse, of mere improvement of administrative conditions. But the same writer cannot in fact find his way beyond advocating more management analysis, more competent management, more managers. The paradox is only too clear: on the one hand a search for change via administrative means, on the other a suspicion, a dissatisfaction, a distrust of administration, and at times a specifically anti-administrative position.

## WHAT IS ADMINISTRATION?

Our concepts of what administration in general is about are inadequate. Almond's idea of administration as merely an output-structure or rule-application function will not do at all.[2] Almond himself admits that he was not particularly interested and that his notion was derived from Frank Goodnow, and so back to his discussion of the separation of powers. If administrative structures are public servants working together, then they also have quite clearly to do with interest articulation, with communication between specialized interest groups and authorities, with communication within authoritative structures, with socialization and with allocation also. Older concepts were scarcely more helpful. They left quite unanswerable questions about a dichotomy of policy and administration, politics and administrators, appointed and elected personnel and so forth. They were unanswerable, no doubt, because the questions were wrongly conceived.

Administrative personnel can, amongst other things, be seen as one sort of political team, but that seems to be neither distinctive nor comprehensive enough. Political teams have to be recruited and so do the members of an administrative team. But it is clearly inadequate simply to say that administrative recruitment is like political recruitment and no more.

Certainly, personnel in offices or employed as public servants, civil, police or military, do act together as teams for political prizes from time to time, and control significant resources. This is central in the contemporary experience of new states. But what is striking is that it is members of *that*

[1] G. F. Gant, 'A note on applications of development administration', *Public Policy* 15 (1966), 200.
[2] Gabriel A. Almond, Introduction, at pp. 52 ff. in Almond and J. Coleman (eds.), *The politics of the developing areas*, Princeton 1960. See pp. 52 and also 14 esp.

sort of team who are acting together in *that* sort of way, with *that* sort of prize, and not members of other political teams.

Nonetheless, this way of analysing administration can be operational-ized. It is altogether better than thinking of administration as explained by a distinction between policy and implementation. Policy is, after all, a commitment of resources in particular patterns; decision-making is the act of choice about the use of resources. What is or is not a policy decision is primarily a way in which the actor himself perceives the significance of what he is deciding. All actors in organizations who perceive themselves as participating in the control of important resources participate in policy decision-making. So the separation of powers, a distinction between decision-making and implementation, is not at all helpful in understanding what administration is about.

To conceive of administration is, rather, a way of looking at certain relationships or acts. As Riggs puts it '...administration and politics are always analytically distinguishable aspects of certain relationships found in any government, but never separate in the sense that one act or role is exclusively administrative and another exclusively political. Cooperative acts become politico-administrative as soon as the relationship between two roles becomes asymmetrical'.[1]

But, still, how are we to distinguish the administrative aspects? They are certainly common. In any political system relationships which include these aspects are more or less inevitable. Where political systems employ formal organizations they are all the more apparent, as such organizations attempt to deal with the problems of scale, decentralization, the complexity of matter and context, the weight and timing of programmes. A political system which has a degree of centralization or hierarchy, institutionaliza-tion and specialization, almost inevitably requires asymmetrical or agency relationships. The system needs it as soon as it moves beyond the utterly diffuse and acephalous.

Hence the advice of Jethro to his son-in-law Moses, 'What is this thing that thou doest to the people? Why sittest thou thyself alone, and all the people stand by thee from morning until even?...Thou wilt surely wear away, both thou, and this people that is with thee; for this thing is too heavy for thee; thou art not able to perform it thyself alone...Thou shalt provide out of all of the people able men, such as fear God, men of truth, hating covetousness; and place such over them, to be rulers of thousands, and rulers of hundreds, rulers of fifties, and rulers of tens: And let them judge the people at all seasons: and it shall be, that every great matter they shall bring unto thee, but every small matter they shall judge: so shall it be easier for thyself, and they shall bear the burden with thee.'[2] So, as soon as agency is provided, problems of recruitment, of relations between

---

[1] F. W. Riggs, *Administration and a changing world environment*, mim. Bloomington 1968, p. 8 esp.
[2] Exodus 18:14–22.

administrators and leaders, of access and of rules of reference rapidly emerge. In other words, we can detect an administrative element in any political relationship which has the characteristics of that between principal and his agent—it is in this sense asymmetrical.

Now the facts of interest, of organizational life and of decision-making, entail that these administrative aspects of a political system will have three general characteristics, each with its own difficulties. There is, in fact, a check list of relevant questions about those situations, organizations or personnel which we tend to think of as 'administrative', having to do with administration in the public sector. In the *first* place there will be close, complex, but asymmetrical relations between leaders and administrators. The asymmetry has to be established, accepted and institutionalized. Bureaucratization is one solution, such as civil service rules about anonymity; in other styles poverty and chastity were also required. But if the members of a public service as a single group are, in fact, also going for better conditions of service, better jobs and for amendments of the restrictive rules, very quickly that raises problems for the other groups in the political arena. One answer is to require administrators to sacrifice some degree of civil rights.[1] Another is to build up a sense of obligation to the political leadership by the manufacture of a sense of favours received or sanctions unexercised.[2] As the asymmetry becomes more specialized, so the particular pattern of inducements for relevant contributions and sacrifices becomes more complex.

Those are the inward-looking relationships between leaders and administrators: the internal mechanics of asymmetry. There is, *secondly*, the effect on those relationships of the environment and the maintenance of the relationship within the environment. The network of 'official interest' constitutes an investment of resources. There is the official job and the official decision which may be made. In some systems, the prize may simply be the award of further jobs: courtly office or sinecure. Office is the point of office. It is a piece of property to gain and to keep.

In some systems, then, administration actually constitutes part of the prizes. In all systems it also constitutes a guardianship of prizes. Hence there are rules of access which govern who may approach the administration, where and how. The rules may be depersonal and bureaucratic, but there are many alternatives: traditional, ascriptive, arbitrary; the gamble, purchase, favour or partisanship. An appointed courtier meets a peasant boy on the road; he may choose to give him a letter to the king, but he may not. Administration means a problem of access to resources and relations between office-holders and clients from the community. But these relations are quite different from the political relationship of leader and support:

[1] E. Shils, *Torment of secrecy*, London 1956; A. T. Dotson, 'A general theory of public employment', *Public Administration Review* 16 (1956), 197.

[2] P. M. Blau and W. R. Scott, *Formal organisation*, London 1963, p. 142.

relations between administration and client tend to be both specialized and discrete. Relations between leaders and supporters are more ideological and on the whole more delayed exchanges.

*Thirdly*, for all the parties involved in relationships around administration—the leaders, the officials, the clients—the relationship is instrumental: the administrative aspect is perceived. But the perceptions of the instrumentality of the relationship cannot very well coincide. The courtier and the peasant boy do not hope for the same thing and do not see the situation in the same way, nor do the king and the courtier (or the man who hopes to be one).

From time to time the potential participants will thus be provoked to judge the administration. In the interim, between the judgements, administration tends to be not merely misleading, but also somewhat overwhelming. Administrators are servile, but also forceful. Administration is a matter of provisional means, but it is also a more or less unavoidable sorcerer's apprentice.

The administrative aspects of political relationships, therefore, have characteristic difficulties by which we recognize them. There are relations between the officials and the leaders, organizations and goals. There are inducements and contributions of interest and of loyalty. There may be combinations of high or low rewards for high or low service; the great soldier rewarded with glory, the clerk with his pittance. Secondly, whatever public office may bestow there will be some means of access to it, whether universalistic or arbitrary. Thirdly, whatever the communications and perception of the instrumental exchange, as long as we recognize an administrative aspect a distinctive instrumentality will be there. There may be the heavy hand of parliamentary questions or the high degree of independence of the trustee. There may be what has been called the peasant-like process of annual appropriation or the quinquennial freedom of the grant-in-aid. The perceptions of the exchange may be shared as in a temporary, Jacksonian, rotating or representative system, or conflicting as between the demotic and the esoteric; but, unlike relations between leaders and followers, and unlike political prizes, administration is instrumental. What we mean by an administrative sub-system, then, is these aspects of relationships in the political system, the places where we expect to find these sorts of problems. No particular structure will ever be wholly administrative. A particular public service does not only provide administrative aspects of relationships, nor will 'the administrative' in a political system be present only in one particular structure.

## THE BUREAUCRATIC STYLE OF ADMINISTRATION

Administration is a set of political relationships and bureaucracy is a particular set of solutions for its expected problems, a distinctive style in which the relationships can be conducted. It is not the only possibility and it is unfortunate if the term is employed as a synonym for administration. Irrespective of prescriptions, non-bureaucratic administration has, after all, worked and survived as much in the West as in the rest of the world. There can be conciliar as well as monocratic structures, recruitment by patronage as well as by proficiency. The office need not be separated from the domicile. Many alternatives are possible and almost none wholly without merit. There were good administrators in Britain before the Trevelyan–Northcote report and many recruited in many ways to different sorts of contracts; the James Stephen, the Chadwick or the Trollope type, as well as the placemen and the Treasury idiots.

There are, in other words, non-bureaucratic ways of administration. What we mean by bureaucracy is one style of administration. The point is familiar but neglected and there are some aspects of the bureaucratic style which could do with elucidation in relation to the agenda of concern about development administration. The inheritance of the extraordinary process of nineteenth-century public service reform dominates our practice and understanding of bureaucratic administration, but it was peculiar, contingent, different from place to place, not only a feature of the middle of the nineteenth century, and employing a wide variety of motives and solutions: an emphasis on superannuation here, on parliamentary appropriation there; a replacement of fees by salaries; an alteration of recruitment methods; a distinction between clerical and administrative needs here, between professional or technical and administrative there; the recovery from the disasters of war and defeat, the example of Napoleon or the fear of him; the fear of plague or the fear of taxation; a desire for judicialization or an escape from it; management as punishment and control or management as fairness and obligation.[1]

It is likely that administration in less developed conditions will not be bureaucratic. Nor is it at all surprising that it will not be wholly satisfactory. Administration is an inherently difficult set of relationships. Bendix has reminded us that each system has its characteristic tensions: the patrimonial system has tension between the inviolability of tradition and the supremacy of sanctioned arbitrariness, the bureaucratic system between the equity of the rule and the equity of the case.[2] The point of the concern

---

[1] F. M. Marx, *The administrative state*, Chicago 1957, for four types. For Weber's own meaning see, e.g. S. Udy, 'Bureaucracy and rationality in Weber's theory', *American Sociological Review* 24 (1959), 791; or H. Constas, 'Max Weber's two conceptions of bureaucracy', *American Journal of Sociology* 63 (1958), 400. For an apposite and unusually valid critical point, A. Stinchcombe, 'Bureaucratic and craft administration of production', *Administrative Science Quarterly* 4 (1959), 168. A famous critical essay is A. W. Gouldner, 'Metaphysical pathos and the theory of bureaucracy', *American Political Science Review* 49 (1955), 496. Two very helpful discussions of alternatives are R. Presthus, in *Administrative Science Quarterly* 6 (1961), 1, and in R. Ward and D. Rustow (eds.), *Political modernization in Japan and Turkey*, Princeton 1964, M. Inocki, *The civil bureaucracy: Japan*, pp. 283 ff., esp. at p. 286. For a general bibliographical discussion, S. N. Eisenstadt, 'Bureaucracy and bureaucratization', *Current Sociology* 7 (1958), 99.

[2] *Nation building and citizenship*, New York 1964.

with development administration remains what sort of administration could and should be prescribed for development situations.

There may certainly be features of Western and bureaucratic administration that development might use; but there may also be others that it cannot tolerate; costs that it cannot afford. The style of adminstration which development does need will be one which minimizes (if it does not wholly avoid) those costs, bearing in mind that any style will have a balance of advantage and disadvantage. Some of the characteristic demands of the bureaucratic style are well understood: the 'punishment morale' of large-scale industrial organization, for example; the conflict between the need of the individual to develop his own personality and the need to adapt it to the demands of the organization; the dysfunctions and unanticipated consequences of specific bureaucratic devices of control; the bureaucratization of personality; the institutionalization of means and procedures; the displacement of goals.[1] What particular aspects of the advantages and disadvantages of the bureaucratic style are relevant to the development agenda, to the conditions of less development and the needs of change, is a somewhat different question.

Bureaucracy is a particular form of decision-making and allocation; expert, universalistic, professional, computative, depersonalized, disenchanted and routinized. Within the organization particular patterns tend to be reiterated. A pattern of hierarchy emerges, for example, because the acquisition of expertise and the known commitment to the reiterated and fairly exclusive use of past cases as precedents to determine present ones make possible appellate supervision. This is what gives rise to the familiar pyramid. Rules about data storage, feedback, and search limit the information available to guide the choices to be made. The choices will, accordingly, tend to be repetitive or, at the most, adaptive. The risks of venturing beyond the well-known areas will appear to be very great and the costs will seem very unlikely to look worth while. The style lays particularly heavy emphasis on sets of rules about clientele and community access.

So, with the development agenda in mind, the following points can be made about the costs of bureaucracy. The bureacratic model is not really an *efficiency* or 'output' model. The emphasis is on repetition and reiteration rather than on innovation. Inevitable tensions of administration are solved by personality bureaucratization and institutionalization. The prime concern is not the product but the value of certainty. Certainty requires controls.

Control-orientation is not the same as programme-orientation. It is true that Weber can be paraphrased as explaining the concept of jurisdictional

---

[1] R. Merton, 'Bureaucratic structure and personality', *Social Forces* 18 (1940), 560; C. Argyris, *Personality and organisation*, New York 1957; A. W. Gouldner, *Patterns of industrial bureaucracy*, Glencoe, 1954.

areas as bundles of specific tasks and duties emerging out of a logical process of breakdown and definition from an overall programme of objectives. But it becomes '*wertrational*' to institution rather than '*zweckrational*' towards a programme.[1] That is partly because of the requirements of bureaucratization of personality. It is partly also because of the complexity, the slow but sure incremental alteration, the inner life and organizational cost of programmes. Competitiveness at any one moment within any one organization is met by a sacrifice of output to maintenance functions. The organization tends to be maintained on the one hand because of institutionalization and on the other because its overall values are preferred to any particular programme achievement.[2]

Yet bureaucracy is a style which maintains the possibilities of scale, of scattered but continuous relationships, of accepting a degree of coincidence, inconvenience and the unexpected into the running of affairs. It allows for the expert but inner directed, the non-arbitrary, and the authority of supervision as a right of appeal. The rules are both formalized and accepted in practice. That provides stability. Behaviour is expert and therefore reliable and also impersonal. The style is, then, instrumental; but not necessarily for programme achievement.[3] That was the main positive advantage of the Weber model and also of those Western and later nineteenth-century reforms which, as it happens, coincided with the model, like changes in recruitment, function and parliamentary appropriation.

### BUREAUCRATIC COSTS AND DEVELOPMENT

What are the costs and demands of this style which are most relevant to the development agenda?[4] Bureaucracy is adaptive rather than innovative, and the ways in which the bureaucratic style attempts to emphasize

[1] The distinction is, broadly, between an overwhelming commitment to a value, against which all means and actions will be judged, and the adoption of one means rather than another towards some interstitial goal. The point is that the bureaucratic style becomes more concerned to maintain the institution, come what may, than with selecting particular means for particular programmes. See A. Henderson and T. Parsons, trans. *Max Weber: the theory of social and economic organisation*, London 1947, pp. 115, 130, and 14. Of course, it is not true that the bureaucratic style is 'absolutely *wertrational*'; it is a matter of trend and balance. The point argued here is that there are factors which move bureaucracy away from a pure concern with programme achievement and economy.

[2] E.g. *The Guardian*, London 21 February 1968, quoting H.M. Treasury O. and M. Bulletin on the difficulty of defining objectives in government departments.

[3] R. H. Hall, 'Inter-organisational structural variation', *Administrative Science Quarterly* 7 (1962), 95.

[4] R. Presthus, 'Weberian versus welfare bureaucracy in traditional societies', *Administrative Science Quarterly* 6 (1961). On the possibilities of traditional resources for development, see in J. LaPalombara (ed.), *Bureaucracy and political development*, R. Braibanti, *The judiciary and bureaucracy in Pakistan*, and in Braibanti and Spengler (eds.), *Tradition, values and socio-economic development*, B. Hoselitz on the forms of tradition-oriented behaviour which might not be adverse to development.

incremental rather than other sorts of change has been much commented on.

Two points of a somewhat different nature will be particularly emphasized here. The first is the notion of 'compartmental' organizational decision-making and its costs and demands in clientele relations. The second is its reliance on one particular sort of official or instrumental role which, using English terminology, may be called that of 'the administrator' himself.[1]

## Compartmentalism

Bureaucratic behaviour is amongst other things a particular style of decision-making in formal organizations. The style means the acceptance of three sorts of rules: a rule of simplification, a rule of jurisdictional area and a rule of simulation or metaphor. 'Simplification' here means the acceptance of what Herbert Simon called the habit of satisficing rather than maximizing. In so far as the bureaucratic style is thought to be 'rational', it is supposed that its habit is to optimize. That, in fact, is not the case. The choice sought is not the best possible, but one that is good enough. Great ranges of ends, of interstitial values and of data are excluded from consideration.

Compartmentalization, then, is the acceptance of the possibility of a generous application of the rule of *ceteris paribus*. But this simplification of choice has two aspects. It narrows the search for data. It also narrows the grounds on which choices will be evaluated. But in many development situations it is especially important that both the search and the evaluation should not be too narrow.

The second aspect of compartmentalized decision-making is that individual officials will not merely narrow the area of data search and the evaluation on the basis of which choices will be formulated, but will also narrow the area within which they will make choices at all. They will make choices about some issues, but not about others. In popular parlance, they will pass the buck.

The third point about the bureaucratic style of decision-making is that it carries to the greatest height the equity of the rule; and, consequently, the gap in perception and communication between the decision-maker and the client from the community. What the official can see, hear, or listen to is only a part of the 'real' situation. He sees a 'case', a case that can (or cannot) be brought within the scope of a rule, and not the whole human situation which gives rise to it.

There are good reasons for that. In the first place, it is in his interest to anticipate his defence, as an agent who will sooner or later be called to account. His defence is to abide by what has been called the golden rule

[1] B. B. Schaffer, 'The distinction between executive and administrative work', *Public Administration* (Sydney) 17 (1956), 112.

of public administration: like treatment for like cases. It is in the interests of the bureaucrat to see the issue as something which is wholly familiar, completely precedented and therefore a case completely (not merely adequately) covered by an existing and not-to-be-changed rule. But it may be in the interests of the client to maintain as far as he possibly can the unique characteristics, urgency and difference of his own situation, or at least its unique urgency. There is thus an inherent conflict between the interest of the bureaucratic official and the interest of the client. In the second place, the combination of the rules of simplification, specialization, and area mean that any one bureaucratic decision-maker, however well intentioned, can see in fact only one part of what may appear to the client to be relevant and indeed essential.

A bureaucratization of personality is required for decision-making behaviour of this sort. It is what is meant by 'depersonalizing' the choices made. The applicant's letter, say, is written from one point of view with one set of motives, and with other ranges of data present in his mind and surely, he must feel, more or less expressed by what he says. The interest of the official and the rules of procedure which he must follow place the letter as the last document on the file. Only certain parts of the data which the applicant expresses, and maybe none of the data which the applicant implies, can conscientiously be taken into account. Even supposing that it needs to be said, it can in no way be detected by the administrator. There is much that he does not, cannot and must not hear. What he does hear or see is something different; in fact a simulation or a metaphor. His choices are the next and proper step, a restrained and restricted one, along the departmental line.

Now the interesting question is under what conditions people will find this sort of decision-making tolerable. For it to be tolerable two things are necessary. The first is that the unconsidered facts, the unanticipated consequences, and the choices not made are either insignificant or primarily eufunctional. Hence compartmentalized decision-making cannot operate in situations where either the unanticipated results or the dysfunctions are likely to be more significant than the eufunctional. The second requirement of compartmentalization is that the width of the gap of perception, the communications problems between the bureaucratic administration on the one hand and the client or community on the other, does not matter too much, can be tolerated, or else can somehow be reduced.

There are many factors which may make this so. In developed societies we are conditioned to understand a simplification of choice. It is what we all do. The rule of *ceteris paribus* lies at the heart of the emergence of disciplines for research, of professional behaviour and of much vocational activity. The interpersonal relations of the adaptive society are in any case specialized and in that sense 'blind'. The developed society makes relatively small demands on empathy. Specialized organization means precisely the overlooking of many implications of action. It may be wrong to carry that fashion into different sorts of society. 'Important implications of action in terms of relatively nonspecialised organisation tend to be overlooked because as members of relatively modernised societies we habitually overlook them.'[1]

Further, the formal organizational rules creating jurisdictional areas, and the breakdown of decision-making on whole entities into metaphorical cases and specialized issues, assumes some fit between the jurisdictional areas and simulation and the real world. That will be more or less true, granted some degree of stability in the organization and its environment. Bureaucratization, as we have said, means a relatively high degree of acceptance by the public of the organization's norms, and this is only possible in conditions of stability.[2] And stability of organizational–environmental relations demands a relatively low rate of occurrence of critical decisions.[3] This helps people to recognize these decisions as critical and to transfer them from the 'administration' to the 'political level' so that responsibility for taking them can be lifted from the bureaucratic agency.

Compartmentalism, therefore, demands ready processes for referring issues elsewhere and relatively high degrees of stability. It is stability which makes possible formal organizations; their own continuity which allows compartmentalism. It is in its turn that compartmental behaviour which allows the strain of the informal and unanticipated in the formal organization to be tolerable. But an essential part of this possibility is the concept of the marginal itself. That is what an incremental output means. It is not that choices about change cannot be made, but they can only be made at the margin of the service being provided. If we take such a matter as a school building programme we see that for compartmentalism to be possible, a decision about building the $n$th school and about its location as between place $x$ and place $y$ must not be critical. The question must be dealt with technically rather than politically. Secondly, while the decision might well make some difference to the environment of the organization like a difference of more or less convenience for its potential clients, it cannot be a difference about a total way of life. Compare a decision about locating a school in the London Home Counties, for example, with such a decision in the New Guinea highlands. In the one case it may make, at the most, a difference of a school journey; in the other case it is likely to make a difference of an absolute nature about participation in one of two quite different ways of life.

There are two other points to be made about the sort of perception required for compartmentalized behaviour. In the organization there will

[1] Marion Levy, *Modernisation and the structure of societies*, Princeton 1966, p. 25.
[2] See F. G. Bailey's work on political anthropology, esp. *Stratagems and Spoils*, Oxford 1969.
[3] P. Selznick, *Leadership in administration*, Evanston 1957, for the concept of critical decisions.

be patterns of recruitment and training, and rules about allocation of work, access and flows of information, about what will be heard and stored. In particular there will be rules about what will be recalled. The first point is that these must all help to create a sufficient degree of sensitivity to secure the right amount of referral upwards, a movement from a position where there are administrative resources to one where there are political resources. This must occur when new cases cease to be capable of being handled under established precedent. The metaphor breaks down; the critical, as opposed to the routine, decision now has to be taken; the world breaks in.

The critical moment can be recognized and dealt with occasionally but not continuously. Ministers, for example, can be responsible for vast quantities of organizational behaviour such as decision-making, precisely because there is so high a coincidence between what the rules dictate and what people are prepared for, and thus a reliable stability. Secondly, they can rely on a perception, somewhere within the organization, of what is potentially critical. The range of ministerial attention demanded is tolerable because of a rather low occurrence of the critical, a relatively reliable perception of it, some degree of coincidence between organizational or administrative perceptions and environmental, political, or community perceptions.

For all this to work it must be possible to recruit into the organization an acceptance of compartments and a perception of their occasionally too costly limits. The political culture and socialization in the United Kingdom, and its formal education system, have in the past met that requirement. A sense of the fitting, of what is not done, and of what is not, need not, or cannot be talked about was cultivated. The inculcation of these characteristics of behaviour corresponds precisely with the perceptive and cognitive requirements of compartmentalization. In so far as these cultural supports may disintegrate, it would become increasingly difficult for that sort of bureaucratic organizational behaviour to obtain. The organizations would have to come to rely much more on post-entry training than on pre-entry preparation and recruitment, much more on the organization culture and much less on the general political culture.

The second general problem of perception is how the client sees the organization. As I have explained, there is both an inherent conflict of interest between the client and the bureaucrat and an inherent difference of perception. This sort of difference or conflict can obviously be very dangerous for an organization. The danger will nevertheless be tolerable when the behaviour of the official, however it may conflict with the client's interests and perceptions, is at least comprehensible to him. The client, though irritated, will remember that he too understands the distinction between home and office, between the lay and the specialized, and between duty and will. He is a member of an adaptive society in which he himself is not always a client, but sometimes a specialist on his own account. The very irritation may remind him of that. One way of putting this would be to say that the client will tolerate bureaucratic behaviour and, in particular, its peculiar rules of access, in societies where people know how to 'queue'. Such a society is, ideally, neither one in which riot has to be met with 'pacification', nor one in which a different availability of time, a different conception of time, or low valuation of it, leads people to vitiate the rules of 'queuing' for access by a sort of 'camping out'.[1] (Hence studies of the conditions under which civil violence occurs are suggestive as ways of setting the extreme limits.[2])

Bureaucratization thus demands sacrifice by the client. It also means the surrender of a range of interests by the official. His satisfaction assumes an identification of his remaining interests with the interests of the organization, perhaps their further identification with those of the service, programme, goal or output itself. It also demands a sacrifice in the acceptance of a particular style of access and exchange by the client and the community. Bureaucratic access assumes a functional coincidence between its rules of storage and recall and the minimalization of the search for relevance. On the other hand, the rules of access are supposed to be stable, in that sense potentially familiar and public, and thus neutral and instrumental. In fact, they serve various sections of the community unequally. They favour some categories at the expense of others.

There is, moreover, an inherent tension between the need of the organization for depersonalization, and its need for a degree of sensitivity to the extrinsic, the critical, and the unexpected. Non-political organizational behaviour has to some extent to be politicized just so that it can be maintained. There has to be some sort of recourse to non-bureaucratic types of organizational behaviour to make sure that critical decision-making will be initiated in time, and a safety-valve thus provided to prevent adverse reactions by the public leading to the destruction of the organization. Hence social work organizations use highly *informal* appeals in procedures. These are precisely the organizations in which the bureaucratic requirement of non-arbitrary decision-making coincides most uncomfortably with the pressure of the individual client for something quite different. If we have to go beyond bureaucracy in administration to provide a welfare state, it is scarcely surprising that we may need to go beyond it for development purposes too.

The costs and limits of bureaucracy are indeed severe. They may be tolerated, granted a combination of three particular conditions: where the demands both of executive and of administrative work can be met,[3]

---

[1] R. Apthorpe, 'The introduction of bureaucracy into African politics', *Journal of African Administration* 12 (1960), 15.

[2] T. Gurr and C. Ruttenberg, *The conditions of civil violence*, Princeton 1967.

[3] See above, p. 192, n. 1.

where the client will be provoked up to a point but not beyond it and where the need for critical decision-making is not too frequent and choices of predominantly incremental change will be accepted and perceived. Two of these three conditions entail the recruitment and acceptance of one particular sort of bureaucrat, the administrator.

### The administrator

A bureaucratic administrator is not so much a man who wins arguments about choices, as one who detects the need for and then wins arguments about the limits within which choices must be made. He is a man who indicates and delineates the issue, who sees that it is his or at any rate his department's metaphor that is chosen.

Now there is a sort of bargain in bureaucracy between the organization and its environment. The system will allow the organization to be sustained if in the end the costs are just worth the output. On the other hand, the organization will be fairly well institutionalized. It will provide an output in the terms of what the system wishes in so far as it is necessary to maintain itself. The reference processes and the leadership function of detecting the critical moment and acting appropriately are therefore the most important requirements of organizational survival.

The bureaucratic style thus requires leadership within rather severe limits. The political role in the policy decision-making drama provides one element. The bureaucratic administrator provides another. The key element in his particular contribution is precisely his institutionalization; that is to say, his commitment to maintain the organization. The bureaucratic style means a high degree of institutionalization. Institutionalization requires effective articulation of the interest of instituted organization maintenance in the critical decision-making process itself. That is the administrator's concern, rather than programme output. It is an expensive condition of the bureaucratic style.

Let us emphasize just what the administrator is expert about; what his characteristic contribution is. The whole justification of his position is that he is a professional, a specialized and expert person; but it is a local, not a cosmopolitan, expertness. He is an expert in that particular organization, not in the social system except in so far as the environment affects the institution; he understands and operates certain sets of rules about access, storage, recall, selection, and referral. Above all, he knows the delicate rules for determining when the routine rules must be changed, when and how critical decisions must be made.

The administrator must suppose these rules to be exact, complete, reliable, and stable. But they may become none of these. At that moment the administrator is no longer a help but an obstacle, and that moment can come at almost any time and in surprising ways. If the rules he knows about critical detection are no longer appropriate, disaster may follow.

o

He is supposed to anticipate the occasions for considering defensive adaptations; but if he fails to detect some radical or sudden change, owing to his degree of contentment with the existing set of rules (e.g. by miscalculating the tolerance or the resources of the disappointed) the very identification of his institution with those rules will put it in jeopardy. He goes beyond routine to discretion, but the discretion is not arbitrary. The guarded discretion is meant to save the institution; it may endanger it.

Here is the abyss at the edge of which this extraordinary role perpetually stands. The abyss would disappear if stability were more assured or prediction easier than we can suppose it ever is. The administrator's rules about the anticipation of the critical are, after all, still the rules of experience. Rules of experience are rules of thumb. Neither the actual achievements of social science nor the degree of their use by administration has yet served to alter that. Of course, conditions in a developed society are precisely those in which we can most easily suppose that the network of rules of thumb will keep the administrator from the abyss. The situation in new political systems, however, is markedly different. The stable political system is one in which this role, both identifying with the rules and yet in some way rising above them, may be just manageable. But the tolerance of such a role cannot be universal and is generally rather unlikely in new political systems.

Hence the compartmentalism of bureaucracy and its requirement of an administrative role are highly contingent and more likely to be tolerable in some societies than others. Bureaucracy is not always completely tolerable in Western societies. It may be all too easily tolerated in less developed conditions where the sorts of services and structures represented by public organization are of marginal value to the small-scale social structures of the underdeveloped society. But in post-colonial societies attempting development, it does *not* seem likely that there will be an environment conducive to peaceful queuing. If we consider bureaucracy as a particular kind of solution for the various requirements of administration, we see that it is particularly difficult to afford in less developed societies where rapidly induced change is being sought. It deals with the problem of access, for example, by a peculiarly high compartmentalization of reception and very radical processes of simplification.

It is in the diffuse society that unanticipated consequences of outputs are likely to be highly significant and the compartmentalization of behaviour unacceptable, all the more so where the provision or alteration of services is likely to proceed by changes which are perceived as significant rather than marginal. This is likely for three main reasons: the significance of any change at all where initial levels are low; the wide dispersal of the effects; and above all, the lack of public empathy with the bureaucratic style of administration. Further, bureaucracy means the investment of very heavy resources for rather a small degree of change. An efficient bureaucracy, in fact, involves a high degree of institutionalization in exchange for incremental changes; yet these are societies which cannot afford the resources for which the institutionalization is inappropriate and for which incremental changes are largely irrelevant.

The bureaucratic style also means maintaining a balance of interests between employees of the organization on the one hand, and the organization or programme on the other. But the creation of the administrative role which can secure such a balance is exceptionally hard in a diffuse society going through a developmental process.

Yet the unhappy paradox remains that the bureaucratic style and the administrator, so expensive and so unsuitable for the ex-colonial states in process of development, are highly respected by them as a result of the colonial inheritance. But bureaucratic administration was tolerable in colonial situations in so far as the bureaucrats were providing what has been called good government rather than development. This was typical of those situations where the bureaucratic structure could be tolerated by the diffuse society because the society consisted of a large number of small-scale systems, each relatively autonomous, and the administration, seen from the outside, was in any case making only a marginal impact.

### The pyramid

Before leaving the costs of the bureaucratic style, we may derive from them a possibly constructive line of approach to the structure and style of administration which may, perhaps, be appropriate for development. I have mentioned executive and administrative work. By administrative I mean the sort of work in which the 'exception principle' is not relevant, and by executive the sort in which it is.

The exception principle is the supposition that rank and file operation can be run normally without constant supervision; intervention will be 'exceptional'. Executive work can occur when there is insulation from the environment or where the job descriptions, the orders of the day as it were, are accurate, reliable, and sufficient. Administrative work, as we have seen, occurs where decision-making is rather heavily involved in external factors or cannot be adequately planned: critical tests of discretion occur. Organization for each type produces a different sort of pyramid: the executive wide and flat, with few levels and more functional specialization in supervision; the administrative narrow and high, with more levels and less specialization.

The programming of work can certainly be increased as techniques improve, but the area of the non-programmed remains significant. It may even grow just as the techniques improve; there may be an ever-receding horizon. The problem then would be whether development administration can be organized on the exception principle with that sort of pyramid or can be separated from the administrative with the other sort of pyramid; can the administrative role be more or less avoided in that way?

The development administration movement and its sources, colonial inheritance, administrative development, and technical assistance, have not concerned themselves with that question but on the contrary with attempts at recruiting, creating by training, and improving the conditions of the administrator. Yet he represents one sort of rationality rather than another: institutional rather than craft, for example; a man of the centre even when he is in the field, where he may see himself as representative and yet tends to represent only those people who exploit the rules of access, and who are in this as in other respects not representative of the whole public.

The heavy costs of placing the administrator at the top are only justified, then, if the most important work is done in the headquarters. If it was the hived-off executive organization that mattered more, there would have to be a quite different strategy for careers, awards and prestige, and for the whole machinery of government.

Can we find ways in development of relying on the research station, the field service, the output organization more, and the administrator less? I have questioned whether or not there might have to be a sort of politicizing of the administrative role. The other side of the argument may be a need for a form of low-level 'technologizing' of administrative agencies. One of the conditions, insulation from the environment, which makes executive work possible, is likely to be absent; we may have to experiment instead with the other conditions. More job sheets and programming, for instance, will alter the whole balance of training; they will also pull the shape of organization away from administrative departmentalization.

### THE PROBLEM AND NEEDS OF ADMINISTRATION
### FOR DEVELOPMENT

The fact that the bureaucratic style is not appropriate does not mean that the administrative relationship is not required for development. The political leader who sees his problem as mainly a shortage of public servants may not be wholly off the mark. The problems of public administration in less developed countries are not irrelevant to development, nor is it irrelevant that the various strategies for development which should have concerned themselves with administration have not done so, or have done so inadequately. What requirements must an administration for development aim to meet? Reviewing Geoffrey Bing's book *Reap the whirlwind,* President Kaunda wrote, 'Bing diagnosed Ghana's major handicaps as the fragility of its mono-economy and the inexperienced and understaffed public service with which he had been endowed; Zambia struggles today under precisely the same handicaps'.[1]

An inadequate and inappropriate preparation is certainly part of the problem. There was an inheritance of a strongly control-oriented establishment which assumed a steel frame between the field and the central secretariat. It did employ relatively high degrees of decentralization, but of a special sort. As Kaunda said, 'The system and not the people dominated all aspects of life'. Delegation was possible partly because of the limitation of what was being sought. It was also possible partly because of the dominance of technical by administrative services, and the selective content, the small numbers and the oblique impact of administration. There were also strong inner identifications of a public service system, highly trained and separate from the society it was ruling.

There was in many countries a sudden move towards the new public service system, recently recruited, rapidly promoted, undertrained and small. There was now a sharp contrast between its acquired admiration for its predecessors' administrative style, and the demands enunciated from the new and partly hostile, partly incoherent, political system. Such demands from the periphery which had previously been illegitimate were now strong and clear, but there were now also the often all-too-explicit demands of central urban elites, parties, and national political leaderships. Furthermore, if these new demands were actually developmental, they were in conflict with the style which the inheriting administration knew about and copied. If they were not, they were represented as if they were. Incoherent in expression, the demands for administrative resources were overwhelming, especially in terms of the range of the projects required, from the large-scale and central to projects requiring maximum, scattered coverage of the entire community.

The inheriting administrations have also gone through the experience of overseas collaboration. That was partly because of the modernizing ambitions of the political elites which involved them in intimate overseas relationships and a local effort at imitation. Capital aid meant experience of collaboration, negotiation, bargaining, and competition about programmes. Actual technical assistance commonly meant what might be called a superstructural elaboration, to rival, to imitate, or to deal with the advisers, the teams, and the projects of the missions. It has left an institutional deposit.

There was now a strong political norm about delegation, community involvement, and decentralization. Unfortunately, this coincided with a wholly inadequate preparation of junior and executive staff. The actual staff and technology required for delegation, for hiving off executive work, was minimal. But, as in other fields, it was precisely the absence of that low technological level which was the problem. In that situation, it was

[1] *Sunday Times*, London 9 June 1968.

unlikely that those possessing the rare resource of lower-level technical competence would be prepared to devote it to the humbler rewards of the appropriate roles. Relations between the centre and the locality present difficulties for the Western bureaucratic style. They were at least as difficult in developing conditions. They aggravated the problems of the political–administrative relationship itself. They enhanced the problem of a change of style. They were themselves enhanced by the type of output required and the community reception available, and by the inadequacy of a community or grass-roots ideology to support the actual relations between administration and community in a programme.

It was difficult to recruit people with the appropriate motivation and resources unless the rewards were altered. It was also difficult to get the new sort of information which was required flowing from field, peripheral, or research operations to headquarters, between party and official bureaucracy, between those concerned with controls and others concerned with projects, between leaders and representatives. Allocation in conditions of extreme scarcity was exceptionally difficult, and coincided with the severe problem of structuring wholly new patterns of communication. For example, if it was agreed that local administration was now more important, it was necessary still to decide what it should actually look like and actually be doing: representing the locality in the centre, building a new sort of community, reinforcing or altering local leadership, institutionalizing programmes or advancing a particular project, recruiting resources of taxation or resources of labour. Here were elements in the political system which had been excluded from the colonial bureaucratic domination, or at least unrepresented in it. For them perhaps the colonial system had not always mattered very greatly. Now if they were not in fact to be central, at any rate the ideological message was that they should be, and messages do matter. The actual gaps between the administrator and the field or community seemed in no sense to have been reduced by the mere political changes at the centre arising from the transfer of power.

If this was the agenda of difficulties which the inheriting administration faced, it is not surprising that there has been a series of somewhat panicky searches for panaceas: central planning, public service training, technical assistance for public administration, community development. The nature of the deadlock can be seen in the combination of the continuing validity of the need behind the various searches and hopes, with the actual record of successive disappointments. Some of the consequential debates have been illuminating. The whole debate about the record and the strategies, the validity and the possibility of technical assistance for public administration is one outstanding example.[1] Let us consider briefly the particular example of community development.

[1] J. Montgomery and W. Siffin (eds.), *Approaches to development: politics, administration and change*, New York 1966, esp. the essays by D. S. Brown and R. Braibanti. Also D. Ashford, *Political linkage of AID instruments*, mim., 1968.

## THE COMMUNITY DEVELOPMENT APPROACH

The central concerns of community development have included things like village organization and other levels of government.[1] Community development has indeed been defined as 'in fact no more than a modern conception of administration'.[2] It was 'modern' perhaps because it seemed deeply concerned about the public administration content of technical assistance, its expensive, elaborate or marginal projects, its subversion of community institutions, and about problems of communication and allocation. Above all, community development claimed to show a way around the whole difficulty of 'projectism' and the communication gap, the unanticipated but significant dysfunctions of imposed public works, with its own techniques for discovering felt needs and for recruiting available participation and means.

Community development has certainly now built up a fascinating record in, for example, Ghana, the Philippines, India and Pakistan, and Latin America.[3] Its origins were partly in colonial preparatory policy for local government and mass literacy education and in the American experience of agricultural extension and home economics taken together.[4] Since decolonization, there has been a wide variety of experiments: clubs, village resettlement, low-level political institutionalization.

The approach looks highly relevant. The record shows that it has in fact been a heavy user of administrative resources: an addition rather than a solution to the administrator's burdens.[5] The point, however, is not primarily that the record, for all its interest, has been disappointing, but that it is important to understand why it cannot in fact provide a solution for development administration at all.[6] Bureaucratic administration, I have argued, is committed not to output but to institution maintenance.

[1] *International co-operation administration, community development review*, December 1956. S. C. Dube, 'Some problems of community development', *Economic Development and Cultural Change* 5 (1957), 129.

[2] Governor of Uganda, despatch 490/52, 22 July 1952.

[3] U.N. Seminar, *Administrative aspects of community development*, Hague 1959; B. M. Villanueva, 'The community development programme of the Philippines government', *Philippines Journal of Public Administration* 1 (1957), 144; A. Mayer, McKim Marriott, and R. L. Park, *Pilot project, India*, Berkeley 1959; I. Narain, 'A fundamental approach to the administration of the rural community development programme', *Indian Journal of Public Administration* 5 (1959), 159 and 274. Indian Planning Commission Evaluation Organisation, *Evaluation of the Working of Community Projects*, New Delhi 1964; R. N. Adams, *et al.*, *Social change in Latin America today*, New York 1960.

[4] U.N. Mission, *Community development in Africa*, New York 1956. Colonial Office, London, Ashridge Conference, Social Development in the British Colonial Territories, London, Col. Misc. 523, 1954; and Mass Education in African Society, 186, 1935; and Visual Aids in Education and Community Development, 527, 1956. H.M.S.O., Community Development, London 1966, p. 9. H. Belshaw, *The communities project strategy approach to economic development*, mim., n.d., Noumea (South Pacific Commission), 2.

[5] B. Narain, 'Health programmes in the community project areas', *Indian Journal of Public Administration* 1 (1955), 104.

[6] D. Hapgood (ed.), *Policies for promoting agricultural development*, Cambridge, Mass., p. 5.

Community development is committed, too: it is concerned not with its projects or their ends 'but what happens in the process of achieving them'. That, in the event, turns out to be 'the strengthening of the community togetherness, its organic coherence'.[1] The approach is political, not administrative: ideologically committed and suited to mobilization and aggregation rather than to the requirements of feedback, evaluation, and instrumentality. It could not be put more sharply than this: that once that 'primary focus' (on the transcendence of the local group) is lost, 'the emphasis shifts from getting people working together to getting concrete things done and the movement begins to assume more and more the character of administration'.[2]

The approach is thus heavily ideological. It employs myth freely.[3] Its arguments are self-proving: every human group, *by definition*, possesses 'the opportunity and capacity' for self-help and 'the liberty to adopt new ways of living'.[4] This convenient notion of 'latency' is almost millenarial. There is a method which the approach possesses; the End is bound to be achieved, for the Method *is* the End, and the means are always (even if only 'latently') there; failure can only be due to extrinsic obstacles, not to the Method itself.

And behind the egalitarian colour of its normative themes lies something very different: hierarchical, biased, committed.[5] This can be explained in part by the origins and history of the approach.[6] The main point, however, goes further than that. In the first place, the approach assumes the reification of a particular view of the community, its virtue, its resources and structure, its potentialities, and its priority as a value against all others.[7] It is a political movement, not an administrative strategy at all. Secondly, the approach assumes an appropriate fit, a harmony and absence of conflict between the central and the local community and the list of what each wants and provides. It is, in the end, an essentially romantic movement, by an intelligentsia, for 'the people', like that of the *Volia i Zemlia* of the *narodniks*—with all the potential authoritarianism that that implies.

Yet its actual view of the community is highly open to criticism: the poorer the community the less its cooperative resources, in fact. Projects may reinforce factional conflict rather than strengthen coherence. The

[1] I. C. Jackson, *Advance in Africa*, London 1956; S. K. Dey, *Community development: a bird's eye view*, New York 1964; J. McAuley, in *Bulletin of the South Pacific commission*, July 1964.

[2] J. McAuley, *loc. cit.*

[3] Secretary-general, Message to the Trusteeship Council, U.N., 19 June 1956.

[4] U.N., 'Social progress through community development 1955', p. 6; K. L. Robinson, *International Conference of Agricultural Economics Proceedings*, 1956, p. 515.

[5] A. T. Dotson, 'Democratic decentralization in local self-government', *Indian Journal of Public Administration* 4 (1958), 38.

[6] *Community development*, see above, p. 203, n. 4.

[7] A. B. Lewis, 'Local self-government. A key to national economic advancement and political stability', *Philippines Journal of Public Administration* 2 (1958), 54; L. R. Bundagaard, 'Philippines local government', *Journal of Politics* 19 (1957), 262; S. C. Dube, 'Cultural factors in rural community development', *Journal of Asian Studies* 16 (1956), 19.

truly-felt needs may be inadequate, impossible or, in any case, quite irrelevant to the community development list. Resources put into projects which are on that list may well aggravate local problems of maintaining the continuity of previously initiated services. The record shows much greater change through quite other agencies, like immigration, market towns, urbanization, which indeed actually accompany deterioration of community relationships.[1]

Thus, in so far as the approach concerns itself with an administrative agenda at all, it is an inadequate statement of what development administration has to deal with. It is concerned explicitly only with the one matter of the gap in communication between government as a whole and the client in the guise of the local community. The agenda is, we have seen, much more complex than that, and the problem is its complexity: clientele access, the organization and the employee, and maintaining the usefulness of the agency and its commitment to its proper purposes.

Apart from this inadequacy, the approach does not provide a solution for development administration partly because it is actually anti-administrative. That is so not so much because of its frequent and apparently normative hostility to certain sorts of administrative agency and officials, on whom it happens, in fact, to rely.[2] It is more because of its ideological defences against evaluation and feedback, the most urgent requirements of a development administration style.[3] It also fails to provide a solution because it seeks a mere blotting out of the problem: on the one hand it seemed to make evaluation unnecessary; on the other hand it sought, not to solve the problems of communication, allocation and access, but to be an alternative to administration. It bridged the gap by abolishing it from view.

The approach did reveal one part of the problem of administration for development. Its contribution could at best have been partial; it has tended, in fact, to be obstructive. The record shows that it relied at least as heavily on imposed solutions, and was as much obsessed with 'projects',

---

[1] E. C. Banfield, *The moral basis of a backward society*, New York 1958, pp. 151–9; H. Miner, 'Culture change under pressure; a Hausa case', *Human Organisation* 19 (1960), 164; Tito C. Firmalino, 'Political activities of Barrio citizens as they affect community development', *Philippines Journal of Public Administration* 4 (1960), 151; P. Selznick, *TVA and the grassroots*, Berkeley and Los Angeles 1949; R. E. Ward, 'The Socio-political role of the Buraku in Japan', *American Political Science Review* 45 (1951), 1025; Inayatullah and Q. M. Shafi, *Dynamics of development in a Pakistan village*, Peshawar 1963.

[2] Contrast the careful evaluation by A. C. Mayer, 'An Indian community development block revisited', *Public Administration* 30 (1957), 35, with H. W. Beer and D. Ensminger, 'The development block as a social system', *Indian Journal of Public Administration* 5 (1959), 135; for the heavy administrative demands, see B. Narain, see above, p. 203, n. 3. See also H. Orenstein, *Gaon: Conflict and cohesion in an Indian village*, Princeton 1965, p. 13 and p. 298 esp.

[3] For a study of the village settlement idea as an example of a commitment, see G. B. Mansfield, 'Comparison between settlement in villages and isolated homesteads', *Journal of African Administration*, 7 (1955), 64. See, generally, Henry C. Hart, *The village and development administration*, Bloomington 1967, esp. p. 34.

as any of the other governmental agencies; and it remained simply an extrinsic structure for inducing some changes rather than others.[1] But above all it implied mere escape: to achieve community–administrative relationships, which are inevitably specialized and limited, as though they were multiplex;[2] to solve the problem of allocation by pretending that it was a function of demand; and to solve the problem of communication by acting as though the specialized messages of administration were idioms familiar to the whole community. The consequence has been as much waste, disappointment and imbalance as with any other technique. The approach has become, in the end, a sort of masquerade, at least as far as the problems of development administration are concerned.

## CONCLUSIONS

There is nothing in the requirements which development imposes to suggest that a system facing them needs administration less than other political systems do. The whole difficulty is the attempt to work out how the requirements can be met when we bear in mind both the heavy costs and limited tolerance of the bureaucratic style, and the breakdown of various other proposed solutions such as community development.

The effort to work out the necessary prescriptions has been exciting,[3] particularly the debate on the degree to which administration can be altered more or less independently of other changes, and about strategies for alteration. The debate has concerned the degree of independence of the administrative aspects, the appropriate agencies for designing and assisting change and a problem of balance or imbalance which is strikingly comparable with similar debates going on elsewhere in development studies.[4] However, it has also been tantalizing. Apart from the problem of dependence and strategy, the actual prescriptions themselves have either been ignored or have expressed what was irrelevant, Western, and far too expensive, on the one hand, or anti-administrative on the other. The prescription has either reiterated the intolerable or disguised the requirement. The gap between the critical and the prescriptive remains.[5]

---

[1] Indian Planning Commission, Reports, see above, p. 203, n. 3; K. Nair, *Blossoms in the dust*, New York 1962.

[2] Henry C. Hart, *The village and development administration* uses some of F. G. Bailey's work (see above, p. 194, n. 2) in an unusually helpful and brilliant fashion.

[3] Warren Ilchman, 'Rising expectations and the revolution in development administration', *Public Administration Review* 25 (1965), 314.

[4] Ilchman and R. C. Bhargava, 'Balanced thought and economic growth', *Economic Development and Cultural Change* 14 (1966), 385.

[5] The essays by L. Pye and J. Westcott, in Swerdlow (ed.), *Development administration, concepts and problems*, at pp. 25 and 45, indicate the range of disagreement. A. Diamant, *Bureaucracy in development movement regimes; a bureaucratic model for developing societies*, mim., Bloomington 1964, shows the difficulty of prescription. His assumption that the central higher public service is the modernizing element, and that local officials have merely what he calls the 'simple' tasks of 'education', 'health' etc., is unhelpful.

Are there in fact any possibilities of actually working out prescriptions for administration for development in the special and difficult conditions with which we are concerned; or at any rate of working out ways in which research towards this end could be conducted? Bear in mind the categories of requirements which administrative aspects set up: first of all a balancing of inducements against contributions, so as to recruit and retain agents, and so that in consequence certain sorts of career, various types of organizational membership and various types of sacrifice of interest and of reward are provided. Secondly, there must be rules of information and communication, about reception, storage, feedback and recall, and about consideration, like the bureaucratic set about radical simplification, jurisdiction, and simulation; and on the other hand rules about access, what can be communicated and what can be allocated, like the bureaucratic system of queuing. Thirdly, there are the ways in which the instrumentality of the exchange, its asymmetry as it were, will in the end be enforced.

There have been alternative styles for each of the requirements and there must be future ones which have yet to be designed, or will tend to emerge. A mere statement of the received ideas of medium-level theory within any particular system could be used to suggest them.[1] The Western prescription is for single supervision, a division of 'staff' from 'line', independent personnel controls. One could look at opposites as alternative arrangements: multiple supervision, teams instead of departments, and so forth. As a first step that would be free from some dangers and prevent one from going happily on to some third level of purely exotic devices.

It is also possible to use the general analysis of administration as a check list of requirements, and then to see behind most second-level administrative prescriptions the findings of diagnostic criteria with which they are, in effect, attempting to deal. Thus, while we should avoid a commitment, say, to O. and M. as a panacea, the questions for which things like O. and M. were meant to be answers may still be a part of the requirement for development administration. For example, we will still have to deal with the conflicting need for, on the one hand, limiting the numbers of things an official must consider and the number of people he must deal with, and on the other, for limiting the distance between the point of leadership and the point of treatment. We must still deal with the opposed needs of different types of official interest and contribution, as line and staff may be called. We still need to work out ways in which the bits of work to be done are distributed and brought together again. Line and staff, the span of

---

[1] Sayre and Kaufman, *A research design for a pilot study in public administration*, list the hypotheses of the American public administration movement and relate them, interestingly, to the requirements of organization, control, and compliance, which may be compared with the three requirements of interest, instrumentality, and access used in this paper.

control and the range of attention, the allocation of functions used purely as diagnostic criteria, could still be very helpful indeed.

This is true as long as we see quite clearly why, in terms of the requirements of interest, access and instrumentality, quite different answers will have to be given for administration for development. O. and M. could be replaced by more concentration on smaller (methods) and larger (machinery of government) questions. Personnel functions like assessment must still be performed, but in different ways: the received methods may be both too elaborate and quite deleterious.

Thirdly, administration is an exchange of resources for contributions. We should take a fresh look at the resources it does possess. So far it has suffered from an emotive rejection of certain resources because they are inherently extrinsic: a good example is the rejection of research as a precondition for selecting effective interventionist tactics. Yet it was exactly that approach, a research and development approach as he called it, which Holmberg employed at Vicos in working out a device (giving hot school lunches) before utilizing the many other resources which he happened to have available.[1] That was quite a different approach from the community development strategy. It is one that has been much used in population policy.

We must also be prepared to accept that effective administration is not necessarily the most humane. If there are resources, say, for counter-insurgency, for resettlement, or for a highly selective policy for allocating some scarce resource like housing, the designer of development administration should not reject them a priori. Again, the unanticipated consequences of specialized projects like road-building may be, if not optimal, at any rate functional; granted the resources, it may be best to go ahead, after all. The prescription is not for hesitation, rejection, or anticipation, but for feedback. Of course, the actual programme or output for which there are administrative resources will not necessarily be developmental at all: that is another matter.

Administration as decision-making will always be compartmentalized. The compartmentalization does not have to be bureaucratic. So a new sort of compartmentalization is required: processes of programming and research have been suggested as non-bureaucratic ways of selecting data and evaluating choices. There are also ways of initiating non-incremental choices by providing more powerful extrinsic rights of appeal. If one gives up the bureaucratically compartmentalized ways of choosing, it then becomes very important indeed to work out other ways in which choices should be rationally made; resources still have to be husbanded. Precedent, departmentalization, and the set lines of the expert are not suitable;

---

[1] 'The research and development approach to the study of change', *Human Organisation* 17 (1958), 12. See also Holmberg, 'Changing community attitudes and values in Peru', in R. N. Adams, *et al.*, *Social change in Latin America today*, see above p. 203, n. 3.

if they are to be replaced, a feedback of the evaluation of results and wider ways of considering data become all the more important. Further, development administration must seek to avoid the elaborate. Different but simple devices may be discoverable only by sophisticated means: it may be, for example, a complex strategy which would replace the administrative with the executive. As Clausewitz said of war, 'Everything is simple in war, but the simplest thing is difficult'.

There is a second implication of alternative compartmentalization, concerning the problem of career interest. What is suggested here is a quite different structure of status, rewards, and prizes. If one is prepared to work out new sorts of organizational structure, there is no reason why one cannot work out new sorts of career. Maximum rewards for the administrator suit central headquarters, monocratic, departmental, or secretariat organizations. Maximum rewards for the field, the project, or the *ad hoc* team would go with a different sort of machinery of government.

There is also the requirement of access and of community perception. The most promising experiment here has to do with the notion of administration as 'directive education'. Administration is not politics and it is wrong if it seeks to recruit support by ideology. It is rather part of a response to demands, but there is no reason why its response should not be made more comprehensible by education. The 'directive educator' is quite distinct from the community development worker; that was the most distinctive contribution of the Comilla approach.[1]

But neither that nor anything else in the record justifies optimism about the sufficiency of development administration alone. The whole lesson is that development administration works only in conjunction with other factors of change. In any case further research is required into the way in which the new rules for a development style of administration could be worked out. A build-up of the results of field studies is promising, in particular through the possibilities of coding the reports. That is quite different from institutionalized recall processes, like precedent, and much nearer to the ways in which further use of programming techniques can move away from the restrictions of bureaucratic compartmentalization.[2]

To take one example: it could be argued that we now have sufficient field reports on national planning and population control to suggest a combined conclusion. The choice of public decision-making styles is a

---

[1] There is now a large bibliography on Comilla. For a general study of its results, see H. Schuman, *Economic development and individual change*, Cambridge, Mass. 1967.

[2] See esp. the work of Frank Young: F. and R. Young, 'The sequence and direction of community growth', *Rural Sociology* 27 (1962), 374; F. Young and I. Fujimoto, 'Social differentiation in Latin American communities', *Economic Development and Cultural Change* 13 (1965), 344. For another striking research method, F. Young and E. D. MacConnell, 'Structural differentiation of communities and aerial photography', *Rural Sociology* 32 (1967), 334. Generally, see Glenn D. Paige, *Proposition-building in the study of comparative administration*, mim., Bloomington 1963.

factor in growth.[1] Style is affected by organizational structure (as I have just argued). Where there is a high degree of uncertainty in the relation between the goal of a programme and the technology available, the structure employed ought to be innovatory rather than adaptive.[2]

Whether or not output innovation is actually required, bureaucratic compartmentalization certainly needs to be replaced in development administration. Politicization is not necessarily the way.[3] It is true that the nature of the political framework of reference is precisely that it is more open and general than any other.[4] There is also no reason why a particular public service official should not be very good at certain aspects of representation. The field officer often sees himself in that way. He is, sometimes in contrast to the formal political representative, actually present in the field. He has information; he is in a good communications position between the field and headquarters levels. He can certainly be a functioning part of the network of relations with the centre. However, in the end he will either be part of a central institution or identified with it, or he will sink into community politics, unless some depoliticization is enforced on him, if only by a rival for the political role.

Nevertheless, alternative styles to cope with interest, access, and instrumental exchange can be worked out: research for evaluation and intervention; alternative career orientations with different sorts of attitude to environmental information and reception; different information processes about feedback assessment and exchange. As far as exchange between the administration and its political environment is concerned, for example, it would certainly be possible to work out alternatives to the overall, continuous but devised forms of control with which we are familiar. Similarly, as far as internal organizational exchanges are concerned, occasional and inherent controls, as in executive organization, may be possible.

For organization–clientele relations we must certainly move away from any reliance on the 'queue' model. The word queue, after all, came into the English language in 1837 about the same time that Palmerston had to explain the meaning of bureaucracy to the new young queen. Its full and elegant flowering is seen only in those regulations of the Second World War which enacted it and included the acceptance of priorities within the queue itself. This was too much to ask of diffuse societies undergoing development. There the avoidance of either 'riot' or 'camping out' as a mode of client access, demands not so much the community development strategy as something more like a *cafeteria*; where a very important yet at the same time minimal service is possible as a result of the technologically simple but available contributions from the clients themselves.

[1] A. H. Hirschman, *Journeys towards progress*, New York 1963.
[2] J. Finkle and R. Meade, *Organisational adaptation and social change*, mim., Ann Arbor 1967.
[3] A. Zolberg, *Creating political order*, Chicago 1966, pp. 139 ff., esp. for 'patrimonial bureaucratic' aspects of effective political machines in new states.
[4] P. Appleby, *Policy and administration*, Alabama 1949.

Structural invention has always been possible in administration: the ministerial department, the multi-purpose local authority, then the public corporation, then the *servicio*. So it ought to be possible to go on: the temporary posting, the *ad hoc* team, the crisis model, the research academy model suggested by Hart ('District officers must, for a long time to come, keep their prestige, at least in reserve for emergencies. They cannot afford to fail. They cannot, therefore, afford genuinely to experiment. Posted for a year or more to a pilot academy whose mission is to learn by identifying its mistakes, they can innovate and err without failing.')[1]

Yet one cannot sensibly expect much or suppose that the problems can be easily solved. Administration never has been easy. A new need to contain innovation and to employ contradiction[2] is not going to be any easier than the old need for the sensitive but institutionally identified bureaucratic administrator; but it is not necessarily going to be harder.

In any case the best will not happen. If public offices in Jakarta are open only between 9 and 11 in the morning because officials have to leave to do many other jobs, one cannot expect much from them. Yet much has to be expected. A recent report in Honduras about the failure of the 1965 five-year plan says, 'the private sector cannot indefinitely maintain a satisfactory dynamism if the public sector does not provide in an opportune way the basic works and services that private businessmen need'.[3] It had fallen down, the report concluded, for various reasons: a lack of feasibility studies; a slow processing of projects; a 'lack of intense and sustained interest in accelerating development at all levels of public administration'; and no doubt, above all, because of what the report called appointment for political rather than technical qualifications. A good inquiry, no doubt, but its author was dismissed precisely for promoting, it was said, his own political interests.

Hopes are dashed sooner or later even if there is some moment at which, as is not always the case, they can be expressed. In Mexico two generations of land distribution in Guerrero have produced overcrowding, low productivity, landless peasants, meagre crops, idleness, low credit. Peasant copra growers have now had a long experience of that favourite technique, the cooperative association. It ended recently outside the association's headquarters in Acapulco in a gun battle with the leaders and with twenty-seven dead members. Yet in the search for an effective style, for a relevant structure, for new information processes, for ways of utilizing available community perceptions, as elsewhere in development one must continue.

[1] H. C. Hart, *The village and development administration*, pp. 43–4.

[2] F. Schurmann, *Ideology and organisation in Communist China*, New York 1966; H. A. Simon, 'The decision maker as innovator', in S. Mailick and E. H. von Ness (eds.), *Concepts and issues in administrative behaviour*, Englewood Cliffs'1962; J. G. March and H. Simon, *Organisations*, New York 1958, c. 7; E. M. Rogers, *Diffusion of innovation*, New York 1962. I am indebted to Professor L. Joy for a reference to T. Kuhn's *The structure of scientific revolutions*, Chicago 1962, on this point.

[3] Ribera Report, High Planning Council, Honduras, May 1967.

# THE MILITARY AND POLITICAL DEVELOPMENT[1]

## ROBERT E. DOWSE

From Sparta to Surinam, from Napoleon to Neguib, from theories of political and economic development to typologies of military intervention, the variety of military intervention and the range of ideas about it and its causes make analysis difficult. Yet looking at it from a slightly different perspective, that of the actual impact of the military as a ruling group upon the political system, one is immediately struck by the shortage of detailed case studies, as opposed to typologies and 'theories'.

Perhaps the first problem to tackle is whether or not there is a significant subject for study contained in the title of this paper (apart from squabbles about the meaning of the word 'development'). One may well doubt whether soldiers' political activities can be distinguished analytically from those of any other political group; whether, from the viewpoint of systems analysis or of functional analysis, or alternatively from a problem-solving perspective, anything unique to the military is likely to emerge. If this is so, the impact of military rule on development is clearly an aspect of the more general study of political and economic development.

### WHY MILITARY RULE IS COMMON IN DEVELOPMENT CONDITIONS

A great deal of work has been done on the conditions under which the military comes to power. I am not thinking of what Eckstein has called 'precipitants', the advent of which sparks off the violence, but rather of 'preconditions'.[2] Here we enter a veritable jungle of mostly pseudo-theory, a great deal of which need not long detain us.

The most widespread, persuasive, but in the end unsatisfactory account would go something like this: modernization produces disorientation or conflict of values in traditional societies, it leaves power vacuums, economic maladjustments, and dysfunctional stratifications with which the incumbent politicians cannot cope. The result is disequilibrium and uneven development, a situation presenting the military with the opportunity to

[1] I wish gratefully to acknowledge help received in writing and revising this paper from: James Barber, John Hughes, Jeffrey Stanyer, Douglas Pitt, and Richard Rathbone.
[2] 'On the etiology of internal wars', *History and theory* IV, 2 (1965), 133–63.

P [213]

intervene.[1] There then occurs an expansion of the role of the military. 'The army intervenes because other elites are absent, impotent or indifferent; it improvises and expands its role to carry the burden created by a modernisation crisis.'[2]

An alternative formulation of the same basic theme is that there may be sharp differences in the levels of technical development between sectors of society. If the bureaucratic apparatus is technically more competent than the policy-making organs (executives and parties) then a displacement of the functions will occur so that: 'Inter-bureaucratic struggle becomes a primary form of politics. But when the political arena is shifted to the bureaucracy—a shift marked by the growing power of military officers in conflict with civilian officials—the consequences are usually ominous for political stability.'[3] Another version of the same point stresses the 'disrhythmic' patterns of change throughout different geographical areas of the underdeveloped country, arising from different traditions, differential market access, differential educational penetration, etc.[4] We are now far more inclined to stress the variety of responses to modernization, its patchy and adaptive character, and to reject the idea of a homogeneous response.[5] And we are, in consequence, less likely to regard military intervention as a deviation from some natural developmental sequence; indeed the concept of developmental sequences—Marx's, Rostow's or Parsons's—has itself been rejected.

The case of those propositions at a lower level of generality which relate to the yawning gap between military competence and/or morality and civilian bungling and corruption, is rather similar. The mechanisms creating this technical and moral gulf are numerous and include the military's relatively early establishment, its inherently easier task, the absence of a potentially degrading clientage relationship with the public, and the relatively high competence level of the military due to foreign training and comparisons.[6] This list is not by any means exhaustive, but

---

[1] These theories recur frequently in e.g. J. J. Johnson, *The role of the military in under-developed countries*, Princeton 1962. See also M. Halpern in *Annals of the American Academy of Political and Social Science*, March 1965; F. von der Mehden, *Politics of the developing nations*, New Jersey 1964, p. 98.

[2] A. Perlmutter, 'The Israeli army in politics', *World Politics*, XX (July 1968), and also M. Lissak, 'Modernisation and role-expansion of the military in developing countries', *Comparative Studies in Society and History*, VI (April 1967), 233–55.

[3] F. Riggs, 'Bureaucrats and political development: a paradoxical view', in J. LaPalombara (ed.), *Bureaucracy and political development*, Princeton 1963, p. 20.

[4] C. S. Whitaker, 'A disrhythmic process of political change', *World Politics* XIX (January 1967), 190–217.

[5] A. R. Zolberg, *Creating political order*, Chicago 1966; H. Bienen, *Tanzania: party transformation and economic development*, Princeton 1967; C. Anderson, F. Mehden and C. Young, *Issues of political development*, New Jersey 1967; and D. Brokensha, *Social change in Larteh, Ghana*, Oxford 1966.

[6] M.I.T. study, 'The transitional process', in C. E. Welch (ed.), *Political modernisation*, California 1967; S. E. Finer, *The man on horseback*, London 1962; M. Janowitz, *The military in the political development of new nations*, Chicago 1964; Mehden, *op. cit.*; P. J. Vatikiotis, *The Egyptian army in politics*, Indiana 1961.

the lesson is clear: 'The more the army was modernised, the more its composition, organisation, spirit, capabilities and purpose constituted a radical criticism of the existing political system.'[1] The gap may, of course, also be a social one where the army recruits more broadly than other social organizations and hence becomes a haven for the disadvantaged: 'The seismic zones of military intervention...tend by and large to be areas where social stratification is marked...the army provides one of the few avenues of social advancement.'[2] Intervention then can be seen as an attempt to redistribute social status or as one of a variety of possible responses by the military to a tension-creating situation; others would be total withdrawal into professional military interests or indulging in the ideological satisfactions of anti-civilianism.

Systems theorists and those functionalists who are able to accommodate change and revolution tend to widen their perspective: 'Any society is simultaneously a host for tensions and a network of tension-management devices' and 'an aspect of revolutionary potential is its intimate relationship with social change'.[3] Hence, military intervention, rebellion, riots, etc., are seen as aspects of the same phenomenon: 'they signify failures, small or large, of the political system'.[4] For those who argue on these lines the eventual removal of the military from politics depends on the gradual emergence of intermediate strata and cross-cutting status or role positions, economic development, wider social catchment areas for officers and political and economic development.[5]

The military will be reduced to their barracks and their professional functions alone only when Latin American countries develop sufficiently complicated power structures and a society sufficiently flexible and integrated; when social and geographical discontinuities have been greatly lessened and isolated or marginal masses incorporated into the national body; when economic and social conflicts have found institutionalized expression within a common framework of shared norms.[6]

Recent writings on Latin America appear to take a rather different perspective, arguing that the total culture and early socialization experience take a violent form (e.g. *machismo*). Violence there can be seen as a symptom of the underlying social-psychological formation and it may be functionally appropriate behaviour: 'Political violence cannot be regarded as aberrant behaviour in Latin America' since there is a 'compatibility

[1] Halpern, *Annals* (1965) p. 258.
[2] Finer, *The man on horseback*, p. 56.
[3] A. S. Feldman, 'Violence and volatility: the likelihood of revolution', in H. Eckstein (ed.), *Internal war*, Glencoe 1964, p. 115.
[4] W. Kornhauser in Eckstein, *op. cit.*, p. 142.
[5] For example E. Lieuwen, *Arms and politics in Latin America*, New York 1961, chs. 2 and 3. The thesis has been explored at some length in S. M. Lipset, *Political man*, London 1960.
[6] Germani and Silvert, 'Military intervention in Latin America', *Archiv. europ. sociol.* II (1961), 81.

between the values and styles imparted by non-political institutions and the perpetuation of patterns of political violence and revolutions in Latin American political behaviour'.[1]

The Freudian theme about the significance of primary socialization patterns is a clear underpinning of this position; extra-governmental structures are compatible with, reinforce, or are a reflection of a political socialization process saturated with violence both actual and symbolic. We have, then, an inter-generational replication of violence.[2]

And Huntington, with Latin America in mind, suggests that frequent 'reform coups' are actually a sign of political health since they are mechanisms of gradual change and that anyway 'virtually all reforms are produced by coups'.[3] This may be described as the 'revisionist' position, and as well as the above proposition, it also claims that: (a) democratic consent *must* include the consent of the military since it is a significant expression of the culture; and (b) Anglo-Saxon norms of political neutralism for the military may not be appropriate everywhere.[4]

But on the whole the assumption is that military intervention is an indicator of malaise within a society; the problem then becomes one of constructing indicators, of giving various factors a weighting in explaining military intervention. Before examining some of these attempts, however, one point needs to be made.

The general analysis of why military regimes emerge is very similar to the analysis of why one-party states emerged in Africa. A good recent example of this begins: 'One-party states emerge in societies in which traditional authority...has been seriously weakened' and 'One-party states tend to emerge in post-traditional societies as a consequence of the rapid breakdown of existing patterns of social and political authority'.[5] We appear to be at grips with a 'theory' that explains everything: thus Professors Coleman and Rosberg, in analysing the emergence of single-party systems in terms of the general problems of political and economic mobilization, suggest the possibility that these problems may overcome the parties and that one result, amongst others, could be the rise of military regimes.[6]

[1] M. Kling, 'Violence and politics in Latin America', in P. Halmos (ed.), *Latin American sociological studies* (Sociological Review Monograph 11), pp. 119–31.

[2] See R. Linton, 'The concept of national character' in A. Stanton and S. Perry (eds.), *Personality and political crisis*, Glencoe 1951, p. 146: 'Nations with authoritarian family structures inevitably seem to develop authoritarian governments...Latin American countries with their excellent democratic constitutions and actual dictatorships would be a case in point.'

[3] S. Huntington, *Changing patterns of military politics*, New York 1962.

[4] L. M. McAlister, 'Changing concepts of the role of the military in Latin America', *Annals of the American Academy*, July 1965, pp. 85–98. See also L. Coser, *The functions of social conflict*, New York, 1954, and *The functions of social conflict revisited*, New York 1967.

[5] S. Rothman, 'One-party regimes: a comparative analysis', *Social Research* XXXIII (1967), pp. 682–3.

[6] In J. S. Coleman and C. G. Rosberg (eds.), *Political parties and national integration in tropical Africa*, California 1964, pp. 655–80.

There is, in short, a highly unsatisfactory vagueness, or at least too high a level of generality, about this theorizing. The literature on the military, on revolution, and political violence abounds with propositions like 'The seizure of control by the military junta normally does not occur when officers recognise civilian control of the armed forces as legitimate'.[1] Or, in an otherwise excellent discussion, the author suggests that 'It is more likely that a general theory can be reached in the context of a general rather than a restrictive definition'.[2] In an article already cited, the author roundly suggests that 'Revolutions result from unsuccessful tension management'.[3] And in one widely cited textbook on the military, everything to do with intervention in politics hinges upon a definition of 'professionalism' which specifies that a professional soldier does not intervene.[4] Lest I appear too smugly critical, I would suggest that most of the looseness in the formulations stems not from any intellectual shortcomings of the exponents, but rather from the totally overwhelming variety of events that the theorists attempt to embrace. For example, in the last 10 years almost every African state has experienced a coup, a political assassination, or political violence, etc., and it is surely vain to look for valid or even tenable generalizations about things like 'one-party' or 'multi-party', 'type of colonial experience', 'levels of socio-political development', 'attitudinal structure' and so forth. Indeed, the one general statement that can be accepted with some confidence is that new states are always poised on a knife edge of political violence. No generalizations are likely to reach a useful level of specificity and at the same time embrace all relevant material.

Bearing this in mind we next need to consider the various attempts which have been made, mainly by Americans, to operationalize concepts or construct indices in order to get beyond or beneath mere assertions about relationships between societal developments and military intervention, influence or civil strife. These writers take statements like *'Coups d'état* and military intervention in politics are one index of low levels of political institutionalisation'[5] and attempt to construct an index of political institutionalization. Quite clearly the effort to do this is worth while since the theoretical vagueness I have complained of is unlikely to get us anywhere. It is doubly valuable, I would suggest, when the almost overwhelming and frequently contradictory hypotheses about civil

[1] C. E. Welch, 'Soldier and state in Africa', *Journal of Modern African Studies* V, 3, 320. See also Finer, *The man on horseback*, p. 21 : 'Where public attachment to civilian institutions is strong, military intervention in politics will be weak'; but Finer does not offer criteria by which to judge.

[2] P. H. R. Calvert, 'Revolution: the politics of violence', *Political Studies* XIV (February 1967), 3.

[3] Feldman, 'violence and volatility.'

[4] See Finer, *The man on horseback*, pp. 24–5 and W. H. Morris-Jones, 'Armed forces and the state', *Public Administration*, XXXIV (1957).

[5] S. Huntington, 'Political development and political decay', *World Politics* XVII (April 1965), 386–430.

violence are considered. Eckstein, in a list by no means exhaustive, has collected twenty-one hypotheses under five headings and shows very clearly indeed that there are contradictions.[1]

Although factor and regression analysis is not committed to theory-building (hypotheses are all that is needed), many analysts using statistical techniques have tried their hand at it. Possibly the most popular of these theories are drawn from social psychology. Aggression is seen as a consequence of frustration, and civil violence as a consequence of socially created frustrations which the society is not able to alleviate and 'manage' with a regular flow of satisfaction. The theory falls into two parts: the creation of demands and satisfaction of demands. Under the first heading would appear demands aroused by politicians, demands created by national and international reference-groups, and expectations of future satisfactions based on past satisfactions (wind-fall or otherwise). Under the second heading, the system's ability to satisfy demands, might be considered factors such as the level of institutionalization and differentiation; the ability to cope with information flow; the availability of channels of communication; material resources; level of economic development; level or type of cultural development; education; the need to achieve and other attitudinal configurations more or less 'functional' for innovation; the degree of bureaucracy, etc.[2]

The theory then takes the form, 'if social want formation exceeds social want satisfaction then the consequence will be social frustration which may lead to violence'.[3] Feierabend suggests that at most stages of development social want formation is far more rapid than want satisfaction, owing to people's exposure to high consumption possibilities through the radio, films, newspapers, advertising, etc., which are cheaply and easily established, whereas economic development is difficult (indeed initial growth may lead to a decline in living standards owing to the need for a high level of capital investment).[4]

The suggestion here, and it is not a novel one, is that there may well be

[1] Eckstein, 'On the etiology of internal wars', *History and theory* IV, 2 (1965). See also the comprehensive list of assumed relationships in M. Lissak's contribution to M. Janowitz (ed.), *The new military*, New York 1964.

[2] Not all of these appear in all the articles or books; but see, e.g., the many articles by Deutsch and collaborators in the *American Political Science Review* and *World Politics*. See also D. McCelland, *The achieving society*, New York 1961; V. Le Vine, *Dreams and deeds*, Chicago 1966; D. Apter, *The politics of modernisation*, Chicago 1965.

[3] I. and R. Feierabend, 'Aggressive behaviours within politics, 1948–1962: a cross-national study', *Journal of Conflict Resolution* X, 2 (1966), 249–71; R. Tanter and M. Midlarsky 'A theory of revolution', *Conflict Resolution* XI, 3 (1967) and T. Gurr, 'Psychological factors in civil violence', *World Politics*, XX (January 1968) 245–78.

[4] Mancur Olson, 'Rapid growth as a destabilising force', *Journal of Economic History* XXIII (December 1963), 529–52, and J. J. Spengler, 'Economic development: political preconditions and political consequences', *Journal of Politics* XXXI (August 1960) 367–416. See also Russett, Alker, Deutsch and Lasswell, *World handbook of political and social indicators* (Yale 1964), p. 9, and diagram on p. 307.

a close correlation between the incidence of domestic violence and military intervention. Naturally, the problem is to construct indicators of violence, but here the work of the factor analysts has been satisfactory and we have fairly complete statistics of domestic violence variables—strikes, riots, political murder, political arrests, political executions, etc.—and these have been very carefully analysed and factorized, thus reducing them to strongly associated clusters.[1]

A development of the basic theory which ties it in a little more closely with economic development is that of J. C. Davies, as modified by Tanter and Midlarsky.[2] This is designed to take care of the observation that revolutions and civil violence tend to occur after a relatively long period of economic prosperity has ended; that is, they coincide with short-term economic recessions.

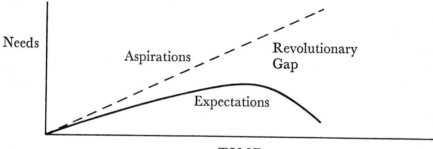

It is at this point of theory formation that the statisticians come into their own.[3]

'There is no dearth of suggestions about what factors are causally related to military intervention in politics. The problem is to subject this array of propositions to some sort of empirical testing.'[4] The first problem then is to define military intervention. This Putnam does on a scale from o to 3 which works as follows: a regime in which there is no military intervention at all scores o; essentially civil rule subject to significant military influence in civil matters scores 1; civil–military coalitions with real civilian influence score 2; regimes in which the civilians are simply supplicants score 3. Clearly there is room for dispute here, but on

---

[1] Feierabend, *op. cit.*; R. J. Rummel, 'Dimensions of conflict behaviour within nations, 1946–59' *Journal of Conflict Resolution* X, 1 (1966), 65–73; R. Tanter, 'Dimensions of conflict behaviour within and between nations, 1955–60', *Conflict Resolution* X, 1 (1966), 48–73; 'Turmoil and internal war', *Peace Research Society Papers*, Chicago 1965.

[2] J. C. Davies, 'Toward a theory of revolution', *American Sociological Review* XXVII, 1 (February 1962), 5–19.

[3] Although I have stressed revolutionary or violence potential, the theorists—especially Eckstein—have also concerned themselves with methods of containing violence by, for example, government coercion, by acts against other nations, by strategic concessions, by allowing individual as opposed to group violence, or by various diversionary mechanisms.

[4] R. D. Putnam, 'Toward explaining military intervention in Latin American politics', *World Politics* XIX (October 1967), 88.

the whole the index is unambiguous; i.e. a panel of experts would be unlikely to disagree seriously on overall placings. Putnam then takes five variables of social mobilization: percentage of population in cities over 20,000, percentage of literate adults, newspapers per 1,000 population, university students per 1,000 population, and radios per 1,000 population (these are highly inter-correlated) and finds that, as most students expected, the higher a country is on this index the lower is its score on military intervention. An index of economic development composed of *per capita* G.N.P. derived from agriculture, percentage of labour force earning wages or salaries, and percentage of labour force in industry (intercorrelation of ·72) was found also to correlate negatively ($-·32$) with the degree of military intervention. But when he controlled for social mobilization, he found that the economic development index correlated *positively* with the military intervention scores.[1] Of course, the implication here is that the mobilization and development indices are not perfectly correlated—otherwise they could not make *independent* contributions to intervention.

To this point I imagine that most political scientists would follow the factor analysts; after all, most of the indices are fairly well based (assuming —heroically—that the national statistics are not too wild), but beyond it many might be inclined to demur.[2] For example, one cannot imagine that too many will be completely happy with an index of political development that includes items as qualitatively disparate as percentage of voting-age population voting, interest articulation by parties, interest articulation by associations, stability of party system, interest aggregation by parties, etc. Nor is one altogether happy about the actual measuring of articulation and aggregation or even stability of party systems. However, for the moment setting aside these difficulties, 'Interest articulation by parties and pressure groups does not necessarily inhibit military intervention'. On the other hand, party stability and party interest aggregation are negatively associated ($-·36$ and $-·63$). The final political proposition considered is the one relating deaths from domestic violence to military intervention. Five weighted factors varying from warfare and turmoil down to small-scale terrorism were used, and the result was practically nil correlation.[3] Given the limitations of data, etc., it would appear that none of the relationships of a 'political' nature are of much significance in ex-

---

[1] Putnam proceeds well beyond this point of statistical sophistication into causal path analysis, but at least one reader here parts company.

[2] I am unhappy at what appears to be the grim determination of some statisticians to make their hypotheses work; e.g. 'Although the relative rank of the bureaucratic measure is low on both lists, when it is compared with the other factors in terms of the values of the contingency coefficients, its relationship with the economic factor is one of the highest.' J. Forward, 'Toward an empirical framework for ecological studies in comparative public administration', in N. Raphaeli, *Readings in comparative public administration*, Boston 1967, p. 461.

[3] The raw material was drawn from A. S. Banks and R. B. Textor, *A cross polity survey* (Massachusetts 1963).

plaining or rather correlating with military intervention in Latin America.

Nor does Putnam confirm that many of the other hypotheses advanced are at all statistically viable (although he does not examine the considerable literature that exists on the first stages of economic development and its relationship with instability). The size of army is not associated with military intervention and the percentage of adult population in the army is negatively associated with intervention; there is no worthwhile association between foreign training and intervention—except a slight negative one with German training; and Putnam's comparison of possible random geographical distributions of coups with the actual distribution of coups suggests that they were not 'contagious'.

The statisticians, then, have certainly contributed a valuable element to the testing of hypotheses. We have a fairly clear idea of what to leave out, and factor analysis is a formidable example of Occam's Razor in action.[1] They cannot, however, be expected to produce the theories from which the hypotheses—statements of relationships—are drawn. Unfortunately, as I have attempted to show in the previous section, we do not yet possess theories logically tight enough to yield anything other than hypotheses whose key terms tend to be rather vague. There is a danger that the statisticians may contribute an aura of specious accuracy to hypotheses that are themselves intrinsically vague: anyone who has a knowledge of how statistics on national income, income distribution, agricultural production, etc., are actually gathered in the underdeveloped countries will be inclined to hesitate before entirely accepting the figures. (The recent controversy in the U.K. and the U.S.A. on the redistribution of national wealth might reinforce this hesitation.) We need to be very careful indeed that the entities we factorize exist in the real world in any quantifiable sense. The difficulty is a two-fold one. First, the information which in principle can be 'hard'—income, its distribution, urban population, racial composition, and so forth—is notoriously shaky for the areas we are interested in. Secondly, there is a category of 'soft' information which is even more difficult to define, and when defined, to measure; e.g. interest articulation or interest aggregation. When we look at the principal source for these we are rightly warned that 'estimates made on the basis of such intangible criteria must necessarily be highly intuitive'.[2] And, one might add, to run the intuitive against the only just probable is to take a real risk. Yet more than one sophisticated analyst has taken the risk.[3]

[1] See, for example, J. Sawyer, 'Dimensions of nations: size, wealth and politics', *American Journal of Sociology* LXXIII (September 1967), where 'three dimensions suffice to account for 40% of the variation among 236 variables'.

[2] Banks and Textor, *A cross-polity survey*, p. 96. See also P. Cutright, 'National political development', *American Sociological Review* XXVIII, 2 (April 1963), 253–64, where political development is defined in terms of competitive party systems.

[3] R. Tanter, 'Towards a theory of political development', *Mid-West Journal of Political Science* XI, 2 (May 1967), 145–72, and J. Forward in Raphaeli, *Readings in comparative public administration*.

It will be suggested below that there may well be a connection between the degree of bureaucracy in a system and military intervention; where the former is high (effective), the latter may be difficult, or at least less likely without bureaucratic support. Although the evidence one way or the other is skimpy—unless we lump intervention in with *all* forms of instability —a recent correlation analysis of the effects of some variables of bureaucratic performance has been published.[1] It is not necessary to go into detail, but one important conclusion of the analysis is that 'the data appear to support the assumption that it is effective bureaucracy which is the precondition for representative and stable government, rather than *vice versa*. Effective bureaucracy is seen to be highly dependent on a relatively advanced level of economic development, literacy, urbanisation and communication capacity.'[2] These partly coincide with Putnam's index of mobilization: hence, the higher the level of mobilization/bureaucratic effectiveness, the lower the rate of overt military intervention? Or alternatively, the higher the level of mobilization/bureaucratic performance, the greater is the weight of the bureaucracy in a military–bureaucratic coalition?

Back to the drawing-board! Or at least, back to an attempt to operationalize some of the concepts that have not yet been confronted with statistics partly because they remain so vague: social consensus, social cleavage, elite alienation, military ethos, social want formation, and so on. Again, although the literature abounds with references to the military as a socializing agency we have no study of the 'before-and-after' attitudes of officer recruits other than in America. Or we can try scattergram analysis to isolate the exceptions to the generalizations, and look at them much more closely. Or we might try straight historical studies! At least the need for historical studies of the actual conditions of actual military intervention seems to be the implication of the many doubts that students have expressed about generalizations concerning military intervention.[3] There is a difficulty here since on the whole armies are not anxious to be investigated (except in the U.S.A.), but if even a student of Gutteridge's stature could argue of Ghana in 1964 that 'it is likely that any political initiative would come from outside rather than from inside forces', then the case for more detail is clear.[4]

There is a possible intermediate position here. We may be on the lookout for second-order generalizations of the type, 'military intervention

[1] J. Forward, in Raphaeli, *Readings in comparative public administration*, pp. 450–72.

[2] See also P. Cutright, 'National political development', where for all nations excluding African ones communications development is strongly associated with political development and is a better indicator of political development than is economic development.

[3] See W. Gutteridge, *Military institutions and power in the new states*, London 1964, pp. 16, 44, 115, and 129; V. Le Vine, 'Independent Africa in trouble', *Africa Report*, XII 9 (December 1967), 19–24; von der Mehden, *Politics of the developing nations*, p. 98.

[4] *Ibid.*, p. 144.

leads to lower economic growth rates'; 'military intervention leads to higher military budgets'; 'military intervention is led by middle-rank officers but may encourage bottom-level counter-interventions'; or 'once a military has intervened decisively it will do so again'. My own feeling is that it might also be wise to confine our attention to one continent or sub-continent at a time, since I cannot see any real hope for wider correlations where the backgrounds are so different. For example, in South America most countries have had some sort of an officer corps for over 100 years; in British West Africa there were nine native officers in 1948. In none of the sub-Saharan African states did the military play any role at all, as an organized body, in gaining independence—not so in Asia and South America. Social stratification was far looser in Africa than in either Asia or Latin America and most commentators speak of military politics in Latin America as a bloody game played between a 'parasitic' upper class and a 'parasitic' military, at least until recently; whereas most African states did not have to clear away a powerful land-owning aristocracy before *any* reform could be introduced. For these reasons (and others can be thought of) one is inclined to opt for more modest comparisons.

On the theoretical level it would seem that our work on the conditions for military intervention has not been adequate and has been overtaken by statistical analysis.[1] And whilst on the subject of inadequacies it is well to insist that the shortcomings are those of general theorizing about economic and political underdevelopment; theorizing about military intervention is drawn from often grossly inadequate theories of societal development, most of which actually neglect, for example, external economic or political control and are frequently deficient on simple logical grounds.[2]

Fortunately we are not in the same position when talking about the politics of the military once they have intervened, for here we are at a pre-theoretical level where typologies abound. Here the most satisfactory work has been done by Professor S. E. Finer, who attempts to relate a considerable number of variables in a consistent pattern which includes actual military government. I am not sure that Finer succeeds in tying up all loose ends; for example, in his discussion of military 'mood', where we are told that 'different armed forces have different flash points'; or in his discussion of the popularity of the military, where he says 'it is im-

---

[1] In studying African developments we are in very little danger from the statisticians for the simple reason that there are few statistics worth using. See P. Cutright, 'National political development', *American Sociological Review* XXVIII (April 1963), 255 n. 4; and J. Sawyer, 'Dimensions of nations', *American Journal of Sociology* LXXIII (September 1967), 146 n. 16.

[2] See the devastating critique of contemporary American sociology of underdevelopment by A. G. Frank, 'Sociology of development and underdevelopment of sociology', *Catalyst* no. 3 (Summer 1967); and R. E. Dowse, 'A functionalist's logic', *World Politics* XXII (July 1966), 607–22.

possible...to generalise about the factors on which the popularity of the army depends'; or in his discussion of 'political culture'.[1] But the attempt to spell out a *relatively* unambiguous set of criteria for political culture, to derive or infer a four-point typology from this set and to relate levels of intervention to this typology, is clear and effective. 'The levels to which intervention is pushed vary according to the group into which a society falls.'[2]

This seems to be one of the most useful formulations in the literature, and if combined with his four-point formulation of the possible 'interests' represented in the military (class, regional, corporate, and individual) it might yield interesting propositions. For West Africa, to take the area which I know best, I have a strong feeling that class interest is not important, and one might be inclined to cut it out or include it under 'regional' (with that term widenened to embrace Shils's category of 'primordial' attachment). Class, in any useful sense of the term, is probably only marginally appropriate at present in a few West African towns like Lagos, Ibadan, and Accra, and even there 'elites' might be a better term. On similar grounds, one is inclined to doubt the operation of individual self-interest as a major causal factor in military intervention in West Africa since the army has no monopoly of avenues to upward social mobility; the party, the civil service, the universities, the party auxiliaries, and the liberal professions all provide perfectly adequate substitutes. For 'British' West Africa at least, the evidence points to corporate and regional interest: the second Nigerian coup; the Ghanaian coup (and the abortive counter-coup); the second Sierra Leone coup and the result of the first. But it does not follow from the fact that a coup is precipitated by these interests that it is supported only by these interests, nor that it benefits only these interests.

Unfortunately, yet another *caveat* is necessary at this stage: we have spoken of the 'army' as though it is an actual entity. I am not thinking of the age divisions and career blockages that have frequently been remarked upon, but of whether or not it makes sense to refer at all to armies in some African states, in the sense of disciplined entities rather than congeries of interest groups. Certainly the Nigerian Army now seems to be in this position; in April 1967 there were rumours of internal army divisions in Ghana; and after the spate of work on African single parties which assumed that the parties were in reality the monolithic structures that they aspired to be, one must beware of reifying.

However, most interest in military regimes has focused upon their dynamics. Once again Finer is most satisfactory, arguing that there is a

---

[1] Finer, *The man on horseback*, pp. 62, 80, and 136–7. The major difficulty here seems to be that we can only know for sure what the cultural level is if we never have an intervention or if there is a resisted intervention (the Kapp *putsch*, for example); at all other levels we must be unsure. I owe this point to Norman Miners, a research student in Exeter working on the Nigerian military.

[2] *Ibid.*, p. 89.

kind of logic of intervention driving the military to intervene more and more intensively at all levels below that of influence at the mature political culture stage.[1] Although this is implicit in Finer, I cannot detect an explicit formulation of the actual dynamic force. Here we may turn to Janowitz who formulates a five-point intervention scale with the 'basic assumption that the military operates at each level of political intervention...as incomplete agents of political change'.[2] Hence a pattern of 'broadening commitment' can be detected. By this I understand him to mean that the military must necessarily seek allies since it does not possess the technical capacity to rule alone.[3] It is this process that leads to a widening of commitments and to the military becoming involved in the general difficulties of ruling states that are not yet nations, and hence in the general problem of solving the still apparently largely unsolvable.

There is another more traditional method of analysing revolutionary change, the Marxist. It has not been widely used in Africa, but some work has been done on Ghana.[4] In these analyses there are two main (though sometimes disconnected) themes: that militarism is an element in a concerted worldwide imperialist plot against the economic independence of the Third World, and that Ghana was not really a socialist state at all. Both themes can be developed at various levels of sophistication,[5] with Dr Nkrumah's own conspiracy theory at the lower level: 'The beginning of 1966 found Ghana poised for a breakthrough in her national economy. As Ghana's economic progress gained momentum so did the imperialist neo-colonialist intrigues and subversion increase.'[6] Perhaps an intermediate level is the one which suggests that some military coups may be a consequence of local conditions but 'this coup is not an ordinary one. It is a desperate effort to reverse the path Ghana has chosen to secure its economic independence—the path of neo-capitalist development...for the path of Ghana symbolized for all the new emerging nations how to break out from dead-end dependence on the imperialist ravages of their natural wealth and resources.'[7]

A much higher level of sophistication is reached by Roger Murray in the *New Left Review*.[8] Murray suggests the need for an explicative scheme—

---

[1] *Ibid.*, pp. 183–190.

[2] Janowitz, *The new military*, p. 7.

[3] For a very useful discussion of the potentially unstable nature of such an arrangement see W. H. Riker, *The theory of political coalitions*, Yale 1962, especially chapters 1 and 2.

[4] R. Fitch and M. Oppenheimer, *Ghana: the end of an illusion*, New York August 1966; and R. Murray, 'Militarism in Africa', *New Left Review*, July–August 1966.

[5] The latter theme was most strongly and originally developed by Frantz Fanon, *The wretched of the earth*, London 1965, especially chapter 3.

[6] In *Africa and the World*, April 1968.

[7] Cited in Fitch and Oppenheimer, *Ghana*, p. 113, from *Political Affairs*, a theoretical journal of the American Communist Party.

[8] R. Murray, 'Militarism in Africa'.

not a typology—and insists that such a theory must be both inclusive and precise: he does not succeed, however, in formulating one. He does not insist that everything can be explained in conspiratorial terms but argues, almost certainly correctly, that 'Paucity of domestic capital formation, dependence on trade for budgetary revenue, absence of effective control over commodity prices, shortage of exchange, leave these countries open to externally catalyzed political crisis'. Whatever the variations in the forms of the coups, he argues that they converge in making the state more hospitable for foreign capital or stable for foreign and domestic capital, since the 'political–institutional structures...were incompatible with even minimal bourgeois rationality and efficiency, an impediment to contemporary forms of capitalist operation'.

In the case of Ghana, Murray believes that a squeeze was put on the economy[1] and that President Johnson took a consistently hostile attitude, withholding aid and grants and using his influence to negate applications for funds to I.M.F. and the International Bank. Against a background of falling world cocoa prices and 'well advanced schemes for structural transformation of the economy towards state-controlled industrialisation' the military took over and 'the *political* objective of the state department had been attained'. My own feeling is that some of this may be true, but it is clearly very difficult to demonstrate; but we should note that Murray only argues that the socio-political objectives of the military and those of the U.S. state department *coincided*. There is no hint of a plot, and in the case of Ghana I am fairly sure there was none.

Balancing, but not negating, Murray's thesis, are those commentators who insist that Ghana was in no meaningful sense a socialist country. At this stage the details are unnecessary, but all the evidence suggests that in the main they are correct: the Convention People's Party *was* a patronage party, it *was* penetrated by obviously non-socialist elements, the bulk of commerce *was* foreign-owned, President Nkrumah *was* corrupt, it *was* the poorer sections who were most exploited, etc.[2] Ghana was not developing, it was just about standing still, and all the evidence suggests that the general level of administrative efficiency was falling. President Nkrumah's verbal intransigence, his leaning towards the Soviet Union and his passionate interest in other countries' affairs can hardly have endeared him to the C.I.A. The relatively large Ghanaian 'bourgeoisie' also disliked

[1] All of the evidence suggests that the fall in cocoa prices down to 1966, and its subsequent rise, was simply a coincidence; a cruel one for Nkrumah, but nevertheless a coincidence.

[2] The evidence for all these assertions is overwhelming—see, for example, the Azu Crabbe and Apaloo reports, 'Report of the commission to inquire into the properties of Kwame Nkrumah (The Apaloo Report), Accra, Ministry of Information, January 1967; Report of commission to inquire into the affairs of Nadeco (The Azu Crabbe Report), Accra, Ministry of Information, 1966; the somewhat indignant but fairly accurate volume by H. L. Bretton, *The rise and the fall of Kwame Nkrumah*, London 1967; Fanon, *The wretched of the earth*; R. Dumont, *False start in Africa*, London 1966; Fitch and Oppenheimer, *Ghana*; and R. E. Dowse, *Ghana and the U.S.S.R.; a study in comparative development*, London 1969.

Nkrumah and his regime. When Nkrumah fell, both were delighted: there was a coincidence of interest, but neither was responsible for his fall from power. Nonetheless, it would be wrong to ignore the questions asked by the Marxists: they too point to the overriding need for more detailed and precise study of the circumstances of particular cases.

## THE MILITARY AS A GOVERNING ELITE

So far as I have been able to discover very little attention has been paid, outside Latin America at any rate, to the actual operations of the military as rulers. Interest has focused upon the military as a sociological entity, upon the society within which the intervention takes place and upon the conditions necessary for withdrawal.

Discussion of the sociology of the military has mainly centred upon two areas of interest: the 'ideology' of the armed forces, and their social structure, training patterns, and life styles.

On the whole, the academics' opinion of military political ideologies has been somewhat disparaging. Edward Shils, for example, writes that 'military oligarchies have no definite conception of the kind of regime to which they wish to transfer power or toward which they wish to move'.[1] In the same volume, Pye writes of the military as believing that 'all problems can be overcome if the right orders are given'.[2] This very widely held belief about the ideas of the military appears to be derived from the idea that the military is an ideal–typical Weberian bureaucratic organization within which rationality is almost everything.[3] The case is especially clear 'under relatively non-modernized conditions [where] the armed forces are more likely to be a focus of pre-occupation with rationality, universalism, functional specificity and the like than anything else'.[4] That is, underdeveloped armies—like most armies in peacetime—are underemployed and are left with very little to do except burnish bureaucratic efficiency and develop anti-political attitudes.

This seems rather confused; students of the military seem undecided whether or not to allow their subjects true ideological credentials. Janowitz allows them 'more or less common ideological themes'[5] and suggests that they have greater interest in organizational forms, and yet goes on to elaborate what seems to be a fairly coherent and related set of attitudes and ideas. Shils suggests that they lack definite ideas, but prefaces his analysis with the claim that 'the military conception of the right order of society is

[1] In Johnson, *The role of the military in under-developed countries*, pp. 58–9.
[2] *Ibid.*, p. 80 and M. Janowitz, *The military in the political development of new nations*, Chicago 1964, p. 66.
[3] See, for example, the M.I.T. study, 'The transitional process' in Welch (ed.), *Political modernization*, pp. 39–42, and Von der Mehden, *Politics of the developing nations*, p. 99.
[4] Marion Levy, 'Patterns of modernisation and political development', *Annals of the American academy of political and social science*, March 1965, p. 38.
[5] *Ibid.*, p. 63.

business-like'.[1] But in more recent writings there has been less hesitation; thus Anderson, Von der Mehden and Young argue that 'throughout the developing world, reformist military leaders have sought to stimulate development through organisation, social mobilisation, and a vigorous assertion of governmental power and economic activity'.[2] In other words, the Afro-Asian military emphasize the same policies and values as most of the politicians.

If there has been some confusion concerning the contents of military ideology, there certainly has been none concerning the derivation of officers' political ideas: they are nearly always held to be a direct reflection of 'the rise of the middle class'. Thus Von der Mehden, in discussing Latin America, argues that the younger officers were identified with emerging middle-class reformers about 1945: 'The high-ranking military officers generally maintained their alliances with the historically dominant groups ...the junior officers identified more closely with the middle-class leadership of the social democratic movements.'[3] Of the United Arab Republic, Leonard Binder writes that its policies 'may be seen as an adaption of the practical choices of the Egyptian political–military elite to the exigencies of the opinion of the (politically) participant Arab classes'.[4] On the role of the army in the Middle East and North Africa, Manfred Halpern suggests that 'As the Army officer corps came to represent the interests and views of the new middle-class, it became the most powerful instrument of that class'.[5] And, generalizing from Latin American experience since 1930, Johnson claims that 'the social and economic orientation of the politically active officers has been away from that of the old ruling groups and toward that of the civilian middle sectors'.[6]

One could add to this list, but the point is fairly clear: there is something resembling a set of ideas, they tend to be adopted by the younger officers, and the ideas are held in common by large sections of the middle class and the officers. Naturally, it is not argued that military training is an exact complement or copy of civilian experience, although Janowitz specifically states that skills are transferable to 'middle-level civilian administration', but it is strongly suggested that there are sufficient modal patterns of experience to ensure sympathy between the two groups.[7]

[1] E. A. Shils, 'The military and the political development of the new states', in J. J. Johnson (ed.), *The role of the military in under-developed countries*, p. 42.

[2] *Issues of political development*, New Jersey 1967, p. 179. See also Coleman and Brice in Johnson, *op. cit.*

[3] Von der Mehden, *Politics of the developing nations*, p. 112.

[4] 'Nasserism: the protest movement in the Middle East', in M. A. Kaplan (ed.), *The revolution in world politics*, New York 1962, p. 154.

[5] M. Halpern, *The politics of social change in the Middle East and North Africa*, Princeton 1963, p. 258.

[6] J. J. Johnson, *Political change in Latin America*, Stanford 1958, p. 13.

[7] But see C. Barnett in the *Journal of Contemporary History* II (July 1967), pp. 15–36, on the education of officers, who protests that too much stress has been laid upon training similarities.

What gives rise to these similarities of outlook? In the literature one can detect two broad 'determinants'. First, a very considerable amount has been written on the primary socialization and educational patterns of the two groups (and here the middle class tends to become equated with the bureaucracy). Secondly (and in a sense this is a development of the first point), the structural positions of the bureaucratized middle class and the officers *vis-à-vis* the politicians are in many ways similar.

The most obvious shared educational characteristic is simply that both army officers and bureaucratized middle class are literate in societies that are predominantly illiterate. They are actual or potential members of the local elite and aware of this. Their educational experiences are similar because of the restricted educational opportunities. This is especially clear in West Africa, where no country has more than half a dozen prestigious secondary schools, so that it is indeed likely that they went to these schools together. Nor has this shared experience always ceased after school; some officers are university graduates and until recently most officers and their civilian peers were educated abroad, mainly in Western Europe and America.

It is, however, the similarity between the positions of the two groups in the social and political structure that seems to be most striking. Both groups belong to the most Westernized sectors of the developing social systems and both belong to country-spanning institutions. Not only are the officer corps and the bureaucracy now the most modernized of all the sectors of society, but historically they are the ones where long-term associations with European superiors or technical assistance may well have resulted in some internalization of Western bureaucratic values.[1] They contrast sharply with the cadres of most political parties in Asia and West Africa, which developed after the civil and military bureaucracies in which promotion certainly involved no nonsense about merit, in which a spoils system was obvious (and probably 'necessary') and within which it was sometimes the most servile who were rewarded.

Both officers and civil servants are organized in relatively rigid hierarchies with limited scope for initiative, relatively ordered promotion, etc. Depending upon a stable society for continued livelihood, both groups have a firm interest in ordered modernization and economic growth, and both are well placed to see that this is what the politicians have often failed to secure. Most students of political development have pointed out that the army and the bureaucracy are alternative elites, committed to growth, unity, stability, etc., and if the politicians cannot provide these, then one or both of the alternative elites *must* try.[2] Associated with this belief is

---

[1] But in West Africa the localization of the officer corps was later and slower than that of the state bureaucracy.

[2] For example, see J. S. Coleman in Johnson, *The role of the military in under-developed countries*, pp. 398–405.

Q

another which sees the decision to join the army not as adherence to martial or heroic values but 'as the pursuit of a career in the most powerful, dynamic and expanding bureaucracy the country offered'.[1] That is, having no strong commitment to the army, the officer can easily slip into a political slot.

Another structural similarity between armed forces and the bureaucracy concerns the so-called 'generation gap'. Those Africans, especially, who were fortunate enough to be born earlier than others and to have entered the institutions at the right time, were catapulted into positions of responsibility and prestige at an early age and the prospects for latecomers are gloomy. Brigadiers and principal secretaries a few years older than those below them are likely to be regarded as the enemy and may well be less 'qualified' academically than their potential successors. There is always considerable pressure from below and resistance from above: Lieutenants Arthur and Yeboah in the 'abortive counter-coup' in Ghana were about to murder all above the rank of colonel.

There are also reasons, drawn from general bureaucratic theorizing, for suggesting that the military and the bureaucracy are at least potential allies. In a standard work it is suggested that organizations fall into four categories based upon the criterion of 'who benefits': mutual benefit organizations, business organizations, service organizations, and organizations benefiting the public-at-large.[2] Into the last category are placed the police, the state bureaucracy and the army. Further, such organizations can enter into coalitions to further their own interests or to defend them when attacked.[3] That is, a bureaucracy is not simply instrumental, but is placed 'in what may be called a power situation in which it has to cast its influence and to generate processes of power on its own behalf and in which it is under pressure from different centres of power in the society which would control it'.[4] Although Eisenstadt (from whom these words are taken) does not discuss the possibility of a civilian/military bureaucratic coalition, he is clear that under attack a bureaucracy has alternative strategies open to it, one of which is 'displacement of its service goals in favour of various power interests and orientations. Examples are military organisations that tend to impose their rule on civilian life.'[5] One should also stress that theorists do not insist that a bureaucracy need be politically challenged for it to spread: 'in most developing countries [bureaucracies]

---

[1] Halpern, *The politics of social change*, p. 275. See also P. T. Vatikiotis, *The Egyptian army in politics*, Indiana 1961 p. 214. 'To the new group of middle and lower class Egyptians...the career of an army officer meant, first, economic security. To many of these men it also meant belonging to an institution which reflected national independence and sovereign power.'

[2] P. Blau and W. R. Scott, *Formal organisations*, London 1963, p. 43.

[3] *Ibid.*, pp. 196–7.

[4] S. N. Eisenstadt, 'Bureaucracy and debureaucratization', *Administrative Science Quarterly* III, December 1959, p. 307.

[5] *Ibid.*, p. 364.

seek autonomy and reinforce both their administrative and social positions when challenged by the diversity of development'.[1]

Obviously propositions about military–bureaucratic coalitions are too general to be intellectually satisfactory since it is perfectly clear that there are different kinds of army and different kinds of bureaucracy. One would hardly expect the relationship between these varieties to be the same. Clearly, the social and geographical structure, the training patterns, the burdens of administration or war vary enormously and will affect the relationship between the two organizations. Although some work has been done on differing patterns within the military and the bureaucracy separately, no attempt has been made to combine the separate results into any sort of pattern.

However, leaving this weakness aside, not only are there good reasons in theory for expecting the military as a bureaucracy to combine with civilian bureaucracies, one can detect signs of it in the developing world. Thus, in the Sudan, 'experience has shown that the authoritarian rule of the military, in conjunction with a civilian bureaucracy, is not necessarily an ephemeral arrangement; indeed it may be a substitute for party government'.[2] And, similarly, in Pakistan one student has suggested that 'The transfer of power from a politician-dominated regime to a military regime may have the paradoxical result of reinforcing the influence and authority of civilian administrators'.[3] In Ghana, at any rate, the military regime can certainly be shown to be a civil/military bureaucratic coalition.

Clearly, the argument is not that administrators and army officers plot coups with one another, carry them out, and proceed to rule a country in a more efficient manner than their predecessors. The need for secrecy would exclude such an arrangement. The contention is that each group *needs* the other; that they have a great deal in common and can work together and, most importantly, that they occupy a similar social role *vis-à-vis* the politicians. The initial relationship may be one of outright suspicion and dislike, as was the case in Pakistan, of moderate authoritarianism, as in Egypt, or of celebration, as in Ghana; obviously there is a great deal of work to be done in investigating the various possible responses and the conditions and structures underlying them. But that the military and the bureaucracy must somehow work together would appear to be certain.

The reason for this is simple. On the one hand, the army does not have the expertise or the numbers to run a country and if they did run it, it might cease to be an army. On the other hand, the bureaucracy cannot

[1] D. E. Ashford, 'Bureaucrats and citizens', *Annals of the American Academy of Political and Social Science* LXXV (March 1965), p. 91.

[2] Coleman and Rosberg (eds.), *Political parties and national integration in tropical Africa*, California 1964, p. 678.

[3] M. Fainsod in J. LaPalombara (ed.), *Bureaucracy and political development*, Princeton 1963, p. 236.

bring down a government: that is the army's task. But when the government has been displaced, the bureaucracy is still necessary and hence by no means powerless. There must be a coalition of sorts, and hence an accommodation between the partners; whatever the conditions of the coalition, the fact of its existence is a certainty.

### THE GHANA COUP: A CASE STUDY

The previous sections have attempted to go as far as possible in drawing from the literature of this subject what general understanding has been gleaned about the conditions of military intervention and the character of military rule in developing countries. In the remaining section, the experience of Ghana is considered in the light of this review. Given the limitations of the theories of intervention that have been discussed, no effort will be made to explain the coup of February 1966 in other than historical terms. I shall, however, try to show that the ensuing government has been a coalition between the military and the civil service.

Before looking at the more immediate causes of the coup, it might be useful to glance at the background. Ghana is not an especially poor country by world standards, ranking third in Africa in terms of *per capita* G.N.P. in 1965 ($229), with almost three times the average for the developing world, and far above the projected African and Asian average for 1985 (best assumption). Its past growth rate and potential projected growth is the best in tropical Africa.[1] But it still falls well within Feierabend's 'low stability zone' of states in which, for example, there is less than 90 per cent literacy (in Ghana, 40 per cent of people under 40 are literate); less than 2,525 calories a day *per capita* (the Ghanaian average is about 2,000); G.N.P. *per capita* of under $300 p.a. (the Ghanaian figure is $229); less than 45 per cent of population urban (in Ghana, 24 per cent are defined as urban)[2]. However, Ghana is far ahead in every respect (except calorie intake, a suspect figure) of any of its neighbours, so if 'relative deprivation' is a clue to unrest it follows that Ghanaians have very high aspirations indeed. This is indeed probably the case with the elite, and arguably with most of the population who have been shown, on radio, in films, and in newspapers, levels of educational opportunity and consumption patterns with which the country cannot possibly provide them. For example, in 1960 about 484,000 children were in primary schools: 31 per cent of these could expect a middle-school place, and of these 13 per cent could

---

[1] *Agricultural commodities projections*, F.A.O. 1968, vol. 1, pt. 1, pp. 13–14 and 21.
[2] Index from Feierabend, 'Aggressive behaviours', 261; figures from P. Foster, *Education and social change in Ghana*; W. Birmingham, *et al.*, *A study of contemporary Ghana*, London 1966; F.A.O. West African pilot study of agricultural development, 1965; Russett, *et al.*, *World handbook of political and social indicators*, and 1960 Population Census of Ghana.

expect a secondary-school place.[1] In a country where education is highly valued, this pattern is potentially explosive.[2]

Under Nkrumah's government the rapid growth of educational and welfare facilities seems likely to have raised popular expectations still further. Ghanaians were led to expect free schooling, free medicines, free agricultural advice, etc., and the recent withdrawal of the first two caused widespread adverse comment. Any government must now take this into consideration—as, indeed, Nkrumah did when he came to power.

One can regard Nkrumah's regime as an exercise in social and political control for the purpose of extracting a surplus; whether the surplus was extracted in order to develop the economy or line pockets is irrelevant, although it must be insisted that he did introduce a large number of valuable and potentially valuable schemes. However, people do not like to be 'exploited', even to develop an economy. Hence, the expropriator needs either an exceptionally compliant or fragmented population or a very powerful apparatus of social control. Although it is arguable that President Nkrumah had more than his fair share of the former, he was singularly lacking in the latter.[3]

Ghana had a middle stratum of fairly considerable size by the early 1960s, composed of a group of absentee cocoa farmers, a number of coastal families with European education going back to the 1850s, a very rapidly expanding group of professionals such as lawyers, doctors, grammar school and university teachers, middle and top grades of the civil service and managers. Although all these categories were numerically insignificant (not more than fifteen thousand families in all, in a population of about seven million), all but the farmers came from a relatively small part of Ghana and had very largely been educated together.[4]

Until Nkrumah took power it is hardly an exaggeration to say that Ghanaian national politics mainly concerned the activities of these people —and on the whole they did not send their children into the army. Nor, according to the one survey of secondary student aspirations of young Ghanaians, was a career in the army thought very desirable, ranking fourteenth in a list of twenty-five possibilities, six of which no Ghanaian with secondary education would dream of entering.[5] Of the members of the national liberation council only Colonel Afrifa went to one of the

[1] P. Foster, *Education and social change in Ghana*, London 1965. Calculated from ch. 6. But Ghana has considerable regional variations.

[2] See Cameron Duodu, *The Gab boys*, London 1968, a novel which focuses on a group of young men after they leave middle-school in Ghana.

[3] It is interesting that many Ghanaian intellectuals concur with ex-governors on the ease with which Ghanaians can be governed; see, e.g., the *Legon Observer*, 5 August 1966.

[4] A glance at the Ghana Year Books before and after the coup ('Personalities in Ghana') will quickly reveal the overwhelming importance of about ten schools in or near Accra—including Achimota, Accra academy, and the Accra government school—plus about six others including Adisadel and Prempeh college.

[5] P. Foster, *Education and social change in Ghana*, pp. 272 and 276.

elite schools (Adisadel); the other military members attended second-level Catholic and Protestant denominational schools, and the same is true of the police members.[1] All of the N.L.C. members received their training in the U.K., one at Sandhurst, two at Eaton Hall Officer Cadet Training School, and all three policemen at the Hendon Police College—a new institution in the revolutionary academic pantheon.

There exists at present only the very scantiest evidence about the education and social composition of the officer corps. By 1966 the army had about 600 officers, and it is very unlikely that they came from a wider social catchment area than did the members of the N.L.C., five of whom were promoted from the ranks. It is possible, though, that the geographical distribution is wider as a consequence of the introduction of cadet training units in Prempeh College, Kumasi, and the Government School in Tamale; however, similar units established at Achimota, Adisadel, and St. Augustine's will almost certainly ensure that recruitment becomes more socially exclusive rather than less. Unlike the earlier generation of officers, the great bulk of the younger officers (under 35 years) have not served in the ranks.

It was the older elite whom Nkrumah squeezed economically by means of rapidly increasing tax levels, the dramatic taxes put on imports of conventional luxuries and the enforced savings *via* bond buying and the compulsory purchase of cocoa crops. By contrast the very rapid expansion and localization of bureaucracy and army meant that neither of these groups did at all badly in crude economic terms; by 1966 both were totally Ghanaian manned. Also it was planned to expand these sectors quickly, and in terms of the growth of local educational opportunity—from which they particularly benefited—a great deal was achieved.

The evidence available suggests that it was the cocoa farmers who bore the main brunt of the expropriation, together with the employed workers who were victims of inflation and the threat of unemployment. Ghana managed to produce both inflation and rising unemployment and thus to maintain hourly wage-rates steady.[2] Government minimum wages policy (6s. 6d. a day for the unskilled since July 1960), coupled with the rise in the cost of living index from 364 in July 1960 (based on 1939 = 100) to 486 in December 1963, led to a decline in the living standards of the unskilled worker. In addition the rapid rise in the cost of living and the general shortage of consumer goods from the beginning of 1964 cut down most of the gains that more skilled workers had previously obtained.[3]

[1] See the biographies in K. H. Bediako, *The downfall of Kwame Nkrumah*, Accra 1966. Gutteridge, *Military institutions* . . . , pp. 101–2, cites Achimta as important, yet not one of the officers involved in the coup, nor any of the previous top men, was educated there (except Otu as a teacher).

[2] W. Birmingham, *et. al.*, *A study of contemporary Ghana*, vol. I, London 1966, p. 141, and R. W. Norris, 'On inflation in Ghana', in T. J. Farer (ed.), *Financing African development*, Cambridge, Mass. 1965, p. 104.

[3] W. Birmingham, *et al.*, pp. 136–53.

These losses followed a period of rising standards and cannot have made the regime popular with the workers.

By comparison the military was *not* badly treated. It was the largest in West Africa and eighth in Africa as a whole, the fifth highest in total expenditure.[1] And in many ways Nkrumah favoured the armed forces—but he also attempted to bring the military to heel as he had brought all the other institutions of Ghanaian life. It was this more than anything else that the military resented: the attempt to introduce party cells amongst the soldiers, the establishment of the Soviet-trained president's own guard regiment (P.O.G.R.), the sending of officers to train in the U.S.S.R., the abrupt dismissal of Ankrah and Otu—and, most important of all, the appointment of a personal nominee (Brigadier Hassan) in charge of military intelligence and the 'people's militia' in December 1965.[2] The military may have been offended by corruption, by the suffering of the population and the general incompetence of the regime and by first-hand knowledge, through relatives, of the general decline of the rural areas, but my impression is that it was a corporate threat that finally aroused them.[3]

Clearly Nkrumah was attempting a control operation and the army struck before it was too late; Nkrumah 'had wicked plans to disband the Ghana armed forces and replace them with a militia formed by his C.P.P. Fanatics'.[4] The P.O.G.R. was taken into the army shortly after the coup, military intelligence reverted to a regular officer, and the dismissed officers were brought back. Similarly the police had been under attack since a bomb plot in the north led to the dismissal of Commissioner Madjitey; and the removal from police control of the border guards, together with the transference of the special branch from the police to the president's office in October 1964, clearly showed the drift.[5] Both were taken back by the police in May 1966.[6] There is also a suspicion that two of the leading police officers were about to be arrested on criminal charges and acted in self-defence.[7]

Thus the coup looks like self-defence and the most cursory glance at the tribal composition of the N.L.C. demonstrates that at least tribalism or regionalism was not a primary factor. So far as one can judge by press

[1] D. Wood, *The armed forces in African states*, London 1966, pp. 28–9.

[2] Major-general (later Lieutenant-general) J. A. Ankrah, Commander-in-chief of the army, and Major-general S. A. A. Otu, chief of the defence staff, were dismissed in July 1965: no reason for the dismissal was given, and both were subsequently made directors of the Bank of Ghana. In 1965 Colonel Hassan was head of counter intelligence: he was subsequently promoted to brigadier and given the title of director of military intelligence.

[3] See A. A. Afrifa, *The Ghana coup*, London 1966; interview in *London Observer*, 13 March 1966.

[4] Police Commissioner Harlley, *Daily Graphic*, 11 March 1966.

[5] As a matter of fact Harlley illegally established a secret Special Branch.

[6] See *Africa Research Bulletin*, May 1966, col. 538c.

[7] Speech by Nkrumah from Guinea, *Africa and the World*, May and June 1966.

reports and very *post hoc* interviews, the coup was a popular one, but the population was in no way involved: hence the very low level of violence.

The bureaucracy had also been under attack for a number of years; it was 'infiltrated' early on by C.P.P. branches and a number of its administrative responsibilities were taken into the president's office. And many of its most experienced members—A. L. Adu and Robert Gardiner for example—preferred to leave or were dismissed. All senior members had to take courses at the Ideological Institute at Winneba. Consultation with senior administrators was lacking.[1] When the list of contracts for short-term credit schemes was put together after the coup it was discovered that millions of cedis' worth of contracts had been signed by ministers without consultation.[2]

In short, the coup could not but benefit the civil service, but one sees no evidence of direct collusion, rather an identity of outlook: 'In Ghana... many of the civil service's members are more educated than politicians and have internalised the British liberal–bureaucratic outlook; they can be thought of as constituting a permanent but relatively latent "rightist" opposition to government.'[3] The regime came up against institutions which it did not entirely succeed in controlling and which predated the regime by many years. These institutions flourish (on the whole) in an ideologically neutral atmosphere where at least a strong element of predictability is present; it was not present in Ghana, and Nkrumah ignored or did not understand the economic situation as it was understood by a group of very able civil servants.[4]

These bureaucrats, who as a matter of fact owed their educational and social opportunity in considerable measure to Nkrumah's Ghana, were certainly undermined in terms of living standards by the rapid inflation from 1963 onwards, but, by Ghanaian standards, they were not doing at all badly; they enjoyed cheap houses or rent allowances, car loans and allowances, relatively pleasant working conditions, and very reasonable hours of work. One may also conjecture that they had political and social objections to the party. They must have found Nkrumaism shallow, the personality cult can hardly have appealed to them, their style of dress (they did not wear 'political suits') and speech differed from those of the party cadres; their approach to politics was cautious and administration-biased. But they were helpless without the armed forces.

Nkrumah also came up against another set of factors in attempting

---

[1] Omaboe, in Birmingham *et al.*, pp. 460–1.
[2] Bretton, *The rise and fall of Kwame Nkrumah*, pp. 98–100, suggests that Nkrumah deliberately created administrative chaos to make himself indispensable.
[3] A. Zolberg, *Creating political order*, p. 71. See also L. S. Tiger, 'Bureaucracy in Ghana', unpublished Ph.D. thesis, London 1963.
[4] See the evidence of these men before the many commissions; perhaps a pinch of salt is necessary, but the broad drift is unmistakable.

to restructure Ghana. These factors are connected with the lack of flexibility of the Ghanaian economy whose dominant features were established during the 'economic miracle' of the late nineteenth and early twentieth centuries.[1] Ghana is totally dependent upon foreign trade, mainly with Europe and America, and thus is sensitive to changes in world patterns or terms of trade for its staple imports and major exports. A glance at the situation after 1960 is instructive. Industry is only weakly developed in Ghana: most of the material used by industry is imported with only about 25 per cent of final product made by or processed by Ghanaian industry. This means that Ghana sustains a relatively well-developed managerial group, but lacks a strong entrepreneurial class.[2] Having few investment outlets in local industry the 'middle class' historically has been driven to enjoy much of its income in immediate satisfaction, or building houses, which means a very strong income elasticity of demand for imports. In 1953 the Gold Coast had the third highest imports of food, textiles and tobacco of all African countries.[3] Even in 1962 non-durable and durable consumer goods accounted for 48 per cent of imports by value with probably another 3 per cent to be added for private sector fuels, although this was *after* the introduction in 1961 of exchange control and import licences to cut down 'inessential' imports.[4]

A section of the Ghanaian population had thus for many years enjoyed a very high standard of living, reinforced by a European education, frequent visits to Europe, the inheritance of expatriate standards, and considerable wealth going back to the early years of the 1900s. The educated or official Ghanaian tended to insist on standards which in Europe are the prerogative of the middle-aged middle-class. And it should be remembered that the post-1961 austerity followed many years of rising prosperity which had accelerated after 1957.

Not only did Nkrumah cut imports, he also raised taxes and levied compulsory savings which hit all sections of the population.[5] At the same time the actual discouragement of Ghanaian enterprise (as opposed to the theoretical co-existence of national, foreign, joint and private enterprise) hit again at the farmer and the small indigenous businessman, especially in sawmilling and fishing, and at the more important trading mammies by making credit scarce and granting import licences mainly to the large foreign firms. No doubt the idea was to do away with the 'Kulaks' in the

[1] R. Szereszewski, *Structural changes in the economy of Ghana, 1891–1911*, London 1966.

[2] Richard Rathbone has suggested that the small Ghanaian entrepreneurial class is politically more significant than its size might indicate. This is true—in fishing, plant-hire, building contractors, and a number of factories—but the import pull of this group is certainly small in proportion to the rest. On business men in the C.P.P. see Rathbone's important paper, *Education and politics in Ghana*, Institute of Commonwealth Studies 1968.

[3] P. L. Yates, *Forty years of foreign trade*, London 1959, pp. 196–7.

[4] Birmingham *et al.*, p. 334; *Economic survey*, 1962, Government Printer, Accra 1963, p. 64.

[5] St. Clair Drake and L. H. Lacy, 'Government versus the unions', in Gwendolen Carter, *Politics in Africa*, Harcourt 1966, esp. pp. 73–81.

interest of controlled growth, but that task requires something stronger than the C.P.P. ever was.

I do not wish to labour the point, but I believe that most of the academic commentators on the C.P.P. have allowed typologies and theories to come between them and a close look at the party on the ground. This does not mean swinging to the extreme of calling the regime a Fascist one, or saying that it was a purely personal system of rule.[1] It was neither. The C.P.P. was a political chameleon taking on the coloration of any particular part of Ghana where it existed. In other words, the social structure of Ghana tended to absorb the C.P.P. rather than be altered by it in any radical way; just as it adjusted to changed circumstances in 1956–7, so it adjusted after independence. The party became deeply involved in the many and intricate stool disputes in Ghana; its membership regarded it, in so far as they took it seriously, as a source of favours and promotion rather than as a mobilizing party; on the Kumasi city council it became embroiled in a series of purely local disputes of no relevance at all to its purported objective of socialism.[2] It became a haven for rogue and idealist alike. At the centre it suffered from bureaucratic elephantiasis and at the periphery it often just disappeared into the local scene: the district of Larteh, recorded Brokensha, 'has shown a remarkable syncretic capacity to absorb new institutions so that even the powerful C.P.P.... emerges as a Larteh rather than a national institution'.[3] There seems no reason to suppose, in the absence of evidence to the contrary, that the party was essentially different in other parts of Ghana. In so far as it was anything, it was a barrier to communication, it was noise in a system already sufficiently noisy; and here the implications of Apter's suggestion that there is 'an inverse relationship between information and coercion in a system' might be considered.[4]

But coercive power was just what the system was running out of, since the C.P.P. was a weak reed and the armed forces and police—at least on the levels which counted—were rapidly running out of patience. Thus, when the coup took place in the early hours of 24 February 1966, only Colonel Zanlerigu's P.O.G.R. offered any resistance at all and the C.P.P. fell apart almost at a touch.

[1] T. Szamuely, introduction to A. A. Afrifa, *The Ghana coup*; Bretton, *Kwame Nkrumah*.

[2] See D. Austin, *Politics in Ghana, 1946–60*, London 1964, esp. pp. 293–7 on the Brong–Ahafo dispute; and this is not a novelty in Ghana since precisely the same fate was met by the far more disciplined colonial service in the Gold Coast, the major part of whose work 'was concerned with chieftaincy disputes, and, above all, boundary and land disputes' (R. E. Wraith, *Guggisberg*, Oxford 1967, p. 221).

[3] D. Brokensha, *Social change at Larteh, Ghana*, Oxford 1966, p. xix. In a recent article David Apter grasps the point that 'In the first stages of Nkrumah's rule, the presence of the CPP organizations simply enlivened the dispute—the pre-existing pattern of conflict and argumentation which had been going on for generations'. But he greatly overestimates the capacity of the party to rise above these absorbing issues; 'Nkrumah, charisma, and the coup', *Daedalus* (Summer 1968), 791.

[4] In *The politics of modernisation*, Chicago 1965, p. 40.

The touch was applied by a very small number of men, 600 in all, under a very limited number of officers (Afrifa names only four and, given the Ghanaian army ratio of officers to men, some six or nine others might well have been actively involved). Hence, we have no idea what the younger or less senior officers might have felt, since they were probably not consulted. Nor have we any idea of what the police officers felt. They were instructed to arrest a number of people and did so, and that is all we know for sure.[1]

Ideologically there is not a great deal to be said about the members of the junta except that they fell into Huntington's category of 'reformers' who are 'eclectic and pragmatic'.[2] But their pragmatism stopped short of socialism or communism; like so many leaders of African coups, their first action was to get rid of Chinese and Russian 'experts', both the useful and the harmful. The N.L.C. adopted a democratic stance, and, by contrast with the previous regime, the claim was justified. It would accept aid from wherever it was available, but certainly veered to the West. It had a touching faith in the power of words—constitutions, exhortations to honesty and civic consciousness and hard work—and, as usual, resented the criticisms of the wordmongers, the journalists. Politics to them was indeed the giving of correct orders; problems arise from failing to understand the orders. Strikes were the work of agitators. The N.L.C. was anti-socialist, but perforce it relied on the state. Its political ideal was stability and liberal constitutionalism.

For the new government the question of legitimacy, one stressed by all students of the military in politics, did not really arise, at least if legitimacy means popularity and widespread acceptability. Not a single section of the population rallied to the displaced regime, and more than one hand was raised against leading C.P.P. members. When the new regime was threatened by a counter-coup in April 1967, the students were preparing a march on Accra and there was a violent popular demonstration against the would-be coupists at Osu Castle.

To run the government the N.L.C. immediately fell back on the civil service, with a heavy admixture of people from the old United Party. Unlike every other organization connected with the previous regime, the

---

[1] So far as I can ascertain there is no evidence at all of external intervention or collusion, although one may be quite sure that no tears were shed in American or British official circles. The British official response was lukewarm, and felt to be so in Ghana. America was more forthcoming and its aid was stepped up, though modestly, from about $17·5 million a year between 1957 and 1965 to about $20 million a year in 1966-7, and loans did increase between 1957 and 1965 (Ghana obtained some $65 million and since 1966 some $40 million). This higher level of assistance was freely acknowledged and American private enterprise was sought—with some, but not much, success. Nkrumah's followers named a man from the Accra U.S.I.S. as the chief liaison between the state department and the plotters, but their sole published evidence was that he departed from Ghana two weeks before the coup: see *Africa and the World*, March 1968.

[2] S. Huntington, *Changing patterns of military politics*, p. 34.

bureaucracy remained unscathed. An economic council to advise the
N.L.C. was formed on the day of the coup, consisting solely of government
officials, together with the governors of the Bank of Ghana and the Ghana
Commercial Bank. Soon after, an administrative committee and a political
committee were established. 'These committees consist mainly of civil
servants, and it is they who have been wielding effective executive power
in the country.'[1] Since the N.L.C. was also concerned with running the
armed forces and the police, it is almost certain that 'the new pattern of
control places great authority in the hands of the civil servants'.[2] The
maze of boards, offices, secretaries, etc., was drastically cut and the
number of ministries reduced from 32 to 18 and principal secretaries were
placed in sole charge of them, under the N.L.C. The nine regions of
Ghana were headed by military or police officers who were told to observe
the rule of law and listen to the regional administrative officers.[3] Hence it
was with considerable justification that Afrifa mentioned as one of the
N.L.C.'s achievements that it 'tried to recreate the independence of the
civil service' and the one independent newspaper stated that 'when
the armed forces and police succeeded in restoring freedom to this country,
the N.L.C. demonstrated their appreciation of the proper role which top
civil servants should play in a democratic country'.[4]

Also popular with the bureaucracy was the policy decision to hand a
number of the state industries over to private ownership. They were a
burden on administrative capacity and led to serious misallocation of
economic and administrative resources.[5]

At the same time the C.P.P. and its subsidiary organizations were
abolished, as were all other political parties. Clearly an administrative
state was emerging, but in alliance with—of all people—the traditional
rulers! 'We shall respect the institution of chieftaincy and recognise the
role that the chiefs will play in the development of the new Ghana.'[6]
And to a chiefs' conference in Kumasi, Commissioner Harlley explained
that 'chieftaincy is an essential element in Ghana's life', after which he
showed he was in earnest by ratifying the destoolment of numerous pro-
C.P.P. chiefs in December 1966. The proposed constitution also buttresses
the power of chiefs, especially in local councils where they will be in a two-
thirds majority over elected members.

Closely paralleling this 'alliance' with the chiefs was the more obvious
alliance with the old U.G.C.C.–N.L.M.–United party axis, which itself

[1] B. D. G. Folson, in the *Legon Observer*, 8 July 1966.
[2] D. Austin, 'The Ghana case', Institute of Commonwealth Studies Papers, *The politics of
demilitarisation*, London 1966, pp. 41–54.
[3] *Daily Graphic*, 15 March 1966.
[4] *Legon Observer*, 31 March 1967, and *Ashanti Pioneer*, 22 January 1968; the statement is by
Mr H. Osie, Ghana's auditor-general.
[5] K. Gyasi-Twum (Principal Secretary, Ministry of Finance), 'Reflections on some aspects
of fiscal policy', *Economic Bulletin of Ghana*, 1966, no. II.
[6] Ankrah, *Daily Graphic*, 5 March 1966.

had considerable connections with the chiefs, and which was manifest in the appointments to the N.L.C. political committee in July 1966. Of the twenty-three members no less than twelve were ex-members of the U.P. and most of the rest were people who had no associations with the C.P.P. Another element in the old alliance which soon surfaced in Ghana was the judiciary, which had been politically opposed to Nkrumah and which now assumed the chairmanships of the many commissions of investigation into the former regime. Similarly, the University of Ghana, which had resisted Nkrumah, soon emerged as a warm—if sometimes critical—friend of the new regime, and obtained a large pay increase.

Thus, the immediate effect of the coup was to put the clock back to about 1951–4 and to reverse the electoral results of those years. The social groups which had expected to inherit the political–administrative kingdom of British colonialism finally did so with the help of the armed forces.[1]

The immediate result was to eliminate completely from the political scene—assuming they were ever really on it—the masses whom Nkrumah was supposed to have mobilized. Politics were banned, and in their place arose influence and covert pressures and strikes, the last being normally attributed to 'subversive elements among the workers'—to ex-C.P.P. and Winneba 'Socialist Boys'.[2] Attempts were made through centres for civic education to interest the 'masses' in the Commissions and in the proposed new constitution, but without any very great success, although it must be admitted that there was a widespread response to the appeal for suggestions for the new constitution. There was some suspicion of the 'masses'. For example, it was suggested that only the literate should be given the vote, and the authorities' constitutional proposals were certainly geared towards the chiefs, the older generation, and especially the judiciary (which might emerge as a 'guardian' group); and against the illiterate, who would not be allowed to stand for election (this would exclude about 70 per cent of the population).[3] It is also clear that the alliance feared a revival among Nkrumah's supporters, a strong possibility since they possessed almost a monopoly of political organizing ability; and for this reason, if no other, everyone of any significance in the party was excluded from active participation for 10 years. The stage was set for victory by the responsible moderate elite. This could have been predicted from Finer's work: 'the leadership always tries to control the political product of any successor regime they establish'.[4]

Economically also it is these groups which benefited most. As far as

---

[1] See also E. Feit, 'Military coups and political development', *World Politics* XX (January 1968), 179–93.

[2] Kotoka in the *Ghanaian Times*, 20 December 1966, Afrifa on the bank strike, in *Africa Research Bulletin*, December 1967, col. 939c, and Ankrah in the *Ghanaian Times*, 27 May 1968.

[3] See *Report of the Constitutional Committee*, Accra 1968.

[4] 'Military disengagement from politics', in the collected seminar papers on *The politics of demilitarisation*, Institute of Commonwealth Studies Papers, April/May 1966, p. 3.

possible, the older structure of state monopolies was broken down into either completely private or joint enterprise; but this was not so much a matter of 'bourgeois attitudes' as a reflection of the fact that the Ghanaian administration simply did not command the range and level of skills needed to run a socialist economy. Very severe retrenchment in state industries and expenditure and a policy (not at the time of writing successful) of leaving new industry to develop privately, led to a growing problem of unemployment. In 1968 it was unlikely that there were less than 80,000 people out of work whilst the unemployment of school-leavers was assuming the proportions of a catastrophe; some 40,000 of 52,000 middle-school leavers of 1967 were unemployed.[1] But university intakes have increased.

The N.L.C. has also attempted, within the crippling limitations imposed by Ghana's external debts, to help local enterprise by allocating import licences on a public basis to Ghanaian businessmen, by diverting resources to agricultural feeder roads, and by liberalizing the loan policy of the National Investment Bank. Both civil servants and university lecturers had substantial salary increases—whilst day labourers got a 5 per cent raise. Devaluation of the cedi from an equivalent of 10s. to 7s. Sterling by June 1967 was designed to reduce imports (raising their cost by 43 per cent) and at the same time encouraging Ghanaian exporters.

But there was evidence that the N.L.C. could not satisfy its allies. The outcry over the agreements with foreign companies, Abbott, Norcement, etc., came mainly from the universities, especially Legon, and led to the dismissal of the editors of the three major newspapers whom the N.L.C. had appointed. Despite price increases for cocoa, it was certain that anything up to 20,000 tons was being smuggled to Togo and the Ivory Coast. Most of the handover to private enterprise was to *foreign* enterprise, and the age-old Ghanaian demand 'to transfer the control of...trade from the hands of resident foreign nationals into those of Ghanaians' was again loud in the land.[2] There were also criticisms of the failure to provide employment.[3]

One could detect signs that the N.L.C. was beginning to recognize the problems associated with the return to barracks. The would-be inheritors of political power, who appeared to be polarizing around Busia and Gbedemah, were beginning to press for further steps to civilian rule and for a rapid return to civilian rule. Yet the N.L.C., with the probable exception of Afrifa, was formally committed to staying until the financial mess and corruption was cleared up—a very distant prospect

---

[1] *West Africa*, 22 April 1967 and 10 February 1968. See also *Legon Observer*, 22 December 1967.
[2] *Ghanaian Times*, 27 March 1968. In June 1968 the N.L.C. announced a policy of restricting the ownership of a wide range of distribution and manufacturing concerns to Ghanaian nationals, *Africa Research Bulletin*, 15 June 1968, pp. 1058–9.
[3] By Busia; see *West Africa*, 4 May 1968.

indeed, and one which General Ankrah dismissed in 1968 as 'hardly bearing realistic examination'.[1] Ghana's economy was pledged to the developed world for many years if it was to pay its debts and service the debt charges; it had succeeded in turning a trade deficit of $116 in 1965 to a credit of $24 million in 1967 mainly by cutting imports, but this could not go much further without completely undermining the economy. At the same time the country has actually got further into debt and although the repayment period for most of the debt has been substantially increased the country will need external support into the 1970s.[2] Hence, the period of 'tutelary democracy' is likely to be extensive.[3]

The N.L.C., like any other government in Ghana, was very closely restricted by the sheer weight of problems and the need to maintain some sort of alliances. To give two trivial examples of the constraints on the N.L.C.: it would have liked, and said so, to get rid of the workers' brigade, but it cannot throw these people on to the labour market; it would also have liked to get rid of more of the state enterprises, and publicly asked for bids, but for some of them no bids were received. The larger constraints are too well known to need repeating. There were signs that within the N.L.C. tension has been felt between the army and the police, especially after 17 April 1967, when two junior army officers nearly seized power.[4] And there is no doubt that many Ghanaians believed, rightly or wrongly, that the N.L.C. is pro-Ewe, a sentiment that occasionally gets into print, as in the N.L.C. press release on the day of the 'abortive counter-coup': 'there are rumours going round to the effect that the insurrection was planned by Ashantis and Fantis against Gas and Ewes. This is a wicked rumour which is absolutely untrue.'[5]

The Ghanaian businessman, then, has reasons to support the N.L.C., and the university does so with reservations: 'On the evidence available, it would not be surprising if our present negotiators are accused by a future

---

[1] *Daily Telegraph*, 18 March 1968.

[2] *Ghana's economy and aid requirements in 1967*, Accra April 1967.

[3] A further step was taken in July 1967, when fourteen civilian commissioners were taken on to the N.L.C. as quasi-ministers.

[4] See the strongly partisan, but uncontradicted, reports in *Africa and the World*, May, June, and July 1967.

[5] See also Zolberg, *Creating political order*, p. 91, on plots against Nkrumah: 'it is striking that many individuals allegedly involved tend to belong...to the Ga and Ewe peoples, who...have long opposed what they regard as Akan domination of Ghanaian politics'. See also Afrifa in *Legon Observer*, 27 October 1967. But there is no statistical justification for this feeling so far as public appointments to commissions of inquiry and N.L.C. committees are concerned. However, Ewe people may well be regarded as the Ibo of Ghana. They are 7·5 per cent of the total population, but occupy about 19 per cent of army and brigade positions; as a tribe they are well above the national adult literacy level and have double the national average percentage of higher education; and since they are very prone to migration they may well be more in evidence than other tribes. Curiously, they are *not* significantly above the national average in professional, administrative, and managerial workers; whether there has been a post-coup adjustment it is impossible to tell. *1960 Census Report of Ghana, Special Report E*, Accra 1964, pp. 61, 87, 101, and 109.

civilian government with careless dissipation of funds.'[1] But it realizes that the very fact of an open and free debate on known and public facts is a massive move towards rationality and a large minority (43 per cent) of students thought in 1967 that civilian rule within 5 years was undesirable.[2] More impressive evidence came from a national poll of over 8,000 people in December 1967; 45 per cent did not want a return to civil rule, 44 per cent wanted a return in 1970 and 31 per cent wanted it in 1971 or 1972, or were uncertain.[3] Unfortunately, the poll did not use breakdowns by socio-economic status; but it is a fair guess that the leaders of the civil service are by no means anxious for a return to civil government 'because they are afraid that the politicians might turn the enquiries on them'.[4] Of the likely contenders for power, the ex-C.P.P. officers had been banned, which only left the older generation of U.G.C.C., N.L.M., and U.P. politicians and a few 'defectors' from the N.L.C. The difficulty here is that Harlley, a possible political leader, was a kinsman of Gbedemah who had been excluded (both are Ewe); Busia, clearly groomed for leadership, appeared in some sort of alliance with A. A. Afrifa who was posted to a non-fighting command at the Teshie Officer Cadet School.[5] Busia had considerable support in the universities, but it was numerically insignificant.

Whatever the answer to these conundrums, one thing is perfectly clear: the armed forces and police cleared up the worst of the mess, and succeeded in introducing a measure of administrative order, in shuffling off a range of administrative tasks beyond the capacity of the Ghanaian or any other African bureaucracy to shoulder, and getting the agricultural priorities right. But they did not solve any of Ghana's most intractable problems. And they may even, inadvertently, have allowed the *almost* buried 'tribal' feeling to resurface. Further, if we regard the military as an interim solution to societal problems, in what sense can it contribute to institutional differentiation and communicational clarity? It does often, though by no means always, clear away corrupt parties and disentangle them from the bureaucracy. Yet it may still be that there are some ultimately indispensable functions that only a party can perform—some communication is provided between rulers and ruled, some psychological satisfactions are offered to the public—Ghana as Africa's Black Star, Ghana on the front page, O.A.S. Conferences, volunteers for Rhodesia, etc.—things which a grey alliance of the military and bureaucracy cannot provide. Parties must, however, achieve a reasonable level of economic performance, and the best the N.L.C. can do is to lay some sort of groundwork to make this

[1] *Legon Observer*, 8 December 1967. The reference is to the very attractive terms given to foreign investors.
[2] Sample opinion survey in *Legon observer*, 9 June 1967.
[3] Jeafan Ltd., Public Opinion Poll, Accra 1967, by permission.
[4] *West Africa*, 27 April 1968.
[5] Afrifa and Busia are both from Ashanti. Afrifa has consistently emphasized the danger of tribalism and urged the need for a quick return to civil government.

possible. Meanwhile, with price rises following devaluation, it is quite certain that overall living standards will decline. Can the N.L.C. clear up corruption? Although the army apparently believed that exhortation plus a bit of rough justice would do away with corruption, it is unlikely that it does so any longer. It may be that corruption *is* a form of communication.[1] One other remark is apposite: the N.L.C. has not solved the major problem of its position in a new regime. It is to this, in conclusion, that I would briefly like to turn.

'The army and the police are the custodians of the nation's constitution.'[2] Although one should not make too much of a random remark, the meaning is clear and it fits well with the reported attitudes of other intervening military. If the military move from direct intervention to a supervisory role, as is apparently the case in Turkey and Brazil, how are they to decide what is proper constitutional behaviour and what is not? The civilian government is hamstrung unless it can control the armed forces somehow, but how is this to be done? How can it reduce the military budget assuming that it is too large? Ghana's almost certainly is: what is the purpose of an air force equipped with jet fighters or a navy with admirals and millions of pounds' worth of installations, in a country threatened by nobody? Why an army of some 10,000 men and 600 officers in a country that apparently cannot afford to import enough medicines or insecticides or build feeder roads for its farmers? Such questions occur to any detached observer and will certainly occur to any new civilian regime—not that the size of the army affects its ability to intervene (Togo had about 200, Dahomey and Sierra Leone about 1,000 men). But the simple fact is that they are expensive; Ghana was spending about £16 million a year in 1965 (about 8·4 per cent of total budget) and had spent £200 million on defence since 1954.[3] At the same time it is difficult to imagine that the armed forces will be content with less than under the Nkrumah regime, even though their intervention may not have been about the amount of money allocated to them.

Similarly, it is difficult to imagine that intervening armies in Africa will move from Finer's most 'extreme' position (i.e. direct military rule) to one of simple influence; in his terms, none of Africa's political cultures are sufficiently advanced or complex, although if any country in black Africa approaches his category of 'developed' political culture it is Ghana; probably Ghana must be classified with Finer's third order, of 'low' political culture, where military intervention is endemic (yet Ghana is *not* Guatemala). At the time of writing, there was no overt split in Ghana between the 'military politicians' of the N.L.C. and the military proper,

[1] See, e.g., M. McMullen, 'A theory of corruption', *Sociological Review* n.s. VIII (July 1961), 181–201; and C. Leys, 'What is the problem about corruption?', *Journal of Modern African Studies* III, 2 (August 1965), pp. 215–30.

[2] A. A. Afrifa, *The Ghana coup*, p. 99.

[3] J. Kraus, 'The men in charge', *Africa Report* XI, 4 (April 1966), pp. 16–22.

R

but there were obvious signs of strain within the N.L.C. and the regime cannot avoid more and growing discontent with its inevitable failure to provide higher living standards. It seemed likely that the army would in the end want to have elections under something like the proposed constitution, leading perhaps to the withdrawal of the army from government and a new alliance between the incoming politicians and the police.

We have no detailed age, tribe, or socio-economic status breakdown of any West African army, although one is currently being undertaken on the Nigerian Army. We have no 'before-and-after' attitude survey of any African officer corps in terms of cadet training. We have no idea whether or not African officers enter the army as a first career choice, whether it is regarded simply as a career not essentially different from any other, whether their choice meets with parental approval; we do not know the amount of an officer's time spent in extra-military secondary associations, what their societal reference groups are, what is their level of satisfaction with promotion prospects compared with similarly bureaucratized career patterns, etc. The point is very clear: before we are in a position to generalize about military intervention we need to scale down our theoretical perspectives to embrace smaller units and get down to work on the details of middle-level hypotheses. The wider theories seem so boundary-blurred as to be capable of absorbing almost anything. There is no royal road, no short cut. We do have an enormously powerful tool in statistical analysis and we must ensure that it is neither neglected nor abused. The task of securing the right kind of information and of testing its worth by statistical analysis is formidable, and only good theory at the right level of generality can enable us to tackle it with any confidence of success.

# THE ANALYSIS OF PLANNING

## COLIN LEYS

A club of states without national plans would be an interesting one (including, for instance, Luxembourg, Monaco, and the U.S.A.) but its membership would probably not run to double figures and it would not include any of the less-developed countries, all of which are included in the list of 193 countries with national plans compiled by Dr Waterston and his colleagues at the World Bank in 1965. What significance, if any, does this fact have?[1]

While the publication of a plan or a series of plans may be enough to qualify for membership of the planning club, the variety of actual practice, from countries which have invested heavily in planning and where it has led to important changes in the political and administrative structure, to countries where it is little more than a public relations exercise for foreigners, is so great that distinctions must be drawn and classifications made. We need to ask what sorts of roles have been created in the name of planning, how they relate to older-established structures, what sort of people are recruited to them, with what resources for exercising influence, and what structural changes have been set in motion as a result; in other words, a systematic and comparative inquiry. This has not been tried.[2] The literature is mainly of a practical, how-to-do-it orientation, as heavily dominated by economists as the new roles created by planning itself, and one looks to it in vain for a framework of ideas with which the comparative task might be begun. In most of this literature, the notion of planning has in fact been overlaid by the notion of 'optimal policy-making'.[3] The distinction is fundamental, both for understanding what is involved in planning, and because two very different approaches to policy-making are implied. To put the matter crudely, good planning

---

[1] A. Waterston, *Development planning: lessons of experience*, Baltimore 1965, pp. 589–643. I am very grateful to Dr B. B. Schaffer for generous help in the revision of this paper.

[2] The major exception to this is the national planning series of monographs published by Syracuse University Press under the direction of Professor B. Gross, a list of which is given on pp. 26–7 of B. Gross (ed.), *Action under planning*, New York 1967. A number of major investigations of planning in particular countries by political scientists also exist, the most outstanding of which is A. H. Hanson's *The process of planning: a study of India's five year plans, 1950–61*, Oxford 1966.

[3] The writing of some Eastern bloc planners stands apart in this respect, possibly because they are preoccupied with the limitations of the 'command economy' in the 1960s; it is curious how Western planners confronted with strictly parallel problems (the limitations of the market interventionist system in less developed countries) have tended to remain preoccupied with the effect of this on their notions of optimality; see, for instance, W. F. Stolper, *Planning without facts*, Cambridge, Mass. 1966, pp. 309–21. The other curious feature of most of this literature is its apparent lack of contact with the literature on decision-making, which in turn, however, rarely discusses planning.

may be bad policy-making and *vice versa*. This all too simple point, because it is so often overlooked with serious results, is the theme of the first half of this paper.

Drawing this distinction leads to emphasis on a few rudimentary characteristics of a concept of planning. Reflection on these suggests that 'comprehensive planning', regarded by many planners as its most developed and valuable form, is in practice apt to be rather the most developed form of the confusion of optimal policy-making with planning, and that this underlies much of the current disillusionment with it. In conclusion, this line of thought is tried out on the planning experience of a particular country, Tanzania.

### THE PREVAILING REPRESENTATION OF PLANNING

I take as a leading example of this, because it has been so widely quoted, the formulation of Professor Jan Tinbergen. The version cited here is based on the actual operations of a particular state planning organization, that of Turkey.[1] To begin with, he says, planning is characterized by the following general features:

    (a) A plan refers to the future;

    (b) It is based on a number of aims which have to be specified;

    (c) It requires coordination of the means of economic policy to be used in order to reach the aims.

The aims are specified by the sovereign political body—government, parliament or electorate; so are certain limitations which are set to the 'means of policy' (which are, however, set in the light of the planners' investigations of the probable effects of various means). Planners—the people 'directly responsible' for the planning process—engage in activities which Tinbergen classifies into *phases:* (1) a general reconnaissance of the economic structure; (2) a provisional choice of the optimum rate of growth, implying a necessary rate of savings; (3) an estimation of the expansion of demand derived from (2); (4) a choice of investment projects to produce the income and goods to satisfy (3); (5) an estimate of manpower and hence educational requirements; (6) revisions of steps (1)–(5) in the light of incoming data; (7) specification of the tasks of the public and private sectors and the means to get them done (public investments, subsidies and taxes).

---

[1] J. Tinbergen, *Central planning*, New Haven 1964, pp. 8 and 11–14, which resumes the main ideas of his *Economic policy: principles and design*, Amsterdam 1956. I have omitted a step from his series because it is clearly only an uncomfortable allusion to a large cluster of problems not dealt with in his formulation: 'The choice of projects may, however, also serve other purposes, among them a certain redistribution of investment...over the regions of the country' (p. 13).

Not everyone will agree that this is a good outline of what is involved in planning, and many economists have argued that this is not what economists even try to do as planners, let alone what is actually done by them and all the other actors actually involved in the planning process. Such critics' position is considered below; here one can only state dogmatically that Tinbergen's formulation, with its clear conception of 'planners' as economists and of their activities as a sequence of intellectual operations in the light of information, policy-decisions and the 'coordination potential' offered them, is indeed the model underlying by far the majority of Western writings on planning. It is certainly a good account of what most people mean when they refer to 'comprehensive' planning, and this is itself a political fact of some importance.[1]

## LINDBLOM'S CRITIQUE

Before considering the position adopted by critics of the 'Tinbergen model' on the basis of their allegedly different experience of what is involved in planning, we should look at the much more radical criticism put forward by Professor Charles Lindblom. With David Braybrooke he showed that, in so far as the 'Tinbergen model' involves what he calls the 'synoptic' conception of problem-solving, it represents an 'ideal' which, except for very simple closed systems, corresponds to no procedure or sequence of analytic behaviour which is within the reach of human beings; that is, the ideal of a comprehensive list of alternative policies; a comprehensive analysis of the consequences of each; a comparison of these with respect to a given hierarchy of value preferences leading to the selection of optimal policies.[2] It seems clear that for any system of social behaviour (as opposed to, say, a game of noughts and crosses), the 'synoptic' ideal of choice breaks down on *logical* grounds; even if the problem of determining an unambiguous hierarchy of value preferences can be solved in principle (and the solutions offered are highly artificial as well as wholly academic), there is an infinitely large number of possible consequences; so that a comparison of them can never be made, even in theory, and consequently optimal policies cannot be selected.

This logical defect of the 'synoptic ideal' of policy-selection or problem-solving needs to be distinguished from the *practical* defects which Lindblom also points out (the fact that even with computers, man's intellectual powers fall short of the feats of memory, simultaneous scanning, etc. that would be required; that information is rarely adequate and never complete; and that the costs—both in resources and time—of the analysis

---

[1] Cf. Waterston, *Development planning*, pp. 64–7.
[2] *A strategy of decision*, Glencoe, The Free Press 1963, chs. 2 and 3; see also C. E. Lindblom, *The intelligence of democracy*, New York 1965.

that would be entailed in the synoptic ideal are prohibitive).[1] The distinction is important because, if the 'synoptic ideal' is logically defective, the 'sequence-of-activities' aspect of the 'Tinbergen model' cannot be made intelligible in this way: or rather, if it has to be understood in this way, it would not appear to have much to recommend it.

Lindblom also observes that the synoptic ideal states what the analyst 'should have achieved by the time he calls his problem solved', but says nothing about the procedures which he should follow for getting there. The distinction is illustrated by Polyani's example of a man riding a bicycle; analytically, this accomplishment can be understood as the solving of a number of equations in mechanics, yet no one who took this as a set of rules for how to ride a bicycle would succeed. This observation (which is closely akin to Hirschmann's argument for unbalanced growth, referred to below) is not an objection to the logic of the synoptic ideal but to representing as a behavioural model of an activity what is only a model of the logical relationship between propositions which are made in the course of the activity and which constitute in an important sense its purpose. This criticism (which Lindblom's own decisional model is aimed to overcome) is important. One way of characterizing the weakness of much of the current literature is to say that it is either based on patently non-behavioural models, or lacks any theoretical basis at all.

### 'DISJOINTED INCREMENTALISM'

If the 'Tinbergen model' of planning cannot be a representation of any *possible* reality—i.e. cannot form the basis even of an ideal type of planning —what can be offered in its place? Lindblom's 'strategy of decision'—the so-called 'strategy of disjointed incrementalism'—is a potential candidate, since it is after all intended to overcome the weaknesses of the 'synoptic' idea. It will be recalled that this is a set of behavioural rules corresponding to generalizations about the actual behaviour of policy decision-makers working in an 'incremental-politics' environment. Each of the characteristics identified as making up the S.D.I. can be recommended as a rule of behaviour in so far as it is better adapted than the synoptic ideal to the practical needs and limitations under which people actually make policy choices. At the risk of oversimplification, these rules may be summarized as follows:

1. (a) Consider only those policies whose consequences differ marginally or incrementally from the *status quo*;
   (b) consider only policies which differ incrementally from each other;

---

[1] I have here omitted Lindblom's objection that the synoptic idea is also ill-adapted 'to the diverse forms in which policy problems actually arise' because this turns out to be mainly an observation that much 'policy-making' is really a by-product of conflict management, which is true but opens up a different line of attack—see below.

    (c) consider only those aspects of the consequences which are incrementally different from the *status quo*;

    (d) choose policies by ranking the increments by which the social states resulting from the policies considered differ from each other.

2. Restrict consideration to only a few of the consequences satisfying rules 1(a) and (b).[1]

3. Restrict consideration to only a few of the consequences satisfying rule 1(c).

4. Consider only or primarily those policies which tend to remedy ills, rather than achieve positive goods ('remedial orientation').

5. Reconsider policies constantly ('serial analysis and evaluation').

6. Distribute the process of policy analysis and evaluation among as many agencies and groups in society as possible ('social fragmentation of analysis and evaluation', 'disjointedness').

7. Regard objectives as related to each other through their costs in terms of scarce resources, and hence regard any one objective as subject to continual reformulation and modification in the light of a continuing examination of means.

Lindblom's account of why this strategy is to be recommended cannot be fully recapitulated here. It comes down to this: it is *possible*. Rules 1–3 keep the task within the limited intellectual capacities of policy analysts, the information available, and the costs of analysis. They do this not only by excluding all non-incremental policies, but also by the open-ended rules 2 and 3, which say, in effect, 'and exclude whatever else you like'. Rule 4 offers some additional guidance on how to exclude, but what makes the strategy feasible under all circumstances is the scope of rules 2 and 3. Rules 5 and 6 offset the apparent disappearance of the rational baby with the synoptic bathwater. Rule 5 provides for the constant review of previous decisions so that both neglected policies and neglected consequences can be considered when they are brought to the analyst's attention as a result of experience of the consequences (or lack of consequences) of the original consideration of the problem. Rule 6 seeks to secure that what one analyst excludes from consideration, another will include, and *vice versa*, so that for the system as a whole, policies and consequences which should be considered are considered. Rule 7 takes account of the fact that, even if the analyst could formulate a welfare function in terms of which to apply rule 1(d), it would be constantly altering as a result of, among other things, the achievement of objectives: and of other difficulties involved in the concepts of values and goals.

Leaving aside for a moment questions about the appropriateness of this 'strategy' for leaders in poor countries anxious to accelerate economic

---

[1] I think this is clearly implied on pp. 88–90 of *A strategy of decision*, although not explicitly distinguished from the primary rules 1(a) and (b).

growth, we may first ask whether it implies the same 'sequence of activities' as Tinbergen proposes as the paradigm of the planning process. There seem to be two main ways in which it would imply something different. In the first place, it implies that there is no single, central focus of decision-taking (rule 6); and in the second place, it implies that there is strictly speaking no *sequence* at all (rules 5 and 7). In each agency or place in which policy analysis and choice is occurring there is an ongoing process of review, reconsideration, consideration of new incremental policies and newly perceived consequences, reassessment and reformulation of values, and so on. Any attempt to cast disjointed incrementalism in the mould of a series of analytic activities, each one of which must be completed before the next, would be quite arbitrary and would also forfeit many of its alleged practical merits.

But is there any connection whatever between disjointed incrementalism and planning? Is not this 'strategy' really the art of muddling through presented as a science?[1] He himself considers that it is equally well adapted to policy-making by people anxious for rapid change as by people wishing to conserve the *status quo* (although he concedes that it is an open empirical question whether 'radicals' are less likely than 'conservatives' to use it or want to use it).[2] But his definition of 'incremental change' is one that excludes all changes regarded generally within any particular culture as 'large' or 'important', and among examples of such changes he includes the 'Soviet decision to move rapidly to the collectivisation of agriculture'; and more generally, the use of a cultural criterion is justified by the argument that in any given society people tend to agree on what is a controversial issue, and on what changes are 'structural' and what are compatible with the continuance of the 'structure'. It seems fairly clear, then, that although disjointed incrementalism may not be incompatible with 'planned change' (ignoring for the moment the problem of distinguishing 'planned change', using disjointed incrementalism, from 'unplanned change') it is certainly not compatible with 'planned structural change', which is what many leaders of poor countries say they want. Braybrook and Lindblom also rely, at various points in their argument, on the assumption that disjointed incrementalism takes place in a context of 'incremental politics', in which parties and leaders agree on fundamentals and compete only over policy-differences which are perceived as incremental. Although such a context may not be necessary for the strategy to be useful, and although single party regimes or military states may practise a kind of incremental politics, whatever their claims to the contrary, this does add to the doubts one feels about the entire relevance of the strategy to most would-be developing countries. One also feels some doubt

---

[1] C. Lindblom, 'The science of muddling through', *Public Administration Review* XIX (1959), 79–88.
[2] *Strategy of decision*, pp. 106–10.

whether in conditions of extremely rapid social change the concept of the '*status quo*', with which 'increments' of change may be compared, is really clear, and hence whether the 'strategy' is as operational as it sounds.[1]

## A MIDDLE ROAD?

The actual behaviour of many planners may perhaps be seen as some sort of compromise between the polar extremes represented by Tinbergen and Lindblom; following a sequence of activities which is intelligible as an attempt to operationalize the (unattainable) synoptic ideal, perhaps they follow incrementalist rules in order to establish a manageable agenda for each phase? Some such interpretation is needed to account for the pro-testations of many practical planners that they spend only 10 per cent of their time on the macro-economic exercises involved in the Tinbergen scheme and that the balance is spent mainly on examining the economic implications of particular policy proposals, scrutinizing projects, etc., as these happen to come across their desks with the normal momentum of the administrative machine.[2] This is surely often true: but then what is the difference between planning and giving policy advice (or indeed just thinking about policy)? Is 'planning' no more than a slogan under cover of which economists (or, say, architects—the kind of soldiers inside the Trojan horse will vary according to circumstances) can participate in the established process of departmental policy-making?

The consequences of adopting this position need to be considered. However illuminating it might turn out to be as a way of explaining the historical state of affairs in many developing countries, it does seem to involve a judgement *against* planning that is contrary to the prejudices— if not to the common sense and intuitive experience—of many students of development, for it clearly involves accepting Lindblom's criticism of the intellectual basis of comprehensive planning; this implies that the sequence of activities described in the 'Tinbergen model' has no particular validity.

To arrange the activities of planners in a sequence of activities in this way (if this happens—actual practice may bear only a very distant resemblance to such a series of stages) would be to reduce the scope of 'serial analysis' and 'disjointedness'; that is, it involves imposing a 'guillo-tine' procedure (what cannot be completed by a given time must be dropped and the next sequence started) and it involves centralizing and compartmentalizing the process of policy analysis. This is not an improve-ment; Lindblom's argument (like that of Hayek, and, perhaps, all other opponents of planning) is that the opportunity for reconsidering policies

---

[1] This point is argued by Y. Dror in 'Muddling through—science or inertia?', *Public Administration Review* 24 (1964) pp. 153–7.

[2] See C. Gray, 'Development planning in East Africa: a review article', *East African Economic Review* II, 2 (December 1966), 1–18. The same point of view was expressed by R. Jolly, in dis-cussion at the conference, on the basis of his planning experience in Zambia.

without limitation, the sharing of initiative for analysis among a plurality of centres, etc. is well adapted to the complexity and unanticipatable character of social change.

The policy implications of accepting this apparent compromise position are, therefore, indeterminate. One either thinks it is a good thing that numbers of economists or other new types of personnel are brought into government (even if on somewhat false pretences) or one doesn't. No particular reason seems to emerge for regarding any one type as uniquely useful there. In short, this position seems to imply that there is no distinctive mode of behaviour which need be called 'planning', only a variety of different patterns of recruitment to the policy-making process, the essential nature of which remains ultimately—if in these circumstances only imperfectly—incremental.

Much of the criticism that has been levelled *against* the prevailing representation of planning is caught on the horns of this dilemma. One school consists of other social scientists who see very clearly that the privileged position accorded to economists in the policy-making process leads to special sorts of distortion—the neglect of quite fundamental social or political factors, for example—and so to the ignominious failure of apparently sophisticated projects. These critics, however, have not usually questioned the 'synoptic' model of analysis; consequently this line of criticism results in a more or less explicit assertion that, for planning to become effective, it must somehow incorporate a comprehensive inventory and analysis of the entire political and social systems. To which economists answer that life is too short; decisions are pressing, and they will have to make do with what common sense and experience tell them about the society and polity and their effects on economic change. The economists, however, do not disclose how they keep their own economic analysis within manageable proportions.

Alternatively other (or the same) critics point out that the 'Tinbergen model' largely ignores the political processes involved in planning; and here the emphasis is on the essentially pluralist nature of society, even in a totalitarian party-state (especially when it is a question of reaching goals requiring positive as opposed to negative acts), and hence on the process of consultation, negotiation, bargaining, and compromise which is part even of the 'plan-making' aspect of planning. At this point, however, the critics come close to an entirely incrementalist position; a recent example is the following quotation from Professor John Friedmann:[1]

the blueprint model of planning (ANALYSIS→design→PLAN→implementation →ACTION→feedback→ANALYSIS) must be amended. Plan formulation and plan implementation tend to merge into a single process, synoptic documents are eschewed in favour of fragmented decisions, they are no longer an essential

[1] J. Friedmann, 'The institutional context', in Gross (ed.), *Action under planning*, pp. 36–7.

part of deciding and acting, the whole of planning becomes an extremely fluid, ambiguous and indeterminate network of information flows.

This conclusion is indeed uncomfortable; and Friedmann goes on to say

The model will read as (ANALYSIS→strategic information→ACTION→feedback →ANALYSIS etc.). In this model, strategic information impinges directly on the stream of ongoing activities, providing signals that lead to incremental adjustments. The information consists, for the most part, of a systematic assessment of the future conditions and consequences of action, of system-wide goals and objectives, and of the largest number of functional linkages among critical variables which are capable of being studied with the resources at hand. In this way, planning thought, understood as a form of seeking greater rationality, injects the inputs which allow a system to cope successfully with the future.

This is quite a convincing summary of what one might call a charitable view of the policy-making process in many so-called 'planned' economies, but it makes it too difficult to distinguish planned from non-planned activities. Friedmann's argument is that we should accept that 'planning' refers more to cultural than to structural aspects of collective decision-making; the structural patterns in the Latin American countries which he particularly studied were more readily understood as incrementalism or muddling through to which the adoption of planning offices and so forth contributed at most additional scanning mechanisms, and additional perspectives on the range of incremental options (i.e. more 'disjointedness'). This is no doubt true, but does not help us to discriminate between different degrees of 'success' in attaining 'greater rationality', more or less well-adapted interpretations of the planning 'style' to particular systems' decisional needs. Like too much in behavioural theory, it insists on what differing systems have in common at the expense of the things which differentiate them.

### THE ANALOGY OF PLANNING IN THE FIRM

The need for a set of concepts for discussing planning is obvious. Probably there are several sources from which it could come, of which the most interesting might well be military planning;[1] but the most immediately

---

[1] The most eloquent passages in the literature of anti-planning are unquestionably Tolstoy's critique of military analysts of the Battle of Borodino, who attributed the outcome to poor planning by Napoleon: 'The dispositions cited above are not at all worse, but are even better, than previous dispositions by which he had won victories. His pseudo-orders during the battle were also no worse than formerly, but much the same as usual. These dispositions and orders only seem worse than previous ones because the battle of Borodino was the first Napoleon did not win...Napoleon at the battle of Borodino fulfilled his office as representative of authority as well as, and even better than, at other battles. He did nothing harmful to the progress of the battle; he inclined to the most reasonable opinions, he made no confusion, did not contradict himself, did not get frightened or run away from the field of battle, but with his great tact and military experience carried out his role of appearing to command, calmly and with dignity.' *War and peace*, Oxford University Press edition, trans. L. and A. Maude, 1951, pp. 499–500.

relevant is the business firm. This analogy has been ably exploited by Professor Neil Chamberlain in his *Private and public planning*, on which this section is largely based.[1] Chamberlain summarizes his central ideas as follows:

the conception of planning as the management of assets; the inescapable conflict of objectives between system and subsystem, and the consequent dependence not only on technical–economic but also organisational–political coordination; the ongoing nature of the planning process, with a continuing interplay between intent and event, and the significance of the distinction between what are called specific and categorical social objectives.[2]

The significance of these ideas derives from the fact that the business firm is a social system of intermediate complexity, smaller, more hierarchically integrated, and technically simpler than the nation, but specialized for the successful fulfilment of those functions which planning is supposed to serve in any system.

The managers of a business firm—the professional managers and the directors—are manipulating assets. They must constantly take decisions about not only current income, but also how to preserve assets to produce future income (if necessary by transforming them into other assets by re-investment), and how to acquire additional assets by investing from current income.

The pattern of assets and income aimed at for the future constitutes the objectives chosen for the firm by its managers. These, it is important to note, are entirely specific things such as establishing a particular kind of reputation or a particular position in an industry. All such objectives are, it is true, particular interpretations of the general goals of profit and growth. But since the latter *are* entirely general, the art of goal-setting is the art of choosing goals that will, in the circumstances of the firm, achieve particular rates of return or of growth; and the former cannot de deduced from the latter. The notions of 'rate of return' and 'growth' furnish standards of comparison between firms, and therefore also standards by which the recent performance of a firm can be assessed. But obviously all firms cannot achieve identical rates of return and growth at all times, so that the selection of particular rates, like the selection of other specific long-term goals, is itself a matter for both analysis and the exercise of will. By analogy the objectives of national planning are 'states of the economy'—some aspects of which are spelled out carefully and others left blank. 'The growth rate [sc. of the economy] constitutes only a convenient envelope for all the substantive achievements which are really the objects of planning.'

While we are on the concept of objectives, we may note that Chamberlain also offers a very useful subsidiary classification of objectives into

---

[1] N. W. Chamberlain, *Private and public planning*, New York 1965.
[2] *Ibid.*, p. vi.

specific, categoric, and hypothetical. Specific objectives admit of only one way of being met—300,000 tractors, 10 million tons of steel, tarmac roads connecting all district headquarters; they are 'considered important in their own right or because of their functional relationship to something else considered important'. A categoric objective does not specify what mix of activities is involved, so long as they add up to a stated total; they are economists' aggregates like consumption or exports. Hypothetical objectives are residual and carry the implication that they are really only expectations of what is probable if other (specific or categoric) objectives are achieved; although they may represent desirable outcomes, government will 'not use its always limited powers to attempt to influence the outcome(s) either in kind or amount'.[1] To repeat: it is the specific objectives that make a *plan* possible—that provide targets to which action may be directed—and although for some purposes it may be convenient to conceive of them as means to the attainment of categoric objectives, they are psychologically and causally primary.

There are two distinct aspects to the processes involved in planning for the firm, which Chamberlain calls technical–economic coordination and political–organizational coordination. The former is 'planning on paper'. All the 'things' coordinated in this sense are treated as symbols, including people and their interrelationships. The aim is to identify a path from the *status quo* to the desired objectives that satisfies various technical or economic criteria—minimizes costs, or delays, or the use of particular scarce resources, etc. This type of coordinating activity establishes a standard of efficiency by which subsequent activity can be judged. Political–organizational coordination, on the other hand, is the process of trying to get the people involved to do what would be technically and economically most efficient. Even in the firm, there are conflicts between the interests of subunits and the interests of the managers in achieving their goals, which necessitate compromises in order to strike bargains; the compromises involve concessions to the interests of the subunits (e.g. longer tea breaks) which imply departures from the technically optimum path of future action, but which are necessary to ensure that still less optimal paths do not result (or even that any path is followed at all).[2]

The analogy between the firm and the nation here is complete, and helps to clarify a lot of the difficulties in the literature so far discussed. Among other things, it becomes obvious that if 'the planning process' is to be seen as a sequence of activities it must be seen as at least two sequences, not necessarily with the same periodicity. The firm's management may get new information about sales, for example, which alters parts of

---

[1] *Private and public planning*, p. 74.

[2] 'Productively, such planning adds nothing to an optimum solution: strategically, it makes a solution possible': J. Moris, 'Agricultural planning as a problem of administrative structure', paper read to the Social Science Council Conference, Dar es Salaam, 1968. I should like to acknowledge the influence of this stimulating paper on the views expressed here.

its technical–economic forecast and, hence, its technically preferred future pattern of activities: it does not follow from this that its politically secured programme of action registered in the firm's budget will automatically be revised. For the firm, feedback by no means eliminates the functional utility of blueprints, and in most developing countries the same would apply, for the same basic reason; feedback from experience flows mainly into the technical–economic coordination stream of decision-making, leaving plenty of options open about whether, and if so how and when, to revise the political–organizational programme.[1]

### LIMITATIONS OF THE BUSINESS-FIRM ANALOGY

Of course there are some very important respects in which planning in the firm is not a good analogy for planning in the nation. The management of even a large firm is concentrated and specialized; the determination of the firm's objectives is the responsibility of its directors, who include its top professional managers, and the range of objectives open to them to select is largely bounded by the current or medium-term technical possibilities given by the firm's existing product line, production organization and financial structure, with which the professional managers at least are thoroughly familiar. By contrast the 'management' of a country is a purely analytic construct; the functions involved are diffused among a number of somewhat autonomous groups and institutions (even Gross's term 'central guidance cluster' suggests more integration than commonly exists)[2] and the range of possible objectives technically open to them and likely to be of interest to them (taken as a collectivity) is ordinarily very much wider than that of most firms; while by the same token the degree of familiarity that any one section of the national 'management' can have with the whole range of 'assets' of the nation is, by comparison with the knowledge possessed by the managers of a firm, extremely imperfect.

Secondly, the 'management' of a country includes many roles whose incumbents do not see themselves as 'managers' under the same compulsion to plan as do the managers of a firm. It is true that there has been a growth of interest in planning as a means to international survival, but there are large areas of activity which are perceived by those in leadership or management positions in a different way—as 'maintenance' activities serving 'consummatory' ends such as national security or national unity, for example, and so making prior claims on resources that must be met 'before' or 'outside' the planning process. Sentimental or professionally incompetent business managements may countenance similar behaviour, but rarely with impunity.

[1] Compare Waterston's suggestion that the best use of the idea of 'rolling plans' is to have them but not to publish them (*Development planning*, p. 141).

[2] It is not really Gross's intention to suggest this, although he does not always avoid the tendency to mix prescription with commentary: see p. 266, n. 2.

Thirdly, the 'management' of a country is not always 'in control' of the system planned for to the same extent as the management of a firm. This can be over-stated; some firms have sub-systems (local branches, trade unions, specialized departments, not to mention informal groups, factions and families, etc.) with a good deal of autonomy *vis-à-vis* the management, and some countries have very powerful central governments with large resources of loyal personnel to enforce obedience to commands; and neither may have the resources with which to offer the inducements which may be necessary to secure the achievement of some of their objectives—for instance, those which require more effort from individual workers. Nonetheless, in most poor countries the degree of autonomy and independent initiative of a wide range of institutions and categories of people is very much greater than in a business firm, so that political–organizational coordination becomes relatively more important and expensive (expensive in terms of resources given to it, and in terms of departures from the technical–economic optimum in order to secure it).[1]

These qualifications, however, really tend to reinforce the usefulness of the analogy, which directs attention to basic characteristics of planning by referring to social systems that are quite complex and also under the necessity of planning, and makes it clear how planned activity should be distinguished from unplanned. In particular, it directs attention to the simple fact that analysis is not what characterizes planning but the prior selection of targets and the subsequent manipulation of behaviour to achieve them. What distinguishes planned behaviour from unplanned is not its superior rationality in relation to some criterion of economic or technical efficiency but its specifically purposive character in relation to a predetermined goal. It may be 'badly' planned; unplanned activity, guided by individual initiatives, intuition, or habitual patterns of behaviour, might be more 'efficient', or popular, or even more successful in reaching the objectives conceived of as targets in the plan; but what gives activity its planned character is whether it is calculated to attain pre-set objectives, not whether it does attain them nor whether it does so in a particular way not specified in the objectives.

### SOME IMPLICATIONS

This approach has the elementary merit of reasserting the broadly sequential nature of planning which we associate with the concept in

---

[1] Chamberlain (p. 58) believes that governments, 'as top management for the system', have an advantage over business managements because their orders can have the force of law. This assumes that, relative to the goals pursued by the government, it has sufficient authority to secure compliance with commands to do what is needed. Political scientists would be tempted to say that this advantage is illusory; the reason why Western governments (which Chamberlain has in mind) have the authority they have is that they do not issue commands unless, for most people, or even for important minorities concerned, there is no need to.

everyday life: a plan is something you first make and then try to carry out. The 'phases' of Tinbergen's representation can then be seen not to be chronological sequences (though they may be conventionally adopted as such) but analytic elements, or ways of conceptualizing, certain mental operations that may enter into the first, plan-making, phase of planning. The whole notion of comprehensive planning as it is customarily described is (in Chamberlain's language) a particular mode of 'technical–economic coordination' which is supposed to establish a particular kind of standard of efficiency (according to which all resources are in their most productive possible use). We have considered the reasons for doubting whether, as Tinbergen describes it, it really works like that; it is now clear that it is a double mistake to represent planning as *consisting* of this process, and it may be suggested that this confusion, leading to some very distinctive planning practices and allocations of planning resources, must bear a considerable share of the responsibility for the relative disrepute into which planning in less developed countries has fallen in recent years, as a steady increase in the resources committed to it has gone unmatched by improved results. The argument is that we can plan, and plan successfully, without seeking to optimize; that the reasons for planning may be to some extent independent of the desire to optimize; and that where optimal technical–economic patterns are set up as the basis for planned activity, they must be subordinated to the requirements of planning, and not the other way round: economic policy-making, is, or ought only to be, the slave of the planning process.

Two kinds of support are offered for this view in the sections which follow. The first considers a version of planning without optimizing, and the second considers the Tanzanian experience.

### PLANNING WITHOUT OPTIMIZING

I suggest that an adequate—if excessively simple—notion of planning consists of the following elements:[1]

Stage 1—Making a plan. This has two logically, though not chronologically distinct aspects:

> (*a*) selecting objectives
> (*b*) identifying a possible course to achieve them

Stage 2—Carrying out the plan—securing action in conformity with the course identified in 1(*b*).

---

[1] The framework used here is a primitive variant on the one suggested by early 'scientific management' theorists, such as 'POSDCORB' (see L. Gulick and L. Urwick, *Papers on the science of administration*, New York 1937, Paper 1, pp. 3 ff.) and equally is related to the thinking underlying the Planning–Programming–Budgeting System (P.P.B.S.) adopted throughout U.S. government in 1965.

## 1(a). Selecting objectives

It is not essential to the notion of planning that the selection of objectives should be done in any particular way. One way to select them is to invite a group of economists to suggest what they should be. Another is to have a system of 'majority bent' parties alternating in office so that new objectives can be formulated by intra-party debate when in opposition. Another is to derive them from an ideology regarded as 'true' or, like Joan of Arc, to be told what to do by 'voices'. One certainly may first set up an agency to secure 'comprehensive preliminary information' and make 'projections of long-term consequences based on specified alternatives' and then select from among the alternatives in the light of those projections, but quite apart from the difficulties of interpreting 'comprehensive' and 'consequences' (which consequences?) there is nothing about planning as such which requires this to precede the selection of goals. The selection of goals is essentially an act of will, which as Deutsch has pointed out involves a decision not to admit any new data into the picture past a certain point.[1] This does not rule out the acquisition of a large quantity of information beforehand, but it does not require it either.

Whether objectives obtained by the means recommended by the 'Tinbergen model' will lead to more desirable consequences than arriving at them by other methods seems to me an empirical matter. There are several reasons why most of the literature assumes that they will:

    (i) Assuming that planning *means* 'synoptic decision-making'

    (ii) confusing 'logic' with 'sequences'.

Without appropriate information, it is impossible to tell how far very ambitious (or complex) objectives are attainable, and it is normal for some objectives to alter or even to take shape in the light of the information that emerges about the means of achieving them, their cost in terms of other objectives, and so on. Therefore it seems natural to see the acquisition of information as 'prior' to the determination of objectives, but this is a mistake. At any rate it is possible to plan without this.

    (iii) Assuming that the objectives of planning are the aggregates in terms of which economic growth is expressed.

This particular confusion seems to spring from the nature of economics as a discipline, with its focus on scarcity, and more particularly from the growth models which form the basis of orthodox economic analysis for development. If we know what level of G.N.P. is desired by some future date, we can in theory estimate the level of investment and hence the savings required to achieve it. The distribution of the investment and savings may be used to secure structural changes or other specific goals, but, according to this way of viewing the matter, the datum with which all other projected data must be made consistent is the future income level

[1] K. Deutsch, *The nerves of government*, New York 1963, pp. 105-7.

that is selected. This the economist wants to know and so it is thought of as a supergoal; and naturally enough, in order that it be selected with a view to its feasibility, it is assumed that its selection should be preceded by 'comprehensive preliminary information' and 'projections of consequences of specified alternatives'.

But, as we have seen, a datum like a future income level is only a possible consequence of the pursuit of other goals; these other goals are themselves only an interpretation of an analytically necessary condition for achieving that future income level (i.e. that there must be a certain level of prior investment); they themselves, however, cannot be 'deduced' from the postulated future income level, and their claim to significance does not derive from it. (There is an obvious analogy here with the way in which the Harrod–Domar growth model led to an implicit assumption that the relationships in the model, which are analytic, are underpinned by some more or less automatic forces which operate through time in the real world; an assumption which, as Hirschman pointed out, cannot safely be made for poor countries.[1]) Chamberlain's comments on such 'portmanteau objectives' are very much to the point: '...concern with growth rates and full employment as targets in themselves represents an early and rather unsophisticated stage of development: a percentage increase in GNP is necessarily an ex-post measure...and...cannot be meaningfully used as an ex-ante target except perhaps in a hortatory way'.[2]

This has increasingly been recognized by practical planners.[3] The French planners preparing for the fifth plan decided not to offer the government a set of alternative growth targets as they had done for plans I to IV, but instead made a projection of growth based on recent experience and then examined the probable consequences of 'varying government policies on a series of economic questions *then under current consideration...* These included the possibility of substantial changes in weekly working hours, a farm policy which could accelerate the flow of agricultural labour to other parts of the economy...[etc.]'[4]

The suggestion that the objectives of planning might be provided by 'voices' rather than by economic advisers is not entirely frivolous. If, for example, a large element of charismatic authority is operative in a political system, planning is perfectly possible, and if the objectives are identified with the charisma of the leadership, it may be relatively easy to achieve them. Such objectives may be far removed from economic optima, but

[1] A. O. Hirschman, *The strategy of economic development*, New Haven 1958, pp. 28–33.

[2] *Private and public planning*, pp. 70–1.

[3] Economists' books on planning tend to cover the point with remarks like this: '...ultimately what matters are the individual projects chosen, and the economic policies adopted. One can make a good plan without a macro-economic framework, if the projects are well chosen and the policy measures well designed. Equally a plan may be very bad, even though it meets all the tests of consistency' (W. A. Lewis, *Development planning*, London 1966, p. 241).

[4] Waterston, *Development planning*, p. 165 (italics added).

from the point of view of developing the system's capacity for collective action to achieve collective goals, they may be 'well' chosen. The tendency of planners to regard their categoric objectives as 'the' objectives, and to see specific objectives as means, may be regarded as the exact opposite of this, for it may easily lead to the abandonment of planning when it comes to implementation. The specific objectives, being regarded as 'only' means, are regarded as subject to alteration and in a rapidly changing environment, such as most poor countries have, this means one of two things; either the specific objectives are adhered to, but with rapidly diminishing authority because of their obvious loss of connection with the supposedly 'real' objectives of the plan; or they are constantly modified in the interests of keeping the economy pointed towards the categoric objectives, in which case there is no serious possibility of representing public action as 'planned'. (An example from Tanzania is given below.)

One further point on goal selection seems worth making. It is the nature of a plan to force planners to choose between goals which are in conflict. When they are not absolute, indivisible goals, but can be achieved more or less, they can be traded against each other, but in either case a selection is a selection and not a collection. If the selection is badly done the plan will be threatened by the tendency of neglected options, or faulty trade-offs, to reassert themselves; in effect, people will wish they had planned to achieve something other than the pattern of goals to which the plan is directed, however good a plan it is turning out to be in other respects. This is important in national planning where political leaders not only differ from business managers in having a more complicated and less integrated set of 'top management structures' (and a less manageable and predictable 'labour force'), they also have a much less specialized set of goals to choose from. The goals served by a good national plan must, as far as possible, be a selection from among all the goals aimed at by the leadership, not just a section of them: otherwise the plan will be overwhelmed by the re-assertion of goals which it neglected. (A familiar form of the failure to grasp this point is to conceive of political goals that conflict with technical–economic goals as 'constraints' analogous to the physical constraints of climate or the quantitative constraints of current income levels. This tends to prevent their being closely examined; on closer inspection it may turn out that they conflict less than might be supposed with goals which embody technical–economic values, or that there are 'cheaper' ways of accommodating them.)

### 1(b). Identifying a 'possible' course to achieve objectives

This resembles the idea expressed in rule 7 of the strategy of disjointed incrementalism in that objectives are subject to modification in the light of knowledge of their probable consequences, their probable tendency to conflict with each other, their costs, and so on. It also implies a combination of the two streams of coordination, the technical–economic and the political. The former comes in, as far as the nature of planning is concerned, as a means to find 'routes' of activities—i.e. a series of sub-goals—which are likely to lead to the outcomes posited in the objectives. If any such route can be found, this is enough to enable a plan to be made. It need not be 'optimal' for it to yield a plan, and in some circumstances, it may be necessary to choose a route without regard to its optimality in order to have a plan at all.[1] This was almost the spirit of the first five-year plan in India: 'Their motto—a very sensible one under the circumstances—was *on s'engage et puis on verra*.'[2] This is not the same as saying it may have to be less than optimal—though considerations of time, lack of data, etc., may mean that the course selected falls short of some technical or economic ideal: but rather that, in order to plan action, all that technical–economic coordination needs to do is find *a* course.

In calling such a course a 'possible' course one is deliberately using language that points *both* to the technical–economic coordination involved —how much concrete, what flow of expenditure, what mix of skills, etc., —*and* to political–economic coordination—what interests are affected, what effective inducements will be required, what time will be consumed in negotiations, etc. The distinction between these two kinds of coordination is important, but it does not mean that they are unconnected. There is no such thing as a completely 'dehumanized' set of data for technical– economic coordination. The data used—from productivity data to such vast compounds as incremental capital–output ratios—all contain more or less conventional, more or less valid assumptions of a sociopolitical nature. Conversely there is no such thing as 'completely' political bargaining by leaders; some idea of the technical–economic implications of the basis on which they secure support for programmes is always present, otherwise they would bargain too 'softly' and soon run out of resources. (For this reason, to say that such costs of political coordination involve departures from the optimum courses indicated by technical criteria is not very meaningful: it is to say that, if people behaved differently from the way they probably will, a course other than the one actually to be adopted would be better from a technical or economic viewpoint.)

But this is to go beyond the matter in hand; to make a plan, one need only feel some confidence that it can be made to happen: that it is a forecast on which one can bet with some confidence; that it is a programme announcing a play one can expect to see, in which the actors will follow their cues (being 'all right on the night' is the stage equivalent of what eastern bloc planners call 'planners' tension'; the hopeful doctrine that

---

[1] J. Heyer illustrates a natural economists' reaction to this aspect of Kenyan planning: 'Projects are justified, not as the best use of resources, but as good on their own ... The question is not whether [a project] is good but whether it is the best;' 'Kenya's agricultural development policy', *East African Economic Review* II (N.S.) 2 (December 1966), p. 45.

[2] Hanson, *The process of planning*, p. 98.

'only when the screw is being applied will results—even inadequate ones—be squeezed out').[1]

How planners operate this process of identifying 'possible' courses of action which will lead to the desired objectives is surely a matter for investigation. Incrementalism obviously plays a part, as do the specific structures and procedures of decision-making established by the constitution, by administrative practice, convention, and culture. What is clear is the important part played by social-scientific 'models' once social scientists are brought into the decisional process. They may be seen as a particular device for following incremental rules (they exclude consideration of factors not reflected by the variables of the model and they often rely heavily on the concept of marginality), but this is contingent and the policies suggested as a result of using such models may be the opposite of 'incremental' in Lindblom's sense of the word (e.g. the economic policies followed by Nkrumah in the early 1960s as a result of high-level professional economic advice). What does seem likely is that the adoption of planning, introducing economists and perhaps other social scientists into the policy-making process on a larger scale or in more influential roles, tends to shift the agenda of discussion in directions indicated by models drawn from social theory and away from those indicated by the models used by civil servants and politicians. What characteristic differences this makes—whether it alters the time perspectives, the implicit values attached to various sectors or strategies, and so on—seems a feasible and useful line of study.

## 2. Securing action in conformity with the plan

'Plan implementation' means what it says—operating all the inducements or 'activators' (to use Gross's expression) that have been calculated to produce the planned pattern of activity. Activators can be changed to keep behaviour in line with the plan, i.e. to see that the planned targets are hit. This does not mean that the *plan* is modified automatically; a decision to change the plan is only required where it appears that a changed plan would be more likely to achieve the objectives of the original plan and this is a fairly rare situation where the unit planned for is of any complexity. If a 'variance'—i.e. a departure from a planned outcome—occurs it may be 'offset' by variances in other sectors, or in the same sector at a later date, and if this happens or is thought likely it can be neglected; if it is not offset, it may be corrected by changes in the pattern of activators at the disposal of the government—tax or subsidy changes, exhortations or threats—that are within the limits of flexibility of the original plan; and if it cannot be corrected, it may still be better to accept it than to modify the plan, unless it arises in a somewhat 'isolated' sector. Otherwise it means consequential modifications elsewhere in the plan; and this is liable to have serious

[1] Hanson, *The process of planning*, p. 263.

disadvantages, involving at the least the abandonment of the plan as a measure of performance. The political coordination which lay behind the original plan must be re-done; this takes time and may in fact not lead to a new plan which comes as close to securing the objectives of the original plan as continued operation of the original plan would have done. As Wiles puts it:

The essential criteria of not being epiphenomenal [i.e. representing as planned what is in reality no more than a forecast of what is actually going to happen] are that (1) the blueprint is altered only at discrete intervals, (2) it is altered more to suit local conditions than simply because the planners have changed their minds, (3) it is, in any case, enforced, where it is materially possible to do so.[1]

To sum up: although maximizing the attainment of technically or economically determined goals is in practice part of the planning process, it is possible to define planning without reference to this except when one considers the process through which a possible route to the attainment of goals is identified. Then optimizing comes in if resources prove inadequate to achieve all the goals selected, until a set of redefined goals is chosen which seems reasonably likely to be attainable with the resources at hand. In practice, of course, optimizing comes in not merely where no possible route can be found to attain the selected goals; one of the goals is normally at least something like 'value for money'. But the fact that some of the goals of the plan are thought of as tending to maximize economic growth is not a specification of the way in which planning will assist their attainment (if it will). And if all the goals in the plan are thought of as tending to this effect, it is highly unlikely that the first requirement of planning, namely selection from among all the relevant goals, has been fulfilled.

If there is any value in this approach it should be possible to construct a number of ideal types of the planning process with which to analyse and compare the experience of different countries, and to go some way beyond the rather eclectic and pragmatic commentary, however shrewd, which has characterized the approach of most political scientists to the subject so far.[2] The starting point would be the type and distribution of authority throughout the various sectors of the social system, and at the different levels; the nature of the 'activators' available to the holders of authority; the mechanisms through which decisions on collective objectives are made; in short, the nature of the system through which both stages of planning can be undertaken, and which will determine what sorts of economic optimizing can be attempted, and how. A glimpse of these possibilities ought to be obtained from even a partial critical examination of the experience of a particular country.

---

[1] P. Wiles, 'Economic activation, planning and the social order', in *Action under planning*, p. 153.

[2] This comes out clearly in the pioneering work of Professor Gross; see particularly his *The administration of economic development planning: principles and fallacies*, U.N. New York 1966.

### THE FIRST TANZANIAN FIVE-YEAR PLAN (1964–9)[1]

This plan, published in May 1964, is described in the text as 'a comprehensive plan because all the sectors of activity, Public and Private, Economic and Social, National and Regional...have been assigned objectives, the technical and economic feasibility of which has been checked in advance'.[2] The plan contains a description of how it was made. This process took one year. First, a directorate of planning staffed by (expatriate) economists examined past growth rates, diagnosed the main obstacles to progress and prescribed structural changes to overcome them, using a long-term perspective to 1980. 'Higher growth rates were then tested against the...resources likely to be available and...the conditions likely to be encountered in world markets.' After 3–4 months this yielded a report to the economic development commission (virtually the whole cabinet); the report apparently proposed one or more growth targets together with 'the policies to be adopted...for the achievement of these long-term objectives'. The E.D.C. accepted this report in all essentials, and in the next 5 months the Directorate worked out the level of activity implied by the 1980 targets for 1970; the sectoral investment levels needed between 1964 and 1969 to achieve this level in 1970; and tested these for consistency. This led to a draft outline plan submitted to the E.D.C. in January 1964. This was again broadly accepted ('...the EDC ...did at least take most of the necessary difficult decisions')[3] and permitted 'drawing up as far as possible specific and coordinated development programmes within the outline plan and finalising the [plan]', which was done under great pressure by May.

This was in many ways a fair example of comprehensive plan-making, and it should therefore be possible to see whether what happened in Tanzania is illuminated by the thesis advanced in this paper, that mistaking this for planning tends in practice to make planning difficult or even impossible. The story will be considered under the same headings as were adopted in the previous section.

### 1(a). Selecting objectives

(i) In an important sense the 1964–9 plan had no goals; everything it contained was presented as an 'implication' of the perspective objectives accepted for 1980; and even these were more categoric than specific. The plan listed as three 'main' objectives to be attained by 1980:

---

[1] The main materials used here are *The five-year plan*; R. C. Pratt, 'The administration of economic planning in a newly independent state; the Tanzanian experience 1963–66', *Journal of Commonwealth Political Studies*, March 1967; and H. Bienen, *Tanzania: party transformation and economic development*, Princeton 1967, pp. 281–306, and 320–33.

[2] Introduction to the plan by Minister of State A. Z. N. Swai, p. 1.

[3] Pratt, 'The administration of economic planning', p. 46.

(a) to raise *per capita* income from £19·6 to £45;
(b) to be fully self-sufficient in trained manpower;
(c) to raise life expectation from 35–40 to 50 years.

The first of these expresses the end-consequence in 1980 of what the planners thought was the maximum rate of growth which could be attained by the economy until then (6·7 per cent). Some inkling of the *ex-post*, derivative and unspecific character of this objective evidently led to the formulation of the other two objectives. Self-sufficiency in trained manpower is only a specific target if one has a fairly sophisticated idea of what the manpower needs of 1980 are likely to be; raising life expectancy is less clearly specific and was almost certainly a 'hypothetical' objective— i.e. not one that government would actively seek to reach if it turned out not to be likely to be attained. Cranford Pratt, in commending the plan document, concludes a little uneasily (note the 'perhaps'): 'Despite its technical detail and professional competence, the plan identifies its central objectives in terms at once comprehensible to the general public and also perhaps capable of enlisting widespread commitment to the achievement of the plan', and lists these 1980 objectives.[1] Later on, however, he comments on 'the failure initially to present the plan in a form intelligible to the middle and lower ranks of the party and the administration, and to the local authorities'. Actually the specific objectives of the plan were on the whole described as 'policies', or as 'features' of the plan; the most important of these were dramatic increases of agricultural production, a very large increase in the share of industry in total production, and improvements in the commercial and distributive system. Targets of physical output were set for all agricultural and mining products. These, however, were evidently determined by inference from the postulated rate of growth, rather than worked up to from estimates of the probable effects of various activators on each sector and industry, and so they remained for some time in the form of national aggregates. As a result it is not surprising that 'at the local level [the plan] provided no immediate and specific targets'.[2] The focus was on consistency rather than on planning and as a result the first requisite of a plan—specific plan objectives—was, if not missing, heavily obscured.

(ii) If 'comprehensive planning' led the planners to work 'backwards' towards specific objectives—even if they did not quite get there—there was also the fundamental weakness that the objectives that were chosen were selected from among a range largely determined by the economic models being used by the planners, not from the range of the 'revealed preferences' of the political leadership. As Bienen has pointed out, shortage of time, lack of experience in interpreting the political implica-

---

[1] 'The administration of economic planning', p. 39.
[2] *Ibid.*, p. 50.

tions of 'economic aggregates', the lack of an associational group basis of power for the national leaders, all conspired to make the leadership accept the 'planners' priorities'.[1]

Of these factors the second seems the most interesting: as we have seen, French political leaders, after experience with four successive plans, were still unable to make effective translations from economic aggregates into political choices, and this is not surprising since it is the nature of an aggregate target to be compatible with a very wide range of possible combinations of strategies and activities which will add up to the aggregate. As a result, the political leaders endorsed, in the E.D.C., goals which they approved in themselves but which were in conflict with other goals to which they were in fact also committed. These included rapid africanization; the pursuit of non-alignment; the control of urban workers' politics by large wage concessions. Each of these implied a lower rate of investment than was needed for the growth rate chosen in the plan: none of them appears to have been brought into consideration in the process of plan formulation. Pratt discloses that two goal-conflicts *were* revealed in the E.D.C.'s discussion of the directorates' first proposals; the E.D.C. declined to approve a policy on population control, or free competition between the cooperative movement and the private trading sector (it is not recorded how the planners adjusted to these refusals). The other goal-conflicts, however, which were to reveal themselves as critically important within the first year of operation of the plan, were not elicited at all.

(iii) Bienen, whose study particularly concerns the party, makes another important comment when he notes that the TANU national executive committee was not involved in the process of plan-making at all, although to a much larger extent than in most developing countries it was and is the main policy-making institution in the system, representing the 'middle level' leadership of the powerful regional and district party machines. In neglecting this organ the planning process failed to include, one might say, a large part—perhaps a majority—of the 'board of directors' (not to say the branch managers). To the extent that, in making a plan for others, a structure must be found which bears some equivalence to the role of management in the firm, those who have the power and authority to determine goals for those who are being planned for must be included in it. The N.E.C. of TANU would certainly have had to be part of this structure; just as the T.U.C. and C.B.I. must be in the N.E.D.C. in Britain, and the major interest groups in the modernization committees in France or the C.N.P.E. in Italy. Thus in so far as goals were set for the plan, and in so far as they were selected from among a range of objectives to which the leadership was in fact committed, the leaders concerned in the process were not sufficiently representative of the 'relevant' leadership.

[1] *Tanzania*, pp. 291–4.

(This question of relevance is bound up with the exploration of means and activators and is discussed again briefly below.)

(iv) A final point about the process of goal formulation that is well illustrated by the Tanzanian case is the effect of treating categoric objectives as if they were the 'real' objectives, and the specific objectives as only 'implications'. It was argued above that if the environment changes rapidly, this would make planning highly vulnerable, and this is indeed what happened in Tanzania. Wiles remarks that the methods to be used to secure plan fulfilment 'necessarily cast their shadows before them, over blueprint-drawing up'; and so, evidently, do notions of optimality, for in the five-year plan there are constant warnings that, because of uncertainties about, e.g. commodity prices, the plan is not 'an infallible forecast of the economic evolution of Tanganyika over the next five years: it would be wrong to regard it as a revelation of the future which cannot be altered even though the circumstances in which it was compiled might have changed materially...it can have no more than a conjectural character...' The President, introducing the plan in parliament, made the same point: 'Many of the facts which this plan has to take into account are outside our control...The plan is therefore a flexible one, and periodically we shall examine progress in the light of new circumstances, making adjustments as required.' The circumstances did alter drastically (not all for reasons outside the government's control) and Pratt was led to conclude: 'For all these reasons it was inevitable that the five-year plan would need early revision if its implementation was to remain a central preoccupation of Government policy.'[1] Pratt suggests that annual plans would have been an appropriate response to this problem; but as is well known, 'in most fields or sectors short-term planning is really equivalent to prognosis';[2] one has only to look at the experience of countries using so-called 'rolling plans' (a perspective plan that is re-written every year as the past year is dropped out of it and a new, say fifth year, is added on at the end) to see the truth of this.[3]

It is hard not to conclude, without underrating the value of the economic analysis that is done in 'comprehensive planning' as a means of establishing canons of economic–technical efficiency, that it is inherently apt to make *planning* impossible in countries liable to rapid changes in the environment if it leads to the formulation of categoric objectives as the primary objectives of the plan. The external changes that occur in aid flows, commodity prices, harvests, etc., and which are characteristic for primary-producing countries such as Tanzania, all tend to alter the attainability of the aggregate objectives precisely because they are aggre-

---

[1] 'The administration of economic planning', p. 42.

[2] Chamberlain, *Private and public planning*, p. 76.

[3] See, e.g. S. Okita and I. Miyazaki, 'The impact of planning on economic growth in Japan', in *Development plans and programmes*, O.E.C.D., Paris 1964, p. 61.

gates and therefore register every fluctuation that occurs. In a developed and well-integrated economy, not only is the external environment typically less important relative to factors more or less within the government's means of control, but there are likely to be more 'offsets' within the economy (e.g. a decline in one industry due to foreign competition releases labour required in another industry) because it is relatively well integrated and all factors are relatively highly used. In a country such as Tanzania, however, offsets will be less likely to occur and categoric goals will either become unattainable or too 'easily' reached, so that they, and hence policies to achieve them, seem to need constant re-setting. In Tanzania, at any rate, within a year of the plan's publication it was commonly felt that it was no longer relevant, although in reality some of the (hidden) specific objectives can be seen to have been as important as before and not necessarily less attainable (especially the increases in agricultural production).

### 1(b). Identifying a possible course—means and ends

(i) The essence of the technical–economic coordination undertaken by the planners was to check the consistency of aggregate inter-sectoral demand and supply under their given growth-rate assumptions, i.e. to determine what pattern of investment and consequent increases in output would secure the desired overall rate of growth at least cost. They did not ask whether alternative, if more costly, routes existed to reach the various objectives they derived from the global rate of growth, routes which at least could be regarded as feasible. Partly this was due to shortage of time, partly (one may surmise) it was due to the absence in Tanzania of the highly articulated apparatus of interest-representation which forms the sounding board for the viability of the planners' computations in France's *economie concertée* (the director of planning was recruited from the French *Office du Plan*). But they did brush aside what was, in Tanzanian circumstances, the closest substitute, i.e. the views of the spending departments. The ministry of agriculture, in particular, did not accept the thesis that the so-called 'transformation approach' should replace the 'improvement approach' as the main instrument of rural development (the transformation approach implied settlement and re-settlement schemes in which a complete break would be made with traditional patterns of life as well as of production). The E.D.C. appears to have backed the directorate's view, and the plan budgeted to spend more on settlements and irrigation than on extension services to what it called 'traditional agriculture'. This policy was a virtually complete failure, both economically and politically, and was largely abandoned in early 1967 after the Arusha Declaration.

It is tempting to see the 'transformation approach' as a particular expression of 'planners' tension', filling the large gap that existed between the crop targets derived from the selected growth-rate and the possible courses of action to achieve increased output which the planning process did not seriously explore. The targets themselves are interesting. Sisal, in 1963 almost wholly an estate crop, was set to achieve an increase of 30 per cent by 1970, whereas cotton, a peasant farmer's crop, was set to achieve an increase of 130 per cent. The planners' rationale for this was that 'a great potential still exists for increasing agricultural output by spending more time in the fields, rationalising the use of land and by applying the fundamentals of better crop husbandry'.[1] It seems a reasonable guess that the 'transformation approach' (first propounded by the World Bank Mission in 1959) represented a formula for sweeping away all the social and cultural constraints which barred the way to surmounting these simple technological hurdles. Whereas the sisal industry's constraints were seen as physical and economic, those of peasant producers were seen as primarily attitudinal, a familiar set of quarter-truths which only a procedure of building 'upwards' to production targets from the formulation of feasible programmes for change could have put in proper perspective. Such a process would, however, have meant reconsidering the growth-rate objective of 6·7 per cent, almost twice that which had been achieved in the 7 years 1954–61. Such a process of interaction between those who could assess the available activators and resources in relation to suggested targets, and those who were responsible for technical coordination to achieve the proposed plan goals, was never seriously put in hand, however, and consequently the courses specified in the plan for reaching its objectives were optimal in some sense but not possible courses.

(ii) What has been said might seem to be contradicted by the planners' gestures (sincerely meant) in the direction of planning 'from the bottom up' as well as 'from the top down', as it is usually described;[2] i.e. the creation of village, district, and regional development committees and the call for the formulation of regional plans to be incorporated in the final plan (after being rendered mutually consistent and consistent with the plan's overall targets). It seems, however, that this was mainly seen as an exercise in securing commitment to the plan, presumably on the basis of the very common (though often questionable) belief that there is nothing to beat participation in making plans for ensuring that they will be implemented. The regional plans did not prove of much value, and thereafter the development committees did not operate as parts of any national planning process.[3]

Two comments seem relevant here. First, although the adjustment of

---

[1] *The five-year plan*, p. 19.

[2] This phrase has two different meanings. In one it refers to building a plan out of properly prepared projects, as opposed to inventing projects to fill a predetermined set of aggregate targets in the plan; in the other it refers to a specific form of mass participation, in which people at or near the 'grass-roots' are invited to say what should or could be done within the broad objectives of the plan. The latter meaning may or may not involve sending up to the central planners projects worked out in the lowest level councils.

[3] An interesting record of the activities of village development committees in Bukoba has been compiled by Göran Hyden in *TANU YAJENGA NCHI—Political development in rural Tanzania*, Lund 1968, pp. 173–7.

ends to means is part of a single chronological stage in the planning process, the structures used must evidently be such that a distinction, and even a tension, is maintained between the proposing of goals and the search for means. If these functions are fused, a rational process of approximation of ends and means is unlikely to occur. This is what happened: the political leaders on the development committees saw their task as one of formulating suitably ambitious production targets with the result that the proposals that emerged exceeded in total the targets derived from the already ambitious growth objectives of the plan, and far exceeded what the administrators in the regions thought was feasible.[1]

Secondly, in a country where there is substantial under-utilization of physical resources the technical–economic aspect of the search for means to achieve proposed ends may be relatively slight compared with the political–organizational aspect; or to put it another way, the assumptions about behaviour which must necessarily be built into any analysis designed to find optimal paths really constitute the problem of development. For instance, it is not a question of finding out what inputs of labour, etc. will be needed in a district to produce a given tonnage of cotton, but what available inducements might produce the inputs of labour which would do the trick. This information, which is necessary for any useful exercise of technical–economic coordination, is not discoverable by inspection but by experiment; but to acquire some advance ideas about it, a process of consultation and even bargaining can be undertaken which foreshadows the process of implementation which comes after it. This is the main reason for 'cutting in' lower-level organs on the process of plan formulation; not to secure their support through identification with the agreed targets, although this may be worth something; but to get them to disclose the 'price' at which the activators in their control, which may be apt to produce the desired economic activity, will be put into operation. (The 'price' may be a given level of crop prices, but it may equally be credit facilities or more extension services or schools or more sanctions.)

This process was not part of the formulation of the five-year plan: for instance cooperative unions, in which all cash-crop farmers are organized, are not recorded as playing any part at all. The plan had in fact little basis for its assumptions about production increases, mixing hope with threats: 'Attitudes will evolve through social emulation, cooperation and the expansion of community development activities. Where incentives, emulation and propaganda are ineffective, enforcement or coercive measures of an appropriate sort will be considered.'[2]

### Implementation

Because the five-year plan lacked some of the necessary characteristics of a

---

[1] Bienen, *Tanzania*, pp. 330–1. But some regions met the increased targets.
[2] *The five-year plan*, p. 19.

national plan, much of it was not implementable; after the publication of the document, it did not so much fail to work as become less and less relevant. The machinery established to make the plan, which was supposed also to supervise its implementation, fell into partial disuse, and the directorate itself was allowed to run down in the first year of the plan period. This can in retrospect be explained by the non-implementable character of the plan, at least as much as by other factors to which much attention has been given. In particular, considerable emphasis has been laid on the absence of a proper system of reporting on progress under the plan, which was certainly a striking shortcoming of the implementation stage; but the intention behind this criticism is misdirected when it is assumed that, given such a system, there could have been a 'continuous process of revision of the plan', rather than a continuous adaptation of the measures used to secure conformity with it.[1] The latter approach may mean making still greater efforts to achieve what may turn out to have been unattainable (or even undesirable) objectives, but that is the nature of carrying out a plan; the former approach will ensure that the current plan document contains a version of optimal future behaviour that reflects the latest information but is unlikely to furnish an effective tool of management and control.

Some other conclusions actually drawn from the reasons for the plan's failure similarly strike one as in need of revision: for instance, Pratt's conclusions that the 'planning authority' must be located under the direct responsibility of the president or his most powerful deputy, the implicit reason being that the directorate should have enough power to assert the discipline of the plan over the too independent ministries. One feels that what was required was not so much to arm the technical economic planners in the directorate with powers superior to those of the ministries, as to secure a dialogue between them and the ministries (conceived of as the political–organizational planners—the directorate was not staffed to fulfil this function). It is clear from Pratt's account that the problem was that both the directorate and the ministries came to assume that the task of getting these two 'streams of decisions' to flow together was essentially one of *making* the political–organizational stream follow the course of the technical–economic stream, whereas in the nature of the case, only a stream which first disclosed the genuine constraints on the possibilities of political–organizational coordination, and then accommodated them, could hope to succeed.

In the same way one is troubled by the conclusion that the political commitment to planning in Tanzania in 1964–5 may have been too weak for 'effective economic planning'. What is surely clear is that no structures

---

[1] Pratt, 'The administration of economic planning', pp. 56–7. While Pratt's conclusions are used here as a focus for criticism of too pragmatic an approach, his study is exceptionally intimate and penetrating.

were established which would effectively 'scan' the range and interrelationships of the goals cherished by the politicians at all the relevant levels and seek to ensure that these were appropriately accommodated in the plan; the politicians were, perhaps, not so much uncommitted to planning as to the limited set of goals which the five-year plan embraced.

### CONCLUSION

It is always easy with the advantage of hindsight to say what practical planners should have done.[1] All the same it is difficult not to feel that a radical shift in the approach to planning is required—from logical models of the end-product to behavioural models of plan-making: and from models of plan-making to models of planned behaviour.

The main argument of this paper might not unfairly be summarized as a proposal to define planned behaviour as behaviour which is subject to and reflects a decision only to change the objectives which it is intended to achieve at more or less fixed intervals. Defining 'planning' this way emphasizes its periodicity and seeks to distinguish it from patterns of action which permit a constant adjustment of the 'mix' of goals and time preferences to the constantly shifting pattern of perceptions and feelings and the shifting balance of political forces. Seen in this way, planning appears not as a mode of decision-making which will necessarily produce technically or economically optimal outcomes, but as one which has other features—such as the periodic sharp definition of issues, legitimizing 'campaignism' and the 'focused' (i.e. highly uneven) application of governmental resources, the provision of specific norms for judging performance in the public sector, etc.—which may outweigh its disadvantages in the eyes of political leaders. It would not help matters to insist that such a definition of planning should replace others; what is suggested is that we might understand actual planning practice better if we thought of it as distributed over a spectrum between two ideal types; one of them a behavioural model with approximately the characteristics of Lindblom's disjointed incrementalism (where 'planning' becomes largely a cultural or stylistic component of the decisional process), the other similarly a behavioural model, the main elements of which would follow the pattern sketched in this paper. It would seem otiose to re-emphasize the lines of thought involved in this proposition, which are very far from new, were it not for the almost complete dominance of the literature on planning by the synoptic model of plan-making. A more appropriate line of analysis would, one hopes, help to make 'planning' more engaging to political scientists and, conceivably, more fruitful for developing countries.

[1] Especially when discussing a *first* plan, formulated by a very small number of people who are new to the country and working against the clock and in a context of almost complete inexperience of planning on the part of everyone else.

# BIBLIOGRAPHICAL INDEX

Aberle, K. G. *Anthropology and Imperialism*. Ann Arbor, The Radical Education Project 1967. – 61

Adams, R. N., *et al. Social change in Latin America today*. New York 1960. – 203, 208

Afrifa, A. A. *The Ghana coup*. London 1966. – 235, 238, 245

Ahumada, J. 'Hypothesis for the diagnosis of a situation of social change; the case of Venezuela', *International Social Science Journal* 16 (1964). – 63

Almond, G. A. and Coleman, J. S. *The politics of the developing areas*. Princeton 1960. – 4, 116, 185

Almond, G. A. and Powell, G. B. *Comparative politics: a developmental approach*. Boston 1966. – 115, 121, 122

Amin, S. *Le Développement du capitalisme en Côte d'Ivoire*. Paris 1967. – 140, 141, 142

Amon d'Aby, F. J. *Le Problème des chefferies traditionnelles en Côte d'Ivoire*. Abidjan 1958. – 143

—— *Croyances religieuses et coutumes juridiques des Agni de la Côte d'Ivoire*. Paris 1960. – 153

Anderson, C. W., von der Mehden, F. R. and Young, C. *Issues of political development*. New Jersey 1967. – 38, 51, 55, 214, 228

Appell, G. N. 'The structure of district administration, anti-administration activity and political instability', *Human Organization* 25 (1966). – 62

Appleby, P. *Policy and administration*. Alabama 1949. – 210

Apter, D. E. and Andrain, C. 'Comparative government: developing new nations', *Journal of Politics* 30, 2 (1918). – 2

Apter, D. E. *The Gold Coast in transition*. Princeton 1955. – 1, 4

—— 'Theory and the study of politics', *American Political Science Review* 51, 3 (1957). – 6

—— 'The role of traditionalism in the political modernization of Ghana and Uganda', *World Politics* XIII, 1 (1960). – 158

—— *The politics of modernisation*. Chicago 1965. – 2, 5, 116, 119, 238

—— *The political kingdom in Uganda*. Princeton 1967. – 9

—— 'Nkrumah, charisma, and the coup', *Daedalus* (1968). – 238

Apthorpe, R. *From tribal rule to modern government*. Lusaka 1959. – 44

—— 'The introduction of bureaucracy into African politics', *Journal of African Administration* 12 (1960). – 44, 196

Argyis, C. *Personality and organisation*. New York 1957. – 190

Ashford, D. E. 'Bureaucrats and citizens', *Annals of American Academy of Political and Social Science* LXXV (1965). – 231

—— *Political linkage of AID instruments*, mim. 1968. – 202

Austin, D. *Politics in Ghana, 1946–60*. London 1964. – 1, 238

—— 'The Ghana case' in Institute of Commonwealth Studies Papers, *The politics of demilitarisation*. London 1966. – 240

Bailey, F. *Caste and the economic frontier*. Manchester 1957. – 45

—— *Tribe, caste and nation*. Manchester 1960. – 36, 39, 139

—— *Politics and social change*. Berkeley 1963. – 35, 53, 139

—— *The peasant view of the bad life*. Presidential address delivered to the Nottingham Meeting of the British Association, 2 September 1966. – 169

—— *Stratagems and Spoils*, Oxford 1969. – 47, 194

Balandier, G. 'La Situation coloniale: approche théorique', *Cahiers internationaux de sociologie* II (1951). – 61

Banfield, E. C. *The moral basis of a backward society*. New York 1958. – 205

Banks, A. and Textor, R. B. *A cross polity survey*. Massachusetts 1963. – 220, 221

Banton, M. (ed.) *Themes in economic anthropology*. London 1967. – 91, 98

Barnett, C. 'The education of military elites', *Journal of Contemporary History* II (1967). – 228

Barth, F. 'Ecologic relationships of ethnic groups in Swat, North Pakistan', *American Anthropologist* 58 (1956). – 40

—— *Political leadership among Swat Pathans*. London 1959. – 35, 47

—— *The role of the entrepreneur in social change in northern Norway*. Bergen 1963. – 47, 53, 97, 139

—— *Models of social organization*. London 1966. – 48, 51

—— 'On the study of social change', *American Anthropologist* 69 (1967). – 48

Beattie, J. 'Checks on the abuse of political power in some African states', *Sociologus* 9 (1959). – 44

—— *Bunyoro: an African kingdom.* New York 1960. – 46

Bediako, K. *The downfall of Kwame Nkrumah.* Accra 1966. – 234

Beer, H. W. and Ensminger, D. 'The development block as a social system', *Indian Journal of Public Administration* 5 (1959). – 205

Belshaw, H. *The communities project strategy approach to economic development*, mim., Noumea (South Pacific Commission), n.d. – 203

Bender, G. J. 'Political socialization and political change', *Western Political Quarterly* 20 (1967). – 60

Bendix, R. *Nation building and citizenship.* New York 1964. – 189

—— 'Tradition and modernity reconsidered', *Comparative studies in society and history* 9 (1967). – 39, 41

Benedict, B. 'Factionalism in Mauritian villages', *British Journal of Sociology* 8 (1957). – 43

Bennett, C. and Rosberg, C. G. *The Kenyatta election, Kenya 1960–1961.* London 1961. – 7

Biebuyck, D. and Douglas, M. *Congo tribes and parties.* London 1961. – 59

Bienen, H. *Tanzania: party transformation and economic development.* Princeton 1967. – 110, 214, 267, 269, 273

Binder, L. *Iran: political development in a changing society.* Berkeley 1962. – 4

—— 'Nasserism: the protest movement in the Middle East', Kaplan, M. A. (ed.) *The revolution in world politics.* New York 1962. – 228

Birmingham, W. *et al. A study of contemporary Ghana*, vol. 1. London 1966. – 232, 234, 236, 237

Black, C. E. *The dynamics of modernization.* New York 1966. – 49

Blau, P. M. and Scott, W. R. *Formal organisation.* London 1963. – 187, 230

Blondel, J. *Voters, parties, and leaders: the social fabric of British politics.* London 1963. – 117, 121

Boissevain, J. 'Patronage in Sicily', *Man*, new series I (1966). – 43

Bottomore, T. B. *Elites and society.* London 1964. – 114

Boutillier, J. L. *Bongouanou, Côte d'Ivoire: étude sociologique d'une subdivision.* Paris 1960. – 153

Braibanti, R. and Spengler, J. J. (eds.) *Tradition, values and socio-economic development.* Durham N.C. 1961. – 182

Braibanti, R. (ed.) *Asian bureaucratic systems emergent from the British imperial tradition.* Durham N.C. 1966. – 183

Brain, J. L. 'The position of women on settlement schemes', and 'Observations on settler productivity and discipline at Kabuku with special emphasis on the role of women', unpublished papers, nos. 34 and 40, Syracuse University Village Settlement Project. – 107

Braithwaite, L. 'Social stratification and cultural pluralism', *Annals of the New York Academy of Sciences* 83 (1960). – 52

Brams, S. J. 'Transaction flows in the international system', *American Political Science Review* LX, 4 (December 1966). – 23

Brass, Paul R. *Factional problems in an Indian State; the Congress Party in Uttar Pradesh.* Berkeley 1965. – 5

Bretton, H. L. *The rise and fall of Kwame Nkrumah.* London 1967. – 226, 236

Brierly, T. G. 'The evolution of local administration in French-speaking West Africa', *Journal of Local Administration Overseas* V, 1 (January 1966). – 161

Brokensha, D. *Social change in Larteh, Ghana.* Oxford 1966. – 214, 238

Buck, A. E. *Administrative consolidation in state governments.* New York 1919. – 180

Bundagaard, L. R. 'Philippines local government', *Journal of Politics* 19 (1957). – 204

Busia, K. *The position of the chief in the modern political system of the Ashanti.* London 1951. – 44

Calvert, P. H. 'Revolution: the politics of violence', *Political Studies* XIV (1967). – 217

Campbell, A., *et al. The American voter.* New York 1960. – 10

Campbell, J. *Honour, family and patronage.* Oxford 1964. – 43

Campbell, M. J., Brierly, T. G. and Blitz, L. F. *The structure of local government in West Africa.* The Hague 1965. – 161

Capell, A. 'The Walbiri through their own eyes', *Oceania* 23 (1952). – 59

Carr, E. H. *A history of Soviet Russia*, vol. 2. *The Bolshevik Revolution*, 2. London 1952. – 67

Carter, G. *Politics in Africa.* New York 1966. – 237

Carter, W. *Aymara communities and the Bolivian agrarian reform.* Gainesville 1965. – 63

Chamberlain, N. W. *Private and public planning.* New York 1965. – 256, 257, 259, 262, 270

Chapple, E. D. and Arensberg, C. M. 'Measuring human relations', *Genetic Psychology Monographs* 22 (1940). – 40, 62

Chapple, E. D. and Coon, C. *Principles of anthropology.* New York 1942. – 40

Charlesworth, J. C. (ed.) *The limits of behaviouralism in political science*, American Academy of Political & Social Science. Philadelphia 1962. – 2

Clamens, R. P. 'Essai de grammaire sénoufo-tagouana', *Bulletin de l'I.F.A.N.* XIV, 4 (1952). – 153

Codere, H. 'Power in Ruanda', *Anthropologica* 4 (1962). – 56

Cohen, P. 'Models', *British Journal of Sociology* 17 (1966). – 45

Cohen, R. 'The strategy of social evolution in British social anthropology', *Anthropologica* 4 (1962). – 36

—— 'Political anthropology', *Rural Africana* 2 (1967). – 42

Coleman, J. S. *Education and political development.* Princeton 1965. – 4, 60

Coleman, J. S. and Rosberg, C. (eds.) *Political parties and national integration in tropical Africa.* California 1964. – 216, 231

Colson, E. *The Makah Indians.* Manchester 1953. – 59

Colonial Office, London, Ashbridge Conference. *Social development in the British Colonial Territories.* London, Col. Misc. 523, 1954. – 203

Constas, H. 'Max Weber's two conceptions of bureaucracy', *American Journal of Sociology* 63 (1958). – 189

Corbett, D. *Politics and the airlines.* London 1965. – 24

Coser, L. *The functions of social conflict.* New York 1954. – 216

Côte d'Ivoire: see Ivory Coast.

Cowan, L. G. *Local government in West Africa.* New York 1958. – 143, 144

Crowder, M. 'Indirect rule—French and British style', *Africa* 34 (1964). – 44

Cutright, P. 'National political development', *American Sociological Review* XXVIII, 2 (April 1963). – 221, 222, 223

Dahl, R. A. 'The behavioural approach in political science: epitaph for a monument to a successful protest', *American Political Science Review* 55 (1961). – 2

—— *Who governs? Democracy and power in an American city.* New Haven 1961. – 9, 117

Dalton, G. 'Traditional production in primitive African economies', *Quarterly Journal of Economics* 76 (1962). – 91

David, P. T., Goldman, R. M. and Bain, R. C. *The politics of National Party conventions.* Washington 1960. – 118

Davies, A. F. *Private politics.* Melbourne 1966. – 119

Davies, J. C. 'Toward a theory of revolution', *American Sociological Review* XXVII, 1 (1962). – 219

Delavignette, R. *Freedom and authority in French West Africa.* London 1950. – 143

Despres, L. A. *Cultural pluralism and nationalist politics in British Guiana.* Chicago 1967. – 52, 54

—— 'Anthropological theory, cultural pluralism and the study of complex societies', *Current Anthropology* 9 (1968). – 52

Deutsch, K. 'Social mobilization and political development', *American Political Science Review* LV, 3 (1961). – 22

—— *The nerves of government.* New York 1963. – 261

—— *The integration of political communities.* Philadelphia 1964. – 44

Dey, S. K. *Community development: a bird's eye view.* New York 1964. – 204

Diamant, A. 'The relevance of comparative politics to the study of comparative administration', *Administrative Science Quarterly* 5 (1960). – 178

—— *Bureaucracy in development movement regimes; a bureaucratic model for developing societies,* mim. Bloomington 1964. – 206

Diamond, S. and Burke, F. *The transformation of East Africa.* New York 1966. – 61

Diaz, M. *Tonala: conservatism, responsibility and authority in a Mexican town.* Berkeley 1966. – 63

Dinnerstein, H. S. 'Soviet policy in Latin America', *American Political Science Review* LXI, 1 (1967). – 22

Dobb, M. *Russian economic development since the Revolution.* London 1928. – 67

Dotson, A. T. 'A general theory of public employment', *Public Administration Review* 16 (1956). – 187

—— 'Democratic decentralization in local self-government', *Indian Journal of Public Administration* 4 (1958). – 204

Dowse, R. E. 'A functionalist's logic', *World Politics* XVIII (July 1966). – 4, 223

—— *Ghana and the USSR; a study in comparative development.* London 1969. – 226

Dror, Y. 'Muddling Through—Science or Inertia?', *Public Administration Review* 24 (1964). – 253

Dube, S. C. 'Cultural factors in rural community development', *Journal of Asian Studies* 16 (1956). – 204

—— 'Some problems of community development', *Economic Development and Cultural Change* 5 (1957). – 203

Dumont, L. 'Village studies', *Contributions to Indian Sociology* I (1957). – 53

Dumont, R. *False start in Africa.* London 1966. – 28, 226

—— *Terres vivantes: voyages d'un agronome autour du monde.* Paris 1961. – 28

Dunbar, A. *A history of Bunyoro-Kitara.* Oxford 1965. – 46

Duodu, C. *The Gab boys.* London 1968. – 233

Duverger, M. *Political parties*. London 1954. –
124
Dyson-Hudson, N. *Karimojong politics*. Oxford
1966. – 60

Easton, D. 'Political anthropology', B. Siegel
(ed.), *Biennial Review of Anthropology*. Stanford 1959. – 44
—— 'The current meaning of 'behaviouralism'
in political science', Charlesworth, J. C.
(ed.), *The limits of behaviouralism in political
science*. – 2
Eckstein, H. and Apter, D. *Comparative politics*.
New York 1963. – 30
Eckstein, H. (ed.) *Internal war*. Glencoe 1964. –
215
—— 'On the etiology of internal wars',
*History and Theory* IV, 2 (1965). – 213, 218,
219
Eisenstadt, S. N. 'Bureaucracy and Bureau-
cratization', *Current Sociology* 7 (1958). – 189
—— 'Bureaucracy and debureaucratization',
*Administrative Science Quarterly* III (1959). –
230
—— *Problems of emerging bureaucracies in develop-
ing areas and new states*. Chicago 1960. – 178
—— *'From generation to generation'*. London
1964. – 30
—— 'Modernisation and conditions of sus-
tained economic growth, *World Politics* XVI
(1964). – 4, 141
Eldersveld, S. J. *Political Parties: A Behavioral
Analysis*. Chicago, 1964. – 117–19
Emmerich, H. *Administrative road blocks to
co-ordinated development*. New York 1961. –
177
*Encyclopedie mensuelle d'outre-mer* 70 (juin 1956),
250, 'L'africanisation des cadres en Côte
d'Ivoire'. – 143
Esman, M. *Education for development administra-
tion*. Pittsburgh 1962. – 182
Etzioni, A. *Political unification*. New York
1965. – 44
—— *The active society: a theory of societal and
political processes*. New York 1968. – 14, 49
Evans-Pritchard, E. *The Sanusi of Cyrenaica*.
Oxford 1949. – 44
—— 'The Zande state', *Journal of the Royal
Anthropological Institute* 93 (1963). – 46, 47
Eulau, H. *The behavioural persuasion in politics*.
New York 1963. – 2

Fallers, L. 'The predicament of the modern
African chief', *American Anthropologist* 57
(1955). – 44
—— *Bantu bureaucracy*. Chicago 1965. – 44, 46
—— 'Political sociology and the anthropological study of African politics', *Archiv. europ.
sociol* 4. (1963). – 45

Fanon, F. *The wretched of the earth*. London
1965. – 139, 225–6
Feierabend, I. and R. 'Aggressive behaviours
within politics, 1948–1962: a cross national
study', *Journal of Conflict Resolution* X, 2
(1966). – 218, 219, 232
Feit, E. 'Military coups and political development', *World Politics* XX (1968). – 241
Feldman, A. S. 'Violence and volatility: the
likelihood of revolution', in Eckstein, H.
(ed.) *Internal war*. Glencoe 1964. – 215, 217
Fenton, W. *Factionalism at Taos Pueblo, New
Mexico*. Washington, Bureau of American
Ethnology Bulletin 164 (1957). – 43
Finer, S. E. *The man on horseback*. London 1962.
– 214, 215, 217, 224, 225
—— 'Military disengagement from politics',
Institute of Commonwealth Studies, *The
politics of demilitarisation*. London 1966. – 241
Finkle, J. and Meade, R. *Organisational adapta-
tion and social change*. Ann Arbor 1967. – 210
Firmalin, T. C. 'Political activities of Barrio
citizens as they affect community develop-
ment', *Philippines Journal of Public Administration* 4 (1960). – 205
Firth, R. 'Introduction to factions in Indian
and overseas Indian societies', *British
Journal of Sociology* 8 (1957). – 43
—— *Essays on social organization and values*.
London 1964. – 36, 45, 46, 48, 61
Firth, R. 'The influence of social structure
upon peasant economics', unpublished paper
presented at Agricultural Development Corporation conference, Honolulu 1965. – 93
Fitch, K. and Oppenheimer, M. 'Ghana: end
of an illusion', *Monthly Review* 18, 3 (1966). –
171, 225–6
Foltz, W. J. *From French West Africa to the Mali
Federation*. New Haven 1965. – 146, 148
Forde, D. 'Anthropology and the development of African studies', *Africa* 37 (1967).
56
Forde, D. and Kaberry, P. (eds.) *West African
kingdoms in the nineteenth century*. London
1967. – 38, 48
Fortes, M. and Evans-Pritchard, E. *African
political systems*. London 1940. – 29, 42
Fortes, M. Introduction, Goody, J. (ed.) *The
development cycle in domestic groups*. Cam-
bridge 1958. – 36
Forward, J. 'Toward an empirical framework
for ecological studies in comparative public
administration', Raphaeli, N. (ed.),
*Readings in comparative public administration*.
Boston 1967. – 220, 221, 222
Foster, G. 'The dyadic contract in Tzintzunt-
zan', *American Anthropologist* 65 (1963). – 43
Foster, P. *Education and social change in Ghana*.
London 1965. – 232, 233

Frank, A. G. 'Sociology of development and the underdevelopment of sociology', *Catalyst* (1967). – 54, 223

Freedman, M. 'The growth of a plural society in Malaya', *Pacific Affairs* 33 (1960). – 52

—— 'A Chinese phase in social anthropology', *British Journal of Sociology* 14 (1963). – 41

Frey, F. W. *The Turkish political elite.* Cambridge, Mass. 1965. – 117, 119

Fried, M. H. 'On the evolution of social stratification and the state', Diamond, S. (ed.), *Culture in history.* New York 1960. – 39

—— 'Anthropology and the study of politics', Tax, S. (ed.), *Horizons of anthropology.* Chicago 1964. – 39

—— 'On the concept of tribe and tribal society', *Transactions of the New York Academy of Sciences* 28 (1966). – 59

—— *The evolution of political society.* New York 1967. – 39

—— 'The state', *International encyclopedia of the social sciences.* London and New York 1968. – 39, 61

Gable, R. *Plan for research and publication in public administration.* Washington 1961. – 178, 180

—— *Development administration and assistance, an annotated bibliography.* Washington 1961. – 181

Gant, G. F. 'A note on applications of development administration', *Public Policy* 15 (1966). – 185

Garbett, G. K. 'Prestige, status and power in a modern valley Korekore Chiefdom, Rhodesia', *Africa* 37 (1967). – 39

Garvin, P. L. 'Comment on the concept of ethnic groups as related to whole societies', Austin, W. (ed.), *Report of the Ninth Annual Meeting on Linguistics and Language Studies.* Georgetown 1958. – 59

Geertz, C. *Old societies and new states.* New York 1963. – 61

—— *Agricultural involution.* Berkeley and Los Angeles 1963. – 38, 40

—— 'Politics past, politics present', *Archiv. europ. sociol.* 8 (1967). – 60, 63

Germani and Silvert. 'Military intervention in Latin America', *Archiv. europ. sociol.* II (1961). – 215

Gerschenkron, A. 'Agrarian policies and industrialisation, Russia, 1861–1914', *Cambridge Economic History*, vol. 6, part II. Cambridge 1965. – 66

Glickman, H. 'Dialogues on the theory of African development', *Africa Report* 12 (1967). – 39

Gluckman, M. *Analysis of a social situation in modern Zululand.* Manchester 1958. – 61

—— 'Civil wars and theories of power in Barotseland', *Yale Law Review* 72 (1963). – 41

—— 'The utility of the equilibrium model in the study of social change', *American Anthropologist* 70 (1968). – 36, 45, 48

Goldman, I. 'Status rivalry and cultural evolution in Polynesia', *American Anthropologist* 57 (1955). – 58

Goldschmidt, W. *Man's way.* New York 1959. – 37

Goldsmith, R. W. 'Russian economic growth, 1860–1913', *Economic development and cultural change* (1961). – 65

Gonidec, P. F. 'Les Assemblées locales des territoires d'Outre-Mer', *Revue Juridique et Politique de l'Union Française* VI (1952); VII (1953). – 144

Goody, J. (ed.) *The development cycle in domestic groups.* Cambridge 1958. – 36

—— (ed.) 'Feudalism in Africa', *The Journal of African History* 4 (1963). – 41

Goswami, U. 'The structure of development administration', *Indian Journal of Public Administration* 1 (1955). – 182

Gouldner, A. W. *Patterns of industrial bureaucracy.* Glencoe 1954. – 190

—— A. W. 'Metaphysical pathos and the theory of bureaucracy', *American Political Science Review* 49 (1955). – 189

Graham, B. D. 'Change in factional conflict: The case of the Uttar Pradesh Congress Party, 1964–65', mim., University of Sussex, 1968. – 10

Gray, C. 'Development planning in East Africa: a review article', *East African Review* II, 2 (1966). – 253

Grinevetsky, E. *Poslevoennye perspektivy Russkoi promyshlennosti.* Kharkov, 1919. – 69

Gross, B. (ed.) *Action under planning.* New York 1967. – 247, 254

Gross, B. *The administration of economic development planning: principles and fallacies.* New York 1966. – 266

Grossman, G. 'Soviet growth, routine, inertia and pressure', *American Economic Review* 50 (1960). – 77

Gulick, L. and Urwick, L. *Papers on the science of administration.* New York 1937. – 260

Gulliver, P. H. 'The Karamojong cluster', *Africa* 22 (1951). – 60

—— 'Land tenure and social change among the Nyakyusa', *East African Studies*, no. 11, E.A.I.S.R. Kampala 1958. – 92–3

—— 'Land shortage, social change and social conflict in East Africa', *Journal of Conflict Resolution* 5, 1 (1961). – 93, 95

—— 'Anthropology', Lystad, R. A. (ed.), *The African world*. New York 1965. – 37

Gurr, T. and Ruttenberg, C. *The conditions of civil violence*. Princeton 1967. – 196

Gurr, T. 'Psychological factors in civil violence', *World Politics* XX (1968). – 218

Gusfield, J. 'Tradition and modernity: misplaced polarities in the study of social change', *American Journal of Sociology* 72 (1967). – 39

Gutteridge, W. *Military institutions and power in new states*. London 1964. – 222, 234

Guttsman, W. L. *The British political elite*. London, 1963. – 117

Gyasi-Twum, K. 'Reflections on some aspects of fiscal policy', *Economic Bulletin of Ghana* 11 (1966). – 240

Haas, E. *Beyond the nation state*. California 1964. – 44

Hacker, A. 'Capital and carbuncles: The "great books" re-appraised', *American Political Science Review* 48, 3 (1954). – 6

Hall, R. H. 'Inter-organisational structural variation', *Administrative Science Quarterly* 7 (1962). – 191

Halpern, J. *The changing village community*. New Jersey 1967. – 62

Halpern, M. *The politics of social change in the Middle East and North Africa*. Princeton 1963. – 228, 230

—— 'The rates and costs of political development', *Annals of the American Academy of Political and Social Science* (1965). – 214, 215

Hammel, E. 'Some characteristics of rural village and urban slum populations on the coast of Peru', *Southwestern Journal of Anthropology* 20 (1964). – 63

Hanson, A. H. *Public enterprise and economic development*. London 1959. – 177

—— *The process of planning: a study of India's five year plans, 1950–61*. Oxford 1966. – 247, 264, 265

Hapgood, D. (ed.) *Policies for promoting agricultural development*. Cambridge, Mass. 1965. – 203

Hart, D. V. and Meadows, P. *Directed social change, field reports and annotated bibliography*. Syracuse 1961. – 181

Hart, H. C. *The village and development administration*. Bloomington 1967. – 205, 211

Heady, F. *Bureacracies in developing countries: internal roles and external assistance*. Bloomington 1966. – 183

Heady, F. and Stokes, S. *Comparative public administration* (2nd edn). Ann Arbor 1960. – 178

—— —— (eds.) *Papers in comparative public administration*. Ann Arbor 1962. – 183

Henderson, A. and Parsons, T. *Max Weber: the theory of social and economic organisation*. London 1947. – 191

Heyer, J. 'Kenya's agricultural development policy', *East African Economic Review*, new series II, 2 (1966). – 264

Hirschman, A. H. *The strategy of economic development*. New Haven 1958. – 24, 262

—— *Journeys toward progress*. New York 1963. – 24, 210

H.M.S.O. *Community development*. London 1966. – 203

Hobsbawm, E. J. *Primitive rebels*. London 1959. – 43

Holas, B. *Les Sénoufo (y compris les Minianka)*. Paris 1957. – 153

Holmberg, A. 'The research and development approach to the study of change', *Human Organisation* 17 (1958). – 208

Huntington, S. P. 'Political development and political decay', *World Politics* XVII (1965). – 4, 34, 217

Huntington, S. *Changing patterns of military politics*. New York 1962. – 216, 239

Hyden, G. *Tanu Yajenga Nchi—political development in rural Tanzania*. Lund 1968. – 272

Ilchman, W. 'Rising expectations and the revolution in development administration', *Public Administration Review* 25 (1965). – 206

Ilchman, W. and Bhargava, R. C. 'Balanced thought and economic growth', *Economic Development and Cultural Change* 14 (1966). – 206

Inayatullah and Shafi, Q. M. *Dynamics of development in a Pakistan village*. Peshawar 1963. – 205

Indian Planning Commission Evaluation Organisation, *Evaluation of the working of community projects*. New Delhi 1964. – 203

Ionescu, G. *The politics of the European communist states*. London 1967. – 163

Ivory Coast. Conseil Economique et Social, *Rapport sur l'évolution économique et sociale de la Côte d'Ivoire 1960–1964*. Abidjan December 1965. – 140

—— Ministère de l'Information, *IVe Congrès PDCI–RDA, 23–24–25 septembre 1965*. Abidjan 1965. – 150, 165, 166, 172

—— Ministère de Plan, Service de la Statistique, *Inventaire économique de la Côte d'Ivoire 1947 à 1956*. Abidjan 1958. – 140, 160

Jackson, I. C. *Advance in Africa*. London 1956. – 204

Janowitz, M. (ed.) *The military in the political development of new nations*. Chicago 1964. – 214, 227

Lienhardt, G. *Social anthropology*. London 1964. – 44

Lieuwen, E. *Arms and politics in Latin America*. New York 1961. – 215

Lindblom, C. E. 'The science of muddling through', *Public Administration Review* 19 (1959). – 252

—— *The intelligence of democracy*. New York 1965. – 249

Lindblom, C. E. and Braybrooke, D. *A strategy of decision*. Glencoe 1963. – 249, 251 252

Linton, R. 'The concept of national character', Stanton, A. and Perry, S. (eds.) *Personality and Political Crisis*. Glencoe 1951. – 216

Lipset, S. M. *Political man: the social bases of politics*. New York 1960. – 17, 215

Lipset, S. M. and Rokkan, S. *Party systems and voter alignments: cross-national perspectives*. London and New York 1967. – 21

Lissak, M. 'Modernisation and role-expansion of the military in developing countries', *Comparative Studies in Society and history* VI (1967). – 214, 218

Lloyd, P. C. 'Traditional rulers', Coleman, J. and Rosberg, C. (eds.), *Political parties and national integration in tropical Africa*. Berkeley and Los Angeles 1966. – 44

—— 'The political structure of African kingdoms', Banton, M. (ed.) *Political systems and the distribution of power*. London 1965. – 42, 56, 58

—— *The new elites of tropical Africa*. London 1966. – 57

McAlister, L. M. 'Changing concepts of the role of the military in Latin America', *Annals of the American Academy of Political and Social Science* (1965). – 216

Mackenzie, W. J. M. *Politics and social science*. London 1967. – 2, 58, 178

McClelland, D. *The achieving society*. New York 1961. – 218

McMullen, M. 'A theory of corruption', *Sociological Review* VIII (1961). – 245

Mair, L. P. 'Chieftainship in modern Africa', *Studies in applied anthropology*. London 1957. – 44

—— *New nations*. Chicago 1963. – 37–8, 39, 42

—— *Primitive government*. London and Baltimore 1962. – 39

—— 'How small-scale societies change', *Penguin survey of the social sciences*. Baltimore 1965. – 35

—— *New Africa*. London 1967. – 60

Mansfield, G. B. 'Comparison between settlement in villages and isolated homesteads', *Journal of African Administration* 7 (1955). – 205

Maquet, J. J. *The premise of inequality in Ruanda*. London 1961. – 56

March, J. G. and Simon, H. *Organisation*. New York 1958. – 211

Marglin, S. A. *Public investment criteria*. London 1967. – 85

Marx, F. M. *The administrative state*. Chicago 1957. – 189

Mason, E. S. 'The role of the government in economic development', *American Economic Review* 50 (1960). – 184

Matthews, D. R. *U.S. senators and their world*. Chapel Hill, N.C., 1960. – 117

Mayer, A. C. 'An Indian community development block revisited', *Public Administration* 35 (1957). – 205

Mayer, A. C., Marriott, McKim and Park, R. L. *Pilot project, India*. Berkeley 1959. – 203

Mayer, A. C. 'Quasi-groups in the study of complex societies', Banton, M. (ed.) *The social anthropology of complex societies*. London 1966. – 43

Mehden, F. von der. *Politics of the developing nations*. New Jersey 1964. – 214, 222, 227

Meillassoux, C. *Anthropologie économique des Gouros de Côte d'Ivoire*. Paris 1964. – 141, 142, 153

Merriam. A. P. 'The concept of culture clusters applied to the Belgian Congo', *Southwestern Journal of Anthropology* 15 (1959). – 60

Merton, R. K. 'Bureaucratic structure and personality', *Social Forces* 18 (1940). – 190

—— *Social theory and social structure*. Glencoe 1957. – 4

Middleton, J. Review of Lofchie, M. *Zanzibar: background to revolution. Africa* 38 (1968). – 56

Middleton, J. and Campbell, J. *Zanzibar: its society and its politics*. London and New York 1965. – 59

Middleton, J. and Tait, D. *Tribes without rulers*. New York and London 1958. – 42

Millikan, M. F. and Rostow, W. W. *A proposal: key to an effective foreign policy*. New York 1957. – 182

Mills, C. Wright. *The power elite*. New York 1956. – 114

Miner, H. 'Culture change under pressure; a Hausa case', *Human Organisation* 19 (1960). – 205

Mitchell, J. C. *Tribalism and the plural society*. London 1960. – 52

Mitchell, W. *Sociological analysis and politics*. New Jersey 1967. – 4

Moerman, N. 'Ethnic identification in a complex civilization: who are the Lue?', *American Anthropologist* 67 (1965). – 59

Montgomery, J. D. 'Field organisation, administrative relationships and foreign aid policies', *Public Policy* 10 (1960). – 177

political anthropology', *Rural Africana* 2 (1967). – 42

Perlmutter, A. 'The Israel army in politics', *World Politics* XX (1968). – 214

Peters, E. 'Some structural aspects of the feud among the camel-herding Bedouin of Cyrenaica', *Africa* 37 (1967). – 49

Petras, J. 'U.S.–Latin American studies: a critical assessment', *Science and Society* 32 (1968). – 54

Pflanze, O. 'Characteristics of nationalism in Europe: 1848–1871', *The Review of Politics* 28 (1966). – 42

Pitt-Rivers, J. *Mediterranean countrymen.* Paris 1963. – 63

Polanyi, K., Arensberg, C. and Pearson, H. *Trade and market in the early empires.* Illinois 1957. – 41

Pratt, R. C. 'The administration of economic planning in a newly independent state', *Journal of Commonwealth Political Studies* (1967). – 267, 268, 270

Presthus, R. 'Weberian versus welfare bureaucracy in traditional societies', *Administrative Science Quarterly* 6 (1961). – 191

Putnam, R. D. 'Toward explaining military intervention in Latin American politics', *World Politics* XIX (1967). – 219, 220

Pye, L. W. *Communications and political development.* Princeton 1963. – 5

—— *Politics, personality and nation-building; Burma's search for identity.* London and New Haven 1962. – 4, 18

Pye, W. and Verba, S. (eds.) *Political culture and political development.* Princeton 1966. – 5

Radcliffe-Brown, A. 'Social evolution', Srinivas, M. N. (ed.) *Method in social anthropology.* Chicago and London 1958. – 36

Ranney, A. *Essays on the behavioural study of politics.* Urbana 1962. – 2

—— *Pathways to Parliament.* London 1966. – 118

Rathbone, R. 'Education and politics in Ghana', *Institute of Commonwealth Studies.* 1968. – 237

Rex, J. 'The plural society in sociological theory', *British Journal of Sociology* 10 (1959). – 52

Ribera Report, High Planning Council. Honduras 1967. – 211

Richards, A. I. *East African chiefs.* New York and London 1960. – 36–7

Rigby, P. 'Political change in Busoga', *The Uganda Journal* 30 (1966). – 44

Riggs, F. W. 'Public administration: a neglected factor in economic development', *Annals* 305 (1956). – 177

—— *The ecology of public administration.* New Delhi 1961. – 183

—— 'The theory of developing politics', *World Politics* XVI, 1 (1963). – 20

—— *Administration in developing countries.* Boston 1964. – 4, 20, 183

—— 'The political context of administrative reform; re-learning an old lesson', *Public Administration Review* 25 (1965). – 180

—— *Administration and a changing world environment.* Bloomington 1968. – 186

Riker, W. H. *The theory of political coalitions.* Yale 1962. – 225

Robinson, K. L. *International Conference of Agricultural Economics Proceedings,* 1956. – 204

Rogers, E. M. *Diffusion of innovation.* New York 1962. – 211

Rogow, A. A. 'Comment on Smith and Apter, or whatever happened to the great issues?', *American Political Science Review* 51, 3 (1957). – 6

Rokkan, S. and Valen, H. 'The Mobilization of the Periphery', Rokkan, S. (ed.) *Approaches to the study of political participation.* Bergen 1962. – 122

Rostow, W. W. *The stages of economic growth.* Cambridge 1960. – 17

Rothman, S. 'One-party regimes: a comparative analysis', *Social Research* XXXIII (1967). – 216

Royal Institute of Public Administration, 'Administrative organisation for economic development', *Proceedings of the Cambridge conference.* London 1959. – 177

Rubin, V. 'The anthropology of development', Siegel, B. (ed.) *Biennial review of anthropology* 1961. Stanford 1962. – 35

Russett, B. M., Alker, H. R., Deutsch, K. W. and Lasswell, H. D. *World handbook of political and social indicators.* Yale 1964. – 218, 232

Rustow, D. A. 'New horizons for comparative politics', *World Politics* IX (1957). – 4

Ruthenberg, H. (ed.) *Smallholder farming and smallholder development in Tanzania.* Munich 1968. – 95

Sady, E. J. 'Community development and local government', *Journal of African Administration* 11 (1959). – 177

Sahlins, M. 'The segmentary lineage: an organization of predatory expansion', *American Anthropologist* 63 (1961). – 40

—— Review of Murdock, G. P., *Social structure in Southeast Asia* (Chicago 1967), *Journal of the Polynesian Society* 72 (1963). – 37

Sartori, G. 'From the sociology of politics to political sociology', Lipset, S. M. (ed.) *Social science and politics.* New York 1969. – 117

Sawyer, J. 'Dimensions of nations: size, wealth and politics', *American Journal of Sociology* LXXIII (1967). – 221, 222, 223

Sayre, W. and Kaufman, H. *A research design for a pilot study in public administration.* Bloomington 1966. – 178, 207

Schaffer, B. B. 'The distinction between executive and administrative work', *Public Administration (Sydney)* 17 (1956). – 192

—— 'Public administration and the political education', *Public Administration (Sydney)* 21 (1962). – 180

Schapera, I. *Government and politics in tribal societies.* London 1956. – 47

Schuman, H. *Economic development and individual change.* Cambridge, Mass. 1967. – 209

Schurmann, F. *Ideology and organisation in Communist China.* New York 1966. – 211

Seligman, L. G. 'Political recruitment and party structure', *American Political Science Review* 55, 1 (1961). – 124

—— *Leadership in a new nation: political development in Israel.* New York 1964. – 122–3

Selznick, P. *TVA and the grassroots.* Berkeley and Los Angeles 1949. – 205

—— *Leadership in administration.* Evanston 1957. – 194

Seton Watson, H. *The Russian Empire, 1801–1917.* Oxford 1967. – 66

Shils, E. A. *Torment of secrecy.* London 1956. – 187

—— 'The concentration and dispersion of charisma; their bearing on economic policy in under-developed countries', *World Politics* XI (1958). – 184

—— *Political development in the new states.* The Hague 1960. – 4

Siegel, B. J. 'Some recent developments in studies of social and cultural change', *The Annals* (of the American Academy of Political and Social Science) 363 (1966). – 35

Siegel, B. and Beals, A. 'Pervasive factionalism', *American Anthropologist* 62 (1960). – 43

Siffin, W. J. (ed.) *Towards the comparative study of public administration.* Bloomington 1957. – 178, 183

Silverman, S. 'Patronage and community-nation relationships in central Italy', *Ethnology* 4 (1965). – 43

Simon, H. A. 'The decision maker as innovator', in Mailick, S. and von Ness, E. H. (eds.) *Concepts and issues in administrative behaviour.* Englewood Cliffs 1962. – 211

Singer, M. *The emerging elite.* Cambridge, Mass. 1964. – 117

Sklar, R. L. 'Political science and national

integration', *Journal of Modern African Studies* 5 (1967). – 53

Smith, D. G. 'Political science and political theory', *American Political Science Review* 51, 3 (1957). – 6

Smith, M. G. *Government in Zazzau, 1800–1950.* London 1960. – 41

—— 'Kagoro political development', *Human Organization* 19 (1960). – 36–7

—— *The plural society in the British West Indies.* California 1965. – 52

—— 'A structural approach to comparative politics', Easton, D. (ed.) *Varieties of political theory.* New Jersey 1966. – 39, 41

—— 'Pre-industrial stratification systems', Smelser, N. and Lipset, S. (eds.) *Social structure and mobility in economic development.* Chicago 1966. – 39, 50, 51, 60

Smolinsky, L. 'Grinevetskii and Soviet industrialisation', *Survey* 67 (1968). – 69

Southall, A. *Alur society.* Cambridge 1956. – 46

—— 'A critique of the typology of states and political systems', Banton, M. (ed.), *Political systems and the distribution of power.* London 1965. – 42

—— 'The concept of elites and their formation in Uganda', Lloyd, P. C. (ed.) *The new elites of tropical Africa.* London 1966. – 57, 58

Southwold, M. *Bureaucracy and chiefship in Buganda.* Kampala 1961. – 46

Spengler, J. J. 'Public bureaucracy, resources, structure and economic development', *Kyklos* 11 (1958). – 177

—— 'Economic development: political preconditions and political consequences', *Journal of Politics* XXXI (1960). – 218

Spicer, E. H. (ed.) *Human problems in technological change.* New York 1952. – 184

Spitz, A. and Weidner, E. *Development administration, an annotated bibliography.* Honolulu 1963. – 181

Stalin, J. *Economic problems of Socialism in the USSR.* Foreign Languages Publishing House, Moscow 1952. – 74

Staniland, M. 'Local administration in Ivory Coast', *West Africa,* 9 March 1968, and 16 March 1968. – 161

Stevenson, R. F. *Population and political systems in tropical Africa.* Columbia 1968. – 29

Steward, J. *Theory of culture change.* Illinois 1955. – 39, 61

—— *Contemporary change in traditional societies.* Chicago and London 1967. – 39

—— 'Comment', *Current Anthropology* 9 (1968). – 53

Steward, J. and Faron, L. *Native peoples of South America.* New York 1959. – 42

Stinchcombe, A. 'Bureaucratic and craft administration of production', *Administrative Science Quarterly* 4 (1959). – 189

Stolper, W. F. *Planning without facts.* Cambridge, Mass. 1966. – 247

Strauss, L. 'Epilogue', H. Storing (ed.), *Essays on the scientific study of politics.* New York 1962. – 2

Swerdlow, I. (ed.) *Development administration, concepts and problems.* Syracuse 1953. – 181, 183

Szereszewski, R. *Structural changes in the economy of Ghana, 1891–1911.* London 1966. – 237

Tanter, R. and Midlarsky, M. 'A theory of revolution', *Journal of Conflict Resolution* XI, 3 (1967). – 218

Tanter, R. 'Dimensions of conflict behaviour within and between nations, 1955–60', *Journal of Conflict Resolution* X, 1 (1966). – 219

—— 'Towards a theory of political development', *Mid-west Journal of Political Science* XI, 2 (1967). – 221

Teaf, H. M. and Franck, P. G. (eds.), *Hands across frontiers.* Ithaca 1955. – 184

Thomas, M. L. 'The Philippines rural development programme', *Social Research* 22 (1955). – 177

Thompson, Victor 'Objectives for development administration', *Administrative Science Quarterly* 9 (1964). – 183

Thompson, Virginia and Adloff, R. *French West Africa.* London 1958. – 148

—— 'Niger', Carter, G. (ed.) *National unity and regionalism in eight African states.* Ithaca 1966. – 140

Thornton, T. P. *The third world in Soviet perspective.* Princeton 1964. – 22

Tiger, L. S. 'Bureaucracy in Ghana', unpublished Ph.D. thesis. London 1963. – 236

Tinbergen, J. *Economic policy: principles and design.* Amsterdam 1956. – 248

—— *Central planning.* New Haven 1964. – 248

Tinker, H. *Ballot box and bayonet.* London 1964. – 14

Tolstoy, L. *War and peace.* Oxford University Press 1951. – 255

Turner, V. *Profiles of change.* Cambridge 1969. – 61

Udy, S. 'Bureaucracy and rationality in Weber's theory', *American Sociological Review* 24 (1959). – 189

U.N. *Standards and techniques of public administration, with special reference to technical assistance for under-developed countries.* New York 1951. – 180

—— *Public administration, current concepts and practice, with special reference to developing countries.* New York 1961. – 180

—— Social progress through community development, 1955. – 204

—— Economic Commission for Africa, *Economic Survey of Africa*, vol. 1, *Western Sub-region—Republic of South Africa.* Addis Ababa 1966. – 141

—— Mission, *Community development in Africa.* New York 1956. – 203

—— Seminar, *Administrative aspects of community development.* Hague 1959. – 203

—— Technical assistance operations, *Public administration aspects of community development programmes.* New York 1959. – 177

Valen, H. 'The recruitment of parliamentary nominees in Norway', *Scandinavian Political Studies* I (1966). – 120

Valkenier, E. K. 'Recent trends in Soviet research on the developing countries', *World Politics* XX, 3 (1968). – 22

Vatikiotis, P. J. *The Egyptian army in politics.* Indiana 1961. – 214, 230

Villanueva, B. M. 'The community development programme of the Philippines government', *Philippines Journal of Public Administration* 1 (1957). – 203

Vine, V. Le *Dreams and deeds.* Chicago 1966. – 218

—— 'Independent Africa in trouble', *Africa Report* XII, 9 (1967). – 222

Vorys, K. von *The theory of political development.* In press. – 22

Wagley, C. and Harris, M. 'A typology of Latin American subcultures', *American Anthropologist* 57 (1955). – 42

Wagret, J. M. *Histoire et sociologie politique de la Republique de Congo (Brazzaville).* Paris 1963. – 30

Wallerstein, I. *Social change: the colonial situation.* New York 1966. – 61

Ward, R. E. 'The socio-political role of the Buraku in Japan', *American Political Science Review* 45 (1951). – 205

—— 'Political modernisation and political culture in Japan', *World Politics* XV (1963). – 4

Ward, R. E. and Rustow, D. (eds.) *Political modernization in Japan and Turkey.* Princeton 1964. – 4, 189

Waterston, A. *Development planning: lessons of experience.* Baltimore 1965. – 247, 249, 258 262

Weidner, E. *Technical assistance for public administration overseas: the case for development administration.* New York 1963. – 183

Weiner, M. *Party building in a new nation: The Indian National Congress.* Chicago 1967. – 5